A HISTORY OF
RUSSIAN
LITERATURE
FROM ITS BEGINNINGS
TO 1900

D. S. Mirsky

A HISTORY OF
RUSSIAN
LITERATURE
FROM ITS BEGINNINGS
TO 1900

Edited by Francis J. Whitfield

VINTAGE BOOKS *NEW YORK*
A DIVISION OF RANDOM HOUSE

Editor's Note

This volume contains Mirsky's *A History of Russian Literature from the Earliest Times to the Death of Dostoyevsky* (*1881*) and the first two chapters of his *Contemporary Russian Literature, 1881-1925,* as edited by me for the one-volume *A History of Russian Literature* published by Alfred A. Knopf in 1949. The editors of Vintage Books have kindly given me the opportunity to correct the errors that have come to my notice since the original printing of that edition. I am indebted, for their advice and help, to my wife and to my colleagues Professors Gleb Struve and Lawrence L. Thomas.

Mirsky dedicated the original two books to JANE ELLEN HARRISON and to MAURICE BARING. This edition is respectfully offered to PAUL McGEORGE.

F. J. W.

Berkeley
January 1958

A Note on Transliteration

THERE is no universally accepted system of transliterating the Cyrillic alphabet. The following tables will permit the reader to compare the system used in this book with that used by the Library of Congress and most American libraries. The third table is representative of systems used by Continental European (and, increasingly, by American) scholars.

	USED IN THE PRESENT BOOK	USED BY THE LIBRARY OF CONGRESS	USED BY SPECIALISTS
а	a	a	a
б	b	b	b
в	v	v	v
г	g	g	g
д	d	d	d
е	e	e	e
ж	zh	zh	ž
з	z	z	z
и	i	i	i
й	y	ĭ	j
к	k	k	k
л	l	l	l
м	m	m	m
н	n	n	n
о	o	o	o
п	p	p	p
р	r	r	r
с	s	s	s
т	t	t	t
у	u	u	u
ф	f	f	f
х	kh	kh	ch, x
ц	ts	t͡s	c

	USED IN THE PRESENT BOOK	USED BY THE LIBRARY OF CONGRESS	USED BY SPECIALISTS
ч	ch	ch	č
ш	sh	sh	š
щ	sch	sh͡ch	šč
ъ	omitted	″	″
ы	y	y	y
ь	omitted	′	′
э	è	ė	è
ю	yu	i͡u	ju
я	ya	i͡a	ja

Final unaccented "ий" and "ый" have been transliterated as "y," and further exceptions from the general rules have been made for the following combinations:

ае	aye		ье	ie
ое	oye		ьи	yi
уе	uye		ью	iu
юе	yuye		ья	ia
яе	yaye		кс	x

The place of the accent in Russian words and names has been indicated throughout. When "e" falls under the accent, it is, in some words, pronounced (approximately) "yo." Where this occurs I have used the symbol "ë."

Many familiar Christian names are given in their English form (thus Peter for Pëtr, Michael for Mikhaíl, and so on).

Contents

A HISTORY OF
RUSSIAN
LITERATURE
FROM ITS BEGINNINGS
TO 1900

1

The Literature of Old Russia
(*Eleventh to Seventeenth Centuries*)

FROM its beginning in the eleventh century to the end of the seventeenth, Russian literature lived entirely out of touch with contemporary developments of Latin Christendom. Like Russian art it was a branch of the Greek trunk. Its germs were brought late in the tenth century from Constantinople, together with the Orthodox faith. But as it was the practice of the Eastern Church to favor the translation of the Scriptures and liturgies into the vernacular, the clergy of the converted nations had no need to learn Greek, and the absence of Greek scholarship in Russia had as its consequence the absence of all acquaintance with secular Greek literature and pre-Christian classical tradition.

THE LITERARY LANGUAGE

The literary language of Old Russia is known as Old Church Slavonic. It is based on some Bulgarian dialect from around Salonika, elevated to the rank of a liturgic and literary language in the ninth century by the apostles of Slavdom, SS. Cyril and Methodius. It was used by the South Slavs and Romanians as well as by the Russians. It was saturated with Greek influence in vocabulary and syntax, and was very different from what we may imagine the spoken language to have been. In the course of time this artificiality increased, and while the spoken languages (in Russia as well as in the Balkans) underwent, between the eleventh and fourteenth centuries, rapid and radical changes, Church Slavonic remained stationary and even tended to approach still closer to its Greek prototype. In the fourteenth century especially, South Slavic clerks made a thorough revision of the Scriptures and liturgies in order to make the Slavonic text more literally adequate to the Greek. This form of Church Slavonic became the literary language of Muscovite Russia.

Though the only literary, Church Slavonic was not the only written language. The administrative offices of the Russian princes and communes evolved a more vernacular form of writing, and towards the end of the fifteenth century the language of the Muscovite chanceries became the official language of the Empire. It is expressive and often picturesque, but it was obviously incapable of displacing Slavonic for literary purposes. As for the literary language, the vernacular element insinuated itself only to the degree of the writers' illiteracy or inability to find Slavonic molds for expressing their stronger feelings. The Russian vernacular was first consciously used for literary purposes in the third quarter of the seventeenth century in the writings of a great and original man of genius—the Archpriest Avvakúm.

LITERARY CONDITIONS

Authorship was not one of the recognized activities of Old Russia. There were no "writers," but only "bookmen" (*knízhniki*). The "reading of books" (*knízhnoye pochitánie*) was a respectable and edifying occupation, but new literary works were written only when some practical necessity called for them. The humanistic tradition, so lively in Constantinople, was not transmitted to Russia, and traces of the acquaintance of Russian clerics with even the names of the ancients are negligible. Imaginative literature formed an insignificant part of the reading of the Old Russians. When he wanted to read, the Russian bookman turned to the holy books and other collections of edifying matter. There was no need for fresh literary invention.

As in the mediæval West, the copying of books was regarded as a work agreeable to God, and was, especially in pre-Muscovite times, carried on mainly by monks. Printing was introduced into Russia very late. The first book printed on Russian territory (in Moscow) appeared in 1564. Even after the establishment of the printing press the cost of printing was so great and printers so few that only books of the greatest importance (Bibles, liturgies, statutes, and official instructions) could be printed. Till about the middle of the eighteenth century there were more manuscripts than printed books in circulation. Not until the reign of Catherine II did mediæval conditions cease to prevail in the Russian book market.

Judged exclusively by its literature, Old Russian civilization cannot fail to produce an impression of poverty. But it would be wrong to regard literature as its principal expression. The very nature of this civilization, traditional and ritual, reduced literary originality to very little. The real expression of the creative genius of Old Russia is its architecture and painting, and those who want to gauge its true value must turn to the history of Russian art rather than to that of literature.

TRANSLATED WORKS

The principal and most permanent part of the verbal impressions of the Old Russian came from the liturgies. It was by attending church services rather than by reading that his mind became saturated with the intellectual food of Orthodox Christianity. The liturgies of the Eastern Church are full of sublime and elevated poetry. The Greek hymns were translated into a beautiful prose, devoid of all metrical construction but carefully adapted to the music to which they were sung. The original hymnology of the Orthodox Slavs is negligible.

The Bible was known chiefly through the liturgy. The Psalms were the most familiar of all books to the Old Russian reader, and he usually knew them by heart. Of the other Old Testament books the favorites were those which presented a philosophy of life agreeable to the taste of the Old Russian bookman—Ecclesiastes, Proverbs, the Wisdom of Solomon, and Sirach. As the Psalms were his treasure house of poetry, so were these his mine of wisdom. Copies of the Prophets and of the Apocalypse were usually accompanied by the commentary of the Greek Fathers. The historical books of the Old Testament were little read. Expositions of the Old Testament story known as *Paléya* (Greek παλαιά) were the ordinary sources of the Old Russian's knowledge of Biblical history. The books of the Slavonic Bible were copied out and circulated separately. The first Bible printed in Russia was that of Ostróg (1581), and the first complete edition to appear in Moscow was that of 1663. The final "Authorized Version" of the Russian-Slavonic Bible appeared almost a century later, in 1751.

Next to the liturgies and the Bible, the Fathers were the most authoritative books. The most widely read was St. Chrysostom, the great moral teacher and the great examplar of eloquence. The highest theological authority was St. John Damascene. The lives of saints were extensively read. Some were the works of reputed and highly authoritative authors, and these were copied with particular care and exactitude. One of these was the story of Barlaam and Josaphat, ascribed to St. John Damascene. This Byzantine version of the life of the Buddha deeply impressed itself on the Russian religious mind. The form in which saints' lives were most frequently read was that of calendars or menologia (*minéi*) where the lives of the several saints were arranged under the dates of their respective feasts. Authoritative and official *minéi* were compiled in the sixteenth century by Macarius, Metropolitan of Moscow, and under Peter the Great by St. Demetrius, Metropolitan of Rostóv. But by the side of these official collections there were others of a more popular and arbitrary composition which were more widely read. Such, above all, was the *Prologue,* a vast collection of the most varied religious readings for every day. It had numerous redactions and contained lives of saints, pious anecdotes, and readings from the Fathers. Its contents varied, and, by the side of a prevailing majority of translations from the Greek, many of its entries were of native origin. Although highly esteemed, it never received the official sanction of the Church. Some of the matter included in it no doubt verges on the apocryphal.

After the great schism of the seventeenth century it began to be looked at askance by the Church, but it remained in favor with the Old Believers and has come down in numerous manuscripts. In recent times the *Prologue* has attracted considerable literary attention, and modern writers, like Tolstóy, Leskóv, and Rémizov, have retold many of its stories.

The *Prologue* is halfway between canonical and apocryphal literature, and so is the *Paléya*, which includes much that is not found in the Bible. Numerous apocrypha, many of early Christian origin, formed a vast mass of Old Russian literature. Those which were not at variance with Orthodoxy were countenanced by the Church and, at times of low learning, hardly distinguished from canonical books. The most popular were those dealing with the future life. One of them, the legend of the Virgin's visit to hell, particularly impressed itself on the Russian imagination:, moved by the suffering of the damned, she implores God to be allowed to share it, and finally obtains from Him that all the damned be henceforth given each year a respite from their torments, from Maundy Thursday to Whitsunday.

The books whence the Old Russians drew their secular scientific information were not the residue of the scientific achievement of the ancients preserved by the Byzantines. The sounder part of the Old Russians' ideas on nature came from the Fathers that had written on the creation. The secular books they had were those current among the lower cultural strata of Byzantine Greece—such as the cosmography of Cosmas Indicopleustes and the *Physiologus*.

Of Byzantine historians, again, the more classical and "highbrow," as for instance Procopius, remained unknown, and Russian bookmen drew their historical information from the more "popular" chronicles, such as those of John Malalas and George Hamartolos. These chronicles presented the history of the world, beginning with the story of the Old and New Testaments, followed by the fall of Jerusalem and the persecutions of the primitive Church; they enumerated the early Cæsars and then gave a more or less detailed history of the Byzantine emperors.

The only author known in Old Russia that may be termed a classic was Josephus. Besides epitomes of his

works in various compilations, there exists a very early
Russian-Slavonic version of the *De Bello Judaico,* apparently made in Russia about 1100. For its intelligent freedom in following the text it is unique among Slavonic
translations. It seems to have been very popular among the
higher intellectuals of the twelfth century, and traces of the
influence of its diction are evident in *The Campaign of
Ígor.* But the Russian Josephus is interesting not only for
its important part in Russian literature. It contains six
passages on Christ and Pilate that are not found in extant
Greek manuscripts, and which appear to be early Christian
interpolations (first and second centuries). Other passages,
expressive of strongly anti-Roman feeling, have even been
explained as going back to an original version that Josephus
afterwards changed to avoid offending his patrons.

In Byzantine and mediæval literature in general it is
not easy to distinguish history from fiction. It is the fashion
today, for instance, to include the mediæval stories of Troy
and Alexander in the department of fiction, but the Old
Russian scribe inserted them in his historical compilations.
Neither story received any romantic development on Russian soil, for the subject of romantic love was alien to the
Old Russians. The same is even more evident in the Russian
prose version of the Byzantine epic *Digenis Akritas.* The
original contains an appreciable element of romance, but
this is entirely eliminated in the Russian version. Another
kind of imported fiction was stories of wisdom, consisting
of dialogues, parables, and apologues, or turning on the
solution of riddles. Most of these stories were ultimately
of Indian or Arabic origin, but all came to Russia via
Greece.

THE KIEVAN PERIOD

From the tenth century to the invasion of the Tatars in the
middle of the thirteenth, the political and cultural center of
Russia was Kíev. The civilization of the period was dominated by two classes: the urban clergy and the military
aristocracy. The former was largely recruited from the
latter. The clergy, especially the higher monastic clergy,
were the principal depositories of culture, and the art and

literature of the time are mainly religious. The military class, headed by a numerous and warlike race of princes, submitted to the authority of the Church and were Christians in their moral ideals, but they retained heathen traditions and loved war, the chase, and the pleasures of the table above all things. They produced the only real literary masterpiece of the period, the prose poem of *The Campaign of Igor*.

The most strictly Byzantine department of Kievan literature is the writings of the higher clergy. As early as between 1037 and 1050 a piece of Russian oratory was produced that is quite comparable to the highest rhetorical achievement of contemporary Greece. This is the *Oration of Law and Grace,* ascribed to Hilarion, Metropolitan of Kíev, the first Russian to occupy that seat. It is a piece of subtle theological eloquence on the opposition of the New and the Old Testament, followed by an elaborate panegyric upon St. Vladímir. The same kind of ornate and subtle rhetoric was cultivated in the second half of the twelfth century by Cyril, Bishop of Túrov. Both Hilarion and Cyril are fully versed in the art of balancing their phrase and constructing their paragraph, and are at home in the whole Byzantine arsenal of trope, simile, and allusion. Their sermons could find evidently but a small public, and the common run of Kievan preachers used a far simpler style. Such, for instance, are the extant sermons of St. Theodosius, Abbot of the Crypt Monastery, one of the founders of Russian monasticism.

The Crypt (*Pechérsky*) Monastery in Kíev, founded in the middle of the eleventh century, was for two centuries the nursery garden of Russian abbots and bishops, and the center of ecclesiastical learning. Néstor (*c.* 1080), a monk of this monastery, was the first notable Russian hagiologist. He wrote the lives of the martyred princes Borís and Gleb and of St. Theodosius. The latter, especially in the part concerning the holy abbot's early years, gives a more intimate and familiar idea of the everyday life of Kievan Russia than any other literary work of the time. Towards the end of the present period Simon, Bishop of Vladímir (d. 1226), wrote down for the edification of the monk Polycarp the lives of some of the Crypt saints. These formed the nucleus of the *Book of the Crypt Fathers* (*Pechérsky paterík*), which, extensively added to in follow-

ing centuries, became one of the most popular hagiographi-
cal writings in the language.

Another Russian monk who has left a name in the
history of literature is the Abbot Daniel, who in 1106–8
went to the Holy Land and described his journey in a
famous *Pilgrimage*. It is written in a simple, matter-of-fact,
but by no means dry or tedious, style and is remarkable for
its exact and reliable account of the Holy Land under the
first Frankish king. It is also interesting for the patriotic
feeling that animates it: in every holy place he visited,
Daniel never omitted to pray for the Russian princes and
all the land of Russia.

Ecclesiastical learning was not confined to the clerics,
and two remarkable works by laymen are full of reflections
of clerical knowledge. One of these is the *Testament* of
Vladímir Monomákh (Great Prince of Kíev, 1113–25), the
most popular and universally respected prince of the period.
Written shortly before his death, it tells of his active life,
full of wars against the nomads and punitive expeditions
against seditious princes, of conferences, of distant voyages,
and of big-game hunting. Vladímir's tone is full of dignity
and the consciousness of his own achievement, but at the
same time free from all pride or vanity. It is humble in a
truly Christian sense. He has been called a "Slavonic
Marcus Aurelius," but there is nothing of the Roman
Emperor's stoical sadness in the Russian King, whose main
characteristics are a simple piety, an honest sense of duty,
and lucid common sense.

Very different is the other secular sermon that has
come down to us—*The Supplication of Daniel the Exile*.
Written probably early in the thirteenth century in the
province of Súzdal, it takes the form of a petition from the
disinherited son of a good serving-family to his prince that
he may accept him into his service. It is primarily a show-
off of reading and consists mainly of quotations from the
gnomic books of the Bible, oriental wisdom tales, and other
sources, including popular proverbs, all welded together
with elaborate rhetoric. *The Supplication* was copied and
interpolated, and finally became a sort of commonplace
book, so that its original form of a petition became entirely
obliterated. It is interesting for the light it throws on the
taste of the average literate Old Russian and on the kind of
wisdom he appreciated.

THE CHRONICLES

The largest and (except for *The Campaign of Ígor*) the most valuable, original, and interesting monument of Kievan literature is the Chronicles or Annals (*Létopisi*). Russian annal writing began about the same time as Russian literature, and its uninterrupted tradition was continued far into the seventeenth, in the case of Siberia, even into the eighteenth, century. The Annals were the work partly of monks, partly of lay bookmen, and, in Muscovite times, of official scribes. Like by far the greater part of Old Russian literature, they are anonymous and have come down to us not in their original and individual forms, but as parts of large codices, varying greatly from manuscript to manuscript. The Annals of the Kievan period are contained chiefly in two compilations, which in one form or another appear at the head of most later codices. These are the so-called Primitive Chronicle (*Nachálnaya létopis*), covering the period from "the beginning of Russia" to 1110, and the so-called Kievan Chronicle, continuing the history to 1200. The former is ascribed in certain late manuscripts to St. Néstor, the hagiographer previously mentioned. Another name connected with it is that of Sylvester, Abbot of St. Michael's in Kíev, who prepared a copy of it in 1116. Whether he merely copied or whether his work was rather that of an editor we do not know, and, in general, the problems of authorship and sources are still matters of the widest conjecture.

The Primitive Chronicle begins with a genealogy of the Slavs "from the generation of Japheth." This is followed by an account of the early history of the Slavs, of their divisions and manners, which is strangely "nineteenth century" in its Panslavist sentiment and its ethnographical interest. Then follows the well-known story of the "invitation of the Varangians" to Nóvgorod, which is curiously similar to that of Hengist and Horsa. The account of events of the later ninth and of the tenth centuries is based on a fairly solid chronological skeleton, but the strictly annalistic entries are very few. They are enlivened by numerous vivid and spirited traditional tales, which form the chief attraction of this part of the Chronicle. The earliest is en-

tered under 882, and they continue as far as the early years
of Yaroslác (1019–54). They are obviously founded on
oral tradition, but there is no ground to believe that this
tradition was poetical. They are just anecdotes, of the same
kind as the anecdotes that are the chief charm of Herodo-
tus. One of the Russian annalist's anecdotes is even identical with one of the tales of the father of history (the story
of the siege of Bélgorod by the Pechenégs and that of the
siege of Miletos by the Lydians). Another, the tale of how
Olég met death from his favorite horse, is a version of a
story found in the Old Norse Qrvar-Odd Saga (Púshkin
later made it the subject of a famous ballad). Besides such
stories the early Chronicle contains more connected and
generalized passages, such as the account of the wars of
the great adventurer Prince Svyatosláv, part of which is
closely paraphrased by Gibbon in The Decline and Fall.
The account of Vladímir's reign includes the remarkable
story of how that prince examined the various religions
before deciding to adopt Greek Christianity. Rejecting
Islam because "it is the Russians' joy to drink; we cannot do
without it," he finally chose Orthodoxy, under the impression of the account given him by his envoys of the beauty
and splendor of the service at St. Sophia in Constantinople,
a motive that throws an important light on the Old Russian's essentially ritualistic and æsthetic conception of his
religion.

The part of the Chronicle subsequent to c. 1040 appears to have been mainly the work of a monk of the
Crypt Monastery, perhaps Néstor. The chronicler writes
in a deeply religious spirit and regards all events as the
direct action of Providence. He takes a keen interest in
portents and omens, and regards all the woes of Russia as a
punishment for the wicked conduct of the princes: the
second half of the eleventh century was one incessant civil
war between the sons and grandsons of Yaroslác. The
annalist exhorts the princes to forget their feuds and turn
their attention to the defense of the steppe marches against
the steadily advancing nomads. He is particularly partial to
Vladímir Monomákh, who alone of all Russian princes
answered to his ideal of a patriotic prince. Inserted in this
part of the Chronicle, under the year 1097, is a narrative
of exceptional merit, the work apparently of a cleric named
Vasíly. It is the story of the blinding of Vasílko, Prince of

Terebóvl (in Galicia), by his cousin and neighbor David of Volynia, and of the events that followed it. The story is told in greater detail than the rest of the Chronicle and is a masterpiece of simple, direct narrative. For its straightforward and comprehensively human manner it may almost be compared with the stories of the book of Genesis.

The Kievan Chronicle of the twelfth century is, like its predecessor, a composite document. Most valuable is its account of the years 1146–54, dealing with the struggle of Prince Izyasláv II (grandson of Monomákh) for the throne of Kíev. It is evidently by a soldier, one of Prince Izyasláv's "companions," and is full of the spirit of military prowess. The ambition of the princes and their desire to win honor in the field are the main motive of their actions. The narrative is lucid, leisurely, detailed, straightforward; the style ample and free from rhetorical devices. It is altogether the masterpiece of Kievan historical literature and can rank with the best examples of mediæval history.

After the decline of Kíev the Annals were continued both in the north and in the southwest, in the Kingdom of Galicia, which flourished in the second half of the thirteenth century and which has an honorable place in literary history owing to its single extant production—the so-called Volynian Chronicle. This Chronicle is different from the others in that its form is not a succession of isolated entries under every year, but a connected account of causes and effects. It is pretty difficult reading and not infrequently obscure. The characters speak almost invariably in proverbs and aphorisms; the literary influence of the Old Testament (Kings and Isaiah) is clearly apparent; the descriptions are full of vivid and hyperbolic imagery. Though not devoid of considerable ecclesiastical culture, the spirit of the story is purely secular and military. The story is carried on till 1290. After that date the southwest of Russia becomes silent for several centuries.

THE CAMPAIGN OF ÍGOR AND ITS FAMILY

The Word of the Campaign of Ígor (*Slóvo o pŭlku Ígorevĕ*) was discovered in 1795 by an enlightened nobleman, Count A. I. Músin-Púshkin, in a (sixteenth-century?) manuscript codex that contained only secular matter, in-

cluding a version of *Digenis Akritas*. The manuscript was
destroyed in the fire of Moscow in 1812, so that the *editio
princeps* (1800) and a copy made for Catherine II are
now our main authority for the text. They were made at a
time when Russian palæography was in its youth, and contain numerous corrupt passages, which we do not know
whether to attribute to the destroyed manuscript or to its
decipherers.

The *Slóvo* was discovered at a time when the Ossianic
question occupied all minds. The admirers of the poem immediately compared it to Ossian, while its detractors
affirmed that it was as much a forgery as "Ossian" himself.
Skepticism, however, was soon silenced, chiefly by the discovery of a verbatim quotation from the *Slóvo* in a dated
manuscript of 1307, and of an early fifteenth-century prose
poem on the battle of Kulikóvo, which was nothing but a
rather unintelligent paraphrase of *The Campaign of Ígor*.[1]

From the first the work stood out as a startlingly
isolated phenomenon, unrelated to anything of its age. One
quite obvious thing was that it had been composed very
soon after the events described, probably within the same
year, and that its account of the campaign was substantially
historical, for it squared most exactly with the account in
the Kievan Chronicle, without there being any trace of
verbal coincidence between the two documents. The problem of the *Slóvo* cannot yet be regarded as finally settled,
and there is still considerable variety of opinion on many
points, but the available internal and external evidence
seems to be best interpreted in the following way.

There existed in Kievan times a secular oral poetry,
preserved by singers belonging to the upper military class
of the prince's companions and similar to, but less professional than, the Norse scalds. This poetry flourished in
the eleventh century; some of the poems were still remembered in the end of the twelfth. They were associated with
the name of a great singer, Bayán, whose songs are quoted
by the author of the *Slóvo*. But it is not clear that at the
time of the composition of the *Slóvo* this oral poetry was
still alive. *The Campaign of Ígor* itself is a purely literary
work, *written*, and not sung. The author, though anony-

---

[1] Professor André Mazon of the Collège de France, has revived
the question of the *Slóvo*'s authenticity, but his doubts are not generally
shared. (Ed.)

mous, has a powerful individuality. He was a layman,
probably the companion of some prince. He was steeped in
books and in oral tradition. The great originality of his
work was that he used the methods of oral poetry in a work
of written literature. There is no reason to believe that he
had had any literary predecessors in this manner of writing, but he has roots in the literary tradition. The similarity
of some turns of phrases and expressions with the Russian
Josephus (*v. supra*) is very striking, and there are more
distant associations with the style of the ecclesiastical orators and that of the Annals. The rhythmic structure of the
poem is not that of verse. The rhythm of prose is different
in *kind* from the rhythm of verse, for it lacks the essential
element of the latter—*the line*. It must be remembered that
the parts of the Slavonic liturgy that are sung are nevertheless couched in prose, and that consequently even if *The
Campaign of Ígor* was actually a song (which is very un-
likely) it need not necessarily have been in verse. Analysis
reveals that the *Slóvo* possesses a very real and efficient
rhythm, but a rhythm far more complex than that of any
metrical pattern. No rhythmical prose I know of in any
language can so much as approach it for infinitely varied
flexibility.

It is not only the nature of its rhythmical prose that
makes *The Campaign of Ígor* unique. It is altogether difficult to classify. Neither a lyric, nor an epic, nor a piece of
political oratory, it is all these blended into one. Its skeleton
is narrative. It relates the story of the unfortunate campaign of Prince Ígor against the Pólovtsy, his initial success, his subsequent defeat, and his captivity. This constitutes what may be regarded as the first part of the poem.
This is followed by a long lyrical or oratorical digression.
The Great Prince of Kíev is described dreaming a dream of
ill omen, symbolic of Ígor's disaster. Then the poet apostro-
phizes, one after the other, the several Great Princes of the
land of Russia, exhorting them to save Ígor. Then Ígor's
wife is introduced, lamenting on the walls of her town of
Putívl—this passage forming one of the most beautiful
summits of the poem. After a rapid and abrupt transition
the third part begins—the account of Ígor's escape from
captivity. Like that of his advance and disaster it closely
agrees in fact with, but differs strikingly in style from, the
Chronicle account.

The spirit of the *Slóvo* is a blend of the warrior spirit of the military aristocracy as reflected in the Chronicle of 1146–54, with a wider patriotic outlook that is more akin to that of Monomákh and of the patriotic clerics, and which regards self-sacrifice for Russia as the noblest of virtues. It is also distinctly secular in spirit. Christianity appears only incidentally and rather as an element of contemporary life than as part of the poet's inner world. On the other hand, reminiscences of an older nature worship are part of the most intimate texture of the poem.

The style of the poem is the reverse of the primitive and barbaric. It is curiously, disconcertingly modern, all suggestion and allusion, full of splendid imagery, subtly symbolic and complex. Professor Hrushévsky has rightly remarked that only now, after a prolonged education in the school of modern poetry, are we really able to feel and understand the poetical methods of the *Slóvo*. It is far too modern for anyone to have been able to forge it in 1795.

Nature symbolism and nature parallelism play a large part in the poem. The movements of men have their "correspondences" in the movements of the "vegetable universe." This feature has been adduced as proof of the kinship of the *Slóvo* to "popular poetry." A vague kinship there certainly may be, but no similarity of detail with later Great Russian or Ukrainian folk song. Besides, a nature parallelism of a very similar kind was a time-honored form of expression in Byzantine sacred oratory.

The Campaign of Ígor, alone of all Old Russian literature, has become a national classic, familiar to every educated Russian and often known by heart by lovers of poetry. The quality of its poetry is entirely different from the quality of the poetry of the Classical Age of Púshkin, but it cannot be regarded as inferior. If Púshkin is Russia's greatest classical poet, the author of the *Slóvo* is the greatest master of ornate, romantic, and symbolic poetry. His work is a continuous succession of purple patches, the least of which has no counterpart in modern Russian poetry.

The language of the *Slóvo* is, of course, antiquated and unintelligible to an absolutely uncultured Russian. It is, with minor peculiarities, the usual Russo-Slavonic literary language of the twelfth century. But the modern Russian reader needs very little preparation to be able to understand it, especially if he has read his Slavonic Bible and understands his Slavonic prayers (achievements which, unfortunately, are becoming ever rarer).

However unique its quality, *The Campaign of Ígor* is not so absolutely isolated as it appeared to be at first sight. I have already alluded to some of its ancestry and direct progeny. Traces have come down to us of other fragments, not directly dependent on it but belonging, broadly speaking, to the same school. One is a small fragment in honor of Prince Román of Volynia (d. 1205) inserted in the Volynian Chronicle. Another, a fragment of little over two hundred words inscribed *Oration* (*Slóvo*) *on the Ruin of the Land of Russia,* is the beginning of what was evidently a long and elaborate lament on the destruction of Russian power by the Tatars.

More important, and different from the rest in its subject matter, is *The Appeal* (*Slóvo*) *of Adam to Lazarus in Hell.* No Greek source of it has been found; and though a priori it is dangerous to admit the absolute originality of its actual matter, there can be no doubt as to the originality of its actual form. Its date is unknown. It has certain affinities of style with *The Campaign of Ígor* and other Kievan writings of the same family. *The Appeal of Adam* is also a prose poem, but its rhythm seems to be less akin to that of the Kievan orators than to the prophetic books of the Slavonic Old Testament. The theme of the poem is Adam's appeal to Lazarus, about to leave hell on his resurrection, on behalf of all the righteous men of the Old Testament, and the oration ends with the descent into hell and the release of the righteous patriarchs. But there is in the questions of Adam a "Jobean" spirit that is rare in Old Russian writings. The powerful eloquence of the poem has deeply influenced the style of the prose poems of Rémizov, a writer saturated with the form and spirit of the Old Russian apocrypha.

BETWEEN KÍEV AND MOSCOW

In 1238–40 the Tatars, as the Mongols are always called in Russian sources, overran practically the whole of Russia, subjected all its eastern part, and destroyed Kíev. Except for the short period during which the Kievan tradition was continued in the Kingdom of Galicia, Russian civilization survived only in the north and east. Its centers there became the great merchant city of Nóvgorod and the principalities of the upper Volga, one of which, Moscow, ultimately succeeded in unifying the nation.

If we consider nothing but its literature, the period that extends from the Tatar invasion to the unification of Russia by Iván III of Moscow may be called a Dark Age. Its literature is either a more or less impoverished reminiscence of Kievan traditions or an unoriginal imitation of South Slavonic models. But here more than ever it is necessary to bear in mind that literature does not give the true measure of Old Russian culture. The fourteenth and fifteenth centuries, the Dark Age of literature, were at the same time the Golden Age of Russian religious painting.

Nowhere is the concretely æsthetic and non-intellectual character of Old Russian civilization so obviously apparent as in Nóvgorod. That wealthy city, for three hundred years the source of Europe's supply of furs and other northern commodities, was ruled by an art-loving merchant aristocracy that succeeded in making it something like a Russian Venice. But like Venice, though it produced great art, Nóvgorod has no literature to speak of. The Nóvgorod Chronicles, though admirable for their freedom from irrelevant talk and their strict matter-of-factness, are not literature. The civilization of Nóvgorod is perhaps the most characteristic expression of Old Russia, and the fact that it produced no literature is certainly significant.

The country ruled by the princely house of Súzdal (later the provinces of Moscow, Vladímir, Kostromá, Yaosláv, and Tver and the district of the White Lake), though culturally and economically inferior to Nóvgorod, produced more interesting literature. The chronicles and the "military narratives" connected with the Tatar invasion are of considerable interest. The *Life of St. Alexander* (d. 1263), Russia's champion against the Latin West, is a particularly remarkable "military narrative" and has left a lasting trace on the national memory.

Still more interesting are the "military narratives" relating to the victory of Kulikóvo (1380). These are the *Zadónschina* ("Trans-Doniad") written in the early fifteenth century by the priest Sophonia of Ryazán, and *The*

Legend of the Rout of Mamáy (the vizier who commanded the Tatars), extant in several later redactions. The former is artistically the finer production. Its style is rhetorically and poetically colored, but its construction is strictly narrative. Its interest, apart from the importance of its subject, lies in the author's genuine gift of poetical atmosphere and his discrete and skillful use of reminiscences of *The Campaign of Ígor*.

Towards the end of the present period a new style of writing was imported by the numerous Serbian and Bulgarian clerics who came to Russia after the conquest of their countries by the Turks. Outstanding among these ecclesiastics was Cyprian, Metropolitan of Moscow (d. 1406). The first Russian bookman to use the new style was Epiphanius the Wise, a monk of the Trinity Monastery and a disciple of St. Sergius. The new style found its chief expression in hagiography. Its main characteristic was a disregard for concrete detail and a conventionalized treatment of the subject. The individual was so reduced to the typical that the writings of the school have practically no value as historical evidence. In Epiphanius's *Life of St. Sergius* this stage is not yet quite reached—he had a too intimate knowledge of his master to let the saint's personality be lost in a conventional pattern. But his other work, the *Life of St. Stephen of Permia,* became the type of such writings for the following centuries. Nor was the influence of the new style limited to hagiography. Its conventional and impersonal rhetoric was adopted by all writers with any literary pretension. The very language was changed under South Slavonic influence, and a stricter and more pedantic standard Church Slavonic replaced the strongly vernacularized language of the thirteenth and fourteenth centuries.

Somewhat off the main track, and probably not intended as literature, is the *Journey beyond the Three Seas,* by Afanásy Nikítin, a merchant of the city of Tver. It is the account of his commercial travels and life in India in 1466–72. It is interesting not only as an account of India a quarter of a century before the discovery of the sea route, but also as a revelatory reflection of the mental experience of an average Russian in unfamiliar surroundings.

THE MUSCOVITE PERIOD

Within less than a generation of the taking of Constantinople by the Turks the Prince of Moscow became the
effective monarch of all Great Russia and threw off the
last remnants of Tatar supremacy (1480). This succession
of events produced a revolution in the state of the Orthodox world, which was immediately taken into account by
the Muscovites and became the basis of their political
philosophy. Moscow became the third Rome, the sole depository of all imperial power and the only receptacle of
unsullied Orthodoxy. The marriage of Iván III to a
Palæologue princess and his assumption of the title "Autocrat" transformed the Prince of Moscow, who had been
little more than a *primus inter pares* among other princes,
into the sole successor of the Cæsars. The official crowning
and assumption of the title of "Tsar" (Cæsar) was the
work of Iván III's grandson and namesake of "Terrible"
reputation.

The first century or so after the accession of the first
Autocrat (1462) was marked by violent political and religious conflicts. They gave rise to an interesting polemical
literature, which, however, belongs to the domain of the
general rather than of the literary historian. The conflict
was at first chiefly between the party of bishops and abbots,
who insisted on the worldly claims of the Church and on
taking an active part in secular government, and the party
of the "Hermits from beyond the Volga," whose headquarters were the monastery of St. Cyril on the White Lake
(east of St. Petersburg) and who favored a more mystical
and ascetic conception of the Church. The chief man of
the clerical party was Joseph, Abbot of Volokolámsk, a
vigorous pamphleteer who wrote in a correct Slavonic full
of expletives. The leader of the Hermits was Blessed Nil
Sórsky, a disciple of Mount Athos and the most remarkable
mystical and ascetic writer of Old Russia. The Hermits
were supported by part of the aristocracy, who regarded
the bishops and abbots as usurpers of their political rights
and desired to limit the growing power of the Tsar.

By the middle of the sixteenth century the religious
controversy was over, the clerical party being victorious,

on all points. But the political controversy between the partisans of autocracy and the oligarchs was continued into the reign of Iván the Terrible (b. 1530, crowned Tsar 1547, d. 1584). Iván was no doubt a cruel tyrant, but he was a pamphleteer of genius. His epistles are the master-pieces of Old Russian (perhaps all Russian) political journalism. They may be too full of texts from the Scriptures and the Fathers, and their Slavonic is not always correct. But they are full of cruel irony, expressed in pointedly forcible terms. The shameless bully and the great polemist are seen together in a flash when he taunts the runaway Kúrbsky by the question: "If you are so sure of your righteousness, why did you run away and not prefer martyrdom at my hands?" Such strokes were well calcu-lated to drive his correspondent into a rage. The part of the cruel tyrant elaborately upbraiding an escaped victim while he continues torturing those in his reach may be detestable, but Iván plays it with truly Shaksperian breadth of imagination. Besides his letters to Kúrbsky he wrote other satirical invectives to men in his power. The best is the letter to the Abbot of St. Cyril's Monastery where he pours out all the poison of his grim irony on the un-ascetic life of the boyars, shorn monks, and those exiled by his order. His picture of their luxurious life in the citadel of asceticism is a masterpiece of trenchant sarcasm.

Iván's principal opponent, Prince Andréy Mikháylo-vich Kúrbsky (c. 1528–83), was one of the most cultured and enlightened men in Muscovy. He played a prominent part in the administration and distinguished himself as a soldier at the siege of Kazán and in the Livonian war. In 1564, during the war with Lithuania, when Iván had instituted his reign of terror, Kúrbsky, fearing responsibility for a reverse of his army, deserted to the enemy. From Lithuania he wrote his famous epistles to the Tsar and a *History* of his reign. The latter work is pragmatic, not an-nalistic, and shows him a man of keen and constructive intellect. He deliberately exaggerates the crimes of his archenemy and is not to be trusted as impartial witness. His style is strongly infused with West Russian, Polish, and Latin influences. It does not reveal any original literary temperament. The same with his epistles: for all their sincere violence, just indignation, and forcible argument, as literature they are inferior to those of his opponent.

The fixation of the Muscovite mentality took place in the middle of the sixteenth century. About that time was undertaken and accomplished a series of compilations that together form a sort of encyclopædia of Muscovite culture. These works cannot all be regarded as falling within the cognizance of literary history. Thus the *Stoglóv* (*Book of a Hundred Chapters*), which contains the decisions on dogmatic, ritual, administrative, and disciplinary subjects of a Provincial Council of the Russian Church held in Moscow in 1551, belongs to canon law rather than to literature. Nor has the *Domostróy* (*House-Orderer*), edited by the priest Sylvester (d. 1566) substantially greater claims to be regarded as literature: it is a didactic work setting down in literary Slavonic, but without literary pretensions, the principles by which the head of the house is to rule his family.

A more literary work is the great *Menologion* or *Saints' Calendar* (*Chetyí-Minéi*) compiled by Macarius, Metropolitan of Moscow (d. 1563). It remained the official calendar of the Russian Church until the reign of Peter the Great. Macarius also gave its final form to another vast work of codification: *The Book of Degrees* (i.e., of generations, *Stepénnaya kníga*), so called because the Russian princes and tsars were grouped in the order of their generations. The collection had been started by Cyprian, the fourteenth-century Serbian Metropolitan of Moscow, but was completed only about 1563. In substance *The Book of Degrees* was a compilation from the Russian Annals, but these were recast so as to suit the literary taste and the historical philosophy of sixteenth-century Muscovy. The Annals, officially conducted throughout this period by Muscovite scribes, also reflect the all-prevading taste for rhetoric, and the political philosophy of the time.

MUSCOVITE HISTORIES

Besides these compilations and official Annals, there was no lack of historical literature in Muscovite times. Prince Kúrbsky's *History* stands somewhat apart, from the fact of having absorbed Western influences. But there was a local tradition of historical narratives of isolated, chiefly military events, with a style of their own that goes back to the *Rout of Mamáy* and the Russian Josephus, and is thus a collateral relative of *The Campaign of Ígor*. An early example is the *Story of the Taking of Pskov* (1510) by the Muscovites, one of the most beautiful "short histories" of Old Russia. The history of the Muscovites' leisurely perseverance is told with admirable simplicity and art. An atmosphere of descending doom pervades the whole narrative: all is useless, and whatever the Pskovites can do, the Muscovite cat will take its time and eat the mouse when and how it pleases.

The series of events that stimulated the most intense historiographical activity was the great political crisis of the early seventeenth century (1604–13) known in Russian historical tradition as the Time of Troubles. Three works especially stand out: that attributed to Prince Iván Katyrëv of Rostóv and those by Avraámy Pálitsyn, Bursar of the Trinity Monastery, and by the scribe Iván Timoféyev. Katyrëv's narrative is the most distinctly literary of the three: it is in the traditional style of the "military story," with very little regard for concrete details, with numerous recurrent stock passages, at times attaining to something like poetry. Pálitsyn's work is the most perfectly written. It is a piece of powerful and skillful rhetoric, inspired with a definite purpose and displaying great ability in the effective arrangement of its climaxes. The passages describing the horrors of civil war and foreign invasion are particularly memorable. Pálitsyn's work was the most popular of the whole family, and up to recent times his interpretation of the facts dominated Russian literary and historical tradition. Timoféyev's work is the greatest curio in all Muscovite literature. His amazingly quaint and elaborate style is the *reductio ad absurdum* of Muscovite rhetoric. On no account will he call a spade a spade. The rich become in his hands "those who have large receptacles." A river is "the element of watery nature." His grammar is complicated and contorted, and his meaning as a rule wonderfully obscure. But he is also the shrewdest and most intelligent of all contemporary historians. His story is a real story with a beginning and an end. Timoféyev has been given high praise as a chronicler and as a trustworthy witness by the greatest of our modern historians, Professor Platónov, who has singled him out as a particular favorite.

A last fruit of the Old Russian "military story" is the *Story of the Defense of Azóv* by the Don Cossacks against the Turks in 1641. It is really the official report of the Cossacks to the Tsar, but it is written as a story with definite literary aims, and as such became widely popular. It is a sort of epitome of all the traditions of Old Russian war narrative, with echoes of the Russian Josephus and all its progeny, of the *Rout of Mamáy,* of the *Tale of Troy*—and, on the other hand, of more modern forms of folklore, as represented now by the so-called *bylíny* and robber songs. It is full of the poetry of war and is one of the most stimulating of Old Russian writings.

The majority of saints' lives written during the Muscovite period are in the style introduced by the Serbs and by Epiphanius, and have no individual interest. An exception is the *Life of St. Juliánia Lazarévsky,* by her son Kalistrát Osóryin. St. Juliánia herself is an exception, being the only Russian female saint who was neither a nun nor a princess but merely a virtuous matron. The fact of a son's writing his mother's life is also unique. The *Life* is full of concrete detail and inspired by an intense feeling of Christian charity. It is one of the most attractive evocations of Old Russian life in the whole of literature.

BEGINNINGS OF FICTION

It is very difficult to draw a line between hagiography and biography, and fiction. There is a whole intermediate region that modern historians usually include in fiction but that the contemporary reader did not distinguish from hagiography. Such are the numerous legends standing in somewhat the same relation to the lives of saints as the Apocrypha stand to the Bible. Some were included in Macarius's compilation, and the unofficial Prologues contain even more. They were of course regarded primarily as books of edification, but the element of marvel and narrative interest is far more prominent than in the approved type of saint's life. Some have a distinctly fairy-tale appearance, as for instance the charming *Legend of Prince Peter of Múrom and of the Maiden Fevrónia,* with its battle against the dragon, and the wise maiden guessing the Prince's riddles.

A further step towards fiction is found in a remarkable seventeenth-century work, *The Story of Sávva Grúdtsyn*. It is in literary Church Slavonic and has all the appearance of a story of pure fact, with dates and place names in abundance, but it is probably a work of fiction written for purposes of edification. Sávva Grúdtsyn is a kind of Russian Dr. Faustus, who sells his soul to the Devil in return, not for knowledge, but for power and pleasure. The Devil serves him well, but finally Sávva repents and saves his soul in a monastery.

Along with these first essays in edifying narrative other types of fiction began to appear. It is probable that Russian narrative folk poetry as we now know it came into existence in the middle or second half of the sixteenth century. It is certain that its first written traces appear in the early seventeenth century, when it begins to exercise an appreciable influence on written literature. We have seen its influence in the *Siege of Azóv*. It is still more unmistakable in the story of *Woe-Misfortune* (*Góre-Zloschástie*), which is an isolated instance of the use of actual folk-song *meter* in a literary work. Like *Sávva Grúdtsyn* it is a work of edification, in a style not derived from ecclesiastical Muscovite literature, but from devotional folk poetry. "Góre-Zloschástie" is a man's ill luck, personified as a kind of guardian devil who accompanies his man from cradle to grave. He leads a fine young man of respectable and wealthy family from his father's house into the wide world, brings him to tavern and highroad and thence well-nigh to the gallows. But the young man finally escapes and ends his days in a monastery, the never-failing refuge of the Russian sinner. The figure of Góre is a powerfully poetical symbol, and the whole work bears evidence of being the work of a talented and original poet. Like all Old Russian fiction it is anonymous and cannot be exactly dated. It seems to belong to the middle of the seventeenth century.

Folk-song influence is again apparent in two romances introduced into Russia from abroad by the first half of the seventeenth century—*Bová Korolévich* and *Eruslán Lázarevich*. *Bová* is of French origin, a descendant of the Carolingian romance *Bueves d'Anston* (English: *Bevis of Hampton*). It came to Russia by way of a North Italian *Bovo d'Antona* and thence through Bohemia and White

Russia. In Russia it was completely assimilated and thoroughly Russianized. It is amusing to see how the French
romance has been transformed into a story of purely fairy-
tale adventure, with all the chivalrous and courtly element
eliminated. *Bová* and *Eruslán* (a distant descendant of the
Persian Rustam) were immensely popular as chapbooks.
It was from them that the poets of the eighteenth and
early nineteenth centuries formed their idea of Russian
folklore, of which they were the principal representatives
before the discovery of the *"bylíny."* Another popular
chapbook was *Apollón of Tyre*, a version of the Greek
romance that is the source of Shakspere's *Pericles*. It
came to Russia rather late in the seventeenth century via
a Latin version, but the Russian reader easily discovered
its familiar Byzantine flavor and rapidly adopted it. Rémizov has made use of it in one of his most delightful
legendary stories.

A curious little production connected, like *Góre-
Zloschástie* and *Bová*, with folk poetry, but again in a different way, is *The Story of a Young Man and a Girl*, a
dialogue between a suitor and a disdainful maiden. He
praises her in imaginative language closely connected with
the language of folk poetry. To every tirade of his she
answers with a tirade of coarse and equally imaginative
vituperation, which is also connected with popular charms
and curses. She ends, however, by yielding. It is a piece
of elaborate verbal art and has no parallel in Old Russian
literature. It seems to have been composed in the north
(where folk poetry was and is most alive) at the end of
the seventeenth century.

These last-mentioned works are entirely secular
and free from all intention of edifying. Still more
distinctly secular and unedifying are the stories derived from, or similar to, old French fabliaux and the
tales of the *Decameron*. A good example is the *Story of
the Merchant Karp Sutúlov* and of his wife, who success-
fully defended her virtue against all the attempts of another
merchant (a friend of Karp's), of her confessor, and of
the bishop. The chief defect of these stories lies in their
language, a rather colorless and illiterate form of Slavonic.
This defect is not shared by the masterpiece of Muscovite
fabliaux—the story of *Frol Skobéyev*. This interesting story
is written without any literary pretenses in a pure col-

loquial language with a simple syntax. It is a piece of vivid and cynical realism, telling in the calmest fashion and with evident, but unobtrusive, relish the tricks by which a low scrivener contrived to seduce and marry clandestinely a nobleman's daughter, and how he succeeded in reconciling himself with her parents and becoming ultimately a man of position. The naked and matter-of-fact simplicity of the story enhances the effect of its cynical picaresqueness.

The only rival to *Frol Skobéyev*'s unique position in the (unconsciously) literary use of the vernacular is the delightful story of the Gremille (*Érsh Schetínnikov*) and of the lawsuit intended against him by his neighbor fishes of the lake of Rostóv. It is also a picaresque story, for it tells of the Gremille's evading by lawful and lawless means all the rightful demands of the other fishes. The story is in the form of a lawsuit and is a delightful parody of Muscovite legal procedure and legal language.

It is impossible to date these with any precision. Some of them may have been written in the early years of the eighteenth century, but in substance they all belong to that latter half of the seventeenth when Muscovy was still Muscovite but when the foundations of its traditional, ecclesiastic civilization were being slowly undermined by a growing and disintegrating tide of secularization.

THE END OF OLD MUSCOVY: AVVAKÚM

Before it came to an end, Old Russian civilization found something like its final and definitive expression in two very dissimilar but, in a way, complementary figures—Tsar Alexis and Archpriest Avvakúm. Alexis (reigned 1645–76) wrote little. A few private letters and an instruction to his falconers are all we have of him. But it is sufficient to make him the most attractive of Russian monarchs. He acquired the surname *Tisháyshy*, which means "most quiet" or "most peaceful." Certain aspects of Russian Orthodoxy, not its most purely spiritual, but its æsthetic and worldly aspects, found in him their most complete expression. The essence of Alexis's personality is a certain spiritual epicureanism, manifested in an optimistic Christian faith, in a profound, but unfanatical, attachment to the traditions and ritual of the Church, in a desire to see everyone round him happy and at peace, and in a highly developed capacity to extract a quiet and mellow enjoyment from all things.

By an irony of fate the reign of this monarch was one of the most agitated in Russian history. Apart from wars and social unrest it was marked by the Great Schism of the Russian Church, a tragic development that split in twain the conservative core of the nation and whose influence has lasted to this day. Its origin was connected with the revision of the liturgic books. In the preceding reign the development of printing had made the fixation of the sacred texts an important matter. In the 1640's a revision of all sacred books, in agreement with the best available Slavonic texts, was carried out under the auspices of the Patriarch Joseph. It was done largely by a group of young secular priests who were full of zeal to purge the Russian Church of the spirit of sloth and laxity and who demanded from clergy and laity a stricter observance of tradition. Their reforms were conservative and intended to revive the good practice of early Muscovite times. Among other things they renewed the practice of preaching, which had been in abeyance for about a century. One of the most fervid of these reformers was the priest (later archpriest) Avvakúm. He was the son of a country parson of the district of Nízhny-Nóvgorod, where he was born about 1620. In his fervor he more than once met with ill treatment at the hand of the laity and worldly priests, who resented his rigorous preaching and his interference with the old-established usages of lazy laxity.

In 1652 the Patriarch Joseph died and was succeeded by Níkon, Archbishop of Nóvgorod. He had been a friend of the reformers. Once patriarch, he decided to go one better in the revision of books and restoration of rituals, and, instead of limiting himself to Old Russian models, he turned to the Greek. This new revision resulted in the publication of texts conforming to the Greek and in certain changes of ritual where Russian practice had differed from that of the Greeks, as, for example, in making the sign of the cross with two fingers and saying alleluia twice instead of the Greek three fingers and treble alleluia. It was such seemingly–unimportant points that led to the schism. Avvakúm and his friends refused to accept them and denounced Níkon as a heretic and a tool of Satan. The main reason for their revolt was that they regarded the practice of the Russian Orthodox Church as one whole, dogma and ritual, of which not a tittle might be changed. Russia was the only repository of the faith and had nothing to learn from the Greeks, whose orthodoxy had been adulterated by dalliance with the heretic and subjection to the infidel. Níkon, who was then practically an autocrat, stood firm, and Avvakúm and his friends were exiled. Avvakúm was sent to Siberia and ordered to join the expeditionary force of Páshkov, whose task it was to conquer Dáuria (the present Transbaykália). Páshkov was a valiant "builder of empire" but had no patience with any religious nonsense. He treated Avvakúm with brutal cruelty.

For nine years Avvakúm remained in Siberia, dragged about from place to place and persecuted in every manner. In 1664 he was brought back to Moscow, where during his absence considerable changes had taken place, Níkon had fallen, and a synod was going to meet to judge both Níkon and Avvakúm. The Tsar was disposed to concessions. But Avvakúm was opposed to all compromise, and Alexis was forced to submit to the guidance of the Greek party. The Synod of 1666-7 condemned Avvakúm's ritual tenets, and thus the schism became final: the conservatives were henceforth schismatics (*raskólniki*). Avvakúm himself was shorn monk and exiled to Pustozérsk in the far northeast of Russia. There he became an even more prominent, active, and dangerous leader than he had been before. It was then he wrote his famous *Life* and his powerful epistles to his friends, in which he urged them to keep faithful to the old faith, to defy their persecutors, and to seek martyrdom. He himself, by writing a violent letter to the young Tsar Theodore, seems to have courted martyrdom. It came at last: he was burned at the stake in April 1682, together with his most faithful and trusty friends, the monk Epiphanius and the priest Lazarus.

Avvakúm's writings are not voluminous. They consist of a *Life Written by Himself* (1672-3) and of a score of epistles, hortatory and consolatory to friends, and abusive to enemies, all written during his last years at Pustozérsk. He is above all remarkable for his language, which is the first attempt to use colloquial Russian for literary purposes. Though we do not know anything of the character of his oral preaching, it is highly probable that his written work had its roots in his spoken sermons. The daring originality of Avvakúm's venture cannot be overestimated, and the use he made of his Russian places him in the very first rank of Russian writers: no one has since excelled him in vigor and raciness and in the skillful command of all the expressive means of everyday language for the most striking literary effects. The freshness of his Russian is enhanced by his use of Church Slavonic, which he employs only in quotations from the holy books or allusions to them. The sacred texts shine like hard and solid jewels in the flexible and living texture of his spontaneous Russian. Avvakúm is a great artist of words, and his example is still full of instruction to every writer of Russian.

But Avvakúm is not only the efficient master of expression. He is a firm and fiery fighter, a good hater and a good friend. Scorn and indignation are mixed in his writings with a fierce and manly tenderness that has nothing sentimental in it: the best lot he desires for his best disciples is a martyr's death. His style is constantly relieved by a delightful humor, which ranges from that Christian humor at one's own expense which is so genuinely akin to humility, to stinging and cruel sarcasm at the expense of his foes, which, however, is never far removed from a smiling pity for the torturers who know not what they do. His masterpiece is his *Life*, in which he relates his striving for the truth, and his sufferings at the hands of Páshkov and of the bishops. It has been admirably rendered into English by Jane E. Harrison and Hope Mirrlees, whose translation should be read by everyone who is at all interested in things Russian or in good literature.

Avvakúm's writings were immensely influential with his followers, the Old Believers or Raskólniks. But his manner of writing found no imitator among them, while outside their communities no one read him before the mid-nineteenth century except for purposes of confutation.

2

The Passing of Old Russia

AFTER the Union of Lúblin (1569) all the west of Russia (White Russia, Galicia, and Ukraine) came under the direct rule of Poland. The Poles, organized by the Jesuits, started a vigorous campaign against the Orthodox faith and the Russian nationality. They easily succeeded in winning over the West Russian nobility, but met with the determined opposition of the middle and lower classes. The most active form this opposition took was the series of Cossack rebellions. Its other aspect was a religious and intellectual movement in the Church and laity. Schools were founded, and there sprung up an active polemical literature to counteract the Roman propaganda.

The early stage of the movement produced an original and talented writer, Iván Výshensky (of Výshnya, in Galicia; *flor.* 1588–1614), a sort of attenuated Ukrainian Avvakúm. He opposed his co-religionaries' tendency to adopt Latin methods in fighting the Latins, which seemed to him in itself a capitulation to the alien civilization. But the advantages of adopting the Jesuits' learning were too obvious, and by the end of the first quarter of the seventeenth century this method of fighting the enemy had finally triumphed among the West Russians. The Kíev

Academy, founded in 1631 by Peter Mohýla (1596–1647), Abbot of the Crypt Monastery and afterwards Metropolitan of Kíev, became the center of all intellectual activity in West Russia.

The Latin culture adopted by West Russia was purely ecclesiastical and scholastic, and so was the literature it produced. Its principal interest lies in its attempts to assimilate Polish and Polish-Latin forms of poetry and drama, which will be discussed later. Apart from these, Kievan literature consisted mainly of polemical writings, sermons, and textbooks. The sacred oratory of the period is a conscientious effort to adopt the forms of classical rhetoric. Its principal representatives were Ioánniky Golyatóvsky, Rector of the Kíev Academy, and Lázar Baranóvich, Archbishop of Chernígov, both of whom flourished in the third quarter of the seventeenth century. More important are the writers of the following period, whose work belongs already to the reign of Peter the Great.

THE TRANSITION IN MOSCOW AND PETERSBURG

In Muscovy Western influences began to play an appreciable part about the year 1669, when the Westernizer Artamón Matvéyev became head of the administration. They came by two channels—one from the southwest, the other via the German Liberty (*Nemétskaya slobodá*) of Moscow. This was a settlement of foreigners in the military or financial service of the government and of foreign businessmen, nearly all of them from the Protestant nations, Germany, Holland, and Scotland. As literature and art were mainly an ecclesiastical business, the predominating Western influence in literature was at first that of the southwestern current.

By the time Peter the Great began his "Reforms," the progress of Westernization had advanced considerably in Moscow. But it had proceeded along familiar lines, Westernizing the fabric of the Church but leaving it the center of all civilization. Peter's reforms were far more revolutionary. They aimed at displacing the Church from its place of honor and at secularizing the whole of the Russian polity. Literature took some time before it fully felt the new state of things, and the literature of the reign of Peter is largely a continuation of the preceding period. Its outstanding men of letters were three prelates of Ukrainian origin, bred in the Latin methods of the Kíev Academy: St. Demetrius Tuptálo (1651–1709), Metropolitan of Rostóv, Stephen Yavórsky (1658–1722), locum tenens of the patriarchal chair, and Feofán Prokopóvich (1681–1736), Archbishop of Nóvgorod.

Demetrius of Rostóv is a particularly attractive character. A great scholar and lover of books and learning, he was a peace-loving, meek, and charitable prelate who won the boundless love and gratitude of his flock. After his death he came to be venerated as a saint and was officially canonized in 1757. He is the most exquisite fruit of the cultural revival of seventeenth-century Kíev. His most voluminous work is his *Calendar of Saints,* which, compiled along more European and scholastic lines than Macarius's, replaced the older work and is to this day the standard compendium of Russian hagiology. He is particularly interesting as a playwright (*v. infra*).

Stephen Yavórsky is chiefly notable as a preacher. His sermons are composed in a simple and manly style, free from excessive rhetorical ornament. They are often outspoken in dealing with current issues. Yavórsky deeply resented many of Peter's innovations and showed sympathy with the Old Muscovite opposition. He dared to rebuke Peter for his divorce, lamented the fate of the Church in a secularized Russia, and dared to raise his voice against the intolerable weight of conscriptions and taxes that ground down the lower classes.

Feofán Prokopóvich, a younger man, was animated with a different spirit. In secularizing his own mentality he went further than any other prelate. Very widely educated, he was the first Russian writer to go direct to the fountainhead of European culture in Italy and not to be satisfied with Polish and Polish-Latin learning. He was a powerful orator, and his funeral oration on Peter the Great remained for over a century the most famous piece of Russian solemn oratory. His sermons and orations are secular in tone, inspired with a cult of enlightened despotism and a hero-worship of the great despot that sounds even less Protestant than pagan.

The secular literature of the age of Peter discarded Slavonic and made Russian the literary language. But it was a curious Russian, full of Slavonic reminiscences and saturated with undigested words of every conceivable foreign origin—Greek, Latin, Polish, German, Dutch, Italian, and French. The formal rupture with the old language was symbolized by the introduction of a new alphabet, in which the Slavonic letters were modified so as to resemble Latin characters. Henceforward Russia had two alphabets: the Church continued using the old alphabet with the old language; the lay society used only the new. The books printed in "civil" characters during Peter's reign and some time afterwards were either laws and official resolutions, or translations. As the nature of Peter's reforms was above all practical, the books translated all referred to practical knowledge.

Of the original writings of the period those of Peter himself are easily the best. His Russian was quaintly mixed with barbarisms, but he used it with vigor, terseness, and originality. His literary originality is evident everywhere —in his journals, in his letters, even, and perhaps best of all, in his official ordinances. The vivid and realistic imagery of his style makes his ukases the most enjoyable literature of the time. He had a genius for pithy and memorable statement, and many of his sayings still live in everyone's memory.

Of the other secular writers of the period the most interesting are Iván Pososhkóv (1652–1726), a tradesman and self-educated man who wrote a book, *On Indigence and Wealth,* and Vasíly Nikítich Tatíschev (1686–1750), whose *History of Russia,* though formless from the literary point of view, is the first really scholarly attempt to tackle the vast material in the Russian Annals together with the evidence of foreign writers. It is quite on a level with contemporary European erudition. Tatíschev was one of the most cultured men of his class and time, a politician, and an administrator. His *Testament,* addressed to his son, is an interesting document, reflecting the high sense of duty and practical patriotism that is characteristic of the men of Peter's school.

THE FIRST LITERARY VERSE

Verse writing was introduced into Russia from Poland in the late sixteenth century. The oldest extant specimens are found in the rhymed preface to the Ostróg Bible (1581). In the seventeenth century much rhymed verse was written by West Russian scholars. The prosody they employed was Polish, which, like French and Italian, is based on the counting of syllables, without any obligatory position for stress accent. The matter of this West Russian poetry is panegyrical or didactic. About 1670 it was imported to Moscow by the White Russian cleric Sýmeon of Pólotsk, who flourished at the courts of Alexis and his son Theodore and who attained considerable elegance in the turning of syllabic verses. But no trace of anything that may, except by courtesy, be styled poetry is to be discovered before the age of Peter. Apart from dramatic poetry the only versifier of the school with a grain of the poet in him was Feofán Prokopóvich. His pastoral elegy on the hard times that befell the men of Peter's making after the death of the Great Monarch is one of the first genuinely poetical literary lyrics in the language.

When young Muscovite laymen became acquainted with the technique of rhyming, they began trying their hand at amatory verse. Doggerel rhymes on amatory subjects are extant from the last years of the seventeenth century (the oldest specimens, interestingly enough, occur in criminal lawsuits), and in the reign of Peter the Great this new art spread rapidly. Manuscript collections of love poems in syllabic verse have come down from the first half of the eighteenth century. They reflect the love songs that were current at the time in Germany. Altogether the Germans played a prominent part in the first developments of Russian poetry. Wilhelm Mons, a German of Moscow who was the lover of Peter's wife Catherine and was executed in 1724, wrote amatory verses in Russian but in German characters. They have a quaint intensity that makes us believe he was something of a poet. The first attempts to introduce regular feet into Russian verse were made by two Germans, the Pastor Ernst Glück (in whose house Catherine I had been a servant) and the Magister

Johann Werner Pauss. They translated Lutheran hymns into a Russian that, though very incorrect, is studiously pure of foreign words. By 1730 Russian society was ready to receive a more ambitious and regular poetry on the European model.

THE DRAMA

The ritual of the Eastern Church, like that of the Western, contained the germs of drama, but in the East they never grew into dramatic representations. Russian drama is entirely an importation from the West. Like most Western things it came by two distinct routes. One leads from the Latin school drama to the Kíev Academy and thence to Moscow; the other comes direct from the strolling secular players of Germany to the German Liberty of Moscow.

School dramas on religious subjects were introduced into West Russian schools very early, before the end of the sixteenth century. By the middle of the seventeenth they were a popular and stable institution. When not in Latin or Polish they were always translations from Latin or Polish. Their style was mediæval—they were the late-born children of the miracle and mystery play. The neo-classical theory of dramatic poetry was taught in the rhetoric class of the Kíev Academy, but before the eighteenth century these theories did not affect the practice. Kievan students continued playing, and their masters translated or adapted, plays of a purely mediæval type. There is little originality in the serious parts of these plays, but the comic interludes early received independent treatment. Native Ukrainian characters—the Cossack, the clerk, the Jew, the braggart Pole, the faithless wife and the comic husband—became traditional types, surviving the interlude and its successor the puppet play and living for ever in the early tales of Gógol. Before long the school drama left the school walls and went out into the wide world. Strolling bands of students performing miracle plays became a popular feature of Ukrainian life in the seventeenth and eighteenth centuries. A further development was the puppet theater, which finally assumed an entirely popular character and became one of the important starting points of modern Ukrainian literature.

When Kievan prelates and clerics came to Muscovy to rule the Muscovite Church, the school drama spread over Great Russia, but it failed to flourish on Great Russian soil and never became a popular institution. One reason was that here it had an important rival in the secular play of German origin. In 1672 Tsar Alexis caused Dr. Gregori, the Lutheran pastor of the German Liberty of Moscow, to form a troupe of amateur players to act before the Tsar's Majesty. Plays from the repertory of the German strolling players were translated by scribes of the Foreign Office into stilted and unidiomatic Slavonic prose (which sounds especially quaint in the comic parts), and a theater was instituted at the Royal Palace. One of the first plays produced was a distant descendant of *Tamburlaine the Great*. It was only after Gregori's first production that Sýmeon of Pólotsk ventured to introduce the Kievan school drama and wrote his *Action of the Prodigal Son* in rhymed syllabic verse. In the last years of the century, with the growth of Kievan influence in Muscovy, the rhymed school drama became predominant, but under Peter the Great the secular prose play translated from the German again took the upper hand. Public theaters were opened and the school drama was relegated to the seminaries and academies.

From the literary point of view, by far the greater part of this early drama is uninteresting and unoriginal. The secular prose drama is outside literature. The same cannot be said of the verse drama. Besides an interesting series of realistic comic interludes, it produced in the plays of Feofán Prokopóvich and Demetrius of Rostóv serious works of genuine literary value. Those of St. Demetrius are particularly attractive. They are quaintly baroque in their strangely concrete representation of the supernatural and their audacious use of humor when speaking of things solemn. The shepherds' dialogue in his *Nativity Play* and their discussion of the appearance of the approaching angels are particularly good.

Feofán Prokopóvich, who had studied in Italy and was much more modern than St. Demetrius, broke away from the mystery-play tradition, and his tragicomedy of *Saint Vladímir* (1705) is the first fruit of classical theory in Russia. Its model is the Italian renaissance drama. It is a *pièce à thèse* dealing with the introduction of Christianity into Russia by St. Vladímir despite the opposition of the

heathen priests. These priests are satirically intended—they
stand for the "idolatrous" Roman Catholics and conservative Orthodox ritualists, over whom triumphs the rational
Christianity of the enlightened despot Vladímir-Peter. Together with his lyric poetry and with the plays of St.
Demetrius, Feofán's dramatic work marks the highest
poetic level reached by the Kievan school.

FICTION AND CHAPBOOKS

The evolution of Russian prose fiction owed little to the
southwest, nor was it connected with the clergy. It
answered to a demand of the educated or semi-educated
laity. Young men of the nobility and gentry, government
scribes (especially those of the Foreign Office), and open-
minded young merchants of Moscow and of the commercial north were the first readers of fiction, the translators, copiers, and authors of the first Russian novels.
Our principal landmark in the early history of Russian
fiction is a group of works translated in Moscow in or
about the year 1677. These stories are not Russianized out
of recognition, as is the case with the earlier *Bová*, and
they retain, in their heavy, unidiomatic Slavonic, traces
of the languages from which they were translated. They
include a number of romances from the Polish that go
back in substance to chivalric romances of the late Middle
Ages and early Renaissance. It was precisely their foreign,
un-Muscovite spirit that attracted the young boyars and
scribes to these stories. What they liked most was the
presentation of romantic, chivalrous, and sentimental love,
so conspicuously absent in Old Russian literature. Fiction
became widely popular and was widely circulated in manuscript far into the eighteenth century, but no novel was
printed in Russia before 1750.

Original novel-writing after these new models began
in the time of Peter. Several manuscript novels are extant
belonging to the first half of the eighteenth century. They
follow a more or less uniform pattern. The subject is
always the experiences of a young Russian gentleman in
foreign countries, where he meets with more or less romantic and sentimental adventures. The style sometimes
inclines to rhythmical parallelism, and the characters are

often made to speak a rhymed doggerel. Together with the love rhymes of the period they were the irruption into Russian civilization of the Western conception of sentimental and gallant love.

Standing apart from this main line of development is the one preserved fragment of what its modern editor has called a "novel in verse." It is unique in kind and impossible to date (except for the use of rhyme there is no formal evidence pointing to a date later than 1670–80). Its meterless doggerel is written in a simple vernacular style with constant parallelism or reduplication and with a certain kinship to popular poetry. The narrator, a woman, tells of her relations with her lover and her unloved husband. The setting is the drab and ordinary one of everyday life. Some passages are outspokenly and coarsely, but not in the least cynically, realistic. There is an unsweetened directness and sense of tragedy in the narrative, which makes one think of some nineteenth-century realist, like Písemsky or Maupassant.

Soon after the death of Peter, Russian literature finally becomes modern and Western. But the new, French-bred literature was confined to the upper classes, and the people remained more or less aloof from it. The later eighteenth century produced a popular literature distinct from both the literature of the upper classes and the unwritten folk poetry. It catered to the lower middle and lower urban classes and was a direct continuation of the literature of the age of Peter.

When, in the middle of the eighteenth century, the printing press became an accessible and universal means of expression, numerous books and inscribed woodcuts began to be published for popular consumption. The publication of popular literature continued into the nineteenth and twentieth centuries, but its really interesting period is the second half of the eighteenth. Many, perhaps most, of these popular publications were books of edification— mainly lives of saints. But these are of little interest, being nothing but more or less modernized and vulgarized reproductions of older versions from the *Prologue* or the official *Menologion*. More interesting are the secular stories. *Eruslán, Bová, Apollón of Tyre,* and several translated romances of the late seventeenth century were first printed soon after 1750 and constantly reprinted. Of original productions that may be assigned to the second half of the eighteenth century, the most remarkable is the story of the famous robber, and afterwards police agent, *Vánka Káin* (Jack Cain). The story is told in the first person. It is an original specimen of the Russian picaresque imagination. Its style is a mixture of rhymed doggerel, cruel jokes, crude puns, and cynically roguish paraphrase and circumlocution. It was exceedingly popular: fifteen editions of it appeared in the last third of the eighteenth century.

Alongside the narrative chapbooks are the explanatory rhymed inscriptions that appear on the cheap woodcuts published for popular circulation in the eighteenth and early nineteenth centuries. In style they are clearly related to the showmen's cries at the open-air shows that were a prominent feature of Russian town life of that time, and which are themselves closely connected with Great Russian popular theater. Like the woodcuts they accompany, the doggerel inscriptions employ a rude and primitive technique. They cover a great variety of subjects. Their ultimate source is usually some book of the late seventeenth or early eighteenth century. Fairy-tale and novelistic subjects are particularly frequent. In the course of time the censorship learned to keep a watchful eye on these productions, but interesting satirical and political prints have come down to us from the earlier times. The most interesting of these is the famous picture of *The Mice Burying the Cat*. Though with the lapse of time its satirical meaning was lost, and it continued popular merely as an amusing bit of fun, it is in substance a savage satire on the death of Peter the Great. It reflects the feelings of the Old Believers and other enemies of the great tyrant, the exultation of the oppressed and martyred mice at the end of their persecutor.

3

The Age of Classicism

MODERN Russian literature dates from the establishment
of a continuous tradition of secular imaginative literature
in the second quarter of the eighteenth century. The adop-
tion of French classical standards by four men, all born in
the reign of Peter, and their variously successful attempts
to transpose these standards into Russian and to produce
original work according to them are the starting point of all
subsequent literary development. The four men were Kantemír, Trediakóvsky, Lomonósov, and Sumarókov.

KANTEMÍR

Prince Antioch Kantemír (1708–44), the son of a wealthy
and cultured noble (his father's history of the Turks,
written in Latin, remained for over a century the standard
work on the subject), was himself, at the age of twenty-
two, probably the most cultured man in Russia. During the
crisis of 1730 he was a leader of the anti-oligarchic party,
and, together with Feofán Prokopóvich and the historian
Tatíschev, persuaded the Empress Anne to cancel the constitution she had sworn to observe. In the same year he
was appointed Minister-Resident to London. In 1738 he
was transferred to Paris, where he remained Russian

Minister till his death in 1744. While in Paris he kept up close relations with many eminent French men of letters, including Fontenelle and Montesquieu.

His literary work is contained in his satires, written between 1729 and 1739. They remained in manuscript till long after his death, and when they were at last published, in 1762 (a French version had appeared in London in 1749), it was too late for them to influence the development of Russian literature, for their language and "syllabic" meter had already become antiquated as a result of Lomonósov's reforms. Kantemír's style is Latin rather than French. Despite the use of rhyme, his verse produces an effect closely similar to that of the hexameter of Horace. His language is racy and colloquial, considerably less bookish and Slavonic than that which was to triumph with Lomonósov. His painting of life is vigorous, and, though he adheres to the main lines of the classic tradition, his characters are living types, taken from the thick of contemporary Russian life. Kantemír has every right to be regarded as the first deliberate and artistically conscious realist in Russian literature. The edge of his satire is directed against the enemies of enlightenment, the unfaithful successors of Peter's work, the old prejudices of Muscovy, and the new foppishness of the semi-educated, Europeanized young nobles.

TREDIAKÓVSKY

Very different were the career and work of Vasíly Kiríllovich Trediakóvsky (1703–69), the son of a poor priest of Ástrakhan. There is an anecdote that Peter the Great, passing through that city, saw the boy and, patting him on the head, called him a "lifelong drudge," a prophecy that sums up Trediakóvsky's whole career. He was the first non-noble Russian to receive a humanistic education abroad (in Paris), and he learned to compose fugitive verses in French that were not beneath the accepted level. Soon after his return to Russia he was appointed Acting Secretary to the Academy. One of his duties in this post was to compose complimentary odes and panegyrics on various occasions and solemn orations in Russian and Latin. Innumerable pathetic anecdotes reflect his humiliating relations with the arrogant nobles of his time, who regarded the professional poet and orator as an inferior kind of domestic servant. His numerous translations are extraordinarily clumsy. His verse is devoid of all poetic merits and began to seem unreadable long before his death. His principal work, a translation in hexameters of Fénelon's *Télémaque* (1766), as soon as it appeared, became a byword for all that is pedantic and ugly. His claim to recognition as an important figure in Russian literary history is mainly based on his work as a theoretician of poetry and prosody. His *View of the Origin of Poetry and of Verse* (1752) is the first statement in Russian of the classical theory of imitation. Still more important are his works on Russian prosody. Although he did not, as was once thought, introduce regular accentual feet into Russian verse, his theories were not only remarkable for their time, but are interesting even today.

LOMONÓSOV

Kantemír and Trediakóvsky were precursors. The real founder of modern Russian literature and of modern Russian culture was a greater man than either of them— Mikháylo Vasílievich Lomonósov. He was born in 1711, the son of a "peasant" of Kholmogóry (south of Archangel) who was a deep-sea fisherman by trade. Much of his boyhood was spent in his father's boat, in the White Sea and Arctic Ocean, where they used to go as far as the Murman coast and Nova Zembla. The boy was early taught the Slavonic alphabet, but his father did not countenance his insatiable thirst for further knowledge. In December 1730, therefore, he left home and went to Moscow, where he entered the Slavo-Græco-Latin Academy as a student. Without any support from his father he persevered and, in 1736, was sent to Germany to complete his education. At Marburg he studied philosophy, physics, and chemistry under the famous Christian Wolff; afterwards, at Freiburg in Saxony, he learned practical mining. It was from Germany that he sent to the Academy of St. Petersburg an *Ode on the Taking of Khótin* (1739), the first Russian poem written in what has since become our classical prosody. In 1741 Lomonósov returned to Russia and was appointed Assistant Professor at the Academy of Science. His connection with the Academy, of which he became virtual head in 1758, continued till his death. From the outset Lomonósov gave proof of an extraordinary working capacity and an incredible range of interest and knowledge. Chemistry, physics, mathematics, mining, the making of mosaics, grammar, rhetoric, poetry, and history were among his principal occupations, and in all except history and mosaics he produced work of lasting value. At the same time he worked at reorganizing the Academy and actively combated the "German party," whose policy it was to make the Russian Academy a snug home for unemployed German *Literaten*. Worn out by his toils and endless strife with Germans and unsympathetic ministers, he became addicted to drink, and in his last years he was little better than a ruin of his former self. He died in 1765.

Two passions reigned in Lomonósov: patriotism and the love of science. To create a Russian science and a Russian literature worthy to rival those of the West was his one dream. His upright, unbending character and his firm sense of dignity won him universal esteem in an age when birth and power were as a rule the only claim to esteem. His hostility to the Academic Germans never prevented him from recognizing the achievement of German scientists. When the physicist Richmann lost his life while experimenting in electricity, Lomonósov used all his influence to save from poverty the widow and children of this martyr of science. The letter he wrote on the occasion to the minister Shuválov is one of the noblest expressions of his faith in the nobility of science. Lomonósov's vocation was to be a scientist. His achievements in physics and chemistry are important, and he is regarded today as an advanced precursor of the methods of physical chemistry. In his lifetime only the most advanced minds, like the great mathematician Euler, were able to gauge the full extent of his scientific genius. To the great majority of his contemporaries he was primarily a poet and an orator. Since then the situation has been reversed, and in the later nineteenth century it became the fashion to praise the scientist at the expense of the poet. We are in a position to give him better justice.

In literature Lomonósov was first of all a legislator. He fixed the standards of the literary language and introduced a new prosody, which, despite numerous revolutionary attempts to dislodge it, still rules the greater part of Russian poetry. Church Slavonic had ceased to be the language of secular literature before Lomonósov's time, but literary Russian was still in a state of standardless chaos. It had freely borrowed from the older idiom, as it had to if it were to become a literary language, but the fusion of the Russian and Slavonic elements was incomplete and unsettled. It was Lomonósov's task to find a *modus vivendi* for the two and to give the new literary language a final form. His linguistic reform is contained in his practice as poet and prose writer and in his legislative writings, which include a *Rhetoric,* a *Russian Grammar,* and a remarkable essay, *On the Use of Sacred Books in the Russian Tongue.* Without entering into details of his reform, suffice it to say that he made the best use of the great lexical and grammatical wealth of Church Slavonic, thus to a certain extent repeating the work done in the Western languages by the humanistic scholars who enriched French, Italian, and English by the infusion of Latin blood. Although Lomonósov's solution of the problem has since been modified, the essentials have survived, and his Russian is in many ways nearer to ours than to the language of his immediate predecessors. An important feature of his linguistic legislation is his—characteristically classicist—doctrine of the three styles of diction: "high," "middle," and "low." They were to be distinguished chiefly by the relative abundance of Slavonic elements. Where there were two words, Slavonic and vernacular, to denote the same thing, the Slavonic was to be preferred in the "high" style, while none but strictly colloquial expressions were to be used in the "low."

Lomonósov's language has, no doubt, become antiquated. Because of the later evolution of the colloquial language it is often his boldest colloquialisms that seem to us most antiquated. Slavonic doubtlets of many Russian words have also gradually been dropped, though they survived in poetry long after the fall of classicism. It is, however, in the syntax, which betrays an excessive influence of Latin and German periodic construction, that Lomonósov's Russian has least survived. Nevertheless his importance as the legislator and actual *founder* of the literary language of modern Russia cannot be exaggerated.

Lomonósov's metrical reform consisted in the introduction of equisyllabic and accentual feet instead of the old syllabic prosody. His system was largely an adaptation of the prosody introduced into German by Opitz and further perfected by Fleming, Gryphius, and Lomonósov's immediate model, Günther. As a theorist of prosody Lomonósov was inferior to Trediakóvsky and Sumarókov, but the force of his example, of his own poetical practice, carried all opposition before it.

In the second half of the nineteenth century it was the fashion to belittle Lomonósov's poetry and even to deny him the title of poet. But the eighteenth century regarded him as a great poet, not only as a "Russian Malherbe," but as a "Russian Pindar"—and we are not very far from reverting to this view. Like a true classicist he rigorously distinguished between the various kinds of poetry, and the style of his didactic epistles is different from that of his odes. In the former he writes a very pure Russian, and though he submits to the eighteenth-century fashion of paraphrase, he conveys his idea with almost scientific precision. The famous epistle *On the Use of Glass,* ridiculed by the nineteenth century for its prosaic subject, might easily be used as a chapter from a textbook, so exact is its language. His principal poetical works are, however, his odes, sacred and panegyrical. They are not the expression of individual experience, but the ideal voicing of the sentiments and aspirations of a nation, or at least of its intellectual elite. The panegyrical odes extol Peter the Great as Russia's "culture hero" and his daughter Elizabeth for continuing her father's work, neglected by his first successors. They sing the glory of Russian armies and the greatness of the Empire, but, above all, the praise of science, learning, and industry. They call on Russia to produce "her own Platos and quick-witted Newtons" that she may eclipse her Western teachers. But Lomonósov's highest range as a poet is attained in the sacred odes, inspired by the rationalistic conception of a legislating God who manifests Himself in the grand, immutable laws of nature. The two *Meditations on the Divine Majesty* are especially fine examples of Lomonósov's philosophic poetry—and of his power to trace in grand, broad strokes the solemn and majestic aspects of nature. But the finest example of his eloquence, his "mighty line," and his "curious felicity" of diction is the admirable

Ode, selected from Job, Chapters xxxviii–xli, where the Jealous God of the Old Testament is with convincing vigor transformed into a Leibnitzian Legislator of the universe.

NARRATIVE AND LYRIC POETRY AFTER LOMONÓSOV

If Lomonósov was the father of modern Russian civilization, the father of the Russian literary profession was Alexánder Petróvich Sumarókov (1718–77). Born of a good family of Muscovite gentry, he was educated at the Cadet School in Petersburg, where he acquired an intimate familiarity with French polite learning. Neither an aristocratic dilettante like Kantemír nor a learned professor like Trediakóvsky or Lomonósov, he was the first *gentleman* in Russia to choose the profession of letters. He wrote much and regularly, chiefly in those literary kinds neglected by Lomonósov. His principal importance rests in his plays, but his non-dramatic work is by no means negligible. His fables are the first attempt in a genre that was destined to flourish in Russia with particular vigor. His satires, in which he occasionally imitates the manner of popular poetry, are racy and witty attacks against the archenemies of his class—the government clerks and officers of law. His songs are, of all his writings, those which still can be expected to attract the reader of poetry. They are remarkable for a truly prodigious metrical inventiveness (not so much as imitated by his successors) and a genuine gift of melody. In subject matter they are entirely within the pale of classical, conventional love poetry.

Sumarókov also pioneered in journalism and literary criticism. His criticism is usually carping and superficial, but it did much to inculcate on the Russian public the canons of classical taste. He was a loyal follower of Voltaire, with whom he prided himself on having exchanged several letters. He used Voltaire's authority in combating the abominations of sentimental taste which, in the form of the English sentimental drama, began to insinuate themselves into Russia towards the end of his life. Vain and self-conscious, Sumarókov considered himself a Russian Racine and Voltaire in one. In personal relations he was irritable, touchy, and often petty. But this exacting touchiness contributed, almost as much as did Lomonósov's calm dignity, to raise the profession of the pen and to give it a definite place in society.

Lomonósov and Sumarókov inaugurated the reign of classicism and established the undisputable authority of "one Boileau" and of his heir on the critical throne— Voltaire. Poetry became the principal field for literary ambition. It was strictly divided into immutably established kinds, each with its prescribed forms, style, and meter. Individual poets might write in every one of these kinds, but they might not mix them. The high kinds were tragedy, epic, and the solemn ode. On a lower level stood the Horatian ode, the song, the satire, the tale in verse (as canonized by La Fontaine), the fable, and the burlesque.

The epic was regarded as the highest form of poetry, and a literature could not pretend to independent importance unless it had produced a national epic. Lomonósov had attempted an epic on Peter the Great, but left it barely begun. Michael Kheráskov (1733–1807), a gentleman of Moldavian origin, a pietist, a Freemason, for many years Curator of the University of Moscow, and one of the most enlightened and universally respected men of the century, renewed the attempt at a national epic. He wrote two vast narrative poems modeled on Voltaire's *Henriade: Rossiyáda* (1779), on the taking of Kazán by Ivan the Terrible, and *Vladímir* (1785), on the introduction of Christianity by St. Vladímir. In the latter the author's pietistic and mystical tendencies come to the fore. Both poems, especially the patriotic *Rossiyáda,* were very popular, and Kheráskov was for a time regarded as the "Russian Homer." He was one of the first poets of the eighteenth century to be rejected by the nineteenth, but readers of Aksákov will remember with what enthusiasm he recited passages from Kheráskov when a small boy in the late 1790's.

The ode in Elizabeth's and Catherine's Russia was an important institution. There was a constant demand for odes at court, and ode-writing brought more tangible results in the form of pensions and honors than any other kind of literary exercise. The average level of ode-writing was naturally low. Except Derzhávin alone, all the ode-writers of the time of Catherine were more or less unoriginal imitators of Lomonósov. The most famous of them was Vasíly Petróv (1736–99), who lived for two years in

England and was an admirer and translator of Pope. A more pleasing and accomplished poet was Derzhávin's brother-in-law, the Ukrainian Vasíly Kapníst (1757–1823). He was the most polished and elegant poet of his time, excelling chiefly in the Horatian ode, a "middle" kind of poetry that stands halfway between the real ode and the frankly frivolous song.

Of the narrative kinds other than the regular epic, two of the most popular, the fable and the tale in verse, had for their origin the amiable genius of La Fontaine. The fable after Sumarókov was brilliantly represented by Iván Ivánovich Khemnítser (1745–84), a friend of Derzhávin and the first Russian fabulist to sound an original note. His fables give something more than a foretaste of Krylóv and are written in an admirable, vigorous, popular language. Some of them are among the few eighteenth-century poems that have remained universally popular ever since. The verse tale is represented by Ippolít Bogdanóvich (1743–1803), a Ukrainian who took the reading public by storm with his *Dúshenka*, an adaptation of La Fontaine's *Psyché et Cupidon*. For half a century *Dúshenka* was regarded as an exquisite masterpiece of light poetry.

The "lowermost" forms of narrative poetry were the mock-heroic poem and the burlesque. The former flourished in the hands of Vasíly Máykov (1728–78), whose *Elenséy, or Bacchus Infuriated* (1771) was the favorite comic reading of two generations of Russian readers. It abounds in crude but virile realism, and is, next to Khemnítser's fables, the best piece of unsweetened, colloquial Russian of its time. The burlesque produced several travesties of the *Æneid*, one of which is of special interest and considerable historical importance. This is the Little Russian *Æneid* of Kotlyarévsky (1798)—the starting point of modern Ukrainian literature.

DERZHÁVIN

Towering above the respectable and derivative mediocrity of all these verse writers stands the greatest poet of the century, one of the greatest and most original of all Russian poets—Gavríla Románovich Derzhávin. He was born in 1743 of a family of small squires of the Province of Kazán, and was educated at the Kazán high school. He acquired there a knowledge of German, but not of French or Latin. From school Derzhávin went to Petersburg, where he became a private in the footguards. Having no powerful protectors he rose but slowly to officer's rank. In 1773 the Pugachëv Rebellion found him on leave of absence in Kazán, where he attracted the attention of persons in power by writing for the nobility of the province an address with expressions of loyalty to the Empress. He became A.D.C. to General Bíbikov and, on the suppression of the rebellion, was given promotion and lands in the newly annexed White Russia. In 1777 he returned to Petersburg and entered the Civil Service. It was only now that he began to devote himself seriously to poetry. By 1780 Derzhávin was enjoying a considerable reputation as a poet. The reputation soon grew into a boom when there appeared, one after another, *Felítsa*, a semi-humorous ode to Catherine, and the famous *Ode to God*. In the former, Derzhávin extolled the virtues of the Empress and satirized the vices of her principal courtiers. It brought him Catherine's particular favor. When, shortly after its publication, Derzhávin quarreled with his superior and had to leave his office, he was immediately given a higher post and appointed Governor of Olonéts. But there again he quarreled with his associate governor and, on being transferred to the governorship of Tambóv, quarreled again. In 1791 he was appointed Secretary to the Empress for the receipt of petitions, but he did not get on with her, and when, after Catherine's death, Paul tried to employ him in a similar capacity, he found the poet equally difficult. Alexander I in 1802 made a last attempt to use him as an administrator and appointed him Minister of Justice. But the liberal spirit of the young Emperor's administration was against the grain of the old poet, who was an outspoken reactionary, and the experiment did not last more than a year. In 1803 Derzhávin left the Civil Service and settled down to enjoy life in his recently acquired estate of Zvánka, in the province of Nóvgorod. His spacious, epicurean, and philosophically quiet life there is described with verve in one of the most charming poems of his old age, *To Eugene, Life at Zvánka* (1807). During his last years Derzhávin's lyric genius remained almost undiminished, and when he died, in 1816, his last lines, the splendid opening stanza of an

Ode on Mortality, had just been jotted down on a slate.

Derzhávin's work is almost exclusively lyric. His tragedies, written in his later years, are negligible. His writings in prose are more important. The *Essay on Lyric Poetry* is a remarkable piece of uninformed, but inspired, criticism. The commentary he wrote to his poems is full of delightfully quaint and illuminating details. His *Memoirs* give a convincing picture of his obstinate and contrary character. His prose is rapid and nervous—quite free from the pedantic involutions of German-Latin rhetoric—next to Suvórov's the most personal and virile prose of the century.

His lyric poetry is great. For sheer imaginative power he is one of the small number of Russia's greatest poets. His philosophy is a joyous and avid epicureanism that does not deny God but admires Him quite disinterestedly. He accepts death and annihilation with a manful thankfulness for the joys of ephemeral life. He combines in a curious way a high moral sentiment of justice and duty with the resolute and conscious decision to enjoy life to the full. He loved the sublime in all its forms: the metaphysical majesty of a deistic God, the physical grandness of a waterfall, the political greatness of the Empire, of its builders and warriors. Gógol was right when he called Derzhávin "the poet of greatness." But though all these features are essentially classical, Derzhávin was a barbarian, not only in his love of material enjoyment, but also in his use of the language. "His genius," said Púshkin, "thought in Tatar, and knew no Russian grammar for want of time." His style is a continuous violence to the Russian tongue, an unceasing, vigorous, personal, virile, but often cruel, deformation of it. Like his great contemporary Suvórov, Derzhávin was not afraid of losses when the issue was victory. His greatest odes (as the famous *Waterfall*) consist too often of isolated and giddy peaks of poetry rising over a chaotic wilderness of harsh commonplace.

Derzhávin's range is wide. He wrote sacred and panegyrical odes, Anacreontic and Horatian lyrics, dithyrambs and cantatas, and even, in his later years, ballads. He was an audacious innovator, but his innovations conformed to the spirit of classicism. In his paraphrase of Horace's *Exegi Monumentum* he adduces as his principal claim to immortality the creation of a new genre: the humorous panegyrical ode. This bold mixture of the sublime with the realistic and comic is characteristic of his most popular odes, and it was largely owing to this novelty that he struck his contemporaries with such force. But apart from this innovation Derzhávin is also the greatest Russian poet in the orthodox classical manner, the most eloquent singer of the great immemorial commonplaces of poetry and universal experience. His greatest moral odes are the magnificent ode *On the Death of Prince Meschérsky,* than where the Horatian philosophy of *carpe diem* was never worded with more Biblical majesty; the short and vigorous paraphrase of Psalm lxxxii, against bad kings, which brought to the poet considerable unpleasantness after the French Revolution (the only way he could answer accusations was that "King David was not a Jacobin, so my poem can be disagreeable to no one"); and *The Nobleman,* a powerful invective against the great favorites of the eighteenth century, where a keen sarcasm goes hand in hand with a stern moral earnestness.

But what makes Derzhávin unique is his extraordinary power of conveying impressions of light and color. He saw the world as a heap of precious stones, and metals, and fire. His greatest achievements in this line are the opening of the *Waterfall,* which is also the acme of his rhythmical power; the astounding *Peacock* (so willfully spoiled at the end by a flat moral maxim); and the middle stanzas of the ode, *On the Return of Count Zúbov from Persia* (which is, by the way, a striking example of Derzhávin's independence and contrariness: written in 1797, immediately after the accession of Paul, who notoriously hated the Zúbovs, it was addressed to the brother of the late Empress's last favorite). It is in such poems that Derzhávin's genius reaches its most triumphant pinnacles. It is very hard to give an idea of them; their effect depends so largely on the extraordinary character of the words, the syntax, and, above all, the metrical divisions. His visual flashes and rhetorical eruptions make Derzhávin the poet par excellence of "purple patches."

A very peculiar division of Derzhávin's poetical work is the Anacreontic poems of his later years (first collected in 1804). Of all Russian poets Derzhávin is alone in striking this note of joyous, sturdy, sane sensuality of a green old age. The poems are not inspired merely by sexual sensuality, but by an enormous love of life in all its forms. Such are *Life in Zvánka,* the gastronomic-moralistic *Invitation to Dinner,* and the lines to Dmítriev on the gypsies. (Derzhávin was the first in the long line of great Russian writers—Púshkin, Grigóriev, Tolstóy, Leskóv, Blok—who did homage to the intoxication of gypsy music and gypsy dancing.) But among the later Anacreontic poems, there are also other poems of wonderful sweetness and melodiousness, in which (as Derzhávin tells us in his commentary) he avoided "the letter *r,* to prove the mellifluousness of the Russian language."

Derzhávin's poetry is a universe of amazing richness; its only drawback was that the great poet was of no use either as a master or as an example. He did nothing to raise the level of literary taste or to improve the literary language, and as for his poetical flights, it was obviously impossible to follow him into those giddy spheres.

THE DRAMA

The continuous history of the Russian drama and of the Russian theater begins in the reign of Elizabeth. The first regular drama, written according to French standards, was Sumarókov's tragedy *Khorév,* acted before the Empress in 1749 by young men of the Cadet School. The first regular troupe of players was founded a few years later in the city of Yaroslávl (on the upper Volga) by a local merchant, Fëdor Vólkov (1729–63). Elizabeth, who was a passionate lover of the theater, heard of the Yaroslávl players and summoned them to Petersburg. They played before her in 1752 to her entire satisfaction. Sumarókov was also delighted by Vólkov, and from their contact was born the first permanent theater in Russia (1756), with Sumarókov as its first director and Vólkov its leading actor. As has more often than not been the case in Russia ever since, the actors of the eighteenth century were superior to its playwrights. The great name in the history of the Russian classical theater is that of the tragic actor Dmítrevsky (1734–1821), one of Vólkov's original cast. He assimilated the French grand style of tragic acting, and heads the list of great Russian actors.

The classical theater rapidly became a popular insti-

tution. The educated and semi-educated, and even uneducated, classes of the time were fascinated by the acting of
classical actors in classical tragedies and comedies. It was
no doubt the good acting that made the reputation of
Sumarókov, as the literary value of his plays is small. His
tragedies are a stultification of the classical method; their
Alexandrine couplets are exceedingly harsh; their characters
are marionettes. His comedies are adaptations of French
plays, with a feeble sprinkling of Russian traits. Their
dialogue is a stilted prose that had never been spoken by
anyone and reeked of translation.

After Sumarókov, tragedy made little progress except
in the fluency and elegance of the Alexandrine couplet. The
principal tragic author of the age of Catherine was Sumarókov's son-in-law, Yákov Knyazhnín (1742–91), an
imitator of Voltaire. Some of his most interesting tragedies
(e.g., Vadím) breathe an almost revolutionary spirit of
political freethinking. Comedy was a much liver business
and, after Sumarókov, made great strides towards a firmer
grasp of the material of Russian life.

The most remarkable playwright of the age was Denís
Ivánovich Fonvízin. Born in 1745, in Moscow, of a family
of gentry, he received a good education at the University
of Moscow and very early began writing and translating.
He entered the Civil Service, became secretary to Count
Pánin, one of the great noblemen of the reign, and, in the
late 1760's, wrote the first of his two famous comedies,
The Brigadier-General. A man of means, he was always
a dilettante rather than a professional author, though he
became prominent in literary and intellectual circles. In
1777–8 he traveled abroad, the principal aim of his journey
being the medical faculty of Montpellier. He described his
voyage in his Letters from France—one of the most elegant
specimens of the prose of the period, and the most striking
document of that anti-French nationalism which in the
Russian elite of the time of Catherine went hand in hand
with a complete dependence on French literary taste. In
1782 appeared Fonvízin's second and best comedy The
Minor, which definitely classed him as the foremost of
Russian playwrights. His last years were passed in constant
suffering and traveling abroad for his health. He died in
1792.

Fonvízin's reputation rests almost entirely on his two

comedies, which are beyond doubt the best Russian plays before Griboyédov. They are both in prose and adhere to the canons of classical comedy. Fonvízin's principal model, however, was not Molière, but the great Danish playwright Holberg, whom he read in German, and some of whose plays he had translated. Both comedies are plays of social satire with definite axes to grind. *The Brigadier-General* is a satire against the fashionable French semi-education of the *"petits-maîtres."* It is full of excellent fun, and though less serious than *The Minor,* it is better constructed. But *The Minor,* though imperfect in dramatic construction, is a more remarkable work and justly considered Fonvízin's masterpiece. As is the rule with Russian classical comedies, it contains a pair of virtuous lovers, who are uninteresting and conventional. All the interest is concentrated in the Prostakóv family and their surroundings. The point of the satire is directed against the brutish and selfish crudeness and barbarity of the uneducated country gentry. Mme Prostakóv is a domineering bully with only one human feeling—her love for her sixteen-year-old son Mitrofán, whom she persists in calling "the child." Her maternal affection is of a purely animal and material nature: her one desire is that Mitrofán should eat his fill, not catch cold, not be bothered by duties or obligations, and that he might marry an heiress. In addition are her brother Skotínin (Mr. Brute), who confesses to a greater family feeling for pigs than for human beings; her sheepish husband Prostakóv (Mr. Simpleton); the nurse, doting on her "baby," who only bullies her; and finally the hero himself, Mitrofán. He is the accomplished type of vulgar and brutal selfishness, unredeemed by a single human feature—even his fondly doting mother gets nothing from him for her pains. The dialogue of these vicious characters (in contrast to the stilted language of the lovers and their virtuous uncles) is wonderful—true to life and finely individualized; and they are all masterpieces of characterization—a worthy introduction to the great portrait gallery of Russian fiction.

Fonvízin is superior to all his contemporaries in the art of drawing character and writing comical dialogue, but he is surrounded by a galaxy of talented comic playwrights, whose works present a lively picture gallery of the times. The most prolific was Knyazhnín, whose comedies are better than his tragedies. They are mostly in verse, and though for character drawing and dialogue they cannot rival Fonvízin's, they are often superior from the point of view of stagecraft. One of the best is *An Accident with a Carriage* (1779), a satire on serfdom that is bolder if less serious than Fonvízin's. Another notable dramatist was Michael Matínsky, a serf by birth, whose comedy *The St. Petersburg Bazaar* (c. 1781) is a vigorous satire on government clerks and their thievish ways. It is in prose, and partly in dialect. But the most famous dramatic satire, next to Fonvízin's, was Kapníst's *Chicane* (1798), in which the amiable author of Horatian odes revealed himself a savage satirist. His victims are the judges and officers of law, whom he paints as an unredeemed lot of thieves and extortioners. The play is in rather harsh Alexandrines and is full of outrages against the spirit of the Russian language, but it produces a powerful effect by the force of its passionate sarcasm. The two greatest Russian comedies of the nineteenth century, Griboyédov's *Woe from Wit* and Gógol's *Inspector General,* owe not a little to the crude and primitive comedy of Kapníst.

Closely connected with comedy, but less ambitious and less serious, was the comic opera, which had a great vogue in the late eighteenth century. Its principal champion was Alexander Ablesímov (1742–83), whose *Miller, Wizard, Quack, and Matchmaker* (1779) was the greatest theatrical success of the century. It is a lively and merry play, with excellent, sprightly dialogue and delightful, genuinely popular songs. Quite free from all social or moral preoccupation, full of unrestrained and purely Russian merriment, Ablesímov's is one of the masterpieces of Russian eighteenth-century literature.

EIGHTEENTH-CENTURY PROSE[1]

The standards of the new literary prose were set up by Lomonósov and remained in force till the advent of Karam-

[1] Russian literary historians usually neglect all ecclesiastical literature after the age of Peter. But the eighteenth century produced an abundant harvest of sermons of a much more ambitious kind than was the rule in Old Russia. There was considerable mutual influence between secular and ecclesiastical literature, all the more so as the prelates of the age of Elizabeth and Catherine were more secular in outlook than their successors in the nineteenth century. The most

zín. Lomonósov's own practice was limited chiefly to the higher kinds—solemn eloquence and rhetorical history. Sumarókov in his periodicals was the first to cultivate the more everyday forms. The age of Catherine saw a great extension in the use of prose, together with the spread of European and modern ideas.

Catherine herself was an author. In the early years of her reign she piqued herself on being one of the most advanced minds in Europe. She was in constant correspondence with Voltaire, Diderot, and Grimm, and did her best to appear enlightened in the eyes of these leaders of European opinion. Her *Instruction* (*Nakáz*) to the Committee of Deputies convened in 1767 was based on the ideas of Montesquieu and Beccaria. It was so openly liberal that in France it was prohibited by the censorship, and a French translation of it could appear only in Neuchâtel. But before long, under the influence of the Pugachëv Rebellion, Catherine's liberalism was greatly damped. In the end of her reign, under the influence of the French Revolution, she finally discarded all liberal pretence and became an overt reactionary. As a writer she is not devoid of merits, but her best is to be found in her French writings. French critics praise her French, which, though less correct than Frederick II's, is personal and vigorous. In her letters to Grimm she is on her best intellectual behavior and tries to show off her native wit and cleverness. Her Russian writings, considering her German origin, are quite respectable. But neither her satirical papers, nor her comedies, nor her tales, nor her historical chronicles (clumsily imitative of Shakspere) are in any way above mediocrity. On the strength of her remarkable memoirs and her correspondence with Grimm she has a higher place in French literature than she can be given in Russian.

It was Catherine herself who started, in 1769, the publication of satirical journals, after the model of the famous English papers. For four or five years (1769–74) this kind of journalism flourished in Russia, until it became too independent and was put an end to by the same Cath-

celebrated preachers of the period were Gedeón Krinóvsky, Bishop of Pskov (1726–63), whose best-known sermon was preached against Voltaire on the occasion of the latter's poem on the Lisbon earthquake; and Platón Lévshin, Metropolitan of Moscow (1737–1812), the most typical representative of the Broad-Church mentality of the Age of Reason.

erine. Its most brilliant representative was Nikoláy Ivánovich Nóvikov (1744–1818), one of the most remarkable men of his generation. He edited the *Drone* (1769–70) and the *Painter* (1772–73), both of which were, like most of the other journals, the almost exclusive work of the editor. But instead of making his papers, as his fellow journalists did, and as Catherine wanted them to do, a collection of harmless jokes at the expense of old-fashioned prejudice, he tried to make them the weapon of serious social satire. He aimed his blows at the very core of contemporary society— the system of serfdom. In his polemics with Catherine's own magazine he dared to disagree with her opinion that satire should smile at foibles rather than chastise vices. It was precisely Nóvikov's witty and earnest attacks on serfdom that made Catherine put a stop to the whole lot of satirical journals. Nóvikov transferred his activities to another sphere. He started a publishing business, which he conducted in a highly public-spirited way, aiming, not at gain, but at the extension of enlightenment. From 1775 to 1789 his press turned out a greater number of books than had been printed in Russia since the beginning of printing. He may be said to have formed the Russian reading public. About the same time Nóvikov became a Freemason—one of the most prominent and respected men of that sect. In his publications he gave occasional expression to his religious and moral views, and this was his undoing. He became one of the first victims of the reaction caused in Catherine by the French Revolution. In 1791 his printing press was closed. He himself was arrested and remained in prison till the accession of Paul, who liberated him, not so much from any liberal impulse, as from a desire to undo all his mother had done. Nóvikov never returned to active life but spent his remaining years on his country place, devoting himself to mystical meditations.

About 1790 there was a short-lived revival of satirical journalism, but, as had happened twenty years earlier, the journals soon assumed an independent tone that caused the authorities to put an end to them. The principal part in this revival was played by the young Krylóv, who was later to become the great fabulist.

Even at their boldest the satirical journals never touched on strictly political matters. But Catherine's own initiative in convening an elected Committee of Deputies in the beginning of her reign (1767), and the effect of the French Revolution in the end, gave rise to some purely political literature. Of the writers connected with the first of these impulses the most remarkable was Prince Michael Scherbátov (1733–90). He was an aristocrat and a conservative, one of the first enlightened Russians who began to condemn Peter the Great for introducing the corrupt morality of the West into the solid family life of Old Russia. His most interesting pamphlet is *On the Decline of Morals,* a lurid account of the misconduct of the eighteenth-century empresses and of their favorites. Scherbátov also wrote a history of Russia, which is inferior from a literary point of view to his other writings, a mere ill-digested compilation of the Chronicles. A much more intelligent historian was I. N. Bóltin (1735–92), who has every right to be regarded as the father of Russian history. His *Notes* (1788) on Leclerc's history of ancient and modern Russia are the first evidence of a critical historical spirit in Russian scholarship.

The second great political stimulus of the reign—the French Revolution—found its expression in a famous book of political invective, *A Voyage from Petersburg to Moscow,* by Alexander Nikoláyevich Radíschev (1749–1802). Radíschev had been sent as a young man to complete his education at Leipzig, where he came under the influence of the more extreme French philosophers—Helvetius, Raynal, and Rousseau. On his return he quietly served in the Civil Service, and nothing predicted the development his career was to take. In 1790 he started a private press and issued from it his famous *Voyage.* The style of the book is one of intense and unrelieved rhetoric, and its Russian is exceptionally heavy and clumsy. It is a furious attack against existing social and political conditions. The brunt of it was directed against serfdom, but it also contained expressions of anti-monarchic feeling and materialistic opinions. The book was immediately seized, its author arrested and exiled to East Siberia. He was released by Paul in 1797 and received back into the Civil Service with complete rehabilitation by Alexander I in 1801. But during his exile he had become a victim to nervous melancholy, and in 1802 he committed suicide. He has come to be regarded by the radical intelligentsia as its first spokesman and martyr. The sincerity of his book has been questioned both by his early

advocates and by his later detractors. It would seem that
he wrote it merely out of literary ambition and that it is
no more than a rhetorical exercise on a subject suggested
and familiarized by Raynal. However this may be, the
book is devoid of literary merit. But Radíschev was also a
poet of no mean talent. He held paradoxical views, pre-
ferring Trediakóvsky to Lomonósov, and tried to introduce
Greek measures into Russian prosody. A short love poem
of his in the Sapphic meter is among the most charming
lyrics of the century, and his elegy (in distichs) on *The
Eighteenth Century* has both poetical power and intellectual
substance.

The eighteenth century has left us an interesting series
of memoirs. First in time and, probably, in human interest
came the memoirs of Princess Nathalie Dolgorúky, née
Countess Sheremétev (1714–71). She was the fiancée of
one of the oligarchs of the Dolgorúky family when the
coup d'état of Anne (1730) restored autocracy and sent the
Dolgorúkys into exile. In spite of this she married the
exile and followed him through all his ordeals. After his
execution she became a nun and in her old age wrote her
life for her children and grandchildren. Its principal attraction, apart from the high moral character of the author,
resides in the great simplicity and unpretentious sincerity of
the narrative and in its beautiful, undefiled Russian, such
as could be written only by a gentlewoman who lived before the age of schoolmasters.

Of the later memorists I have already spoken of
Derzhávin. The memoirs of Bólotov (1738–1833) and of
Danílov (1722–*c.* 90) are priceless historical documents
and agreeable and interesting reading.

Private letters, and even official correspondence of the
eighteenth century, are often of considerable literary interest. Non-literary men were as a rule more independent
of grammar and rhetoric than the men of letters and wrote
a more vigorous and personal Russian. Field Marshal
Suvórov, one of the most cultured men of his time, gave
much attention to the form of his correspondence, and
especially of his orders of the day. These latter are highly
original, deliberately aiming at unexpected and striking
effects. Their style is a succession of nervous staccato sentences, which produce the effect of blows and flashes.
Suvórov's official reports often assume a memorable and

striking form.[2] His writings are as different from the common run of classical prose as his tactics were from those of Frederick or Marlborough. He was, in a sense, the first Russian romanticist—and in his old age his bedside book was Ossian, in the admirable Russian translation of Kostróv, dedicated to the great soldier.

KARAMZÍN

The last years of Catherine's reign saw the beginning of the literary movement that is connected with the name of Karamzín. It was not a violent revolution. The spirit of the eighteenth century continued alive till much later, and the new movement was even to a large extent a further assertion of that spirit. The reform of the literary language, which was its most striking and immediately apparent aspect, was a direct continuation of the Europeanizing and secularizing reforms of Peter and Lomonósov. But, as Europe itself had changed since the first half of the century, the new wave of Europeanization brought with it new ideas and new tastes—the new sensibility of Richardson and Rousseau and the first signs of the beginning revolt against classicism.

The main question at issue, however, was that of language. Karamzín's object was to make literary Russian less like the old ecclesiastical languages, Slavonic and Latin, and more like French, the new language of polite society and secular knowledge. He exchanged Lomonósov's heavy German-Latin syntax for a more elegant French style. While ejecting hundreds of Slavonic words, Karamzín introduced numerous Gallicisms—exact translations from the French of words and expressions denoting ideas connected with the new sensibility or the advance of knowledge. His reform was successful and immediately accepted by the majority of writers, but it was by no means an unmixed blessing to the language. It only substituted one foreign model for another. It even increased the distance between the written and the spoken language, for it did away (virtually) with Lomonósov's distinction of three styles by merging them all in the "middle" style and practi-

[2] One of his rhymed reports is quoted, somewhat inaccurately, by Byron in a note to *Don Juan*.

cally abandoning the "low." It is doubtful whether the language has profited as much as has been supposed by the exclusion of so many Slavonic synonyms of Russian words: they added color and variety. By reforming the language as he did, Karamzín contributed to widen the gap between the educated classes and the people, and between new and old Russia. The reform was anti-democratic (in this a true child of the eighteenth century) and anti-national (in this still more so). But whatever we may say against it, it was victorious and facilitated the coming of an age of *classical* poetry: the ultimate justification of Karamzín's language is that it became the language of Púshkin.

Another aspect of the Karamzinian movement was the new sensibility. It had been prepared by the slow infiltration of sentimental novels and the emotional pietism of the Freemasons, but the cult of feeling, the obedient submission to emotional impulses, the conception of virtue as the outcome of man's natural goodness—all these were first explicitly preached by Karamzín.

Nikoláy Mikháylovich Karamzín was born in 1766, in Simbírsk (on the middle Volga), of a family of provincial gentry. He received a good secondary education at the private school of a German professor of the University of Moscow. After leaving school he was in danger of becoming a dissipated, pleasure-seeking young squire, when he met I. P. Turgénev, a prominent Freemason, who led him from the ways of vice and introduced him to Nóvikov. These Masonic influences had a principal part in framing Karamzín's mind. Their vaguely religious, sentimental, and cosmopolitan ideas paved the way to the understanding of Rousseau and Herder. Karamzín began to write for Nóvikov's publications. His first work to appear in book form was a translation of *Julius Cæsar* (1787). He also translated Thomson's *Seasons*. In 1789 he went abroad, where he remained for about eighteen months, traveling in Germany, Switzerland, France, and England. On his return he started a monthly review, mostly written by himself, called the *Moscow Journal* (1791–2), which marks the real beginning of the new movement. The most important of his contributions was *Letters of a Russian Traveler*, which were received by the public as something of a revelation: the revelation of a new, enlightened, and cosmopolitan sensibility, and of a delightfully new style. Karamzín became a leader, the most important literary figure of his generation.

In the reign of Paul (1796–1801) the growing severity of the censorship forced him to silence, but the liberal beginning of the reign of Alexander I prompted him into renewed activity. In 1802 he started a new monthly, the *Messenger of Europe,* largely devoted to politics. It judged contemporary events from the point of view of a sentimentalized Plutarchian "Virtue," condemned Napoleon, and glorified Washington and Toussaint L'Ouverture. In 1803 Karamzín gave up the editorship of his magazine, abandoned all literary work, and devoted himself to historical research.

The intrinsic value of Karamzín's literary work does not today strike us as great. He was not a creative mind. He was an interpreter, a schoolmaster, an importer of foreign wealth. Besides being the most cultured mind, he was the most elegant writer of his age. Never had Russian prose sought so much to enchant and fascinate, and the sweetness of his style was what struck his readers most of all.

All Karamzín's early work bears the stamp of the New Sensibility. It is the work of a man who has first discovered in his feelings an infinite source of interest and pleasure. He announces the good news of Sensibility: that happiness consists in making the best use of our spontaneous impulses, and that to be happy we must have confidence in our feelings, for they are *natural,* and Nature is good. But Karamzín's Rousseauism is tempered by an innate mediocrity (in the unabusive Aristotelian sense of the term). An elegant moderation and a cultured urbanity are the constant characteristics of his writings. And to remind us that we are still up to the ears in the eighteenth century, his Sensibility is never divorced from an intellect that judges at least as keenly as it feels.

The subject of Karamzín's first and best-known tale, *Poor Liza* (1792), is the story of the seduced girl who is abandoned by her lover and commits suicide—a favorite theme of the sentimental age. The success of the story was immense. A pond in the environs of Moscow where Karamzín located Liza's suicide became a favorite shrine of sentimental Muscovites. Karamzín was the first Russian author to give prose fiction a degree of attention and artistic finish that raised it to the rank of literature. But apart from this the merits of his tales and novels are small. His later stories, *A Knight of Our Times* and *The Sensitive Man and the Cold Man*, are superior to the rest, for they display a genuine originality of psychological observation and sentimental analysis.

Karamzín's poetry is imitative, but important, like the rest of his work, as the indication of a new period. He was the first in Russia for whom poetry was a means of expressing his "inner life." He also left a distinct trace on the technique of Russian verse, both by refining the traditional French verse forms and by introducing new forms of Germanic origin. In all these respects, however, he was but the forerunner of Zhukóvsky, the real father of modern Russian poetry.

After his withdrawal from literature and journalism, Karamzín lived in the quietness of archives, working at *The History of the Russian State*. His historical studies produced a profound change in his ideas. Though he retained his cult of virtue and feeling, he became imbued with patriotism and State-worship. He came to the conclusion, expressed in his memoir, *On Ancient and Modern Russia* (1811), that to be efficient the State must be strong, monarchic, and autocratic. The memoir (published only long after Karamzín's death) was aimed against Speránsky's liberal Francophil policy and constitutional reforms, then under discussion. It is remarkable for its outspoken criticism of the Russian monarchs of the eighteenth century, from Peter to Paul. From a literary point of view, its vigorous clarity of argument, unblurred by rhetoric and sentimentality, make it the writer's masterpiece. It produced a strong impression on Alexander and made its author a political influence to be counted with. In 1816 Karamzín came to Petersburg to supervise the printing of his *History*, the first eight volumes of which appeared in 1818. Three more volumes appeared later, while the twelfth (which brought the narrative down to 1612) remained incomplete and was published posthumously. Karamzín's residence at Petersburg brought him into closer contact with Alexander, and a warm friendship developed between them. The death of Alexander (November 1825) was a severe blow to Karamzín. He did not survive his royal friend very long, but died in 1826. His reputation as the greatest writer of

Russian prose and a great historian became a principal
tenet of the official creed and of all the conservative part
of the literary world. Thus it was that, beginning as a reforming, almost revolutionary, force, Karamzín passed into
posterity as the symbol and perfect embodiment of Imperial
Russia's official ideals.

The success of *The History of the Russian State* was
immediate and universal. Even the liberals, who disliked
its fundamental thesis of the all-efficiency of autocracy,
were carried away by its literary charm and the novelty of
its facts. No one today would revive the ecstasies of the
reading public of 1818. Karamzín's historical outlook is
narrow and crippled by the essentially eighteenth-century
character of his mind. He concentrated almost exclusively
on the political actions of Russian sovereigns and practically overlooked the Russian people. His judgment of the
rulers is often sentimentally moralistic, and his basic idea
of the virtues of autocracy distorts his reading of individual facts.

But these defects have their redeeming points. By forcing on the reader a consistent view of Russian history as a
whole, Karamzín helped to understand its essential unity.
By taking a moralistic view of the behavior of sovereigns,
he was able to condemn their selfish or tyrannical policies.
By concentrating on the actions of princes, he added
dramatic value to his work: the parts that struck the
readers' imagination most powerfully were precisely those
stories of individual monarchs, founded no doubt on solid
fact, but arranged and unified with the consummate skill
of a dramatist. The most famous of these stories is that of
Borís Godunóv, which became the great tragic myth
of Russian poetry and produced Púshkin's tragedy and
Musórgsky's popular opera.

The style of the *History* is rhetorical and sustainedly
eloquent. It is a compromise with the literary conservatives,
who forgave Karamzín all his early sins for having written
the *History*. But in the main it is a development of the essentially French eighteenth-century style of the younger
Karamzín. Abstract and sentimental, it avoids, or rather
misses, all historical and local color. The choice of words
is calculated to universalize and humanize, not to individualize, Old Russia, and the monotonously rounded
cadences convey an idea of the continuousness, but not of

the complexity, of history. Contemporaries liked his style. A few critics found fault with its stiltedness and sentimentality, but on the whole the age was fascinated by it and recognized it as the greatest achievement of Russian prose.

CONTEMPORARIES OF KARAMZÍN

Karamzín's early work met with a strong conservative opposition, led by Admiral Alexander Semënovich Shishkóv (1753–1841), an all-round conservative and patriot, author of the stirring 1812 manifesto on the invasion of Napoleon, and champion of the Greek-Slavonic tradition in the literary language. In his campaign against the Karamzinians, Shishkóv counted among his adherents such men as Derzhávin, Krylóv, and, in the younger generation, Griboyédov, Katénin, and Küchelbecker, but the trend of the times was against him, and he lost his battle. His linguistic writings, though often rather wildly dilettantish, are interesting for his great insight into the shades of meaning of words, for his pious, if uninformed, interest in Old Russian literature and folklore, and for the excellent Russian in which they are written.

The poets that followed the colors of Shishkóv were rather a motley throng and cannot be all bracketed as one school. They are distinguished from Karamzín's followers in that they continued the eighteenth-century tradition of high poetry, for which they were ridiculed by the Karamzinian wits. But at least two poets of Shishkóv's party, Semën Bobróv (1767–1810) and Prince Sergius (Shirínsky-) Shikhmátov (1783–1837), have greater merit than any Karamzinian before Zhukóvsky. Bobróv's poetry is remarkable for its rich diction and splendid imagery, for the soaring flights of his imagination and the sublimity of his design. Shikhmátov's *Peter the Great* (1810), a "lyrical epic" in eight cantos, is devoid of narrative (or metaphysical) interest, but its style is remarkable. Such a saturated and ornate style is not to be found in Russian poetry until we come to Vyacheslád Ivánov.

Karamzín's following was more numerous than Shishkóv's, and it occupies the highway of Russian literary tradition. But before we come to Zhukóvsky and Bátyushkov it is not strikingly rich in talent. The Karamzinian poets abandoned the great themes and "high" style of the Russian eighteenth century and devoted themselves to the cultivation of the *poésie légère* of the French eighteenth century. The most eminent of these poets, Iván Ivánovich Dmítriev (1760–1837) strove to write verse in a style as polished as that of Karamzín's prose. His songs, short odes, elegies, epigrams, fables, and verse tales are all eminently elegant, but long before his death Dmítriev's elegance had become antiquated, and his poetry the quaint rococo toy of a hopelessly irrevertible past. Other poets of the Karamzinian coterie were Vasíly Lvóvich Púshkin (1767–1830), the uncle of a greater nephew, who wrote polished sentimental trifles—and a lively, but very coarse burlesque, *A Dangerous Neighbor;* and A. F. Merzlyakóv (1778–1830), an eclectic follower of senescent classicism, who was particularly successful in his songs.

The vogue of songbooks is a prominent feature of the Karamzinian age, and several poets, including Dmítriev, Merzlyakóv, and Yúry Alexándrovich Nelédinsky-Melétsky (1752–1828), acquired a reputation with their songs, some of which have become folk songs. But only Merzlyakóv's songs are genuinely akin to those of the folk; Nelédinsky's and Dmítriev's are quite as conventional as the older songs of Sumarókov, merely substituting a new, sentimental convention for the classical convention of sensual love, and an elegantly monotonous singsong for the rhythmical variety of the older poet.

A more modern and subjective poet was Gavríla Petróvich Kámenev (1772–1803), the first to follow Karamzín in making his poetry express individual emotional experience. He cultivated the new "Germanic" and rhymeless forms of verse and was under the strong influence of Ossian and Young. But the new subjective poetry acquired only later a really sincere tone and efficient forms of expression. The elegies of the short-lived Andréy Turgénev (1781–1803) and the early work of Zhukóvsky are the first swallows of the Golden Age. But the distinctive quality of that age begins first to be felt in the maturer work of Zhukóvsky, from about 1808 onwards.

There remains to be mentioned Prince Iván Mikháylovich Dolgorúky (1764–1823), who belonged to neither Shishkóv's party nor Karamzín's. Studiously avoiding all

sentiment and sentimentality, Dolgorúky tried to make
common sense and the simple pleasures of domestic life
the subject of his poetry. Garrulous and puerile at his
worst, he is distinguished at his best by ease, raciness, and
a well-bred naïveté. His prose, especially that quaint alpha-
betical dictionary of his friends, *The Temple of My Heart*,
is a good example of pure colloquial Russian, uncontaminated by foreign influence or literary fashion.

In the drama of the period the French classical
standards were giving way to a taste for the sentimental
drama, or *comédie larmoyante*, which had begun to insinuate itself into Russia some twenty years earlier. The
new style did not produce any original work of value, and
the Russian stage had to rely chiefly on the plays of the
famous German melodramatist Kotzebue. The one outstanding dramatic author of the period was Vladisláv Alexándrovich Ózerov (1769–1816), whose tragedies were produced between 1804 and 1809. Their success was tremendous, largely owing to the remarkable acting of
one of the greatest of Russian tragediennes, Catherine
Semënova. What the public liked in these tragedies was the
atmosphere of sensibility and the polished, Karamzinian
sweetness that Ózerov infused into the classical forms. One
of his first successes was *Fingal*, a sentimental tragedy
with choruses in an Ossianic setting. The climax was
reached in *Dimítry of the Don*, first acted within a few
days of the battle of Preussisch-Eylau (1807), when its
patriotic tirades were received with overwhelming enthusiasm. Ózerov's last play, *Polyxene*, was less successful, but
intrinsically it is his best, and no doubt the best Russian
tragedy on the French classical model. The subject is
handled in a broad and manly manner that makes the play
genuinely evocative of the atmosphere of the *Iliad*.

KRYLÓV

At the end of the eighteenth and in the first years of the
nineteenth centuries, fable-writing became a veritable craze,
and the fable plays an important part in Russian literary
development. It was one of the principal schools for training writers in that realism which is the main feature of
later Russian literature. A robust, open-eyed realism is

already the outstanding feature of Khemnítser's fables. It is mellowed down, conventionalized, and gentilified in the drawing-room fables of Dmítriev. It regains all its vigor in the crude, but racy, picaresque fables of Alexander Izmáylov (1779–1831) and in the work of the greatest Russian fabulist—Krylóv.

Iván Andréyevich Krylóv was born in 1769, the son of a poor army officer who had risen from the ranks. He received a very summary education and was a small boy when he entered the Civil Service as a minor clerk. At the age of fourteen he found a post in Petersburg and in the same year began his literary career with a comic opera. Afterwards Krylóv turned to satirical journalism and edited the *Spectator* (1792) and the *St. Petersburg Mercury* (1793). Among much inferior sentimental matter these journals contained several vigorous satirical essays in a manner very different from the skeptical common sense of the fables. The best of these papers is *A Panegyric of my Grandfather* (1792)—a tremendous caricature of a rude, selfish, savage, hunting country squire, who, like Fonvízin's Skotínin, has a greater family feeling for his hounds and horses than for his serfs. The *Mercury* was short-lived, being suppressed for the dangerously violent tone of Krylóv's satire. For twelve years Krylóv practically disappeared from literature. Part of this period he lived as a secretary, a tutor, or simply a parasite in the houses of great noblemen, but for long periods he entirely escapes the eye of the biographer. At this new school of life Krylóv seems to have lost his early violence and acquired the passive and complacently ironic shrewdness of the fables. In 1805 Krylóv returned to literature; he wrote his first translation from La Fontaine and made a fresh attempt to conquer the stage: during the first wars with Napoleon he wrote two comedies satirizing the French fashions of the Russian ladies. Their success was considerable, but Krylóv did not try to improve it, for he had found his right vein in the fable. In 1809 twenty-three of his fables were published in book form and had a success unprecedented in the annals of Russian literature. Henceforward he wrote nothing but fables. In 1812 he received a peaceful and commodious post (practically a sinecure) in the Public Library of St. Petersburg, where he remained for over thirty years. He died in 1844. He was noted for laziness, untidiness, good appetite, and shrewd, malicious common sense. His fat, bulky figure was a familiar feature in the drawing-rooms of Petersburg, where he used to sit for whole evenings without opening his mouth, his little eyes half shut or gazing vacantly, with an air of boredom and indifference to all around him.

Krylóv's *Fables,* most of them written between 1810 and 1820, are contained in nine books. Their enormous popularity was due to both their matter and their manner. Krylóv's outlook was representative of what is perhaps the typical outlook of a Great Russian of the lower or middle classes. It has a foundation of sound common sense. The virtues he respects above all things are efficiency and aptness. The vices he satirizes most readily are self-satisfied inaptitude and arrogant stupidity. Like the typical middle-class philosopher he is, Krylóv has no faith in big words and high ideals. Intellectual ambition finds no sympathy with him. There is a vast amount of Philistine inertness and laziness in his philosophy of life. It is eminently conservative, and some of Krylóv's most poisonous shafts were aimed at the fashionable progressive ideas of his time. But his common sense has no more patience with the absurdities and ineptitudes of the upper classes and of people in power. His satire is a smiling satire. His weapon is ridicule, not indignation, but it is keen and pointed, and can make his victim smart.

Krylóv is a great master of words, and this makes his place in the pantheon of Russian literature impregnable. He did not achieve from the outset that mastery and originality now associated with his name. The 1809 volume contains several fables that are little more than good translations from La Fontaine. But the greater part of the first book already displays his style at its best. Krylóv was no friend of the reforming Karamzinians. He was a thorough classicist, a nationalist, and not averse to archaism. The descriptive and lyrical passages of the *Fables* are quite eighteenth-century in tone. Even the raciness of his colloquial passages is different from the realism of such eighteenth-century writers as V. Máykov or Khemnítser, not so much in kind as in quality. But the quality is of the highest. Krylóv most emphatically "had language." His words are alive. The line is tightly filled with them. And they are real, living words, words from the street and the tavern, used in the true spirit of the *people's*, not of the schoolmaster's, Russian. Krylóv is at his best in condensed epigrammatic statement. The pointed conclusions and morals of his *Fables* are the legitimate descendants of the popular proverb (no language is richer than Russian in the wealth and beauty of its proverbs), and hundreds of them have themselves become proverbs without anyone's now thinking of where they came from.

Some of Krylóv's best fables are pointed against inefficiency and the pretensions of the unskilled man to do skilled work. Others are political pamphlets produced by current events, especially during the war of 1812–14. Several are satires against vain and importunate poetasters and criticasters. Others again are social satires, like the famous one of *The Geese* who protested against being sold at the market because they were descended from the geese that had saved the Capitol from the Gauls. But it is impossible to give any enumeration or classification to Krylóv's fables. Fortunately (although Krylóv would seem on the face of it to be an untranslatable author) they have been admirably rendered into English by Sir Bernard Pares, who has succeeded in finding wonderfully happy equivalents for Krylóv's raciest idioms. The reader is advised to get a copy of Sir Bernard's translations and taste for himself of Krylóv's immense variety.

THE NOVEL

Classical theory did not regard the novel on an equal footing with the drama and other forms of poetry, and no novels were printed in Russia till 1750. After that date translated fiction appeared in increasing numbers, but the first original Russian novel was published only in 1763. For many years original novels remained both exceedingly rare and considerably below the general level of literature. The Russian reader's demand for fiction was met by numerous translations from French, German, and English. The first Russian novelist was Fëdor Emin (*c.* 1735–70), who wrote didactic and philosophical romances of adventure in a florid and prolix literary prose. A more realistic style that had been popularized by translations of Marivaux and Fielding was taken up by Michael Chulkóv (*c.* 1743–92)

in his novel *The Fair Cook, or the Adventures of a
Debauched Woman* (1770), a sort of Russian *Moll Flan-
ders*. This practically exhausts the list of *literary* novels
before the time of Karamzín.

The example and success of Karamzín as a novelist
provoked a somewhat increased output of prose fiction,
but his direct imitators are negligible. Robuster work was
done by men unconnected with the sentimentalist movement. Alexander Benítsky (1781–1809) wrote philosophical oriental tales in the best tradition of Voltaire. His style
surpassed in elegance and lucidity everything written in
Russian prose before Púshkin. The novel of manners is
represented by *Eugene, or the Results of Bad Upbringing*
(1799–1801), an early work of the fabulist Alexander
Izmáylov, a cautionary and moral story, where the author
describes vice with such realistic gusto that his critics were
inclined to doubt the sincerity of his moral purpose.

The most significant, and prolific, novelist was the
Ukrainian Vasíly Trofímovich Narézhny (1780–1825), a
robust and conscious realist in the tradition of Smollett,
Fielding, and Lesage. In his stories of Ukrainian life he
was the first to present to the Russian reader a colorful,
humorous, and realistic picture of Cossack and post-Cos-
sack Ukraine, so much more memorably revived a generation later by Gógol. Narézhny's principal work is *A
Russian Gil Blas,* a novel in six parts, three of which appeared in 1814, while the remaining three were held up
by the censorship. It is a vast and unsweetened picture of
Russian life in the provinces and the capitals, turning
round the adventures of a poor squire, little more than a
peasant, who by an irony of fate bears a prince's title.
Narézhny had a grip on real life, which places him above
all the "prehistorical" Russian novelists. But he was too
little of an artist, and his books, owing to their heavy style
and their diffuseness, are difficult reading. He was in fact
little read, and his influence on the development of the
Russian novel is almost negligible.

4

The Golden Age of Poetry

THE Golden Age of Russian poetry is roughly contemporary with the great age of romantic poetry in western Europe. But its poetry is not romantic; it is far more *formal,* active, selective—in short, *classical*—than any other nineteenth-century school of poetry. It was, in a sense, behind the times, a posthumous child of the eighteenth century. For general tone and atmosphere Púshkin has been compared to Mozart. The western European poets nearest in tone and feeling to those of our Golden Age are poets of the later eighteenth century—Burns, Chénier, Parny. What is particularly important—the technical efficiency of the poets of the Golden Age never lags behind their inspiration. Their poetry is perfect, even when it is minor poetry; and when it is major poetry, it is great without qualification. Its technical perfection marks off the poetry of the twenties both from the primitive rudeness of the age of Derzhávin and from the degenerate laxity of the later nineteenth century.

Though creative and original where the other had been merely receptive, the poetry of the Golden Age was a direct continuation of the Karamzinian movement, its best fruit and chief justification. Being a continuation of that movement, it was "French"—and French of the eighteenth century, for it remained hostile to French romanticism. From 1820 onward the movement called itself romantic and was in open revolt against the rules of French classicism. It desired greater freedom and novelty of forms; it liked originality and picturesqueness. It admired Shakspere for the broadness of his design and for his profound understanding of the human heart, and Byron for his mighty eloquence and effective narrative methods. In comparison with the age of classicism, there was a revival of sentiment and feeling, but the sensibility of most of the poets of the Golden Age was purely classical; only a minority were at all infected by the New Sensibility, and then only by its earliest eighteenth-century forms. Nor was there any "return to Nature." Even the nature symbolism of the Ossianic school is absent from the poetry of Púshkin and his contemporaries. Romantic pantheism and romantic animism do not appear in Russian literature before the thirties.

What still more emphasizes the eighteenth-century character of the Golden Age is its distinct social coloring. It was a movement inside the gentry, a movement of *gentlemen*. Hence, in its early stages, the prevalence of light, society verse, of convivial and Anacreontic subjects: the cult of friendship, of good company, and wine. Socially the age of Púshkin marks the high-water mark of the literary hegemony of the gentry. Higher literature is completely monopolized by men of that class. At the same time the literary press is almost entirely in the hands of the non-noble class—of pedants, hacks, and hucksters. The opposition between the two classes is clearly marked. The gentry, to whatever literary party they belonged, showed a contemptuous united front to the plebeians. The plebeians had their revenge in the thirties.

The Golden Age may be said to begin at the moment when poetry emerges from the placid insipidities of the school of Dmítriev and acquires an independent and original accent in the first mature work of Zhukóvsky, about 1808. A few years later, after the end of the wars, the younger partisans of Karamzín, headed by Zhukóvsky, Bátyushkov, and Vyázemsky, founded the semi-humorous literary society "Arzamás." Its sittings were a parody of the solemn meetings of Shishkóv's conservative literary society. The Arzamasians cultivated poetical friendship, literary small talk, and the lighter forms of verse.

After 1820 the movement becomes more serious. The influence of Byron reigns for about five years after 1821. The tale in verse becomes the principal form of expression. The catchword of romanticism is defiantly accepted in the teeth of the conservatives. The works of Púshkin follow in rapid succession, and meet with loud success, which is rivaled by that of Zhukóvsky, Baratýnsky, and Kozlóv. Poetry almost monopolizes the book market. The gentlemen's party acquires control over all literary opinion. But their day was short and early clouded. The repression of the Decembrist Revolt by Nicholas I (1825 6) was an irremediable blow to the intellectual elite of the gentry. At the same time the clear eighteenth-century atmosphere of the Golden Age is poisoned: young men of a somewhat younger generation introduce the first germs of German idealism. Lower-class journalists, more intellectually ambitious and progressive than hitherto, control the press and rise in the public favor. French romanticism, with its unbridled license of bad taste, infects the air. After 1829 the novel, stimulated by Scott, begins to sell better than poetry. Délvig, the center of the friendly circle of poets, dies in 1831. Púshkin marries in the same year and becomes the leader of a conservative literary aristocracy. The young are no longer young, the summer of the Golden Age is over. After 1831 the front stage of literature is occupied, in Petersburg, by a host of vulgarizers and charlatans; in Moscow, by the Adams of the new intelligentsia, who respect in Púshkin a venerable relic of the past but discard his traditions, despise his friends, and refuse to read his new works. In 1834 appears Belínsky's first article —the manifesto of a new era in the history of Russian civilization. When, in 1837, Púshkin died, Russian literature was far advanced in its new ways. Those who survived him, Zhukóvsky, Baratýnsky, Yazýkov, Vyázemsky, were a small and isolated group in an alien, forgetful, and mainly hostile world.

ZHUKÓVSKY

Vasíly Andréyevich Zhukóvsky, the first pioneer and the accepted patriarch of the Golden Age, was born in 1783, in Túla, the natural son of a country gentleman of the name of Búnin and of a Turkish captive girl. His education in Moscow was dominated by pietist influences. After completing his education he lived on his father's estate, where he gave lessons to his cousins and brought them up in the ways of sensibility. One of them, Marie Protásov (later Móyer) became the object of a Platonic attachment that survived her death (1823). In 1802 Zhukóvsky sent to Karamzín's *Messenger of Europe* a translation of Gray's *Elegy*. The publication of that poem has more than once been declared to be the birthday of Russian poetry. In 1808 appeared Zhukóvsky's first ballad, an adaptation of Bürger's *Lenore*, which gave the signal for a general ballad craze. In 1812, on the invasion of Napoleon, Zhukóvsky joined the militia. He did no actual fighting, but a poem he wrote shortly after the battle of Borodinó, while Napoleon was still in Moscow (*The Bard in the Camp of the Russian Warriors*), made him famous outside literary circles. In 1815–17 Zhukóvsky was the most eminent, though not the most active, member of the Arzamás. About the same time he was invited to give Russian lessons to the Princess of Prussia, then affianced to the future Emperor Nicholas I. The young couple liked Zhukóvsky, and when, in 1818, the future Alexander II was born, the poet was appointed his tutor. He remained in this situation till Alexander's majority. Zhukóvsky's influence on his pupil has generally been regarded as highly beneficial and humanizing. His situation at court and his position as the eldest and, next to Púshkin, greatest poet of the time made him a prominent figure in the literary world. From the first steps of the younger poet he was intimately related with Púshkin and was always helpful when Púshkin got into trouble with the authorities. From 1831, after Púshkin's marriage, the poets exercised a sort of diarchy over what henceforward came to be known as the "literary aristocracy." Zhukóvsky also befriended Gógol, and in 1838 played a principal part in the emancipation from serfdom of the Ukrainian poet Shevchénko. In 1841 he retired from court, and in the same year he married a very young German girl and henceforward lived permanently on the Rhine, working at vast poetical enterprises and only occasionally visiting Russia. He died in 1852, at Baden-Baden.

Up to about 1820 Zhukóvsky was the leader of the

advanced literary movement, and the extent of his influence may be compared with that of Spenser's or Ronsard's. He created a new poetical language on the basis of the Karamzinian reform. Both his metrical methods and his diction remained the standard for all the nineteenth century. Besides these formal innovations Zhukóvsky reformed the very conception of poetry. In his hands it became, for the first time in Russia, the direct expression of feeling. There is no trace in his poetry of raw, unmastered, merely recorded, emotion: the sentimental experience is always completely transformed. But it was a step in the direction of expressive, emotional poetry. The next step was made by Lérmontov. It was not made by Púshkin; the subjective element in Púshkin's poetry is less prominent and more subordinate to the creative design than in Zhukóvsky's.

It is one of the curios of literary history that this first, and for some time to come most, personal and subjective Russian poet was almost exclusively a translator. His original work is small in extent, consisting of a few humorous epistles, occasional elegies, and lyrics. But these last are alone sufficient to give Zhukóvsky a place in the first rank of poets. The æthereal lightness, the melodiousness of his verse and the exquisite purity of his diction reach in them their highest perfection. Romantic melancholy and the resigned hope in a better beyond have never spoken in nobler or more exquisite accents. But it is characteristic of Zhukóvsky that even these lyrics have sources in foreign poetry. Thus the wonderful lyric on the death of Marie Móyer (*19th March 1823*) closely resembles in meter and construction a poem of the German romanticist Brentano. It is the actual words, cadences, and intonation, the very texture of the verse, that make the poem what it is—and those slight touches which are at the hand of only the great poet. Zhukóvsky's poetry of 1808–21 charmed the public by its atmosphere of romantic sensibility, daydreams, optimistic religiosity, and sweet resignation, with a touch of the mildly fantastic paraphernalia of the balladry of terror. But what the initiated most admired was the poet's supreme mastery, his metrical inventiveness, and, above all, the absolutely unheard-of purity, sweetness, and melodiousness of his verse and diction, which were such a contrast to the splendidly barbaric ruggedness of Derzhávin.

The poets Zhukóvsky translated in this period were the romantic, pre-romantic, and even classical poets of Germany and England. His special favorites in Germany were Uhland and Schiller, whose Greek ballads (*Die Siegesfest* and others) are, owing to Zhukóvsky, quite as much classics in Russia as they are in Germany (if not more so). The English poets translated by him were Dryden (*Alexander's Feast*), Thomson, Gray (the *Elegy*), Southey, Scott, Moore, Campbell, and Byron (*The Prisoner of Chillon*). After what I have said of Zhukóvsky's supreme and impeccable mastery in Russian verse it will scarcely be startling if I add that certain of his translations from his English contemporaries (none of whom was really a great craftsman) are very often superior to the original. Southey's *Queen Urraca*, Campbell's *Lord Ullin's Daughter*, Moore's *Death of the Peri*, Scott's *Eve of St. John*, and Byron's *Prisoner of Chillon* have both relatively and absolutely a higher place in Russian than they have in English poetry.

After 1830 Zhukóvsky gradually abandoned the too fluent sweetness that had made him popular. Like Púshkin in the same years he strove after greater objectivity, a more Doric outline and more epic manner. Almost all his later work is either in hexameters or blank verse. He uses both forms with the utmost freedom and variety, placing his words in the most "unpoetical" order, using the most destructive overflows, attaining a style that is "*beau comme de la prose*" and (in blank verse) reminiscent of the later Shakspere. Among the principal works of this period are the adaptations (from the German) of *Rustam and Sohrab* and *Nala and Damayanti*. In both he succeeded in eschewing all sentimentality. In the former, the effect is one of grand, primæval, rude majesty; in the latter, of genuinely Indian wealth and color. Still more remarkable is his adaptation, in very free and enjambed hexameters, of the German romanticist Fouqué's prose romance *Undine*. The atmosphere of the poem is one of optimistic religiosity and romantic fantasy, and akin to that of his early lyrics and elegies, but the story is told with majestic leisure and has a true epic tone. The most extensive task of his old age was the translation of the *Odyssey*, completed in 1847. Though he knew no Greek, and translated Homer from a word-for-word German translation, it is a masterpiece of exactness and reliability. Zhukóvsky's *Odyssey* was intended to complete the Russian Homer, and is, as it were, a sequel to Gnédich's translation of the *Iliad* (1829).

Nikoláy Ivánovich Gnédich (1784–1833) was a poet of considerable merit who wrote a few exquisite lyrics and a much-admired Russian idyl in the style of Theocritus. His *Iliad* is high-sounding and magnificent, full of splendid Slavicisms, with a Virgilian accompaniment of sonorous trumpets and with wonderfully invented composite epithets. It is the most splendid example in Russian poetry of the grand classical style.

The *Odyssey* of Zhukóvsky is very different. He deliberately avoids Slavicism. He makes the *Odyssey* a homely, leisurely, Biblical story of the daily life of patriarchal kings. But Zhukóvsky does not sentimentalize Homer, and, though perhaps it is in the Telemachos and Nausicaa cantos that he is at his best, even in the cruelest parts of the *Mnesteroktonia* he gives a faithful reflection of the true Homer. The two Russian Homers are in a most happy way mutually complementary, and if Gnédich's *Iliad* is our highest achievement in the grand manner, Zhukóvsky's *Odyssey* is unsurpassed as a heroic idyl.

OTHER POETS OF THE OLDER GENERATION

Zhukóvsky was not alone, between 1810 and 1820, in his work of perfecting and refining the instrument of Russian verse. Another most important poet, for some time almost a rival to Zhukóvsky's supremacy, was Constantine Nikoláyevich Bátyushkov. Born in 1787 in Vólogda, Bátyushkov served in the army, was wounded in 1807 at Heilsberg, and took part in the campaigns of 1813 and 1814. After the end of the wars he was a prominent member of the Arzamás. His collected works appeared in 1817. Soon after that date he became a victim to a morbid melancholy. A prolonged stay in Italy failed to cure him, and in 1821 he became a permanent mental invalid. He lived for thirty-four years more in his native town, with only rare and transient luminous intervals. He died in 1855.

Like Zhukóvsky, Bátyushkov was a modernist in verse and language, a continuer of the work of Karamzín, and a resolute enemy of Church Slavonic and archaistic rudeness. But unlike Zhukóvsky, who was more romantic than most of his contemporaries and saturated with German and English influences, Bátyushkov was thoroughly "eighteenth-century" and "Latin." Though he was no stranger to the New Sensibility, the groundwork of his personality was pagan and sensual. His masters were Latin and classical: the Latin and French elegiac poets Tibullus and Parny; Tasso and Petrarch; and the Greek Anthology. Bátyushkov's ambition was to rival in Russian the sweetness and melody of Italian; this in the judgment of his contemporaries he almost achieved. His Russian is miles apart from the barbaric virility of Derzhávin. It is soft and sweet to the point of effeminacy. Bátyushkov's output was not large. It consists of a few elegies and lyrics, where the language of sentimentalism is placed at the service of a purely sensual passion; of some elegies of a more rhetorical character, such as the sometime famous *Dying Tasso* and the exquisite elegy to *The Shade of a Friend*. In 1818 appeared the (free) translations of amorous epigrams from the Greek Anthology, which for beauty of rhythm and diction are his masterpieces. In the years immediately preceeding his madness (1819–21) Bátyushkov wrote some lyrical epigrams in a different manner from that of all his earlier verse. For strange beauty and haunting emotional intensity they are unique in Russian poetry. They are a rare instance of the creative influence of mental illness on poetry.

Another pioneer of form was Pável Alexándrovich Katénin (1792–1853), who began as an early champion of romanticism and, when romanticism became the slogan of the majority, turned classicist and Shishkovian and wrote *Andromache*, the last "regular" Russian tragedy. His principal contention was that poetry should be *national*, and it was this which led him away from the Karamzinians and Zhukovskyites. In his early ballads, written under the impulse of Bürger, he tried to attain nationality by the use of aggressive (and at that time objectionable) realism in diction and detail. These ballads had an appreciable influence on the Russian ballads of Púshkin, who esteemed Katénin highly and was almost alone in doing justice to his poetry. In his later work Katénin became aggressively archaic, finally breaking away from the taste of the day. In all he did he was a genuine master of technique, but he lacked the fire that alone infects and attracts. After 1832 he abandoned literature and lived in the seclusion of his estate, a profoundly embittered and dissatisfied man.

Younger than these poets, but belonging to the same early stages of the movement, was Baron Antón Antónovich Délvig (1798–1831), Púshkin's schoolfellow at the Lyceum and his best friend. Noted for his indolence ("poetical laziness"), kindheartedness, and common sense, he exerted an enormous personal influence on the lives of his poet contemporaries. From 1825 to his death he edited the yearly miscellany of the poets' party, *Northern Flowers*. In 1830 he succeeded in obtaining permission to publish a *Literary Gazette*. His early death in 1831 was a cruel blow to Púshkin and to all the poets of their circle.

As a poet Délvig developed early, but he published little and late, owing chiefly to his famous laziness. He never became popular, though Púshkin and Baratýnsky ranked him very high. Like the poets of the eighteenth century he does not make his inner life the material of his poetry, but takes his subjects from outside. His Russian songs were in his time his most popular work, but his most exquisite poems are those in the classical measures. No one, before or after, ever wrote such perfect epigrams (in the Greek sense) as Délvig did. Still better are his idyls, highly valued by Púshkin: *The Bathing Women* is unquestionably the highest achievement in Russian poetry in the more purely sensuous vision of classical antiquity. Impersonal, unemotional, formal, eminently craftsmanlike, and quite singularly unmeretricious, Délvig's poetry was made to be treated with contempt by the later nineteenth century. Our time has made a great effort to revive him, and he has been restored to his lawful place in history, possibly even more than that. For, like Katénin, though a great master, Délvig lacks that human significance which after all alone makes major poetry.

The younger Karamzinians and Arzamasians cultivated with greatest zest what the French eighteenth century called "fugitive" poetry. Even Zhukóvsky's high seriousness stooped to such light verse, and Bátyushkov made his literary reputation with the epistle *My Penates,* which was considered the masterpiece of the kind. Púshkin's work before his exile to the south of Russia consists almost entirely of fugitive poems.

Two masters of fugitive poetry in the first decade of the Golden Age were Davýdov and Vyázemsky. Though lesser poets than Zhukóvsky or Bátyushkov, these two men are even more characteristic of their generation and more typical of their school. Both are high-spirited, healthy, virile, unromantic, and—ultimately—shallowish. Both were great wits and fond of fun, in life as well as in literature.

Denís Vasílievich Davýdov[1] (1784–1839) was one of the most famous and popular soldiers of his day (he was also a past master in making use of his military celebrity to advertise his literary work,· and vice versa). His early and most popular verses are in a style of his own making, known as the "hussar style." In them he sings the praise of reckless valor, on the field of battle as well as before the bottle. The diction in some is rather unconventional, and occasionally his words have to be replaced by dots, but it is always full of spirit and great rhythmical go. His later poems are inspired by a late love for a very young girl. They are passionately sentimental and as vivid and alive in diction and rhythmical elasticity as his hussar verses. Púshkin had a high opinion of his poetry and used to say that Davýdov showed him the way to be original.

Prince Peter Andréyevich Vyázemsky (1792–1878) was one of the most active members of the Arzamás and became an intimate friend of Púshkin. Their correspondence is a treasure house of wit, fine criticism, and good Russian. In the twenties Vyázemsky was the most combative and brilliant champion of what then went by the name of romanticism. In the thirties, like all the "literary aristocracy," he found himself out of date and out of tune with the young generation. He had the great sadness of surviving all his contemporaries. Though it was precisely in his last years that his poetical talent bore its best fruit, he was forgotten and abandoned by critics and public long before he died. He grew into an irritated reactionary who heartily detested everyone born after 1810. Though he was the journalistic leader of Russian romanticism, there can be nothing less romantic than his early poetry: it consists either of very elegant, polished, and cold exercises on the set commonplaces of poetry, or of brilliant essays in word

[1] Though Davýdov was probably a starting point for Denísov in War and Peace, Tolstóy's creation is, in its final form, entirely unlike the real Davýdov.

play, where pun begets pun, and conceit begets conceit, heaping up mountains of verbal wit. His later poetry is more sober and more significant. It never became strictly personal, like Zhukóvsky's or Púshkin's. It remained universal and typical—essentially classical. But the old and embittered man found new and beautiful intonations for the great eternal commonplaces, and as he approached death, the subject drew increasingly moving notes from him. Such poems as the stanzas to the memory of Davýdov and the one on a funeral in Venice are among the purest gems of Russian poetry.

PÚSHKIN

Alexander Sergéyevich Púshkin was born in Moscow, May 26, 1799. His father's family was one of the oldest of the Russian gentry. His mother, née Gannibal, was the granddaughter of "Peter the Great's Nigger"—more exactly Abyssinian—Engineer General, Abraham Gannibal. The poet was always proud both of his "six-hundred-year-old nobility" and of his African blood. His childhood and early boyhood were spent at home in a French eighteenth-century atmosphere of frivolous and superficial culture. There was no mutual affection between son and parents. In 1811 Púshkin went to school at the Lyceum of Tsárskoye Seló (founded that year). The Lyceum became more of a home to him than his family, and his schoolfellows always commanded the warmest and most permanent of his affections. While still at the Lyceum, Púshkin began writing verses. In 1814 his first poems appeared in the *Messenger of Europe*, and before he left the Lyceum he was a member of the Arzamás, and was regarded as a rival, almost an equal, by Zhukóvsky and Bátyushkov. In 1817, on completing his studies, he became a clerk in the Foreign Office, but the appointment was merely nominal and he did no office work. He lived in St. Petersburg, mixing with the most advanced, brilliant, and dissipated of his contemporaries, and tasting unreservedly of the pleasures of carnal love. All the time he was working at a "romantic epic" in six cantos, *Ruslán and Lyudmíla*, which appeared in the spring of 1820, taking by storm the young generation and being violently censured by the old. Zhukóvsky, on reading

the manuscript, gave Púshkin his portrait with the inscrip-
tion "To a victorious pupil from a defeated master." But
before its publication some of Púshkin's revolutionary epigrams had reached the knowledge of Alexander I, and the
poet was ordered to leave Petersburg. He was transferred
to a government office in Ekaterinosláv. Almost immediately on arriving there he fell ill and was taken to the
Caucasus by General Rayévsky, a famous soldier of 1812,
with whose sons he contracted a lásting friendship and for
whose daughters he held a fervent admiration. The two
months spent in the company of the Rayévskys in the
Caucasus and the Crimea were one of the happiest periods
in Púshkin's life. It was from the Rayévskys also that he got
his first knowledge of Byron. From the end of 1820 to
1823 Púshkin served in Kishinëv, doing very little official
work, detesting the filthy barbarity of the Moldavians, leading the same reckless life he had led in Petersburg, and
having sufficient freedom to pass much of his time at
Kámenka, an estate in the Province of Kíev that was one
of the principal centers of the Revolutionary movement.
But he worked more seriously than in Petersburg. He wrote
The Captive of the Caucasus—which appeared in 1822 and
had an even greater success than *Ruslán and Lyudmíla*—
The Fountain of Bakhchisaráy, and numerous short poems,
and began *Evgény Onégin.* In 1828 he was transferred to
Odessa. He was delighted to breathe the freer and more
European air of a big seaport, but his life became even
more irregular and passionate. His Odessa life is marked
by his love (almost simultaneous) for two women—the
Dalmatian Amália Ríznich, and the wife of the Viceroy,
Countess Elizabeth Vorontsóv. The former seems to have
been the strongest sensual passion in his life and the object of several of his greatest love lyrics. His love for the
latter led him into social entanglements, where he appears
to have been most treacherously served by his Byronic
friend, Alexander Rayévsky—himself a lover of the Countess. In August 1824 Púshkin was suddenly expelled from
the Civil Service and ordered to live permanently on his
mother's estate of Mikháylovskoye in the Province of
Pskov. The pretext for this disgrace was a private letter
intercepted by the police in which the poet expressed the
opinion that "pure atheism," though by no means a com-
forting philosophy, was "the most probable." On arriving

at Mikháylovskoye, Púshkin found his parents there, but a succession of scenes between the poet and his father led to the latter's leaving his scapegrace and dangerous son to himself. Púshkin remained in Mikháylovskoye, alone except for the company of his old nurse, and the neighborhood of Trigórskoye, a country place inhabited by a charming family of ladies—Mme Ósipova and her two daughters. There Púshkin met Mme Kern, who became the subject of a rather trivial love affair with him and of one of his most famous and inspired lyrics. The years spent at Mikháylovskoye were particularly productive.

Púshkin's forced seclusion at Mikháylovskoye prevented him from taking part in the December Revolt of 1825. His connections with the rebels were obvious, but the new Emperor overlooked them and, by a master stroke of clever policy, summoned the poet to Moscow (September 1826), granted him a complete pardon, and promised to be his special protector and patron. Though apparently more free, Púshkin was subjected to an even more meddling supervision than under the preceding reign. What was worse, his inner freedom was forfeited, for he was made to understand that his amnesty was such a signal display of mercy that he could never do too much to live up to it. After several abortive attempts at settling down, in 1829 Púshkin fell in love with Nathalie Goncharóva, a young girl of sixteen, a dazzling beauty, but frivolous and insignificant. He proposed but was rejected. Under the influence of this check he suddenly went off to the Caucasus, where a war was going on with Turkey, but was severely rebuked for doing so without permission. In the winter of 1829–30 he made several attempts to go abroad, but was not permitted to do so by his "protectors." In the spring of 1830 he again proposed to Nathalie and was this time accepted. His own financial affairs were far from brilliant— he got handsome sums for his books, but this was a precarious and irregular income, all the more so because Nicholas's censorship often held them up. Borís Godunóv had been thus prohibited since 1826, but now as a special favor, in order that he might meet the demand of his future family life, he was allowed to print it. It appeared in January 1831, but was met with faint praise and loud blame. The autumn before his marriage Púshkin spent in the country, at Bóldino, and these two months were the most marvel-ously productive in his life. He was married in February 1831. His marriage was, at first, externally happy. But there was no real sympathy between the pair. Nathalie was frivolous and cold, besides being trivial and almost vulgar and quite free from all intellectual or poetical interests. Nathalie's beauty made her an immense success in Petersburg, in town and at court. It was to be able to invite her to court balls that Nicholas in 1834 made Púshkin a "gentleman of the chamber," an honor deeply resented by the poet. No longer the leader of an advanced school, Púshkin was now the head of the "literary aristocracy." He was venerated by the younger generation rather as a relic of the past than as a living force. All he wrote after 1830 met with no success. He half abandoned poetry and devoted himself to a history of Peter the Great, which was never to be written. In 1836 he was, after repeated refusals, allowed to start a literary quarterly, *Sovreménnik* (*The Contemporary*), which, however, like all he had done since 1831, met with no success. Meanwhile his thraldom to the court increased—he became more and more dependent on the royal favor, especially since he had contracted considerable debts to the Treasury. He felt that he was suffocating in a society where a mere poet, in spite of his "six-hundred-year-old nobility," was looked down upon by the great courtiers descended from the favorites of eighteenth-century empresses, and was little more than his wife's husband. He tried to free himself from the noxious and deteriorating atmosphere, but was given to understand that if he left town it would be in disgrace. At last came the tragic end. His jealousy was exasperated by the attention paid to Nathalie by Baron Georges D'Anthès, a French Royalist in the Russian service. Púshkin called him out. D'Anthès at first succeeded in evading a duel by marrying Nathalie's sister, thus pretending to show that Púshkin was mistaken in his suspicions. But a few days after the marriage Púshkin learned that Nathalie and D'Anthès had again secretly met. He called him out a second time, in terms that made all escape impossible for D'Anthès. The duel was fought on January 27, 1837. Púshkin was mortally wounded, and died on the 29th. For fear of public demonstrations of sympathy his coffin was hurried away in the night from Petersburg to the monastery near Mikháylovskoye, which he had chosen for his burial place.

Púshkin began writing early. There is a tradition, founded on the recollection of his elder sister, that he wrote French verse before he left home for the Lyceum. His earliest datable work in Russian belongs to 1814. Only two or three immature and crude poems may be assigned, on internal evidence, to an earlier date. With the exception of these, Púshkin's verse was from the very beginning extraordinarily easy and fluent, almost on the highest level of a time when ease and fluency were the main aim of poets. If till about 1820 he remained inferior to Zhukóvsky and Bátyushkov, it was not for lack of mastery, but rather for the lack of original inspiration. Púshkin's Lyceum verses are imitative and, for a boy's verse, strikingly unemotional and unsentimental. He was a consummate technician before he really became a poet—an order of development not usual with nineteenth-century poets. Some of his Lyceum verses are exercises in the forms practiced by Zhukóvsky and Derzhávin, but by far the greater part belong to the favorite Arzamasian kinds of fugitive poetry, friendly epistles, and Anacreontic lyrics. His style grew up in the school of Zhukóvsky and Bátyushkov, but the direct influence on it of the French classical poets is also considerable, and of these Voltaire was for a long time Púshkin's favorite. Next came the influence of Parny, whose remarkable and long-neglected elegies, inspired with unsentimental, classical, but genuinely passionate, love, were the models for the first of Púshkin's poems in which we can discern the accent of serious passion. By 1818 Púshkin's verse finally acquires that accent which is his alone. The epistles and elegies of these years are already latently great poetry. Through the impersonal brilliance of their Arzamasian wit we distinctly discern a heart and nerves of exceptionally rich vitality. There is a clear and cold atmosphere in these poems—and no feeling underlying them. The same atmosphere pervades *Ruslán and Lyudmíla*. This is a semi-ironic and frivolous romance, where only a few names and the barest skeletons of motifs are taken from the chapbooks of the type of *Bová* and *Eruslán*, but where all the treatment is essentially eighteenth century. There is nothing in it that might have shocked the taste of Voltaire. There is no seriousness in *Ruslán and Lyudmíla* except the seriousness of very conscientious craftsmanship. It is pure play, like the classical ballet, which Púshkin was so fond of at the

time he was writing the poem. It is the work of a confident
and buoyant young man who is already a past master in
the craft of poetry but not yet quite a poet in the highest
sense.

By 1818–20 the essential groundwork of Púshkin's
poetic style was established, and remained unchanged till
the end. It is "French" and classical. Its most characteristic
feature—one that is particularly disconcerting to the ro-
mantic-bred reader—is the complete avoidance of all
imagery and metaphor. Púshkin's images are all dependent
on the happy use of the *mot juste,* and his poetic effectiveness on the use of metonymy and similar purely verbal
figures of speech.

Taken as a whole, the early verse of Púshkin and that
of his later verse which is in the same style are perhaps the
nearest approach outside French poetry to "that tone of
mingled distinction, gaiety, and grace which," says Lytton
Strachey, "is one of the unique products of the mature
poetical genius of France."

The last French master of Púshkin was André Chénier,
whose remains were published in 1819. This was to be the
last external influence that affected the inner texture of
Púshkin's style. Later influences affected only his choice of
subject and his methods of construction.

The principal of these influences was Byron's, which
dominates Púshkin's second period (1820–3). But the
nature of this influence must be clearly understood.
Púshkin had no essential kinship with the English poet.
His exact and logical style is poles apart from Byron's untidy rhetoric. Byron's influence is limited to the narrative
poems of this period, and in these it was the choice of subject and the disposition of the material that are due to
Byron—the actual style remained as classical as before.
The principal Byronic poems of Púshkin are *The Captive
of the Caucasus* (written 1820–1, published 1822) and *The
Fountain of Bakhchisaráy* (written 1822, published 1824).
The success of both of these poems was greater than that
of any other work of Púshkin's. It was they that made
Púshkin the most popular poet of the twenties. They are
very far from giving the full measure of his genius. As in
all that preceded them, the form is consistently greater than
the content. The form (verse and diction) is perfect. In
certain respects, even, it was never excelled by Púshkin

himself, and certainly never approached by any other poet. The public reveled in the sheer beauty of word and sound that the poet so triumphantly upheld at the same flawless level from beginning to end. The effect is all the more marvelous as Púshkin's verse does not "sing." Its beauty and harmony are purely verbal—based on complete mutual adequacy of rhythm and syntax, and on an extraordinarily subtle and complex system of what one might call alliteration if the word might be used to denote anything so variedly and consistently unobtrusive. The perfection of this verbal harmony is reached in *The Fountain of Bakhchisaráy*. Afterwards Púshkin deliberately avoided the too fluent and caressing effects of this manner.

As I have said, the Byronic element in the two Byronic poems is limited to the subject and the narrative construction. The oriental beauty, with her fierce or devoted love, the disillusioned hero, with strong passions in the past, the oriental potentate, grim and silent, the hot atmosphere of "the clime of the East"—these are the elements taken by Púshkin from Byron. The fragmentary and dramatic manner of presentation, with its beginning *in medias res*, the abrupt transitions, and its lyrical epilogues, is the trace of Byron's narrative manner. But the Byronic spirit was only superficially assimilated by Púshkin, and the two poems must be regarded as further impersonal exercises on a borrowed theme. The most original and the most beautiful parts in both poems are the purely descriptive passages: in *The Captive*, the account of the warlike habits of the Circassians, as exact and as reliable in point of fact as those of the shrewdest eighteenth-century travelers; in *The Fountain*, the more lyrical and atmospheric, but always eminently precise and plastic, descriptions of the harem and evocations of the Crimea. Of the shorter romantic and Byronic poems belonging to this period, *The Robber Brothers* (1821), which has less verbal beauty than the two longer poems, is interesting as having attained an exceptional popularity among the people: it has even been incorporated in a folk play.

Púshkin's lyric poetry of the period is conspicuously free from every formal, and almost every emotional, trace of Byronism. It is a continuation of the poems of 1816–19. But it gradually acquires a more passionate and manly tone, becomes more personal and more perfect in form.

The direct influence of Chénier is apparent in a series of descriptive and elegiac epigrams, full of beautiful restraint and plastic expressiveness. The same influence in a more transformed and digested form is present in the greatest lyrical poem of the period (and one of the greatest he ever wrote), the wonderful *Napoleon* of 1821.

The strictly French, eighteenth-century, and Voltairian element persisted in Púshkin some time after his acquaintance with Byron. It was only now that he wrote the most Voltairian of his poems, the blasphemous and lascivious *Gavriliáda* (1821), which brought him much trouble in the next reign and was printed only long after his death (London, 1861). Though quite in the style of Voltaire's and Parny's anti-religious poems, it is different from them in that it is not serious—not intended for anti-Christian propaganda, but merely the froth of an irreverent, sensuous, and unbridled youth.

Púshkin's middle period may be regarded as coextensive with the writing of *Evgény Onégin,* his longest, most popular and influential, and in certain ways most characteristic work. It is a "Novel in Verse," in eight cantos, which are called chapters. It was begun in the spring of 1823 and completed in the autumn of 1830, a few finishing touches being added in 1831. The initial impulse came from *Don Juan,* but apart from the general idea of writing a long narrative poem in stanzaed verse, with a subject taken from contemporary life, and in a tone mingled of gravity and gaiety, *Evgény Onégin* has little in common with Byron's epic. It does not have the qualities of *Don Juan*—its sealike sweep or its satiric power. The qualities it has are of a nature entirely unlike Byron's. It is less loose and, though when Púshkin began it he had not any fixed idea how he was going to finish it, it is a story with a beginning, a middle, and an end. Its unity is not an intended and premeditated unity, but rather like the organic unity of an individual life. It reflects the stages through which the poet passed between his twenty-fourth and thirty-second years. The transition from the boisterously young high spirits of the first chapter to the resigned and muffled tragedy of the eighth is gradual, like the growth of a tree.

The first chapter, written in 1823, is the crowning glory of Púshkin's youth. It is the most brilliant of all his works. It sparkles and bubbles like champagne—a com-

parison long hackneyed but still inevitable. It is the description of the life of a young St. Petersburg dandy (the English
word is used), the life familiar to Púshkin himself before
his exile. It is the only one of the eight chapters where the
gay definitely predominates over the grave. The later chapters are in the same style, but chastened and mellowed
down as years proceed. The mixture of humor (not satire)
and poetical sentiment and the infinite wealth and variety
of the emotional shadings and transitions recall *Tristram
Shandy* (whose author Púshkin esteemed highly), but with
a freedom, a spontaneity, a vigorous go that was entirely
beyond the reach of Sterne.

Evgény Onégin is the crowning glory of Púshkin's
first maturity and the fullest expression of what may be
called his "subjective" manner, as opposed to the objective
and impersonal manner of his latter years. Of all his works
it has the least *apparent* restraint: the poet lets himself go
in digressions, lyrical, humorous, polemical. He makes no
show of artistic economy. More than anywhere else he
relies for his effects on atmosphere. But his sense of measure and his unerring mastery are as present in *Onégin* as
elsewhere.

The actual manner of *Onégin* has been imitated by
numerous Russian poets, never with more than questionable
success. It demanded two qualities that are extremely rare
in conjunction—a boundless, spontaneous vitality and an
unerring sense of artistic measure. When I speak of the
important influence of *Onégin* on later literary developments, I do not allude to the direct and metrical progeny of
this "novel in verse." It is the kind of realism first introduced in it, the style of character drawing, the characters
themselves, and the construction of the story that are to be
regarded as the fountainheads of the later Russian novel.
The realism of *Onégin* is that peculiarly Russian realism
which is poetical without idealizing and without surrendering anything of reality. It is the same realism that will live
again in Lérmontov's novel, in Turgénev, in Goncharóv, in
War and Peace, and in the best of Chékhov—though its
legitimacy outside the perfect poetical form given it by
Púshkin is open to doubt. The character-drawing of *Onégin*
is not analytical or psychological, but poetical, dependent
on the lyrical and emotional atmosphere accompanying the
personages—not on the anatomy of their thoughts and

sentiments. This style of portraiture was inherited from
Púshkin by Turgénev and other Russian novelists, but not
by Tolstóy or Dostoyévsky. Of the characters themselves,
Onégin and Tatiána are the ancestors of a whole race of
characters in Russian fiction; Lérmontov's, Goncharóv's
and Turgénev's, especially, are entirely of this family.
Finally the construction of the story, so different from that
of Púshkin's prose stories, became the standard for the
Russian novel. The simplicity of the plot, its logical development from the essential features of the heroes, and the unhappy, suggestively muffled ending, gave the pattern to the
Russian novelists—especially, again, to Turgénev. Much in
the methods of *Onégin* may be termed romantic. But the
spirit of the poem is not. As in all the mature works of
Púshkin it is dominated by the stern moral law of the
Fates. Onégin's irresponsible self-indulgence and fidelity to
self subtly, inevitably, untheatrically undo him, while the
calm self-command and resignation of Tatiána give her
that unquestionable halo of moral greatness which is forever associated with her name. The greatness of Púshkin in
the creation of Tatiána is that he avoided the almost un-
avoidable pit of making a prig or a puritan out of the
virtuous wife who coldly rejects the man she loves. Tatiána
is redeemed in her virtue by the sadness she will never
conquer, by her resigned and calm resolve never to enter
her only possible paradise, but to live with never a possibility of happiness. The Tatiána-Onégin relation has often
been revived in Russian fiction, and the juxtaposition of a
small and weak man with a strong woman became almost
hackneyed in Turgénev and others. But the classical attitude
of Púshkin, of sympathy without pity for the man and of
respect without reward for the woman, has never been
revived.

During the time Púshkin was at work at *Evgény
Onégin* he wrote numerous other short and long poems, of
varied initial significance but invariable perfection. The
nearest kin to *Onégin* are the tales in verse of contemporary
Russian life: *Count Núlin* (1825), a crisp, clever anecdote
in verse in a more purely realistic and ironic manner; and
The Little House in Kolómna (1830), a poem in octaves, a
kind of Russian *Beppo,* his last essay in the "extensive"
style of *Onégin.*

The Byronic narrative-poem form was continued in

The Gypsies (1824, published 1827) and *Poltáva* (1828, published 1829). These poems are immeasurably superior to the two earlier Byronic tales. Of the influence of Byron nothing remains in them but the merest idea of narrative in verse with a lyrical coloring and with abrupt passages from episode to episode. *The Gypsies* is among the greatest works of Púshkin. It is, with *Onégin*, the first in which he reached the full measure of his genius, and the first, also, in which begins the gradual evolution from the "extensive," melliflu-ous, and caressing style of his youth to the sterner beauty of his later work. Its setting is conventional—the gypsies of Bessarabia are not treated realistically, but merely as ideal representatives of a natural state of human society. The subject is the tragic inability of sophisticated and civilized man to throw away his convention-bred feelings and passions, especially the feeling of ownership of his mate. The poem is, on the face of it, a strong affirmation of free-dom—of the freedom of the woman against the man—and a denunciation of the unnatural wickedness of vengeance and of punishment. It is obviously and patently a plea for anarchism, and has been commented on in this sense by Dostoyévsky (in his famous Púshkin Address) and by Vyacheslav Ivánov. However strangely out of tune this anarchism may be with all the later work of Púshkin, it cannot be explained away and must be accepted as an essential ingredient of his philosophy. But the essentially classical religion of the Tragic Fates, of Nemesis working as an inevitable law of nature, is nowhere more fully ex-pressed than in *The Gypsies*. It was Púshkin's first attempt at tragedy, and one of his greatest. It is too easy to philoso-phize about *The Gypsies*—the most temptingly universal imaginative work in the Russian language. It is less easy to do justice to its poetical beauty, and speaking of it, one is too likely to forget the lesson of restraint that is the best lesson to be learned from Púshkin. The verse, less fluent and voluptuous than in *The Captive* and in *The Fountain*, is tighter, fuller, more saturated with complex expressive-ness. Such passages as the old gypsy's tale of Ovid, the end of the poem (with the speech of the old man on Aléko's murder), and especially the epilogue, are unsurpassable summits of poetry. One can only be deeply grateful to the Fates for allowing us to have such plenty.

Poltáva is a further step towards the objective and

impersonal manner. In it Púshkin deliberately and studiously avoids the fluent loveliness of his southern poems.
To us its stern and harsh style sounds magnificently heroic,
but its first readers were disagreeably taken aback by this
new departure and refused to admire it. It is not a perfect
whole—the romantic love story of the old hetman Mazéppa
for his godchild is imperfectly fused with the national epic
of the struggle of Peter with Charles of Sweden. The epic
itself, which forms the background of the first two cantos
and the prevailing subject of the third (with its famous
description, so exact in its condensed ornateness, of the
battle of Poltáva), is Púshkin's first contribution to that
impersonal, national, group poetry which had inspired
Lomonósov and Derzhávin, and which had been dead since
the triumph of the Karamzinists. After Púshkin it was once
more to die. The great glory of *Poltáva,* apart from this
voicing of national and supra-individual sentiment, is its
diction, magnificent in its very baldness and terseness, so
happily grand and powerful is the choice of words, never
archaic, but always charged with the richest and greatest
associations.

A style similar to *Poltáva,* terse and saturated, is used
in several unfinished narrative fragments of this and the
following period. The most important are *Cleopatra, or the
Egyptian Nights* (begun 1825, resumed 1835) and *Gálub*
(c. 1830). The latter is a story of the Caucasus strikingly
different in style from *The Captive;* the former, one of
Púshkin's most memorable conceptions, a magnificent poem
of death and lust.

The period of *Evgény Onégin* is also the period of
Púshkin's best and greatest lyrical output. With few exceptions (the most notable being the great Napoleon ode) none
of his lyric poems written before 1824 are on the very
highest level of his genius. After that date he often continued to write in the lighter, occasional style of his early
years, and these poems acquire a mellower and subtler
grace, even if they lose the clear, youthful vigor of the
earlier ones. But his serious lyric poetry written between
1824 and 1830 is a body of lyric verse unapproached in
Russian and unsurpassed in any poetry. It is impossible
without quotations from the originals to prove the statement or to give an adequate idea of the nature of this
poetry. Much of it is subjective, occasional, and emotional

—the actual biographical occasion is frequently known. But the occasions are idealized, sublimated, and universalized, and the poems preserve no ragged edges of extrapoetic sentiment or undistilled emotion. Though subjective and demonstrably based on individual experience, they are general in tone, as classical poetry is. They seldom contain any striking psychological observation or any revelation of the all too personal. Their appeal, like the appeal of Sappho, is to common human experience. Their style, which is a further development of Zhukóvsky's, is also of that classical quality which, says Montesquieu in speaking of Raphael, *"frappe moins d'abord pour frapper plus en suite."* The beauty of the style, which, as always in Púshkin, is free from wit, imagery, and metaphor, is a Greek beauty that depends as much on what is left unsaid as on what is said. It depends on the choice of words, on the adequacy of rhythm to intonation, and on the complex texture of sound—the wonderful *alliteratio Pushkiniana,* so elusive and so all-conditioning. It is impossible here to quote or analyze any of these lyrics. I can only enumerate some of the most beautiful: the lines on jealousy beginning: "The stormy day is spent"; the *Lyceum Anniversary* of 1825—the greatest hymn to friendship in all poetry; the stanzas to Mme Kern ("I remember a wonderful moment," 1825) the elegy (sixteen lines) on the death of Amália Ríznich (1826); the *Foreboding* (1828); and the lyrics addressed to a dead mistress, probably Amália Ríznich, written a few months before his marriage (1830), especially, what is perhaps the most intensely perfect of all, *For the Shores of Thy Distant Fatherland (Dlya beregóv otchízny dálnoy).* A group apart is formed by the nature lyrics—the most classical of all—with their conception of inanimate and irresponsive nature. Among the best are *The Storm* (1827), with its famous comparison between the beauty of the storm and the beauty of "a girl on the rock," to the latter's advantage; *The Winter Morning* (1829); and *The Avalanche* (1829). On an even higher level of poetical significance are two poems that are Púshkin's grandest utterances in the grand style—the often quoted and much too often commented-on *Prophet* (1826); and the tense and terrible *Upas-tree (Anchár,* 1828).

To the same period belong Púshkin's best ballads, *The Bridegroom* (1825) and *The Drowned Man* (1828). The style of these ballads is the realistic style introduced by Katénin but perfected and refined with all the mastery of Púshkin.

After 1830 Púshkin's lyrical poetry tends to become impersonally universal and severely bare of all ornament. Henceforward its characteristics are restraint, reticence, and an ascetic avoidance of all that the public associates with poetic beauty—mellifluous ease, melodious tone, attractive sentiment. The most characteristic poems of the thirties are impersonal elegiac meditations, proceeding from a "thinking heart" brooding on the great commonplaces of universal experience. The most majestic of these poems is *The Captain* (1836), an elegy on the portrait of the wronged and misunderstood hero of 1812—Field Marshal Barcláy de Tólly. But by the side of this *odi profanum vulgus* sentiment Púshkin attempted to voice "group feelings," as in his famous retort to the French friends of Poland, *To the Detractors of Russia* (1831). One of the most perfect, unadorned, prosaic, and simplest poems is that noble tribute to the man in the hero—*The Feast of Peter the Great* (1835). But by the side of these high and supra-personal utterances, other sounds came from him—the fruit of his prolonged torture at the hand of Nicholas, Nathalie, and society. The noble restraint of *The Captain* is a striking contrast to the grim and weird irony of the lines on *Madness* (*Ne day mne Bog soytí s umá*, 1833), one of the most poignant "mad poems" ever written. The few lyrics of this latter type were published only after the poet's death.

Most of Púshkin's narrative poems written after 1830 are personative, or "stylized," as we say in Russia. The poet is masked in a borrowed form, or borrowed subject, or both, and his human personality is carefully and effectively hidden. Such is *Angelo* (1833), a paraphrase of *Measure for Measure,* where Púshkin tried to preserve Shakspere's "broad painting of character" while stripping it of the irrelevancies and excrescences of Elizabethan exuberance. Of all Púshkin's poems, *Angelo* has had the least share of praise, but it throws an important light on the workings of his creative mind. More purely impersonal are the *Songs of the Western Slavs* (1832), adaptations of Mérimée's forgeries of Serbian folklore in the style of the Russian folk epic; and, above all, the fairy tales (*Skázki,*

1831–2); the cynically witty *Parson and His Man Baldá*, an admirable revival of the manner of the popular doggerel verse of the eighteenth century; the maliciously ironical *Golden Cockerel;* and the best of all, *King Saltán*. The longer one lives, the more one is inclined to regard *King Saltán* as the masterpiece of Russian poetry. It is purest art, free from all the irrelevancies of emotion and symbol, "a thing of beauty" and "a joy for ever." It is also the most universal art, for it has the same appeal for a child of six and for the most sophisticated poetry reader of sixty. It requires no understanding; its reception is immediate, direct, unquestionable. It is not frivolous, nor witty, nor humorous. But it is light, exhilarating, bracing. It has high seriousness, for what can be more highly serious than the creation of a world of perfect beauty and freedom, open to all?

I fully realize that the claim for *King Saltán* to be accepted as *the* masterpiece of Púshkin has little chance of getting a majority of votes. Such a majority is virtually pledged to the last great narrative poem of Púshkin—*The Bronze Horseman* (written 1833, published posthumously 1841). This poem certainly has very substantial claims to absolute pre-eminence. There is no conception of poetic greatness from the standpoint of which this pre-eminence could be challenged, except that (hypothetic) standpoint which would demand of all poetry that it be as free from human irrelevancies as is *King Saltán*. The classicist, the romanticist, the realist, the symbolist, and the expressionist must all agree in their appreciation of *The Bronze Horseman*. Its actual subject is the Petersburg inundation of 1824 and the effect it had on Evgény, a poor and insignificant clerk, by washing away into the sea his sweetheart's house with all its inhabitants. Its philosophical (or whatever the word) subject is the irreconcilable conflict of the rights of the community, as incarnate in the *genius loci* of the city, the bronze statue of Peter the Great on the Senate Square —and of those of the individual, as represented by the wretched Evgény, who is undone by the mere geographical factor of the site of Petersburg. The greatness of the poem lies particularly in the fact that Púshkin makes no attempt to reconcile the two in any superior harmony. And though the poem begins with a splendid hymn to Peter and Petersburg, and the figure of the great Emperor dominates it in semi-divine proportions, it is a strikingly different figure from the human Peter of *Poltáva* and of *The Feast of Peter the Great*—an inhuman and potent demon who knows no mercy. The poet's essential sympathy for the un-done Evgény is by no means impaired by the greatness of his enemy. And the issue of the moral conflict remains in the balance—unsolved. In style *The Bronze Horseman* is a step further in the direction of *Poltáva*. The concentrated fullness and tightness of the octosyllabics; the vocabulary, strictly realistic, but saturated with the utmost expressive-ness; the elemental majesty of the movement; the endless inward vistas opened by each word and by the whole— give the poem a poetic weight that fully justifies acceptance of it as the greatest example in Russian of great poetry.

Púshkin's first, and longest, play, *Borís Godunóv* (1825, published 1831), was written, like his first stories in prose, primarily as a formal experiment. In writing it he was interested not so much in the doings and destinies of his characters as in the destinies of Russian tragedy and of Russian dramatic meter. *Borís Godunóv* is a first essay in Russian romantic—Shaksperian—tragedy as opposed to the hitherto prevalent French forms. When, in 1826, Púshkin brought it to Moscow, it was acclaimed as his masterpiece by the young idealists whose idols were Shakspere (a German Shakspere) and Goethe. It is hardly possible today to share their view. *Borís Godunóv* must rather be regarded as one of the immature and preparatory works of Púshkin, less mature and less perfect than much that had preceded it—than *The Gypsies,* for instance, or the early chapters of *Onégin*. The subject of the play is taken from Karamzín. It is one of those inset dramatic stories which are the principal literary attraction of his *History*. In his interpretation of the facts Púshkin closely followed Karamzín, and this was a severe handicap. *Borís Godunóv* is a tragedy of expiation, but nowhere else does Púshkin treat the theme with less inevitable mastery. At times it is almost sentimental. The meter, a particularly monotonous form of blank verse, is not quite satisfactory. The diction is somewhat stilted and conventional. And the construction of the play is in many ways narrative rather than dramatic. For a dialogued chronicle, however, to be read, not acted, it is masterly, and one of Púshkin's first triumphs in economy. The characters, especially the False

Demetrius, are admirably drawn. The prose scenes, with their fine irony, are the best in the play and have nothing to compare with them in all previous Russian literature. In two or three places the tragedy attains real dramatic beauty —as in the scene of Borís's death and in the grandly condensed final scene, with the massacre of the Godunóvs (*behind* the scenes—a French touch) and the proclamation of the imposter as tsar. *Borís Godunóv* remained a closet play. Púshkin's dream of seeing it revolutionize the Russian stage never came true. Its influence, both immediate and posthumous, was extensive but not intrinsically significant— Russia never succeeded in producing really original "Shaksperian" tragedy.

On a much higher level of perfection and originality stand Púshkin's later plays—the four so-called "Little Tragedies" and *Rusálka*. The former were written mainly in the wonderful Bóldino autumn of 1830. Two of them, *Mozart and Salieri* and *The Feast during the Plague*, were published shortly afterwards; the third, *The Covetous Knight* (the English title is Púshkin's own), in 1836 (anonymously). *The Stone Guest*, finally revised only in that year, remained unpublished till after the poet's death (1840). Unlike *Borís Godunóv*, the Little Tragedies were not planned as experiments in form. They were rather essays in understanding of character and of dramatic situation. One of the titles proposed and rejected by Púshkin for the whole group was "Dramatical Investigations." The form of the diminutive tragedy was suggested by the similar productions of Barry Cornwall (whom Púshkin, like many of his contemporaries, even in England, valued higher than we do). *The Covetous Knight* bears the subheading "Scenes from the tragicomedy by Chenstone." [2] *The Feast during the Plague* is a fairly accurate translation of a scene of John Wilson's *City of the Plague*. Thus the Little Tragedies may be regarded as largely due to English suggestion.

They are among the most original, characteristic, and perfect work of the poet. In them Púshkin reached his

[2] It is possible that Púshkin had the English poet William Shenstone (1714–63) in mind when he made this acknowledgment. As far as is known, Shenstone wrote nothing called *The Covetous Knight*. Púshkin was probably merely coining a name to avoid any tie-up between his authorship of this work and his own father, a notorious miser. (Ed.)

greatest degree of concentration. With the exception of
The Stone Guest they can hardly be called plays. They are
rather isolated situations, dramatic "points," but points
charged with such significance that they do not demand any
further development. They are the application to drama of
the lyrical method of concentration. Their length varies
from one scene and a little over two hundred lines (*The
Feast*) to four acts and about five hundred lines (*The
Stone Guest*). The least complex is *The Feast*. Púshkin's
creative work in it was reduced to choosing where to begin
and where to end, to translating Wilson's indifferent English
verse into his own supreme Russian, and to adding two
songs, both of which are among his best; one of them, *The
Hymn in Honor of the Plague*, is the most terrible and
weird he ever wrote—one of his rare revelations of the
dark side of things. *Mozart and Salieri* is a study of the
passion of envy, and of the Divine Injustice that endows
with genius whom it will and rewards not the lifelong
labor of the devotee. *The Covetous Knight* is one of the
greatest and grandest studies of the miser—the second
scene, in which the miserly baron soliloquizes in his treasure
vault, is the grandest dramatic monologue in Russian and
perhaps Púshkin's most sustained piece of poetic magnificence. As for *The Stone Guest*, it shares with *The Bronze
Horseman* the right to be regarded as Púshkin's masterpiece. It is less ornate and less apparently saturated than
The Horseman. From beginning to end it never once
abandons the diction of prose, but it even outdoes *The
Horseman* in the limitless psychological and poetic sug-
gestiveness of its severely unornamented verse. It is the
story of Don Juan's last love affair—with the widow of the
man he had murdered—and of his tragic end. It is Púshkin's highest achievement on the subject of Nemesis—his
greatest subject. For the flexibility of the blank verse (so
different from that of *Borís Godunóv*), for the infinitely
subtle marriage of colloquial with metrical rhythm, for the
boundless pregnancy of the dialogue, for the subtly distilled
atmosphere of the south—and of atonement—it has no
equal. In spite of its Spanish subject, it is also of all Púshkin's works the most characteristically Russian—not in any
metaphysical meaning of that much abused word, but because it achieves what can be achieved only in Russian, in
being at once classical, colloquial, and poetical, and because

it embodies in their perfection all the best aspirations of
Russian poetry—its striving towards selective, unorna-
mental, realistic, and lyrical perfection. It is also of Púshkin's works the one that most defies translation—for in it
the poetical and emotional value of every word is put to
the fullest use and fully exhausted, and the natural possibilities of Russian rhythm (*at the same time* colloquial and
metrical) are made to yield all they can. The mere skeleton
of the play will give an idea of Púshkin's sober economy
and restraint but not of the infinite wealth behind them.

The last of Púshkin's dramatic essays, *Rusálka* (*The
River Nymph*), remains a fragment. Were it not for that,
it would be third, with *The Bronze Horseman* and *The
Stone Guest,* in claiming the first place in Russian poetry.
What has been said of the verse and diction of *The Stone
Guest* has to be repeated of *Rusálka.* The difference is that
the subject and atmosphere are Russian. It was also to be
a tragedy of expiation—the revenge of the seduced girl,
who throws herself into the river and becomes "a powerful
and cold water-nymph," on her faithless wooer, the prince.

Púshkin's greatest contemporary successes (with the
general public) were *The Captive of the Caucasus* and *The
Fountain of Bakhchisaráy* and (with the critical elite of his
generation) *Borís Godunóv*—all of them works of immature youth. His later works, beginning with *Poltáva,* met
with increasingly cool receptions, and on the eve of his
death he was regarded by the young generation as a venerable, but obsolete classic, who had outlived his time and
was ossified alive. His death was a signal for his recognition
as a national glory. But the men of the forties were far
from giving him his due—they regarded him as an admirable artist who had formed the language and established
the originality of Russian literature but who was going to
be, or actually had been, superseded by more national and
modern writers. For the Slavophils he was not Russian; for
the radical Westernizers, not modern enough. Both preferred Gógol. Only a minority of men, like Turgénev on the
one hand and Grigóriev and Dostoyévsky on the other, laid
the foundation of that uncompromising Púshkin cult which
is now the common inheritance of every educated Russian.
But if Turgénev was to a certain extent the genuine heir to
the less vigorous and vital, more "feminine," sides of
Púshkin, Grigóriev and Dostoyévsky were men of an en-

tirely alien spirit, and their cult of Púshkin was precisely
due to their awareness of the presence in him of supreme
values that were inaccessible to them. Their cult of Púshkin
was the religion of a paradise lost. The main mass of the
intelligentsia in the second half of the nineteenth century
was either indifferent or hostile to Púshkin. For many years
the rule of utilitarianism prevented them from seeing his
greatness. But among the elect the cult grew steadily.
There can be no doubt that Dostoyévsky's Address in
1880, for all its fantastic un-Pushkinity, was powerfully
effective in promoting it. A further date was the lapse of
the copyright in the poet's works in 1887, which inaugurated an era of cheap and numerous editions. The consciousness of Púshkin's supremacy and centralness in Russian literature and civilization grew apace, unostentatiously,
but irrevocably. The twentieth century received it full-
grown. By the time of the Revolution it was so ubiquitous
and unconquerable that even the Bolshevíks, who are in
spirit as alien to Púshkin as Dostoyévsky was, excluded his
name almost alone from their general oblivious condemnation of pre-Revolutionary Russia.

MINOR POETS

Poetry was more universally popular in the twenties than
it has ever been in Russia, either before or since. The principal form it took was the Byronic tale in verse, whose
vogue was started in 1822 by Púshkin's *The Captive* and
Zhukóvsky's translation of *The Prisoner of Chillon,* and
lasted till the end of the decade. Before the sudden outburst
of novel writing in 1829, tales in verse were even best sell-
ers. The greatest successes were Púshkin's two "Southern
poems" (*The Captive* and *The Fountain*). Almost, if not
quite, equal to Púshkin's was the success of Kozlóv.

Iván Ivánovich Kozlóv (1779–1840) was a man of an
older generation, but he began writing poetry only after
1820, when he became blind. He stands out among the
poets of the Golden Age for the comparative inadequacy of
his technique. His poetry appealed to the easily awakened
emotions of the sentimental rather than to the higher poetic
receptivity. His popularity with contemporaries was based
chiefly on *The Monk* (1825)—a verse tale in which the

darkness of a Byronic hero is sentimentalized and redeemed by ultimate repentance. *The Monk* produced as large a family of imitations as either of Púshkin's Byronic poems. Kozlóv's two other narrative poems, *Princess Nathalie Dolgorúky* (1828), a sentimental variation on the theme of that noblewoman's misfortunes, and *The Mad Girl* (1830), met with a somewhat diminished success. Today the only poems of his still universally remembered are his translations of Moore's *Evening Bells* and of Charles Wolfe's *Burial of Sir John Moore at Corunna*. The latter in particular is both an exceptionally faithful translation and a beautiful piece of Russian verse.

Another poet who won general recognition in the Byronic narrative poem was Kondráty Fëdorovich Ryléyev (1795–1826), who was hanged the suppression of the Decembrist Revolt, of which he was one of the principal leaders. His life belongs to political more than to literary history. Suffice it to say that he was one of the sincerest, noblest, and purest of the revolutionaries. His literary career began in 1820. In 1823, together with his fellow conspirator, the novelist and poet Alexander Bestúzhev, he started publishing a yearly "almanac," the *Polar Star,* which was the first publication to be entirely controlled by the "gentlemen." His patriotic and historical *Meditations,* suggested by the similar poems of the Polish poet Niemcéwicz, proceed from a Plutarchian conception of Russian history as a collection of exemplars of civic virtue. With few exceptions the poems are stilted and conventional. Much superior is the narrative poem *Voynaróvsky* (1825), about Mazéppa's nephew, a champion of Ukrainian liberty, pining away in his Siberian exile. Though not a perfect work of art, and somewhat monotonous in its rhythmical movement, it is a noble and manly poem, inspired by the love of freedom. It was highly valued by Púshkin, who even imitated some passages of it in *Poltáva*. But Ryléyev's best poems are those inspired by his revolutionary eagerness, written in the year of the Revolt: the narrative fragment *The Confession of Naliváyko* and, especially, *The Citizen,* written a few days before the Revolt. This last poem is one of the finest pieces of revolutionary eloquence in the language.

The other kind of verse that was most popular in the twenties was the elegy and the short, semi-society lyric of sentiment. Its greatest (and most popular) masters were Zhukóvsky, Púshkin, and Baratýnsky. But other poets of far less genius wrote short elegies and stanzaed poems of elegiac sentiment that are almost as good as the average of the great masters. These minor poets need not detain us, and I will only just mention, as one of the most pleasantly representative, Peter Alexándrovich Pletnëv (1792–1865)—Púshkin's friend and literary agent, and, after the latter's death, editor of his magazine *Sovreménnik*.

BARATÝNSKY

Púshkin's worthiest rival among his contemporaries, and the only other poet of the twenties who may claim the adjective "great," was Evgény Abrámovich Baratýnsky (or Boratýnsky). He was born in 1800 and, at the age of twelve, was sent to the "Corps of Pages," an aristocratic military school. Being shortly thereafter expelled for theft, he was reduced to becoming a private soldier, at first in a regiment of the footguards in Petersburg. It was then he made his acquaintance with Délvig, who encouraged him, rallied his falling spirits, and introduced him to the literary press. In 1820 Baratýnsky was transferred to Finland, where he remained six years. The poetry written during this period established his reputation. In 1825 he at last received a commission, and the next year left the service and settled in Moscow. He married, and his family life was happy, but a profound melancholy remained the background of his mind and of his poetry. During this period he published several books of verse that were highly valued by the best critics of the "poets' party," including Púshkin and Kiréyevsky, but met with the comparatively cool reception of the public, and violent ridicule on the part of the young "plebeian" journalists, like Nadézhdin. In 1843 Baratýnsky left Moscow for a journey to France and Italy. He died in Naples, of a sudden illness, on June 29, 1844.

Baratýnsky's tales in verse would never have been written without the example of Púshkin, but they are not so much imitations of the greater poet as conscious efforts to write differently. The first, *Èda,* is the simple story of the seduction of a Finnish farmer's daughter by a hussar officer billeted in her father's house—a subject old-fashioned al-

ready in the twenties, and reminiscent of the eighteenth
century. It is treated with careful and consistent avoidance
of rhetoric in a realistic and homely style, with a touch
of sentimental pathos but not a trace of romanticism. It is
written, like all that Baratýnsky wrote, in a wonderfully
precise style, next to which Púshkin's seems hazy. The
descriptive passages are among the best—the stern nature
of Finland was particularly dear to Baratýnsky. But what is
especially pleasing is the delicate psychological drawing of
the heroine—as mere psychology no doubt superior to
everything in Russian literature before it.

His second narrative poem, *The Ball* (1828), is more
romantic. It is the story of the suicide of a fatal and romantic society lioness, abandoned by her lover for "an
affected little minx, with dulcet silliness in her eyes, all in
fluffy curls, like a King Charlie, with a sleepy smile on her
lips"—the favorite romantic contrast of the dark and the
fair beauty. The setting is realistic, but the attempts at
humor are unhappy: Baratýnsky conspicuously lacked that
natural ease without which humor is so hard to stand.
The third tale in verse, and the longest, is *The Concubine*
(1829–30; a later version, *The Gypsy Girl*, appeared in
1842). It is in the same style as *The Ball* and on a similar
subject; only the dark lady is a gypsy, and instead of com-
mitting suicide she inadvertently kills her faithless lover,
believing she is giving him a love drink.

In his earlier lyric verse, which belongs to the
Arzamás school, Baratýnsky is the most brilliant and representative poet of the twenties. The principal influences are
the young Púshkin, the French poets of the later eighteenth
century (Parny, Millevoye), and Bátyushkov. What it has
in common with the later period is the exceedingly clear
and dry atmosphere—dryer and clearer than anything in
the whole of Russian poetry—and the cold, metallic brilliance and sonority of the verse. For anything like the
effect in English poetry one can go only to Pope. It consists
of fugitive, light pieces in the Anacreontic and Horatian
manner, some of which are decidedly the masterpieces of
the kind; of love elegies, where a delicate, but imperson-
alized, sentiment is clothed in brilliant wit; of epistles to
friends, where his wit is made still better use of; of medi-
tative elegies in (roughly) the style of Gray. The longest
and perhaps the best of all these early poems is *Feasts,*

where an epicurean praise of the joys of the table is delicately mingled with a wistful melancholy. This background of melancholy gradually found more original forms of expression and was ultimately transformed into the philosophical pessimism of the mature Baratýnsky.

In his mature work (which includes all his short poems written after 1829) Baratýnsky is a poet of thought, perhaps of all the poets of the "stupid nineteenth century" the one who made the best use of thought as a material for poetry. This made him alien to his younger contemporaries and to all the later part of the century, which identified poetry with sentiment. His poetry is, as it were, a short cut from the wit of the eighteenth-century poets to the metaphysical ambitions of the twentieth (in terms of English poetry, from Pope to T. S. Eliot). As in his earlier work he excelled in the lighter forms of (serious) wit, his later work is saturated with wit in the higher sense, which in his case would not be exactly the sense given to the word either by Donne or by Pope, but would be necessarily included in any definition of poetic wit broad enough to include both Pope and Donne. Baratýnsky's poetry is intellectual in content, but the intellectual content is really transformed into poetry. His style is classical. It always remained fundamentally eighteenth-century, much more so than Púshkin's. But in his effort to give his thought the tersest and most concentrated statement, he sometimes becomes obscure by sheer dint of compression. He had not that divine, Mozartian lightness which produces the (false) impression that Púshkin's work cost him no labor— Baratýnsky's obvious labor gives his verse a certain air of brittleness which is at poles' ends from Púshkin's elasticity. But this is for the real lover of poetry precisely the special charm of Baratýnsky, for one assists all the time at the hardly won, but always complete, victory of the master over the resistant material. Among other things, Baratýnsky is one of the few Russian poets who were, in verse, masters of the complicated sentence, expanded by subordinate clauses and parentheses.

Baratýnsky was a classicist in his manner, but his outlook was, if not romantic, at least semi-romantic. A great intellectualist, he was the victim of intellect, of analytic knowledge. He aspired after a fuller union with nature, after a more primitive spontaneity of mental life.

He saw the steady, inexorable movement of mankind away from nature. The aspiration after a more organic and natural past is one of the main motives of Baratýnsky's poetry. He symbolized it in the growing discord between nature's child—the poet—and the human herd, which were growing, with every generation, more absorbed by industrial cares. Hence the growing isolation of the poet in the modern world, where he is deprived of the popular response that met his highest inspirations in "the market places of the Greek towns." The only response in the modern world that greets the modern poet is that of his own rhymes (*Rhyme*, 1841). He turns away from poetry and seeks for a response from nature by planting trees (*On the Plantation of a Forest*, 1842). The future of industrialized and mechanized mankind will be brillant and glorious in the nearest future, but universal happiness and peace will be bought at the cost of the loss of all higher values of poetry (*The Last Poet*). And inevitably, after an age of intellectual refinement, humanity will lose its vital sap and die from sexual impotence. Then earth will be restored to her primæval majesty (*The Last Death*, 1827). This philosophy, allying itself to his profound temperamental melancholy, produced poems of extraordinary majesty, which can compare with nothing in the poetry of pessimism, except Leopardi. Such is the crushing majesty of that long ode to dejection, *Autumn* (1837). Here and in other poems (as in the famous *Death*, 1829) Baratýnsky is splendidly rhetorical in the grandest manner of classicism, though with a pronouncedly personal accent. But always he is intellectual, and the imaginative wit of these great odes never allows them to be trite or commonplace. In other poems he displays an almost Spinozan power of reasoning, as in *On the Death of Goethe* (1832), which is constructed like a syllogism but is so rich in poetry that even the nineteenth century could not miss it, and it went through all the anthologies.

YAZÝKOV

Nikoláy Mikháylovich Yazýkov (1803–46) was the third major poet of the twenties. Like Baratýnsky he was sponsored in literature by Délvig. His first verses appeared in

print in 1822. The same year he went to the (then German)
University of Dorpat, where he made himself famous with
his riotously Anacreontic verse in praise of the student's
merry life. For his summer vacations he went to Trigórskoye, where he met Púshkin. After leaving Dorpat, without a degree, he lived between Moscow and his Simbírsk
estate. He became intimate with the nationalist and Slavophil circles of Moscow, and as he was of a distinctly
unintellectual turn of mind, their nationalism was reflected
in him in the form of a very crude jingoism. His poetry
was highly esteemed by the Slavophils and by the "poets'
party"—but the young idealists dismissed it as contemptibly
lacking in ideas. This embittered Yazýkov, and in his later
years he wrote some rather tasteless attacks on his enemies.
His health, undermined by the Dorpat excesses, began to
fail very early, and from about 1835 he was a permanent
sufferer from gout and dyspepsia, and a restless wanderer
from one health resort to another. The Genoese Riviera,
Nice, Gastein, and other German *Kurorte* are the frequent
background of his later verse.

Gógol, whose favorite poet Yazýkov was, said of him,
playing on his name (*yazýk*—tongue, language): "Not in
vain was he given such a name; he is master of his language
as an Arab is of his fiery steed." Púshkin protested that the
Castalian fount of which Yazýkov drank ran not with
water, but with champagne. The almost physical intoxication produced by the verse of Yazýkov is an experience
familiar to his readers. His poetry is cold and seething like
champagne or like a mineral spring. There is no human
significance in it. Its force lies not in what it means, but
in what it is. The tremendous—physical or nervous—
momentum of his verse is a thing that can hardly be paral-
leled elsewhere. It must not be imagined, however, that he
was a fountain of word torrents like Hugo or Swinburne.
In all this verbal rush there is a restraint and a master's grip
that prove Yazýkov the true contemporary of Púshkin and
Baratýnsky. His early poetry is devoted to the praise of
wine and merrymaking, and was particularly appreciated by
his contemporaries. But the intoxication of his rhythms is
perhaps even more potent where the subject is less obviously Bacchic. It may easily be imagined what he could
make of such a subject as *A Waterfall* (1830), but his more
peaceful nature poems (*Trigórskoye,* and the one on Lake

Peipus) are as vivid and impulsive in their cold crystalline splendor. Of course Yazýkov had no sympathy with nature. It was purely a dazzling vision on his retina transformed into a dazzling rush of words. In his power of seeing nature as an orgy of light and color he approaches Derzhávin, but he had neither the barbaric ruggedness nor the spontaneous and naïve humanity of the older bard. His later poems are on the whole superior to his earlier ones. His Slavophil and reactionary effusions are rather second-rate, but some of the elegies, written in a state of dejection during his sufferings, have genuine human feeling in them without losing any of his verbal splendor. But his best and greatest poems must be accepted as purely verbal magnificences. Perhaps best of all are the lines *To the Rhine* (1840), where he greets the German stream in the name of the Volga and all her tributaries: the enumeration of these tributaries, an uninterrupted catalogue of about fifty lines, is one of the greatest triumphs of Russian verbal art, and an unsurpassed record of long breath—the recitation of the poem is the most difficult, and, if successful, should be the most glorious achievement of the poetry reciter.

METAPHYSICAL POETS

The poets of the twenties formed a real and, for all its diversity, united movement. They are usually referred to as "the Púshkin Pleiad." But there were also poets who stood outside the movement and consequently remained more or less unrecognized by their contemporaries. Such were Fëdor Glínka and Wilhelm Küchelbecker, of whom the former was almost a major, and the latter, if an imperfect, a very individual poet.

Fëdor Nikoláyevich Glínka (1786–1880), a cousin of the composer, was one of the very few Russian poets who devoted themselves almost exclusively to religious poetry. His originality and independence from contemporary example is startlingly great. Like the other poets of his time, Glínka was a careful and conscientious craftsman. But his poetry is mystical, and, though his religion was strictly Orthodox, his mysticism was in substance of a Protestant type. His style, at once realistic and sublime, is distinctly akin to that of the great Anglican mystics Herbert and

Vaughan. His metaphors are sometimes disconcertingly martial. There is a great swing and go in his verse when he speaks of the last judgment or when he paraphrases the prophets. He was never appreciated at his right value and has not yet been entirely rediscovered, but such a rediscovery is one of the maturest possibilities of Russian literary judgment.

Another poet who was out of joint with the times was Púshkin's schoolfellow Wilhelm Küchelbecker (1797–1846). Though of German blood, he was the most ardent of Russian patriots, and though in reality the most advanced of the romanticists, he insisted on calling himself an extreme literary conservative and a supporter of Admiral Shishkóv. He was an enthusiastic idealist, joined in the December conspiracy, and spent the last twenty years of his life in prison and in Siberia. He was a quixotic figure, ridiculous in appearance and behavior, but all who knew him had a warm affection for him, and Púshkin, who was one of his principal teasers, dedicated to him one of the best and sincerest stanzas of the *Lyceum Anniversary* of 1825.[3] In spite of his ridiculous appearance and comic enthusiasm Küchelbecker was a man of no small brains, and his short career as a literary critic (1824–5) gives him, together with Kiréyevsky, the first place among the critics of the Golden Age. It was courageous in 1825 to write long and enthusiastic articles on Shikhmátov, and it was proof of a singular force of judgment to give equal praise to Shakspere and Racine while denying Byron a footing of equality with them. As a poet, Küchelbecker had a fine, pantheistic vision of the world but did not succeed in giving it a definite expression—like so much of the poetry of the later part of the century, his poetry is an inchoate world awaiting a builder. Only occasionally did he hit on an adequate form, and then he would produce a poem of real beauty. Such is the noble elegy on the death of Púshkin (*October 19*), which is curiously near in time, if not in tone, to Wordsworth's *Extempore Effusion*. It is a *Lament of the Makaris,* closing the Golden Age of Russian poetry.

Küchelbecker's miscellany *Mnemosyne* (1824–5) was the first publication to give place to the young Idealists, who

---

[3] Küchelbecker is the hero of Yúry Tynyánov's biographical novel *Kyúkhlya* (1925), one of the best historical novels in the Russian language.

were to introduce into Russia the cult of Goethe and Schelling's metaphysics. These young men, for the most part of good family and exceptionally good education, lived in Moscow and formed a sort of friendly society, calling themselves the Wisdom-lovers (*lyubomúdry*—Slavonic translation of *philosophoi*). They included Prince Vladímir Odóyevsky, Pogódin, Shevyrëv, Khomyakóv, Iván Kiréyevsky, all of them names we shall meet with again in the following chapter, but their leader was a man whose short-lived career necessarily belongs to the twenties. This was Dmítry Vladímirovich Venevítinov, a distant cousin of Púshkin. Born in 1805, he died in his twenty-second year, carrying away with him one of the greatest hopes of Russian literature. His death was accidental—he caught a chill when driving home from a ball in the winter. It is impossible to predict what might not have come of him. He was a man of dazzling abundance of gifts—a strong brain, a born metaphysician, a mature and lofty poet—at twenty-one. His thirst for knowledge was truly Faustian, and his capacity of acquiring it reminiscent of Pico. At the same time he was a virile, attractive young man who loved all the pleasures of life. There was also in him an essential sanity and balance of all the functions of soul and body that remind one of Goethe. His literary remains are not extensive. His few philosophical and critical articles introduce us for the first time to a Russian mentality modified by the grafting on it of German idealism. But in these propylæa of a new learning there is a sane coolness and broadness of grasp for which we shall look in vain in his successors, the Idealists of the thirties. His poetry is almost perfect. Its style is based on Púshkin's and Zhukóvsky's, but with an individual mastery of his own. His diction is very pure, and his rhythms pure and majestic. His most characteristic poems are philosophical.

THE THEATER

The classical tragedy in Alexandrines died out after Ózerov, but classical comedy survived, and even had a revival. However, with the single exception of the great but isolated comedy of Griboyédov, it produced nothing to compare with the better plays of the eighteenth century. The playwrights worked for the theater and for their own day—not for literature and time. Some of their plays are amusing, especially those where the dramatists (all of them conservatives and classicists) satirized the Karamzinians and the romanticists (e.g. Shakhovskóy's *Lípetsk Spa* and Griboyédov's *Student*), but all are insignificant, frankly and unambitiously so. The futility and absence of serious literary interests in all this world of comedy are admirably pictured in Aksákov's *Literary and Theatrical Reminiscences*. The chief figures of this theater were the versatile and prolific Prince Alexander Shakhovskóy (1777–1846); Michael Nikoláyevich Zagóskin (1789–1852), who afterwards became more famous as a "Waverley" novelist; Nikoláy Ivánovich Khmelnítsky (1789–1846); and Alexander Ivánovich Písarev (1803–1828), the greatest master of stagecraft among them, and a particular friend of Aksákov's. Khmelnítsky and Písarev excelled chiefly in the vaudeville, a dramatic form the craze for which in Russia began about 1820 and reached its maximum about 1840. Griboyédov in his early comedies was nothing but a furnisher of stageable plays: they have curiously little in common with the one great comedy that makes him a classic almost comparable with Púshkin.

GRIBOYÉDOV

Alexander Sergéyevich Griboyédov (1795–1829) was born in Moscow. By the age of seventeen he had taken degrees at the University of Moscow in science and in law, and was preparing for a doctorate when his studies were interrupted by Napoleon's invasion. He enlisted in a cavalry regiment but saw no fighting. In 1816 he went to Petersburg, where he became a clerk in the Foreign Office. Griboyédov plunged eagerly into the animated and excited postwar life of the capital. The theater became (as it was to so many of his contemporaries) the center of his interests. He wrote and staged indifferent comedies and courted actresses. He mixed in the revolutionary circles and was received a Freemason. In the literary quarrels he sided with the Shishkovists. He easily acquired the reputation of being one of the cleverest men and greatest wits in Russia. All the time he did serious work at the Foreign Office; so that when a particularly reliable official was wanted to go as secretary to a mission in Persia, the post was offered to Griboyédov.

Griboyédov passed the years 1818–25 partly in Tiflís, partly in Persia. He made friends with the famous "Proconsul" of the Caucasus, General Ermólov, the most popular officeholder of the day and one of the most remarkable, who liked in Griboyédov a kindred spirit and made him his secretary. It was in 1822–3 that Griboyédov wrote his great comedy *Woe from Wit*. Only the final touches were added during his two years' leave of absence in Moscow and Petersburg (1823–5). *Woe from Wit* was not passed by the censorship for the stage, and only portions of it were allowed to appear in an almanac for 1825. But it was read out by the author to "all Moscow" and to "all Petersburg" and circulated in innumerable copies, so it was as good as published in 1825.

In the end of that year Griboyédov had to return to Ermólov's headquarters in the Caucasus. But he did not remain there long. Immediately after the Revolt of December 14th a courier was sent to arrest him. It is reported that Ermólov (who was popular with the Decembrists) warned Griboyédov of the impending arrest and gave him time to destroy compromising papers. Griboyédov was brought to Petersburg and placed under custody. He was highly incensed by the arrest and wrote to Nicholas a vehement letter couched in such language that the Emperor's A.D.C. did not dare present it to him. At the inquiry Griboyédov behaved with consistent firmness. In spite of his close connections with many of the rebels he succeeded in exculpating himself. He was set free, and, as a compensation for the trouble he had undergone, he was given promotion and a year's salary. The affair, however, remains somewhat mysterious, for it is practically certain that Griboyédov was not innocent in the matter.

He now returned to the Caucasus, where in the meantime hostilities had begun with Persia. Ermólov, disliked and distrusted by Nicholas, had had to resign, but the new Viceroy, the Emperor's particular favorite and intimate friend, Paskévich, was Griboyédov's cousin by marriage, and the relations of the two were most cordial. He joined Paskévich's headquarters at the front and accompanied him throughout the war. He negotiated the Peace of Turkmenchai (February 10, 1828) and took the treaty to Peters-burg for ratification. His arrival at the capital was met with salvos from the fortress; he was given high rewards and appointed Russian Minister to Persia. On his way back, in Tiflís, he fell in love with a sixteen-year-old Georgian girl, Princess Nina Chavchavádze, and married her. At the height of happiness he set off with his young bride to Tab-riz, whence he was to supervise the fulfillment of the treaty by the Persians.

This was no easy and no agreeable task. The treaty provided for the payment of a large contribution and for the repatriation of all Christian prisoners, principally Armenian women in Persian harems. The former clause was impracticable, as Persia was insolvent; the latter was felt by the Persians as a profound insult to the sanctity of the harem, a principal foundation of their religious polity. In December 1828 Griboyédov went to Teheran to negoti-ate more directly with the Shah, leaving his wife in Tabriz. He at once realized (and wrote in his dispatches) that the Russian demands were excessive, but he enforced them with conscientious energy and without respect for oriental susceptibilities. Before long a popular movement was fomented against him, and on January 30 a crowd attacked the legation and massacred all the inmates except one. Griboyédov fell fighting. His stripped and mangled body, it is reported, could be recognized only by his crooked finger, which had been mutilated in a duel some years be-fore. His widow, on hearing of his death, gave premature birth to a child, who died a few hours later. She lived an-other thirty years after her husband's death, rejecting all suitors and winning universal admiration by her fidelity to his memory.

Griboyédov is a *homo unius libri*. This book is the great comedy *Woe from Wit* (*Góre ot umá*). His other comedies, one of which was written after *Góre ot umá*, are negligible and curiously unlike it. The fragments left us of *Georgian Night*, a social tragedy of Georgian history he was working at in his last years, are also very disappointing. Of his few lyrics, some are quite good, but they are only intimations of unrealized possibilities. More important are his letters, which are among the best in the language. It is they that reveal to us the man, but the great imaginative writer is revealed only in *Góre ot umá*.

Góre ot umá belongs to the classical school of comedy —its principal antecedents are in Molière. Like Fonvízin before him and like the founders of the Russian realistic tradition after him, Griboyédov lays far greater stress on the characters and his dialogue than on his plot. The comedy is loosely constructed, but in the dialogue and in the character drawing Griboyédov is supreme and unique. The dialogue is in rhymed verse, in iambic lines of variable length—a meter that was introduced into Russia by the fabulists as the equivalent of La Fontaine's *vers libre* and that had reached a high degree of perfection in the hands of Krylóv. Griboyédov's dialogue is a continuous tour de force. It always attempts and achieves the impossible: the squeezing of everyday conversation into a rebellious metrical form. Griboyédov seemed to multiply difficulties on purpose. He was, for instance, alone in his age to use unexpected, sonorous, punning rhymes. There is just enough toughness and angularity in his verse to constantly remind the reader of the pains undergone and the difficulties triumphantly overcome by the poet. Despite the fetters of the metrical form, Griboyédov's dialogue has the natural rhythm of conversation and is more easily colloquial than any prose. It is full of wit, variety, and character, and is a veritable store book of the best spoken Russian of a period when the speech of the upper classes had not yet been disfigured and emasculated by schoolmastery and grammar. Almost every other line of the comedy has become part of the language, and proverbs from Griboyédov are as numerous as proverbs from Krylóv. For epigram, repartee, terse and concise wit, Griboyédov has no rivals in Russian and is superior even to Krylóv.

In the art of character-drawing Griboyédov is also unique. He had a quality that he inherited from the classicists and that was not possessed by any other Russian realist. He shares it with the great masters of the seventeenth and eighteenth centuries—with Molière and Fielding—and of all nineteenth-century writers, I think, with Thackeray alone. It is a certain universality that makes Tartuffe and Squire Western and Miss Crawley something more than mere individualities. They are persons, but they are also *types*—archetypes or quintessences of humanity, endowed with all we have of life and individuality, but endowed also with a super-individual existence, like that of

the Platonic ideas, or of the *universalia* of the schoolmen.
This is a rare art—perhaps the rarest of all; and of all
Russian writers Griboyédov possessed it in the highest
degree. This is not to say that his characters are not alive;
they are, and very lively too, but they have a life more
durable and universal than our own. They are stamped in
the really common clay of humanity. Fámusov, the father,
the head of an important department, the born conservative of all time, the cynical and placid philosopher of good
digestion, the pillar of stable society; Molchálin, the secretary, the sneak who plays whist with old ladies, pets their
dogs, and acts the lover to his patron's daughter; Repetílov,
the orator of the coffee room and of the club, burning for
freedom and stinking of liquor, the witless admirer of wit,
and the bosom friend of all his acquaintances—all, down
to the most episodic characters, have the same perfection
of finish and clearness of outline. The only exceptions are
the two protagonists, Sophia and Chátsky. Unlike the rest
they are not meant satirically, and as characters they may
be underdone. And yet the play owes much of its unique
charm to them. Sophia is not a type, but she is a person.
She is a rare phenomenon in classical comedy: a heroine
that is neither idealized nor caricatured. There is a strange,
drily romantic flavor in her, with her fixity of purpose, her
ready wit, and her deep, but reticent, passionateness. She
is the principal *active* force in the play, and the plot is advanced mainly by her actions.

Chátsky has often been criticized as irrelevantly eloquent. There is no sense of fitness in his harangues to
Fámusov and his set, and there may be mistakes of proportion in Griboyédov's conception of him. But in spite of this,
Chátsky is the principal thing in the play. He is its imaginative and emotional focus, its yeast and its zest. Not only is
all the best wit put into his mouth, but he gives the tone to
the whole performance. His generous, if vague, revolt
against the vegetably selfish world of Fámusovs and Mol-
chálins is its real spirit. His exhilarating, youthful idealism,
his go, his *élan*, infect and brace you. He is of the family
of Romeo; and it is significant that, in spite of all his apparent lack of clear-cut personality, his part is the traditional touchstone for a Russian actor. Great Chátskys are
as rare and as highly valued in Russia as are great Hamlets.

THE POETS' PROSE

The high-water mark of French linguistic influence in Russia was reached in the reign of Alexander I. All the members of the educated gentry who were brought up during that reign knew French as well as, or better than, Russian. The same conditions obtained for the middle and provincial gentry: Púshkin is careful to record that Tatiána wrote her famous letter to Onégin in French, for, as he says, "to this day our proud language has not been broken to postal prose." To break it was one of the principal tasks of the poets and wits of the Arzamás, and of the other men of the Poets' and Gentlemen's party. Letter-writing between 1815 and 1830 was, for the poets, an important branch of their literary activity, and the Golden Age of poetry is also the Golden Age of letter-writing.

Púshkin is as much the greatest Russian letter-writer as he is the greatest poet. His "postal prose" is an ever fresh source of delight to all who love good Russian. It is the language of everyday conversation, only refined in the laboratory of a great artistic mind. For flexibility, grace, and freshness Púshkin's epistolary Russian has no equals. Moreover, his letters are a mine of keen wit, sound judgment, and good criticism. But Púshkin *never* speaks in them of his feelings, neither to his nearest friends nor to his wife. The only emotions he ever gives vent to are impatience and indignation. This gives his letters a particularly healthy and bracing atmosphere.

Griboyédov stands next to Púshkin as a letter-writer. His Russian is terse and more nervous than Púshkin's. It is full of the dry, pungent wit of *Góre ot umá*, and of a canalized and disciplined passionateness. Griboyédov always knows his mind and says what he thinks in a direct and straight manner. If Púshkin's letters have no equal for flexibility and freshness, Griboyédov is first among Russian writers for pointed and vigorous statement.

Another remarkable body of epistolary Russian is contained in the correspondence of Vyázemsky with Alexander Ivánovich Turgénev (1785–1846)—a friend of all the Arzamasians and one of the most intelligent men of the period. The correspondence forms a sort of running commentary on the Russian literature and life of the time.

In their published prose the poets of the Golden Age continued the work of Karamzín, who, though his reform had been accepted, had not succeeded in creating a universally applicable style of literary prose. The formation of such a style was one of the most difficult tasks before the poets, and here again French was in the way. Púshkin confessed that it was easier for him to express himself in French than in Russian where he had anything to say in prose that was not merely descriptive of fact. The poets applied themselves to their task with painstaking industry. But they failed to establish a canon of Russian prose for the succeeding ages, and all their work was undone by the journalists of the thirties, who are the real founders of modern Russian prose.

The elder generation of poets followed closely Karamzín's example. Zhukóvsky, both in his early stories and in his later moral essays, wrote fluent, agreeable, but somewhat emasculated and placid prose. Bátyushkov in his essays tried to Italianize Russian prose as he had Russian verse. Davýdov and Vyázemsky introduced into literature the manner of their epistolary prose. Davýdov's works include an *Essay towards a Theory of Guerrilla Welfare* (1821), an autobiography prefixed to the 1832 edition of his poems, and a series of recollections of military life. In his autobiography he indulges in a veritable orgy of puns and jokes not always in the best taste. His military writings are fresh, vigorous, and racy, and his memoirs contain some of the best military reading in the language. Vyázemsky is also sometimes exaggeratedly witty, but vigor and raciness are as ubiquitous in his prose as in Davýdov's. His best is contained in the admirable anecdotes of his *Old Notebook*, an inexhaustible mine of sparkling and often wonderful information on the great and small men of the early nineteenth century.

The anecdote was a favorite form in the times of Púshkin, and the great poet himself was a devotee to the art. The anecdotes contained in his (naturally posthumous) *Table Talk* (the title is in English) are masterpieces of the kind, and in a Russian more closely akin to that of his letters than that of his literary prose.

Of the other poets, Baratýnsky wrote very little prose,

but this little contains a quite disproportionate amount of the best things ever said in Russian on the subject of poetry. Two of his utterances should be especially remembered: his definition of lyrical poetry as "the fullest awareness of a given moment," and his remark that good poetry is rare because two qualities, as a rule mutually exclusive, are necessary to the making of a poet—"the fire of creative imagination and the coldness of controlling reason."

THE RISE OF THE NOVEL

The Russian novel continued vegetating rather halfheartedly until in 1829 there was a sudden outburst of novel writing. In that year the notorious Tadéusz Bułháryn published his moralizing picaresque novel *Iván Výzhigin*, which had a record sale; and the same year Michael Nikoláyevich Zagóskin (1789–1852), who had already won a reputation as a comedy-writer, published the first Russian novel in the style of Scott, *Yúry Miloslávsky, or the Russians in 1612*. It is a story of the Time of Troubles, when the Poles occupied Moscow, and of the victory of the national forces. In spite of its conventionality, crude nationalism, cardboard psychology, and lack of real historical color, it is a very good romance of its kind. Its immediate success was enormous, and it set the fashion for "Waverley" novels, a great number of which were turned out in Russia within the next ten or fifteen years. The best of the Russian Scottists is Iván Ivánovich Lazhéchnikov (1792–1869). His knowledge of the past is greater than Zagóskin's. His characters are more complex and more alive, and his moral sense, as clear-cut as Zagóskin's, is less conventional and more generous.

Another kind of romanticism is discernible in the works of Alexéy Peróvsky (1787–1836), who wrote under the pseudonym of Antón Pogorélsky, and was the only man of the Poets' and Gentlemen's party who made a reputation solely by his fiction. His principal work, *The Convent Girl* (1828), is a charmingly humorous picture of the manners of the provincial Ukrainian gentry. The novel is obviously influenced by Fielding, but there is also an admixture of a mild and domestic romanticism. In his shorter stories Pogorélsky is more romantic and fantastic.

The best of them, *The Black Hen*, is a really delightful story. It is plainly as dependent on Hoffmann's *Nutcracker* as *The Convent Girl* is on *Tom Jones*. Tolstóy mentions it as the book that produced the strongest impression on him in his childhood.

The most brilliant of these early novelists was Alexander Alexándrovich Bestúzhev (1797–1837), co-editor with Ryléyev of the early miscellany the *Polar Star*. An officer in the dragoon guards, he took part in the Decembrist Revolt and was exiled to the farthest parts of Siberia. In 1829 he was transferred to the Caucasus as a private soldier. There he was able to resume his literary activity, and his best and best-known novels were published in the early thirties over the signature of A. Marlínsky. As a soldier he soon became noted for exceptional bravery. He was recommended for promotion and for the St. George's Cross, but the same year he was charged with the murder of his mistress, and, though the inquest failed to prove his guilt, the promotion and the cross were withheld. This incident left a profound mark on his mind. He ceased writing and lost all interest in life. In 1837 at the storming of Adler (on the Black Sea coast) he was, literally, hewn to pieces by the Circassians.

Bestúzhev was a poet of no mean talent. But it was his novels and stories that fascinated the public of the thirties. His manner, though showy and superficial, is certainly brilliant. His sparkling verbal imagination makes him show very brightly on the somewhat drab background of Zagóskin or Pogorélsky. His dialogue is especially brilliant, a constant battledore and shuttlecock of pithy epigram and witty repartee. His superficially passionate heroes, with their Byronic pose, are rather cheap. But the stories are thrilling, and the style keeps the reader in constant excitement. His best novel is *Ammalat Bek* (1832), a story of the Caucasian war. It contains the splendid *Songs of Death* of the mountaineers, a thing unequaled of its kind in the language.

THE PROSE OF PÚSHKIN

Púshkin was the first in Russia to write *permanent* fiction, the first really original Russian novelist. But his place in the history of the Russian novel is not comparable to his place in the history of Russian literature as a whole, and his prose, however perfect sóme of his stories and however unique his total achievement, is not of the same order of greatness as his poetry. A principal difference between his poetry and his prose is that he was primarily a poet, and that in verse he spoke his natural language, of which he himself was the supreme standard and judge, while prose was to him a foreign tongue, acquired by more or less laborious learning. He succeeded in mastering the idiom and the intonation of this foreign tongue, and his Parnassian accent can be discerned only by a trained ear. But there is always in his prose a sense of constraint, a lack of freedom, a harking back to some outer rule, which is never the case with his poetry.

It was only after 1830 that Púshkin turned most of his attention to prose. But from the very beginning he had fixed his mind on what it was to be like. In 1822 he wrote in a notebook: "Voltaire may be regarded as an excellent example of sensible style. . . . Precision, tidiness, these are the prime merits of prose. It demands matter and matter, brilliant expressions are of no use to it; poetry is another business." Púshkin's literary prose is rational, analytical, intentionally bald, pruned of all irrelevant ornament, and almost affected in its simplicity. One is most tempted to compare it to Cæsar's prose, for, however comparable to Voltaire's in elegance and purity, it lacks the free, impulsive vivacity and unfettered swiftness of the great Frenchman's. On the whole the eighteenth-century atmosphere common to the whole of Púshkin's work is nowhere more apparent than in his stories, even in those where, like others of his generation, he was influenced by the example of Scott and Hoffmann.

His first attempt at fiction was the unfinished historical novel *The Nigger of Peter the Great* (1828). It was to be the story of his grandsire Gannibal. It remained unfinished, and only two fragments from it were published during his lifetime.

In the autumn of 1830, during his seclusion at Bóldino, Púshkin wrote the five *Tales of Bélkin,* which were published the following year without his name. If not the best, they are in many ways his most characteristic stories. Nowhere did he carry further the principles of detachment, restraint, and self-limitation. The tales are told by a simple, provincial squire: a device to justify the storyteller's impersonality. There is no human, no psychological or descriptive, interest in the stories. They are pure, unadulterated narrative, anecdotes raised to the rank of serious art by the seriousness of the artistic process. As pure narrative they are unsurpassed in Russian literature except by Púshkin's own *Queen of Spades.* They were met by contemporaries' with amazed disappointment, and only very gradually have they become acknowledged as masterpieces. The figure of the supposed author, Bélkin himself, barely outlined in the preface of the *Tales,* was more fully developed in the posthumous *History of the Manor of Goryúkhino,* one of Púshkin's most remarkable prose works. It is also one of the most complex—it is at once a parody of Polevóy's sciolistic and pretentious *History of the Russian People,* a Swiftian satire of the whole social order based on serfdom, and the portrait of one of the most charming characters in the whole of Russian fiction, the simple-minded, naïvely and shyly ambitious Iván Petróvich Bélkin.

After 1831 Púshkin wrote more prose than verse. Only three stories (including *The Captain's Daughter* and *The Queen of Spades*) were completed and printed. But numerous fragments in various states of completion were preserved and published posthumously. They include several alternative beginnings for the story that was to introduce the poem of *Cleopatra* (one of these contains the highly interesting character sketch of Chársky, the poet who, from motives of social vanity and reserve, does not want to be considered a poet) and *Dubróvsky,* an almost completed robber novel with a social background. Had it been finished, it would have been the best Russian novel of action. It is refreshingly (and very consciously) melodramatic, with a virtuous gentleman Robin Hood and an ideal heroine. Like *Goryúkhino* it is full of satire. The figures of the two great noblemen, Troyekúrov and Veréysky—one a rude, old-world bully, the other a Frenchified and refined egoist—are among the glories of the portrait gallery of Russian fiction.

The only full-sized novel Púshkin completed and published during his lifetime is *The Captain's Daughter* (1836), a story of the Pugachëv Rebellion (the great rising of the lower classes in East Russia in 1773). It belongs to the school of Scott in its treatment of the past, but it is curiously unlike any Waverley novel. It is about a fifth of the size of an average Scott novel. The manner is terse, precise, economical, though somewhat more spacious and leisurely than in any other of Púshkin's stories. There is in it, as in *Dubróvsky*, a zest of orthodox melodrama—in the figure of the rebel leader himself and in the frankly conventional character of the villain (the only villain in Púshkin), Shvábrin. It is full of delightful humor, as in the scene of the hero's duel with Shvábrin and the refusal of the old garrison officer risen from the ranks to understand the use of a duel. But the best thing in the novel is the characters: Captain Mirónov and his wife, charming figures of idyllic comedy in time of peace, who, when the rebels come, suddenly reveal an unpretending, modest, as it were casual, courage and die as heroes. Then there is Savélyich, the hero's old manservant, sincerely servile and unbendingly despotic. Besides *Evgény Onégin, The Captain's Daughter* was the only work of Púshkin's that had a powerful influence on the next age—it contains all the essence of what Russian realism was to become—though it is still a story told in the orthodox manner, as a story should be. Its understated, economical, discreetly humorous realism is a striking contrast to another great historical novel that appeared within two years of it—the rhetorical, swollen, magnificent *Tarás Búlba* of Gógol.

The Captain's Daughter is Púshkin's most influential, but it is not his greatest or most characteristic, story—this distinction belongs to *The Queen of Spades* (1834). The story cannot be summarized. Like *The Tales of Bélkin* it is pure art and possesses no human interest except as a whole. For imaginative power it stands above everything else in Púshkin's prose. It is as tense as a compressed spring. There is a fierce romanticism in it—akin to that which inspired *The Hymn in Honor of the Plague* and *God Forbid That I Should Go Mad*. But the fantastically romantic subject has been canalized into a perfect, classical form, so economic and terse in its noble baldness that even Prosper Mérimée, that most fastidiously economical of French writers, had not the courage to translate it as it was, and introduced various embellishments and amplifications into his French version.

Púshkin was a first-class critic, and his serious critiques

and reviews are admirable for the considered soundness of his judgments and for the precise lucidity of his statement. His polemical journalism (in the *Literary Gazette*) is also, in its kind, unsurpassed. His neat, up-to-the-point, closely aimed irony possessed a sting his enemies never forgot. His attacks against Bułháryn, the "reptile" journalist in the pay of the secret police, are admirably and calmly cruel. They contributed to the speedy suppression of the *Literary Gazette* by exasperating its sneakingly influential rival.

After 1832 Púshkin's principal occupation was, at least officially, history. His plan of writing a history of Peter the Great never matured, but in 1834 he published a *History of the Pugachëv Rebellion*. It is a masterpiece of narrative literature, comparable to Caesar's *Gallic War*. Its defect is one of information: it was impossible for Púshkin to know much that was essential to his subject. He was too much of an eighteenth-century classicist to treat history in terms of "mass movement" and "class struggles," but he admirably exposed the social mainsprings of the great Rebellion. In 1836 he published *A Voyage to Arzrum*, an account of his journey to the Caucasus front in 1829, in which he reached the limits of noble and bare terseness.

THE GROWTH OF JOURNALISM

Besides its other claims to literary distinction, the decade 1825–34 is important as the period beginning the uninterrupted history of Russian journalism. Despite severe pressure from the censorship, the journalists of this decade and the two following made a plucky stand for independence, if not in political, at least in general cultural questions. And it was owing to their efforts that a public opinion began to take shape.

The Poets' and Gentlemen's party were not very successful in their journalistic ventures. Délvig's *Literary Gazette* (1830–1) and Iván Kiréyevsky's *European* (1832) were suppressed by the censorship. When in 1836 Púshkin started the *Contemporary*, it was out of date and could not command a paying audience. The journalists proper were despised and disliked by the "Gentlemen," who scarcely distinguished between the different varieties of those plebeians. But the difference was very substantial between the servile Petersburg press and the sometimes unkempt, but independent and enthusiastic, Moscow magazines. In Petersburg a monopoly of political information belonged to the daily *Northern Bee,* founded in 1825 by Tadéusz Bułháryn (in Russian spelling, Bulgárin, 1789–1859). Bułháryn, a Polish deserter from Napoleon's army, had ingratiated himself to the secret police by giving evidence against Decembrist friends of his, and during the reign of Nicholas I he acquired the reputation of a vile sycophant whom all honest men abhorred. He was a clever, but essentially vulgar, journalist. His paper had a far larger sale than any other. His influence was used to combat all that was young, talented, and independent. Púshkin, Gógol, Belínsky, Lérmontov, and the natural school of the forties were in turn the enemies against whom he used all means, public and clandestine.

Very different was the Muscovite journalist Nicholas Polevóy (1796–1846). He was a self-made man, the son of a tradesman. He could never "become a gentleman," and the Gentlemen always despised him. But his enthusiasm (often misguided) did much to spread the new literature and to intensify Russian literary life. His magazine, the *Moscow Telegraph* (1825–34), was an enthusiastic, if undiscriminating, pioneer of romanticism. In 1834 the *Telegraph* was suppressed for printing an unfavorable review of a patriotic play by Kúkolnik. Polevóy was ruined. In his misfortunes he did not show himself a hero—he entered on a compromise with the Bułháryn party, and thus ceased to count in literature. But his memory after his death was deservedly reverenced by the new intelligentsia as that of a pioneer and, in a sense, a martyr.

Another pioneer of the intelligentsia was Nicholas Nadézhdin (1804–56). Also a plebeian by birth, he began his career by publishing a series of scurrilous, though at times witty, articles against the Poets, where he confounded Púshkin and Baratýnsky with their second-rate imitators in a sweeping condemnation. He attacked Russian romanticism from the point of view of Schelling's German romantic idealism, denying all ideological significance to the Russian pseudo-romanticism (as he rightly called it). In a thesis on romantic poetry submitted to the University of Moscow in 1830 he advocated a synthesis of classicism and romanticism. In 1831 he started a monthly magazine, the *Telescope,* where he continued his policy of belittling in the light of philosophical standards the achievement of Russian literature. In 1836 the magazine was suppressed for publishing Chaadáyev's *Philosophical Letter.* Nadézhdin himself was exiled to the north and not till some time afterwards allowed to return to Moscow. After that he renounced literature and devoted himself exclusively to his archæological and geographical studies.

The successor of Polevóy and Nadézhdin was Belínsky, the dictator of literary opinion from 1834 to 1848, and the father of the Russian intelligentsia.

5

The Age of Gógol

THE DECLINE OF POETRY

POETRY early began to decline from the high standards set up by the Golden Age. The harmony, distinction, restraint, and unerring mastery of the great poets from Zhukóvsky to Venevítinov was soon lost. The art of verse degenerated either into an empty and undistinguished tidiness, or into an equally hollow wit unsupported by inspiration, or into a formless rush of untransformed emotion. A veneer of polished versification, covering a void of imagination and substituted for the delicate mastery of the older generation, is the characteristic of all the younger poets who claimed to belong to the older "Poets' party." The Petersburg journalists encouraged poetry of a more meretricious type. Its laureate was Vladímir Grigórievich Benedíktov (1807–73), a clerk in the Ministry of Finance and for ten years the idol of all the romantically inclined officials of every rank throughout Russia. His method consisted in squeezing out of a striking metaphor or simile all it could give. A typical poem of his, *The Belle of Battles*, makes the most of the parallel between the unsheathed saber and the naked woman. Later on, Benedíktov gave up his conceits and developed into a polished versifier of the ordinary type.

Another group of poets had in common with Bene-díktov a love for external brilliancy in rhymes, images, and vocabulary, but differed from him by their higher serious-ness. The most notable of them were Khomyakóv (whose poetry I shall discuss later) and Caroline Pávlova, née Jaenisch (1807–93), the most interesting of the Russian "blues." When a young girl, she had been loved by the great Polish poet Mickiéwicz, for whom she retained a lifelong romantic attachment. Afterward she was unhappily mar-ried to the novelist Nicholas Pávlov. Her literary *salon* was one of the most frequented in Moscow; but her talent was never appreciated by her friends, and she contrived to make herself a bore and a common laughing-stock. Her poetry is deeply attractive, both for the somewhat harsh, but unquestionable, excellence of her technique and for its profound and reticent pathos. The main subject of her poetry is the courage of suppressed suffering. "Grin and bear it" is the pith of her best poems.

The most progressive and modern poets of the thirties rejected the formal discipline of the school of Zhukóvsky and Púshkin and aimed at developing the emotional and expressionist character of poetry. Lérmontov in his early work must be reckoned as one of them. Of the minor poets who may be regarded as first proofs of Lérmontov, the most notable were Prince Alexander Odóyevsky (1802–39) and Alexander Ivánovich Polezháyev (1805–38). Alexander Odóyevsky, a first cousin of Griboyédov and of the novelist Vladímir Odóyevsky, took part in the De-cembrist Revolt, was deported to Siberia and afterward sent as a private soldier to the Caucasus. He is chiefly remembered today for the elegy written on his death by Lérmontov, the most beautiful dirge in the Russian lan-guage. His own poems were first published long after his death. Most of them are concerned with the sorrows of the exile, but one of them, the well-known answer to Púshkin's famous *Epistle into Siberia* (1827), in which the great poet exhorted the exiled rebels not to lose their spirits, is an animated assertion of the undaunted spirit of revolt.

Polezháyev was the natural son of a squire of the name of Strúysky—and thus a *déclassé*. As a student of Moscow University he led a riotous life of drunkenness and debauchery, and described it in the burlesque poem

Sáshka (1825–6). The poem contained some passages expressive of liberal sentiment, and these, much rather than
its obscenity, attracted the attention of the police. The
matter reached Nicholas I, who was then in Moscow fresh
from the trial and execution of the Decembrists. Polezháyev
was summoned into the Emperor's presence. Nicholas, with
his usual consummate stagecraft, played the part of the
kind chastising father—Polezháyev was to serve as a
private soldier, but he was allowed to write direct to the
Emperor if he had any grievances. This Polezháyev did
very soon, for he had plenty of grievances, but the letters
had no effect. He attempted to desert, was arrested for
more than a year, narrowly escaped corporal punishment,
and was told off to the Caucasus. Gradually Polezháyev
sank into degradation—drank heavily and in his relations
with the kind of people who tried to lighten up his hopeless lot behaved with shameless cynicism. At the front,
however, he gave proof of courage and was at last recommended for a commission, but the promotion arrived only
after his death. Polezháyev was strongly influenced by
Hugo and Byron, and romantic grandiloquence and gaudi-
ness had a too great attraction for him. Looseness, turgid-
ness, and garrulity are his besetting sins. Only a dozen or
so of his shorter poems preserve his name in the treasury
of Russian verse. There are in them a passionate force, a
rhythmic rush, and a romantic fire that are his alone. He
was particularly a master of rapid, staccato meters. All his
best poems are concerned either with the lurid romance
of oriental warfare or with the grim despair of his ruined
life. His most famous poems are the remarkably effective
Song of the Sailor Doomed to Wreck (or rather, "in the
process of being wrecked"), in vigorous, three-syllabled
lines, and *The Song of the Captive Iroquois*—bound to the
stake and calmly awaiting the protracted death his captors
are preparing for him.

KOLTSÓV

One of the most interesting developments of the thirties
was the culmination of the school of literary folk song
in the work of Koltsóv. The tradition of the artificial folk
song goes back to the eighteenth century. In the twenties

it was brought to further perfection by the versatile Délvig, whose exquisitely artificial "Russian songs" (as the genre was called) were the most popular part of his work. Less artificial and more spontaneous are the beautiful songs of Nicholas Grigórievich Tsygánov (1797–1831), a wandering actor and the son of a serf. He had no contact with literary circles, and, though the form of his "Russian songs" is dependent on the literary, not on the oral tradition, their spirit is genuinely popular and "folklore." They are personative, most of them placed in the mouth of a woman. Their symbolism, their imagery, their unsentimental sentiment, are all thoroughly popular and Russian. They were published posthumously in 1834, only a year before the publication of the first book of Koltsóv.

Alexéy Vasílievich Koltsóv was born in 1809 in Vorónezh (South Central Russia). His father was a wholesale cattle dealer, and Koltsóv spent much of his boyhood and youth in the Don steppes, accompanying his father's herds to distant markets. His education was desultory. His early verses attracted the attention of Stankévich, the famous head of the idealist circle, who introduced Koltsóv to his Moscow friends. This resulted in a lasting friendship between Koltsóv and Belínsky. In 1835 a first book of songs by Koltsóv was published, which was universally greeted with great warmth. After that, Koltsóv continued living in Vorónezh, managing his father's business and coming to Moscow and Petersburg only in connection with his father's lawsuits. Koltsóv was a man of tact and dignity, and his educated and noble friends highly admired his character. These qualities are always present in his attractive letters, which are also remarkable for the solid common sense displayed in them. He shared the generous aspirations of his idealist friends, though he never quite lost the practical sense and efficiency of the Russian tradesman. But he felt lonely and miserable in Vorónezh. His relations with his father, a selfish, despotic, and unimaginative bourgeois, went from bad to worse, and gradually his family life became a hell to him. He was saved from it by sudden death in 1842. He had almost ceased to write after 1840.

Koltsóv's poetry falls into three distinct sections: his attempts, chiefly belonging to the period before 1835, to write in the accepted literary style of the Púshkin and pre-

Púshkin school; his "Russian Songs"; and the philosophical meditations (*dúmy*) of his last years. Of these three classes, only the second secures for Koltsóv a permanent place as a classic. Koltsóv has been called a Russian Burns. If the title implies anything like equality of genius with the great Scotsman, it is simply nonsense. In *size* of talent Koltsóv comes nearer Hogg than Burns. But in *kind* there is no doubt a certain kinship, not altogether superficial. Like Burns, Koltsóv depended on a literary tradition of quasi folk song. Like Burns, he was in direct touch with the realities of peasant life, though, unlike Burns, he was not himself a peasant. Like Burns, he had a certain freshness and freedom of outlook his more educated and blue-blooded contemporaries were incapable of. Like Burns, lastly, he was a realist, and, like Burns, he had genuine passion. But he is more feminine and sentimental than Burns. Characteristically some of Koltsóv's best songs are placed in the mouth of women. His purely lyrical songs are perhaps the best and have become the most popular among the people; there is in them a typically Russian longing for freedom, adventure, and elbow room. Though they are usually in rhyme and thus more obviously literary in form, they have much more genuine popular feeling in them than the nature and peasant-life songs. As in real folk songs, nature appears as a sympathetic source of symbols for the singer's feelings. In the more elaborate nature songs it becomes rather involvedly personified and philosophized. But there is no more beautiful evocation of the wide steppe than *The Mower*, who goes out to sell his strength to the rich Cossacks of the Lower Don. *Prostór* and *privólye*, two untranslatable Russian words meaning, roughly, space and elbow room, but with an inexpressible poetical over-tone, are the keynotes of some of Koltsóv's best songs. His love songs, with all their range of slightly sentimentalized and romancified, but genuine and strong, passion, are equally exquisite. The beautiful song of the *mal mariée*, beginning "Ah, why did they marry me against my will to an old, unloved husband?" is one of the purest gems of Russian emotional lyric poetry. The least genuinely popular part of Koltsóv's songs is those in which he idealizes peasant life and agricultural labor—a theme entirely alien to actual folk song. But this does not make them less good.

Some of them, such as *A Peasants' Carouse,* are almost Homeric in the simple, unsentimentalized stateliness with which he endows simple life.

TYÚTCHEV

The literary history of Tyútchev is rather curious. His first verse was published only three years after Púshkin's first appearance in print; most of the poems on which his reputation rests appeared in Púshkin's quarterly in 1836–8, but his poetry had to wait for a first critical appreciation till 1850, when he was "discovered" by Nekrásov and it was suddenly realized that he was a very important poet. This recognition came on the eve of the general decline of all interest in poetry, and only the few preserved his cult till the end of the century, when he was again taken up by Vladímir Soloviëv and by the symbolists. Today he is unquestionably recognized as one of the three greatest Russian poets, and the majority, probably, of poetry readers place Tyútchev, not Lérmontov, to the right of Púshkin. Outside Russia, however, though he is much more accessible to the modern romantic taste than is Púshkin, few people have realized his importance. I know from personal experience that when English poetry readers do discover him they almost invariably prefer him to all other Russian poets. This is only natural, for of all Russian poets Tyútchev abounds in those qualities which the English poetry reader has learned to value in nineteenth-century poetry.

Fëdor Ivánovich Tyútchev was born in 1803 of a family of ancient nobility. He received a good education at home and at the University of Moscow. His tutor was the poet Ráich, who afterwards remained his friend and tried to be his literary sponsor. In 1822 Tyútchev entered the diplomatic service and, except for several short visits to Russia, remained abroad twenty-two years. Most of the time he was in Munich, where he met Heine and Schelling, both of whom corresponded with him. He married a Bavarian noblewoman and came to regard Munich as his home. He wrote much; the infrequency of his appearances in print has been explained by his indifference to his poetic work, but the true reason seems to have been his super-

sensitive shyness of criticism. But in 1836 he was persuaded to send some verses to Púshkin's *Sovreménnik*.
From 1836 to 1838 about forty lyrics, all of which (quite
literally) are known by heart today by everyone who cares
for Russian poetry, appeared over the signature of "F. T."
They drew no attention from the critics, and Tyútchev
ceased to publish. Meanwhile Tyútchev lost his first wife
and married a second time, again a Bavarian. He was transferred to Turin. He did not like this change and was
homesick for Munich. While chargé d'affaires of the
legation, he left Turin and the Sardinian States without
permission, and for this breach of discipline was expelled
from the diplomatic service. He settled in Munich, but in
1844 he came to Russia and a little later received a post
in the Censorship. His political articles and memoranda
written in the revolutionary year 1848 attracted official attention. He began to play a political role as a convinced
reactionary and an ardent Panslavist. He began also to
cut a very prominent figure in the drawing-rooms, and acquired the reputation of the greatest wit and most brilliant
conversationalist in Russia. In 1854 his verse at last appeared in book form, and he became famous as a poet.
About the same time his liaison with Mlle Denísieva began,
his daughter's governess. Their love was profound and passionate on both sides, and an infinite source of torture to
both. The young woman's reputation was ruined and
Tyútchev's own gravely tainted, as well as his family happiness. When, in 1864, Mlle Denísieva died, gloom and
despair took possession of Tyútchev. The wonderful tact
and forbearance of his wife in the whole affair only increased his suffering by a profound feeling of guilt. But
his social and political activities never slackened. His slight,
shriveled figure continued appearing in ballrooms, his witticisms continued to enchant society, and he developed a
more than usual pugnacity in politics—becoming one of
the pillars of an unbending nationalist policy. Most of his
political verse belongs to the last ten years of his life. He
died in 1873, after a stroke that left him in a state of
paralysis with only his brain unimpaired.

From the linguistic point of view Tyútchev is a curious
phenomenon. In private and public life he spoke and wrote
nothing but French. All his letters, all his political writings,
are in that language, as well as all his reported witticisms.

Neither his first nor his second wife spoke Russian. He does not seem to have used Russian except for poetical purposes. His few French poems, on the other hand, though interesting, are for the most part trifles and give no hint of the great poet he was in Russian.

Tyútchev's style always remained more archaic than Púshkin's or Zhukóvsky's, and, except his tutor, Ráich, the only Russian poets who influenced him were the classics of the eighteenth century, Derzhávin and Lomonósov, whose oratorical movement is easily recognizable in many of his poems. His style attained its maturity rather early, and the few poems printed in 1829 already display all its essential features. From about that date Tyútchev's poetry is all of a piece (except for the political poems and the love lyrics of his "last love") and may be considered apart from all chronological limits. The greatest number of his best poems belongs to the decade 1830–40.

Tyútchev's poetry is metaphysical and based on a pantheistic conception of the universe. As is the case with every metaphysical poet, Tyútchev's philosophy cannot be stripped of its poetic form without loss of meaning. But the main lines of it must be briefly stated. Its chief difference from that of the great English poets is that it is profoundly pessimistic and dualistic—Manichæan in fact. There are two worlds—Chaos and Cosmos. Cosmos is the living organism of nature, a throbbing and personal being, but it has a secondary and lesser reality as compared to Chaos, the real reality, in which Cosmos is but a slight and precarious spark of ordered beauty. This opposition is one of Tyútchev's fundamental themes. But Cosmos, the vegetable universe, though leading a precarious existence in the womb of Chaos, is opposed as a higher and greater being to the smallness and weakness of the individual consciousness. This theme finds a rhetorical expression (strongly reminiscent of Derzhávin's famous paraphrase of Psalm lxxxi) in the wonderful poem beginning: "Nature is not what you imagine" (*"Ne to chto mníte vy priróda,"* 1836), one of the most grandly eloquent and closely reasoned sermons ever written in verse. It finds another kind of expression in numerous "nature fragments," most of them not over a dozen lines in length.

The two elements of Tyútchev's style—the rhetorical-classical and the visual-romantic—are mixed in his poems in varying proportions. In certain cases the romantic style, saturated with bold, visionary imagery, is given almost free play. Such for instance is the marvelous *Dream at Sea* (1836), the most wildly beautiful poem in the language, for richness and purity of romantic vision comparable to Coleridge's best. But even here the precision of the weird and feverish images is reminiscent of Tyútchev's classical training.

In other poems the classical, oratorical, intellectual element predominates as in the one already mentioned (*Nature is not what you imagine*) and perhaps the most famous of all, *Silentium!* (1833), which contains the famous line: "An uttered thought is a lie." In such poems the romantic vision is recognizable only in the wealth and glow of certain expressions and in the cunning arrangement of the sounds.

Tyútchev's love poetry written at the time of his liaison with Mlle Denísieva has all the unique beauty of his philosophical and nature lyrics but is more passionate and poignant. It is the most profound, subtle, and moving, tragic love poetry in the language. Its main motive is a racking compassion for the woman who has been destroyed and ruined by her overwhelming love for him. The later lyrics, written after her death, are simpler and more direct than anything he ever wrote before. They are cries of anguish and despair, as simple as poetry can be.

Tyútchev's political and occasional poems do not display the highest qualities of his genius, but some of them are splendid pieces of poetical eloquence, and others exquisite examples of poetical wit. Most of his later political poetry (after 1848) is crudely nationalistic and reactionary in sentiment, and much of it (especially after 1863, when he began to write more often than before) is little more than rhymed journalism. But even in this cruder order of ideas he produced such a masterpiece as the lines *On the Arrival of the Austrian Archduke for the Funeral of Nicholas I*, a splendid lyrical invective, one of the most powerful poems ever inspired by indignation.

Tyútchev was famous for his wit, but he made his prose epigrams in French, and he was rarely capable of making his wit collaborate with his art of Russian verse.

But he has left several masterpieces in a more serious style of wit, such as the following poem on the Lutheran service (written in 1834):

> I like the church-service of the Lutherans,
> Their severe, solemn, and simple rite.
> Of these bare walls, of this empty nave,
> I can understand the sublime teaching.
> But don't you see? Ready to leave,
> Faith is for the last time with us;
> She has not yet crossed the threshold,
> But her house is already empty and bare.
> She has not yet crossed the threshold;
> The door has not yet closed behind her.
> But the hour has come, has struck. . . . Pray to God:
> It is the last time you will pray.

LÉRMONTOV

The fact that Tyútchev's poetry passed so completely un-noticed in 1836 was only one of the symptoms of a grow-ing general feeling that the day of poetry was done. It was to have only one more moment of instant and general success in the short, flashlike career of Lérmontov. His early death was accepted as the final closure of the age of verse, but the school of poetry had closed before that date. There is an all-important difference between the conditions in which Púshkin and his contemporaries worked and those in which Tyútchev and Lérmontov were placed. The latter poets lacked the invigorating environ-ment of a literary movement and the sympathetic proximity of fellow craftsmen working at the same task. They were alone in a wasteland. The fact that Lérmontov found an innumerable audience and Tyútchev practically none should not obscure the essential similarity of their situ-ation. Both were cut off from all creative support from the "cultural ambient."

Michael Yúrievich Lérmontov was born October 2, 1814, in Moscow. His father, an army officer and small squire, was a descendant of Captain George Learmont, a Scottish adventurer who in the early seventeenth century entered the Russian service. Learmont, it will be re-

membered, was the surname of Thomas the Rhymer, and
the Learmonts are traditionally descended from him.
Lérmontov, however, seems to have been ignorant of this
poetic ancestry. His mother was an Arséniev, and her
mother, née Stolýpin, was a wealthy landowner and an
important figure in Moscow society. There was a considerable social inequality between the two parents of the
poet. When he was three his mother died, and this led to
a breach between his father and Mme Arséniev, who appropriated her little grandson and brought him up as a
spoiled child. At nine he was taken to the Caucasian waters
—where the mountains and the new environment left a
lasting impression on him. He was thirteen when he began
reading and writing verse and developed a cult of Byron.
He also developed, in a society of numerous, chiefly female,
cousins and acquaintances, a morbid self-consciousness and
highly sensitive vanity. He began taking himself Byronically
and learned to magnify his feelings (such as his adolescent loves) and his circumstances (such as his separation
from his father) on the grand romantic scale. In 1830
he entered the University, but studied little and kept aloof
from the Idealists who were there at the same time as he.
As a penalty for some riotous conduct he was not allowed
to take an intermediate examination, and in 1832 he left
the University of Moscow and went to Petersburg with
the intention of matriculating at the University there. But
instead of the University he entered the School of Ensigns
of the Guards and of Cavalry Cadets. Lérmontov did not
like either Petersburg or the school. But he soon adapted
himself to his new surroundings and became, on the face
of it at least, a typical cavalry cadet. His self-consciousness
was suppressed and became less apparent. His Byronic
pose was transformed into that of a smart and cynical
bully. Romantic love, the dominant sentiment of his Moscow days, was suppressed and driven in, and the surface
was occupied by easy and venal amours, and after school
by callous and calculated Don Juanry. The school brought
Lérmontov in touch with reality, and it was there that
his poetry turned from the magniloquent introspections
of his earlier youth to frankly coarse, unprintable cadet
poems—which, however, are the first germ of his later
realism. In 1834 Lérmontov was given a commission in
the Hussars of the Guard. He was introduced to the best

Petersburg society, but his Muscovite connections were not sufficient to give him a prominent place in it. His vanity suffered from constant pinpricks and was only partly soothed by his victories over female hearts. But under this surface Lérmontov lived his life of a poet and gradually attained his maturity. His poetic and romantic nature burst out at the death of Púshkin. In a memorable poem (which may sound today like rhetoric rather than poetry but is in any case rhetoric of the finest quality) he voiced the feelings of the better side of society—despair at the death of the nation's greatest glory, indignation at the alien murderer, who "could not understand whose life he attempted," and scorn and hatred for the base and unworthy courtiers that had allowed the foreigner to kill the poet. The poem hit its mark—and Nicholas reacted accordingly. Lérmontov was arrested, tried by court-martial, expelled from the Guards, and transferred to a regiment of the line stationed in the Caucasus.

The first disgrace was not of long duration. Before he had been a year in the Caucasus he was pardoned and restored to the Guards. But the short time spent in the Caucasus revived his old romantic attachment for that domestic orient of the Russians and is abundantly reflected in his work. By the beginning of 1838 he was back in Petersburg, this time a famous poet and a lion.

Though a tale in verse by Lérmontov, *Hajjí Abrék*, had appeared in a magazine in 1835, his literary career may be considered to begin with the poem on the death of Púshkin, which (though of course it could not be printed) was widely circulated. In 1837 and 1838 several poems of his appeared in various periodicals, each time attracting considerable attention. In 1839 his friend Krayévsky founded a big magazine, *Otéchestvennye zapíski* (*Notes of the Fatherland*), and only then Lérmontov's work began to appear regularly and frequently. In 1840 a selection of his poems and the novel *A Hero of Our Times* appeared in book form. But like Púshkin, only with more real grounds and more effectively, Lérmontov disliked being regarded as a man of letters. He mixed little with literary circles, and Krayévsky was the only man of letters he ever became intimate with. On the other hand he took a keen interest in political questions, and in 1836–7 belonged to a secret debating society—the Sixteen.

Society life, in spite of all the satisfactions it provided for his vanity, galled and goaded Lérmontov. He had several real and sincere friends in society, but his general feeling towards it was an indignant and bored contempt. His life at Petersburg came to an abrupt end. On a most trivial pretext he fought a duel with M. de Barante, the son of the French Ambassador. No blood was spilled, but all the same the poet was arrested and once again transferred to a line regiment in the Caucasus (1840). This time he took part in several military expeditions against the Chechens and proved himself a brilliantly brave officer. He was mentioned in dispatches and twice recommended for rewards, but these were not approved in Petersburg. In the summer of 1841 he went to Pyatigórsk, the Caucasian watering-place, where he found many acquaintances from Petersburg and Moscow, among them his old schoolfellow, Major Martýnov. Lérmontov and Martýnov paid court to the same lady, and Lérmontov poisoned Martýnov's life by teasing his rival in the presence of the lady. Martýnov bore it for some time but at last called Lérmontov out. Lérmontov was always glad of a duel. They met on July 15, 1841, in the plain near Pyatigórsk. Martýnov was the first to fire, and Lérmontov was killed on the spot.

During his life Lérmontov published very little, and only such of his later work as he considered to be mature. But almost immediately after his death the publication was begun of his early work, strikingly different in quality from what he himself had considered worth publishing. The proportion of this inferior work grew with every new edition and ultimately resulted in swamping the small quantity of his perfect poetry in an ocean of childish effusions. In dealing with Lérmontov it is necessary to distinguish clearly between the immature and the mature, and not to be misled by the (unfortunately, always) *first* volumes of his collected works.

His early poetry is voluminous and formless. To the biographer who is capable of discounting the attitude of the young poet it is valuable, but to the reader of poetry by far the greater part of it is of no use. There occur in it from time to time flashes of genius, bits of song displaying a hitherto unguessed-of power of direct lyrical cry, and piercing passages of self-expression. There is no mastery in this work, no "finer touch," no command of technique—but the raw material of lyric poetry in abundance. Apart from all the rest of the verse of these years stands *The Angel,* written in 1831, which remains one of Lérmontov's highest flights, perhaps the most wonderful *romantic* lyric in the Russian language. It is perfect— though its perfection is not that of maturity. Never has the unconquerable homesickness of the earth-bound soul for its heavenly fatherland been expressed with purer musical truth than in the sixteen lines of this poem by a boy of seventeen.

The following period (1832–6) was less productive than the first. The lyrical output especially is insignificant. At school Lérmontov wrote little more than the obscene cadet poems. They are the antithesis of his early poetry, and it was in a synthesis of the two elements, realistic and romantic, that Lérmontov's true personality was to find its expression. The cadet poems lead on to *Sáshka,* where this synthesis is already half achieved. *Sáshka* is a genuine and lawful son of Byron's *Don Juan*—perhaps the only one of all his progeny who really looks like his father, though he is certainly both more romantic and less polite. Much of the poem is unprintable and goes back, not to Byron, but to the domestic tradition of coarse verse. All the same the general impression is distinctly romantic. *Sáshka* remained unfinished and was published only long after Lérmontov's death. The same realistic vein, but without either the romanticism or the obscenity of *Sáshka,* is apparent in *The Treasurer's Wife* (published 1838), a comic story of provincial life, in the *Onégin* stanza, and directly derived from Púshkin's *Count Núlin.* Lérmontov's first published poem, *Hajjí Abrék* (1835), is a Caucasian tale of revenge, free from Byronic darkness and prolixity, written in a rapid tempo, with a somewhat crude but vigorous martial beat.

With the single exception of *The Angel,* all that constitutes the absolutely valuable part of Lérmontov's poetry belongs to the last four or five years of his life. In Lérmontov's way of working there was a peculiarity that, as far as I am aware, he shared with nobody: numerous themes and passages of various lengths that appear for the first time in his early verses are taken up again and again, in various settings and with various compositional functions, till at last they find an adequate place in some definitive poem of 1838–40. This migration is characteristic of the general abstract character of Lérmontov's poetry. It is not occasional. Reality is an accident. There are permanent visions, permanent knots of emotion, by which he is obsessed; he cannot be at rest until he has freed himself of them. Even in the most deeply felt of his occasional poems, *To the Memory of Alexander Odóyevsky* (1839), the central passage is bodily transferred from *Sáshka*. And the two largest poems of his mature period—*The Demon* and *Mtsýri*—are only fulfillments of conceptions that originated as early as 1829 and 1830.

The Demon, at which he worked from 1829–33, was resumed in 1837 during his stay in Georgia and completed in 1839. The theme is the love of a demon for a mortal. In the early drafts the setting is vague, but in the final form it is Georgia, and the famous descriptive passages of the first part belong to the last period of its creation. The poem could not appear in the reign of Nicholas, as the censorship considered its subject anti-religious, but it was circulated in innumerable copies. In the second half of the nineteenth century it was probably the most universally popular single poem in Russia. It attracted the poetry reader by the same quality that had attracted him in Púshkin's southern poems—its exquisite mellifluousness. Lérmontov's mellifluousness is more purely musical than Púshkin's. It is not tempered by the precise classical training of the elder poet. Our time has greatly reduced its estimate of *The Demon.* The content of the poem is on a level with the Angel-and-Peri poems of Moore. The Demon himself is merely operatic, and the fact that *The Demon* became the libretto of the most operatic of Russian operas (by Anton Rubinstein) is significant. For most Russian poetry readers *The Demon* is a serious drawback in the general appreciation of Lérmontov. But there is in it, after all, a wonderful verbal music, and a haunting magic that had the power of conquering such a man as the great visionary painter Vrúbel and inspiring him to his most memorable imaginings. It is still a source of inspiration to great poets, like Blok and Pasternák, who are able to find more in it than the fastidious uncreative poetry reader can. For behind its obvious puerility and apparent tinsel there is what can hardly be described otherwise than the real presence of demons.

Mtsýri (a Georgian word meaning "novice") has a somewhat similar history. Its theme is the confession at the hour of death of a rebellious young man to his spiritual father—a defiance of the rule and a declaration of unbroken spirit. It is closely related in meter and diction to Zhukóvsky's *Prisoner of Chillon*. Its first draft—*The Confession* (1830)—like the first draft of *The Demon,* is only vaguely localized. Its second draft—*The Boyár Órsha* (1835)—has an operatic "Old Russia" setting and a complicated but incoherent plot. In the final version, as in that of *The Demon,* the scene is laid in Georgia. *Mtsýri* is a poem of great power and may be regarded as the most sustained piece of poetic rhetoric (in the best and highest sense of the word) in Russian. But it is more than that. All that part of the poem which is about nature belongs to the central, small, but priceless, visionary core of Lérmontov—the only Russian poet who knew the "distant land" of the English and German romanticists.

This vision of a "distant land" of eternity shimmering through the visions of this world had already found a definitive expression in *The Angel.* It is the positive side of Lérmontov's romanticism. Its negative side is his passionate contempt for the human herd. Indignation against "empty society" is a dominant note in much of the poetry of his last years. Such poems as *The Death of the Poet, The Poet,* the bitter *Meditation* on his contemporaries, or the invective against the French nation on the occasion of the burial of Napoleon at the Invalides (*The Last Housewarming*) are splendidly effective eloquence, and poetry in so far as they are eloquence in verse. But there is one poem in which *both* the romantic aspects of Lérmontov, the visionary and the rhetorical, are blended in one supreme and matchless unity. That is *New Year's Night:* surrounded by the gay, aristocratic crowd at a ball in town, the poet remembers the pure, transcendent visions of his early years —"the creation of my dream, with eyes full of an azure fire, with a rosy smile like the first brilliancy of the young dawn behind the grove"—and, brought back to reality, ends in a cry of indignant scorn at the mob round him.

But Lérmontov was not only a romanticist. The older he grew, the more he realized that reality was not merely an ugly veil thrown over eternity, not merely a thralldom of his heaven-born spirit, but a world to live in and to act in. The realistic element makes its first appearance in the cadet poems and in *Sáshka*. It continues asserting itself in the work of his maturity, when, parallel to the ridding himself of his romantic obsessions, he gradually developed a new manner, in which he proved himself a greater *master* than in his romantic poetry. For the romantic poems are either a splendid display of effective, rather than refined, rhetoric, which is saved from being bombast and prose merely by the force of the poetic breath that fills it, or gusts of heavenly music overheard from the spheres rather than consciously created. In his realistic poetry Lérmontov is a genuine master, a disciple of Púshkin. By sheer intuition he was able to guess many of the secrets of the poet from whom he was severed not so much by years as by a breach of tradition. For Lérmontov grew up in a world already unfamiliar with French and classical culture and never had the benefit of knowing men who might have taught him. His style was at first strikingly unlike Púshkin's. It was as vague as Púshkin's was precise, as swollen as Púshkin's was terse—it seemed to consist, not of individual words with distinct meanings, but of verbal masses molten into indistinguishable concrete. It was precisely his vagueness, so compatible with music and "heavenly song," that allowed him to achieve his highest romantic effects; but outside these purple patches, his poetry, in his romantic poems, is merely the rush of verbal torrents. In his realistic poems he worked at making himself a new style that would bear no traces either of a heaven-born origin or of romantic untidiness. Beginning with the Russian poems of 1837—the stirring and simple war ballad of *Borodinó*, written in the language and expressing the ideas of an old veteran, and the wonderful *Song of the Merchant Kaláshnikov*, a narrative of Old Russia in a meter and a style taken with admirable intuition from the epic folk songs (though the subject and spirit are frankly romantic)—he achieved style and measure, creating these masterpieces without the elusive aid of heavenly tunes and purple patches. He now became able to treat a romantic theme (like that of *The Fugitive*, 1841) with a concise clarity worthy of Púshkin and with a martial go that was his alone. In a few poems of his last two years he attempted a purely realistic poetry, in the language and diction of prose but on the big themes and with the high seriousness of great poetry. Together with *The Angel* and its kin the poems of this group are his greatest achievement in verse. They bear out his claim to stand in the national esteem by the side of Púshkin. The most remarkable are *The Testament* of a dying officer of the Caucasian Army (admirably translated by Maurice Baring in his *Outline of Russian Literature*), and *Valérik*, a "letter in verse" describing in a style of simple but pregnant realism, a battle against the mountaineers. It is a link between *The Bronze Horseman* and the military scenes of *War and Peace*.

What Lérmontov might have grown into as a poet is a matter of wide speculation. Even as it is, he is oné of the small number of great poets, and, though today his star is under an eclipse, it is probable that posterity will once again confirm the judgment of the nineteenth century and place him immediately next to Púshkin. As a romantic poet he has (with the conceivable exception of Blok) no rival in Russia, and he had in him everything to become also a great realist (in the Russian sense). But it is highly probable also that the main line of his further development would have been in prose, which is regarded today as his least questionable title to a first rank.

THE POETRY OF REFLECTION

The poetry of the Golden Age had been, above all and first of all, "poietic"—in the etymological sense of the word ποιητής (maker). The poets of that age were "makers." Their poetry was not a transcript of their experience, but a creation out of the material of experience. The poetry of Lérmontov was (like all real poetry) also a creation and a transformation, but the element of raw experience and the will to express it play a much larger part in it than in that of his elders. In his later work he certainly turned towards a more "poietic" method of working. But to the reader poetry ceased to be the making of "things of beauty," whose very beauty resided in the fact that they were new and transcended this experience, and became a direct response to his actual—psychological—

emotions, "a beautiful language of emotion"—in short, the beautiful statement of feelings he had actually experienced. When once poetry reaches this stage it ceases to have an independent existence.

Feeling—inner experience—formed the chief interest in life of the better class of Russians in the thirties and forties. Hamlet was their hero, and introspection their principal occupation. The cult of feeling, with the conviction that great feelings are a man's only claim to superiority, was shared by all. But almost invariably introspection failed to detect feelings of sufficient greatness in the introspected subject. Dissatisfaction with one's own self at not finding there the great, ennobling feelings of romantic tradition is the common theme of the literature of the time. In Lérmontov this kind of feeling and this kind of writing were only one side of his weaker—human, not "poietic"—self. But in the minor poets of his generation, the so-called poets of reflection (which in Russian means critical introspection), a similar feeling is practically the only note, while their style is merely a versified transcript of such feelings. The most characteristic of these poets were Iván Pávlovich Klyúshnikov (1811–95) and, especially, Nicholas Platónovich Ogarëv (1813–77), the childhood friend, and for many years the political ally, of Herzen. A man of great but undisciplined nobility of soul, Ogarëv was unhappy in his family life. He emigrated in 1856 and was co-editor with Herzen of the *Bell*. He was to a great extent Herzen's evil angel, not on account of any evilness of his intentions, but because he was entirely devoid of that genius of political tact which was so prominent in his great associate. His poetry (which he began publishing in 1840 and which first appeared in book form in 1856) is typical of the idealistic forties. Melancholy, disillusionment, impotent longing, wistful recollections of missed happiness, are his principal themes. The poetry of Ogarëv is the poetry that might have been expected from a hero of Turgénev's novels.

Turgénev himself began his career by writing verse. His poetic activity lasted from 1838 to 1845. He is far more artistic than Klyúshnikov and Ogarëv, for through the intermediation of Pletnëv he had a direct contact with the Golden Age. But the theme of his poetry is the same as theirs—melancholy, disillusionment, idealistic irony on the falling off and fading of "great feelings." His most memorable (and longest) poem is *Parásha*, which was enthusiastically greeted in 1843 by Belínsky. It is a poem of idealistic irony—the subject is the degeneration of the ideal love of youth into the humdrum realities of middle age. The style is a descendant of that of *Don Juan*, of *Evgény Onégin*, and of Lérmontov (whose prosody is admirably aped). Without being a great poem, or comparable to the best of Turgénev's stories, it is not by any means a contemptible production.

THE DRAMA

The Russian theater in the thirties and forties continued to be adorned by great actors and a high level of acting —but not by great playwrights. The one exception emphasizes the rule—the comedies of Gógol are as isolated and alone in the thirties as the comedy of Griboyédov was in the twenties. The common run of playwriting was by no means superior to that of the preceding period. In tragedy romanticism had triumphed, but its triumph was no benefit to the Russian stage. The plays of Nestor Kúkolnik (1809–68), in blank verse, on romantic themes, and cast in a mold borrowed from Schiller, held the stage with tremendous success, especially in Petersburg, where a public of government clerks found just what it required of romanticism in the cheap and showy tinsel of Kúkolnik. Less obviously meretricious, but in other respects no better than Kúkolnik's, were the romantic and patriotic plays of the unfortunate Polevóy. Nor can anything better be said of Baron George Rosen (1800–66), the author of the libretto for Glínka's great opera *Life for the Tsar* (1836), though, for some reasons that entirely escape us, he was at one time patronized by Púshkin.

The real tragic poet of the thirties was neither Kúkolnik nor Polevóy—but Shakspere. This is true especially of Moscow, where the audiences were more intellectual and more democratic than in Petersburg and consisted of students of the University and of young merchants and city clerks avid for culture and beauty. *Hamlet* especially was the play of the moment. The Idealists found in Hamlet a fellow spirit, while the rest of the audience were carried away by the romantic beauty of the dialogue, and still more by the inspired acting of Paul Mochálov (1800–48), Russia's great romantic tragedian.

At the same time, there was steady progress towards a new, Russian, conception of realism. The growth of realism on the Russian stage is much more regular and logical than in literature, owing to the great personality of Michael Schépkin (1787–1863), who in the second quarter of the century revolutionized comic acting and laid the foundations of the purely Russian realistic style. The comic repertory, especially in Petersburg, was almost entirely dominated by the vaudeville. Though the later vaudevillists chose Russian subjects for their plays and invented Russian plots, the genre was eminently unoriginal and French. It was full of a gay and lighthearted *Scribisme*, and its literary significance is small. But from the theatrical point of view it was an exceedingly grateful kind of play, for it was full of action and gave ample opportunity to the actors to individualize their parts. It has been said that from the point of view of stagecraft the vaudevillists of the thirties and forties have never been surpassed in Russian dramatic literature.

THE NOVELISTS OF THE THIRTIES

The imaginative prose of the thirties and early forties was a chaos, but a fertile chaos. Romanticism and realism, fantasy and everyday life, idealism and satire, construction and style, are all in a state of fertile fermentation, all mixed and jumbled together. The chaos was to take a form only in the second half of the forties, when the Russian realistic school was born.

The main tendencies of the fiction of the period may be classified under three heads: German romanticism, French romanticism, and Russian naturalism. The first is represented by Alexéy Fomích Weltmann (1800–60) and Prince Vladímir Odóyevsky (1803–69); the second by Nicholas Pávlov (1805–64) and Eléna Hahn, née Fadéyev (1814–43; pseudonym "Zinaída R-va"). The third group, represented by Pogódin and Dahl, cannot be considered before we have spoken of Gógol. In Gógol all three tendencies are present, but he transcends them all by the sheer greatness of his originality.

Weltmann's delightfully readable style is based on Sterne, Jean-Paul, and the German romanticists. A blend of imagination and playfully irresponsible humor is the groundwork of his loosely constructed stories. The idealists of the thirties and early forties appreciated Weltmann's romantic humor and his whimsical methods of construction as the expression of "romantic irony"—the irony of the superior poet for the imperfection of the finite world. Prince Vladímir Odóyevsky's best stories are all strongly marked by the influence of E. T. A. Hoffmann. The contrast between the inferior and dubious reality of common life and the higher reality of ideal life is the main subject. All his stories are inspired by a contempt for the low and fleshly life of the Philistine herd. His most ambitious work is *The Russian Nights* (1844), a series of philosophical conversations on the inadequacy of philosophical science when unguided by the higher knowledge to solve the riddles of the universe.

The "French" romanticists cultivated ideas of a simpler and more immediately practical kind—liberty and the cult of passion—and the more forcible forms of rhetoric. The most successful was Pávlov, the disreputable husband of Caroline Pávlova. His *Three Tales* (1835), carelessly passed by the censorship, were one of the greatest literary sensations of the period. Their principal interest lay in a note of strong social protest, a note that had never sounded so strongly in Russian fiction. The most striking of the three tales was the tragic story of a musician of talent who was a serf. Pávlov did not fulfill the promise of his first book. His second book (*New Tales,* 1839) was inferior to it, and after that he devoted himself entirely to gambling and dinner speeches. The influence, shortly to become so powerful, of George Sand made its first appearance in the work of Eléna Hahn. Her husband was an artillery officer, and she spent her life wandering from one God-forsaken billet to another. All her stories are a protest against the sickening boredom, vulgarity, and emptiness of provincial and garrison life. Her sweet, silent, but passionate, heroines are pathetically naïve and helpless, and invariably fall victims to the envy and slander of provincial

gossip. The male characters are either cads who seduce
women by a pretense of love, or cowards whose passions
are too weak to make them act honorably with the women
who love them.

Apart from the main line of development, and parallel
to, rather than in any way dependent on, Gógol, are the
novels of Ukrainian life of Gregory Kvítka (1779–1843),
who wrote under the name of Osnovyánenko. Most of his
work is in Ukrainian and falls outside the scope of the present volume, but his novel *Pan Khalyávsky,* a heavily realistic and heavily humorous picture of the uninspired and
purely materialistic life of the Ukrainian squires, is a
notable landmark in the evolution towards pure physiological naturalism.

GÓGOL

Nikoláy Vasílievich Gógol was born on March 19, 1809,
in the market town of Sorochíntsy, in the Province of
Poltáva. He came of a family of Ukrainian Cossack gentry.
His father was a small squire and an amateur Ukrainian
playwright. In 1820 Gógol went to a provincial grammar
school and remained there till 1828. It was there he began
writing. He was not very popular among his schoolfellows,
but with two or three of them he formed lasting friendships.
Very early he developed a dark and secretive disposition,
mingled of painful self-consciousness and boundless ambition. Equally early he developed an extraordinary mimic
talent, which later on made him a matchless reader of his
own works. In 1828, on leaving school, Gógol came to
Petersburg, full of vague but glowingly ambitious hopes.
They were at once cruelly frustrated. He had hoped for
literary fame and brought with him a poem, very weak and
puerile, of German idyllic life—*Hanz (sic) Küchelgarten.*
He had it published, at his own expense of course, and
under the name of "V. Alov." It was met by the magazines
with deserved derision. He bought up all the copies and
destroyed them. In this state of disillusionment he suddenly went off abroad, with the intention, as he said, of
going to America. But he went only as far as Lübeck. After
a few days' stay there he returned to Petersburg and once
more tried his fortune, this time with better patience. He

entered the Civil Service, still hoping to become a great
administrator, and he began writing prose stories. He came
in touch with the "literary aristocracy," had a story published in Délvig's *Northern Flowers*, was taken up by
Zhukóvsky and Pletnëv, and, in 1831, was introduced to
Púshkin. He was well received in this most select of literary
sets and, with his usual vanity, became enormously proud
of his success and very self-confident. Thanks to Pletnëv's
good offices, he was appointed teacher of history at a young
ladies' institute and at once began to imagine that the way
he was to become great was by writing history. In the
meantime (1831) he brought out the first volume of his
Ukrainian stories (*Evenings on a Farm near Dikánka*),
which met with immediate success. It was followed in
1832 by a second volume, and in 1835 by two volumes of
stories entitled *Mírgorod* (containing *Viy*, *Tarás Búlba*,
Old-World Landowners, and *Iván Ivánovich and Iván
Nikíforovich*), as well as by two volumes of miscellaneous
prose entitled *Arabesques* (containing, besides a variety of
essays, *The Névsky Prospect*, *The Memoirs of a Madman*,
and the first draft of *The Portrait*). In 1834 Gógol was
made Professor of History of the University of St. Petersburg, though, except an unlimited self-confidence, he had
absolutely no qualifications for the chair. This academic
venture proved a signal failure. His first lecture, an introduction to mediæval history, was a brilliant piece of showy
rhetoric, but those which followed it were poor and empty.
Turgénev, who happened to be one of Gógol's audience,
has left a record of the painful impression they produced.
Gógol soon realized his failure (though he does not seem
to have acknowledged his inadequacy) and resigned his
chair in 1835. His good relations with the "literary aristocracy" continued, and Púshkin and Zhukóvsky continued
encouraging him. But there was never any real intimacy
between either Púshkin or Zhukóvsky and Gógol. They
liked him and appreciated his talent, and refused to idolize
him. It is probable, after all, that they undervalued him.
But while the "aristocracy" gave him qualified admiration,
in Moscow Gógol met with the adulation and entire recognition sufficient to satisfy him. The young Idealists, with
Belínsky at their head, carried him to the skies, but it was
not with them he made friends. The set that became his
principal sanctuary were the Slavophils, especially the

Aksákov family, in which he could taste of absolute and unconditioned admiration.

Though between 1832 and 1836 Gógol worked at his imaginative creations with great energy, and though almost all his work has in one way or another its sources in these four years of contact with Púshkin, he had not yet decided that his ambitions were to be fulfilled by success in literature. It was only after the presentation, on April 19, 1836, of his comedy *Revizór* that he finally believed in his literary vocation. The comedy, a violent satire of Russian provincial bureaucracy, saw the stage owing only to the personal interference of Nicholas I. It was met by enthusiastic praise and virulent obloquy. The Petersburg journalists, the spokesmen of the official classes, raised the hue and cry against Gógol, while the "aristocrats" and the Moscow Idealists of every shade of opinion were equally emphatic in admiring it. They received it as more than a work of art—as a great moral and social event. Though hurt by the attacks of the Philistines, Gógol was in much greater degree elated by the praise of his admirers. When, two months after the first night, he left Petersburg for abroad, he was finally convinced that his vocation was to "be useful" to his country by the power of his imaginative genius. Henceforward for twelve years (1836–48) he lived abroad, coming to Russia for short periods only. He chose Rome for his headquarters. He became enamored with the Eternal City, which answered to his highly developed sense of the magnificent, and where even the visions that always obsessed him of vulgar and animal humanity assumed picturesque and poetical appearances that fitted harmoniously into the beautiful whole. The death of Púshkin produced a strong impression on Gógol, especially by emphasizing his conviction that *he* was now the head of Russian literature and that great things were expected of him. His principal work during these years was the great satirical epic (*poèma*, as its Russian subheading goes) *Dead Souls*. At the same time he worked at other tasks—recast *Tarás Búlba* and *The Portrait*, completed his second comedy, *Marriage*, wrote the fragment *Rome* and the famous tale *The Greatcoat*. In 1841 the first part of *Dead Souls* was ready, and Gógol took it to Russia to supervise its printing. It appeared in Moscow in 1842, under the title, imposed by the censorship, of *The Adventures of Chíchikov, or Dead Souls*. Simul-

taneously a collected edition of his earlier work was brought
out in four volumes. The reception of the new book by all
those who counted was enthusiastic. This was the summit
of Gógol's literary career and, practically, the end of his
work as an imaginative writer. The subsequent developments were unexpected and disappointing, and still form
one of the strangest and most disconcerting passages in the
history of the Russian mind.

Gógol's imaginative creation, especially his most ambitious and influential works, *Revizór* and *Dead Souls,* was
satirical. It seemed satire pure and simple, leveled at the
dark and animal forces of stagnant Russia. It was accepted
as such both by the interested side—the bureaucrats and
their journalistic mouthpieces—and by the dissatisfied elite.
To the latter the author of these satires appeared as a
teacher, a man with a great message of moral and social
regeneration, an enemy of dark social forces, and a friend
of progress and enlightenment. There was in this attitude a
great misunderstanding. Gógol's work was satirical, but
not in the ordinary sense. It was not objective, but subjective, satire. His characters were not realistic caricatures
of the world without, but introspective caricatures of the
fauna of his own mind. They were exteriorizations of his
own "ugliness" and "vices": *Revizór* and *Dead Souls* were
satires of self, and of Russia and mankind only in so far as
Russia and mankind reflected that self. On the other hand,
while he was endowed with a superhuman power of creative imagination (in which in the world's literature he has
had equals but certainly no superior), his understanding
was strikingly inadequate to his genius. His ideas were
those of his provincial home, of his simple, childish mother,
modified only by an equally primitive romantic cult of
beauty and of art, imbibed during the first years of his
literary career. But his limitless ambition, stimulated by the
homage paid him by his Moscow friends, urged him to
become more than a mere comic writer, to be a prophet
and a teacher. He worked himself into a faith in his divine
mission, which was to lead sin-bound Russia to moral regeneration.

After the publication of the first part of *Dead Souls,*
Gógol, it would seem, intended to continue it on the plan
of Dante's *Divine Comedy*. The first part, which contained
none but caricatures, was to be the *Inferno*. The second

part was to be the gradual purification and transformation of the rogue Chíchikov under the influence of virtuous publicans and governors—*Purgatory*. Gógol began working at the second part immediately, but it proceeded haltingly and was put aside. Instead he decided to write a book of direct moral preaching that would reveal his message to the world. But he had no message to reveal, apart from the weird mask exteriorized by his subconscious self, or the glowing heroic and romantic images of his creative imagination. The "message" that was embodied in the new book was nothing but a hotchpotch of provincial, very earthly and uninspired, religious flatness, sprinkled by a little æsthetic romanticism and served up to justify the existing order of things (including serfdom, corporal punishment, and so on) and to impress on every man the duty of *conforming* conscientiously and to the best of his might with the present God-ordained order of things. The book, entitled *Selected Passages from a Correspondence with Friends* (though it contained practically no passages from actual letters), appeared in 1847. Gógol expected it to be received with awe and gratitude, like a message from Sinai. He actually believed that it would be a signal for the immediate regeneration of Russians from sin. He was cruelly disappointed before long. His best friends, the Slavophils, were painfully and unmistakably disgusted. Aksákov, the very archpriest of the Gógol cult, wrote to him a letter of bitterly wounded friendship, accusing him of Satanic pride masquerading in the guise of humility. After this and similar rebukes from people whom he regarded as his own, the violent, vehement, and outspoken letter of Belínsky, which accused him of falsifying Christianity for the profit of those in power and of adoring reaction and barbarity, though it hurt Gógol deeply, contributed little to increase his self-disillusionment. His inferiority complex rose in a wave of self-disgust, and Gógol threw himself on the mercy of religion. But he was not made for a religious life, and however despairingly he forced himself to it, he could not succeed. His tragedy entered on a new stage. Instead of trying to proclaim a message he had not got, he now tried to acquire an experience of which he was incapable. His early education made him view Christianity in its simplest form: as the fear of death and hell. But he had no inner impulse towards Christ. His despair of himself was enhanced by the pilgrimage he undertook (in 1848) to the Holy Land. His incapacity to warm himself up to genuine religious experience in the presence of the Lord's footsteps increased his conviction that he was irrevocably lost and damned. From Palestine he returned to Russia and passed his last years in restless movement from one part of the country to another. He met Father Matthew Konstantínovsky, a fierce and narrow ascetic, who seems to have had a great influence on him and strengthened in him his fear of perdition by insisting on the sinfulness of all his imaginative work. However, Gógol continued working at the second part of *Dead Souls,* a first draft of which he had destroyed in 1846 as unsatisfactory. His health gradually gave way. He undermined it by exaggerated ascetic practices, all the time trying to compel himself to a Christian inner life. In an access of self-mortification he destroyed some of his manuscripts, which contained most of the second part of *Dead Souls.* He explained this as a mistake —a practical joke played on him by the Devil. It is not clear whether he really meant to do it or not. After that he fell into a state of black melancholy, and died on February 21, 1852.

The significance of Gógol is twofold—he is not only a great imaginative writer; he is a supremely interesting individuality, a psychological phenomenon of exceptional curiosity. This psychological side still remains, and will probably always remain, very largely a mystery. I am not here concerned with it, except in so far as it is directly connected with the nature of his creative work. But as a writer Gógol is not twofold in the sense Tolstóy or Dostoyévsky is. There is no common *literary* measure between his imaginative work and his miscellaneous and moralistic writings. The latter are remarkable only as they throw light on the psychological, human personality of Gógol. The early essays contained in *Arabesques* are rhetoric pure and simple, of a kind that is but the manure for the really magnificent rhetoric of such early stories as *The Terrible Vengeance* or *Tarás Búlba.* The *Correspondence with Friends* is painful, almost humiliating, reading, in spite of the occasional flashes of imagination that break through its heavy and poisonous mist. The critical pages, with their sometimes genuinely and sublimely imaginative appreciation and impressionistic portraits of Russian poets (especially of his

favorites Yazýkov and Derzhávin), may be alone singled
out for praise. Of the writings of his last years, the commentary on the liturgy is derivative and irresponsible.
While *The Author's Confession* is notable as a human
document of considerable importance, it has no claim to
comparison with the *Confession* of Tolstóy. Still, even in
these writings the unique, unrepeatable personality of
Gógol is always present in the labored, consciously original
style, with its constant suggestion of the presence of un-
conquered chaos and disorder.

His imaginative work is a very different business. It is
one of the most marvelous, unexpected—in the strictest
sense, original—worlds ever created by an artist of words.
If mere creative force is to be the standard of valuation,
Gógol is the greatest of Russian writers. In this respect he
need hardly fear comparison with Shakspere, and can
boldly stand by the side of Rabelais. Neither Púshkin nor
Tolstóy possessed anything like that volcano of imaginative
creativeness. The enormous potency of his imagination
stands as a strange contrast (or complement) to his physical sterility. He seems sexually never to have emerged from
an infantile (or rather, early adolescent) stage. Woman
was to him a terrible, fascinating, but unapproachable obsession, and he is known never to have loved. This makes
the women of his imagination either strange, inhuman
visions of form and color that are redeemed from melodramatic banality only by the elemental force of the rhetoric
they are enshrined in, or entirely unsexed, even dehumanized, caricatures.

The main and most persistent characteristic of Gógol's
style is its verbal expressiveness. He wrote with a view not
so much to the acoustic effect on the ears of the listener as
to the sensuous effect on the vocal apparatus of the reciter.
This makes his prose intense and saturated. It is composed
of two elements, romantically contrasted and romantically
extreme—high-pitched, poetic rhetoric, and grotesque farce.
Gógol never wrote simply—he is always either elaborately
rhythmical or quite as elaborately mimetic. It is not only in
his dialogue that the intonations of spoken speech are reproduced. His prose is never empty. It is all alive with the
vibration of actual speech. This makes it hopelessly untranslatable—more untranslatable than any other Russian
prose.

The other main characteristic of Gógol's genius is the extraordinary intensity and vividness of his *sight*. He saw the outer world romantically transformed; and even when he saw the same details as we do, they acquired such proportions in his vision as to become entirely different in meaning and measure. Gógol's pictures of nature are either romantically fantastic transformations (like the famous description of the Dnepr in *The Terrible Vengeance*) or strange mounds of detail heaped on detail, resulting in an unconnected chaos of things. Where he is absolutely supreme and definitive is in his vision of the human figure. His people are caricatures, drawn with the method of the caricaturist—which is to exaggerate salient features and to reduce them to geometrical pattern. But these caricatures have a convincingness, a truthfulness, an inevitability—attained as a rule by slight but definitive strokes of unexpected reality—that seems to beggar the visible world itself.

I have alluded to the great and exceptional originality of Gógol. This does not mean that numerous influences cannot be discerned in his work. The principal of these are: the tradition of the Ukrainian folk and puppet theater, with which the plays of Gógol's father were closely linked; the heroic poetry of the Ukrainian *dumy*, or Cossack ballads; the *Iliad* in the Russian version of Gnédich; the numerous and mixed traditions of comic writing from Molière to the vaudevillists of the twenties; the novel of manners from Lesage to Narézhny; Sterne, chiefly through the medium of German romanticism; the German romanticists themselves, especially Tieck and E. T. A. Hoffmann; the "furious school" of French romanticism, with, at its head, Hugo and Jules Janin, and their common master, Maturin—a long and yet incomplete list. Many of the elements of Gógol's art may be traced back to these sources. And they are not merely borrowings and reminiscences of motives; most of them had a profound effect on his very manner and technique. Yet they are only constituent details in a whole of more than expectable originality.

The first part of *Evenings* (containing *Sorochínsky Fair, St. John's Eve, The May Night, or The Drowned Girl,* and *The Lost Charter*) together with two of the four stories of the second part (*Christmas Night* and *The Charmed Spot*) are the early Gógol. They are much simpler, less sophisticated and tense, than anything he wrote later. Their fun, which was what attracted the reader above all, is simple and unadulterated. Their romance is somewhat youthfully operatic but free from sophistication. Their devilry is gay and lighthearted. The picture they give of Ukraine is of course quite fantastic, but it was so attractive, at once so prettily romantic and so hugely funny, that not even the Ukrainians themselves (except till much later) remarked all the absurdities, all the supreme disregard for (and ignorance of) reality displayed by Gógol. The prefaces to each of the two volumes, placed in the mouth of the suppositious narrator, the beekeeper Red Pánko, are already masterpieces of Gógol's mimetic art. The stories themselves depend for the humor on the stock characters of the Ukrainian puppet theater; for the spook and romance on the various fictions of chiefly German romanticists. Gógol is present in the blend of the two elements, in the verbal intensity of the style, in the vivid convincingness of the largely fantastical dialogue of the comic figures, in the unique, physical infectiousness of the laughter.

Of the remaining two stories in the second part of *Evenings*, *The Terrible Vengeance* is a creation of the purest romantic imagination. Strongly redolent of foreign romanticism and full of reminiscences of the Cossack songs, *The Terrible Vengeance* is, in a certain sense, a masterpiece. It is Gógol's greatest effort at purely ornate prose. The beautiful rhythmical movement is sustained without breach or flaw from beginning to end. The story is gruesome and creepy, and at a first reading almost intolerably impressive. It is one of his very few stories where humor is entirely absent.

Of the stories contained in the *Mírgorod* volumes, the romantic element is present in *Tarás Búlba* and in *Viy*. The former is a historical romance of Cossack Ukraine. Though suggested by, it is very unlike, the romances of Scott. It is supremely free from considerations of historical exactitude but nevertheless full of the spirit of the old Cossack warriors and echoes of their poetry. It is almost as full, in the battle scenes, of reminiscences of the *Iliad*. Its place in Russian literature is unique—it has had no imitators or followers (except, perhaps, Bábel in his stories of the Red Army). It is heroic, frankly and openly heroic. but it is also broadly humorous and realistic. It is perhaps the only Russian imaginative work that has that many-sided exuberance which might claim the epithet Shaksperian. *Viy* is also a wonderful blend of romantic weirdness with realistic and homely humor. The construction of the story, the absence from it of questionable rhetoric, and, especially, the perfect fusion of the two discordant elements of terror and humor, all make *Viy* one of the fullest and richest of Gógol's stories.

Gógol's stories of everyday life of contemporary Russia are introspective—not in the sense that he analyzed and described his psychic experience as Tolstóy, Dostoyévsky, or Proust did, but because his characters are exteriorized and objectivated symbols of his experience. His inferiority complex and his deep roots in the animal, or rather vegetable, life of a rural squiredom gave these symbols the form of caricatures of grotesque vulgarity. The aspect under which he sees reality is expressed by the untranslatable Russian word *póshlost*, which is perhaps best rendered as "self-satisfied inferiority," moral and spiritual. But other subjective aspects may be discovered in his realistic stories—in particular what we might call a "sterility complex," which makes its appearance in the very first of these stories, in *Iván Fëdorovich Shpónka and His Aunt*, the fourth story of the second volume of *Evenings*.

Until after the publication of the first part of *Dead Souls*, Gógol took scant interest in reality as such but relied for the creation of his characters entirely on his unaided imagination. But he was a realist in the sense that he introduced (as details and as material) innumerable elements and aspects of reality that had hitherto not possessed the freedom of literature. He was (like Tolstóy, Górky, and Andréyev, after him) a great lifter of taboos, a great destroyer of prohibitions. He made vulgarity reign where only the sublime and the beautiful had reigned. This was *historically* the most important aspect of his work. Nor was the younger generation's general concept of him as a social satirist entirely unjustified. He did not paint (and scarcely knew) the social evils of Russia. But the caricatures he drew were, weirdly and terribly, *like* the reality about him; and the sheer vividness and convincingness of his paintings simply eclipsed the paler truth and irrevocably held the fascinated eye of the reader.

In his attitude towards "vegetable life" Gógol oscillated between sympathetic complacency and scornful irony. The sentimental and sympathetic attitude is most fully expressed in the *Old-World Landowners* (in *Mírgorod*), where the vegetable humors of the old pair, their sloth, their gluttony, their selfishness, are idealized and sentimentalized. The purely ironic attitude is expressed with equal purity in the other realistic story of *Mírgorod—The Story of How Iván Ivánovich Quarreled with Iván Nikíforovich*. It is one of the greatest of Gógol's masterpieces. His comic gift (always verging on impossible caricature and impossible farce) appears in its absolute purity. But like almost all his later stories it results ultimately in a vision of depressingly hopeless gloom. The story, begun as a merry farce, grows, towards the end, uncannily symbolical, and ends with the famous words: "It is gloomy in this world, gentlemen" (*"Skúchno na ètom svéte, gospodá"*).

Of the five short stories whose scene is set in Petersburg, *The Portrait* is purely romantic, devoid of humor, and curiously reminiscent of Poe. *The Memoirs of a Madman* (1835) and *Névsky Prospect* (1835), one of Gógol's masterpieces, are romantic in the Hoffmannesque sense, for their subject is the juxtaposition of dream life and real life. *The Nose* (1836) is a piece of sheer play, almost sheer nonsense. In it more than anywhere else Gógol displays his extraordinary magic power of making great comic art out of nothing.

The last in time of the Petersburg stories is *The Greatcoat* (1842), which, together with *Revizór* and *Dead Souls*, turned out to be Gógol's most influential work. It is the story of a poor clerk who lives on four hundred rubles a year and whose only dream in life is to have a new greatcoat. When at last he has the money and the greatcoat is ready, the first time he goes out he is waylaid by thieves and robbed of the greatcoat. He is represented as a pathetically humble and inferior figure, and the story passes through all the gamut of attitudes towards him, from sheer fun to poignant pity. It is this poignancy of pity for the poor and insignificant man that so strongly impressed the contemporary reader. *The Greatcoat* gave rise to a whole literature of philanthropic stories about the poor clerk, of which the most significant is Dostoyévsky's *Poor Folk*.

The plot of *Dead Souls* revolves around Chíchikov

and his roguish plan of buying up "dead souls" (that is, serfs who had died since the last census and for whom their owners continued to pay the poll-tax) for nothing and then getting money by pawning them. The construction is loose, and the narrative spacious. The verbal and visual wealth of the style is as intense as in *The Greatcoat*. The characters are, together with those of *Revizór*, the most memorable and permanent of Gógol's legacy to the Russian mind. Chíchikov is the greatest of Gógol's subjective caricatures—he is the incarnation of *póshlost*. His psychological leitmotiv is complacency, and his geometrical expression roundness. He is the golden mean. The other characters—the squires Chíchikov visits on his shady business—are typical "humors" (for Gógol's method of comic character drawing, with its exaggerations and geometrical simplification, is strongly reminiscent of Ben Jonson's). Sobakévich, the strong, silent, economical man, square and bearlike; Manílov, the silly sentimentalist with pursed lips; Mme Koróbochka, the stupid widow; Nozdrëv, the cheat and bully, with the manners of a hearty good fellow—all are types of eternal solidity. Plyúshkin, the miser, stands apart, for in him Gógol sounds a note of tragedy—he is the man ruined by his "humor"; he transcends *póshlost*, for in the depth of his degradation he is not complacent but miserable; he has a tragic greatness. Among other things the first part of *Dead Souls* contains "The Story of Captain Kopéykin," in which Gógol transcended himself in the wealth of verbal expressiveness.

The second part of the great epic, to judge by what has been left us of it, was a distinct decline. In it Gógol tried to overcome the natural tendencies of his style and to become more objective and realistic. He succeeded only in forfeiting his strength. It contains first-class work in the style of the first part (especially the "humor" of the glutton, Petúkh), but the new manner was a complete failure. The objectively drawn, good-and-bad-mixed characters are comparatively lifeless, and the ideal characters of the good publican and the virtuous governor quite unconvincing and hollow.

Gógol's greatness as a dramatist rests chiefly on the *Revizór*, doubtless the greatest play in the Russian language. It is not only supreme in character drawing and dialogue—it is one of the few Russian plays that is a play constructed

with unerring art from beginning to end. The great originality of its plan consisted in the absence of all love interest
and of sympathetic characters. The latter feature was
deeply resented by Gógol's enemies, and as a satire the
play gained immensely from it. *Revizór* was intended as a
moral satire against bad officials, not a social satire against
the *system* of corruption and irresponsible despotism. But
quite apart from the author's intention, it was received as
a social satire, and in the great oppositional movement
against the despotism of Nicholas I and the system of
bureaucratic irresponsibility, its influence was greater than
that of any other single literary work. In their great symbolic and comprehensive popularity the characters of
Revizór stand by the side of those of *Dead Souls*. They are·
less obviously geometrical, and, the characterization de-
pending entirely on the dialogue, more supple and human.
They are less markedly "humorous," more ordinary, more
average, than Sobakévich and his like. The head of the
local administration, the *Gorodníchy*, is a satirical figure of
immense symbolism and pregnancy. As for the central
character, Khlestakóv, the supposed inspector general himself, he is as subjective and introspective as Chíchikov. If
in Chíchikov Gógol exteriorized all the vegetable elements
of his self, in Khlestakóv he symbolized the irresponsibility, the light-mindedness, the absence of measure, that
was such a salient trait of his own personality. But, like
Chíchikov, Khlestakóv is entirely "transposed," entirely
alive—the most alive of all the characters of Russian fiction
—meaningless movement and meaningless fermentation incarnate, on a foundation of placidly ambitious inferiority.
As for the dialogue of *Revizór*, it is above admiration.
There is not a wrong word or intonation from beginning to
end, and the comic tensity is of a quality that even in
Gógol was not always at his beck and call.

Of Gógol's other plays, *The Vladímir Order*, planned
in 1833 as a satire of the Petersburg bureaucracy, remained
unfinished, apparently because Gógol despaired of seeing
it through the censorship. *Marriage*, begun in 1832 and
completed in 1842, is very different from *Revizór*. It is not
satirical, and it is loosely built, with dialogue greatly
dominating over action. It is pure fun, though undoubtedly
on a Freudian foundation (the same sterility complex as in
Shpónka.) The characters and the dialogue are marvelous.

For here, unfettered by any message, Gógol gave free reign to his grotesque, mimetic imagination and surpassed himself in the exuberance of his comic creation. The remaining play, *The Gamblers,* is inferior to the two great comedies. It is an unpleasant play, inhabited by scoundrels that are not funny, and, though the construction is neat, it is dry and lacks the richness of the true Gógol.

On the stage, as in fiction, Gógol's action, historically, was in the direction of realism. Here as elsewhere he was an opener of doors, an introducer of hitherto forbidden material. *Marriage* especially, with its broad and original treatment of merchant manners, had an appreciable influence on Ostróvsky. And it was in these two comedies (and in *Góre ot umá*) that Schépkin achieved the greatest triumphs of his realistic acting.

LÉRMONTOV'S PROSE

Between the ages of fifteen and eighteen Lérmontov wrote three plays in prose that are on the same low level as his early verse. With a rhetorical style descended from Schiller's *Robbers,* they deal in high-strung passions and melodramatic situations. The most notable thing in them is several strong and realistic scenes describing the serf-owners' abuse of despotic power. In 1835 Lérmontov returned to the dramatic form with *Masquerade,* written in the measure of *Góre ot umá.* Like the early plays, to which it is superior only in its forcible, rhetorical verse, it is a swollen melodrama with unreal personages. Lérmontov's first attempt at fiction—also from his pre-cavalry days—is an unfinished romance of the Pugachëv Rebellion, with a dark Byronic revenger for hero and in the style of the French "furious school," its shrill rhetoric relieved at times by scenes of brutal realism. His second attempt was an unfinished novel of Petersburg society, *Princess Lígovsky,* at which he worked in 1835–6 in collaboration with his friend Svyatosláv Rayévsky. It possesses already many of the qualities of *A Hero of Our Times,* and its principal character is a first draft of Pechórin.

In 1837–9 Lérmontov's creative evolution was in two directions—on the one hand he was ridding himself of the subjective obsessions of his early years, on the other he was evolving a new, impersonal, objective, and realistic manner. Thus it was that the same Causasian impressions of 1839 found their way both into *The Demon* and *Mtsýri* and into their opposite, *A Hero of Our Times*.

A Hero of Our Times (1840) had an immediate success, and a second edition (preceded by a remarkable preface, in which Lérmontov made fun of his readers for believing that in his hero, Pechórin, he had portrayed himself) appeared before his death, in 1841. The novel is one of those works in the valuation of which Russians and foreigners differ most. Russian critical opinion is unanimous in assigning an exceedingly high place to *A Hero of Our Times*, and almost unanimous in considering it of greater importance than Lérmontov's poetical work. Abroad it has failed to kindle enthuiasm, for reasons similar to those which have kept Western people from appreciating Púshkin at his true worth: Lérmontov is too European, too human, too insufficiently Russian, to please the spice-craving palates of Latin and Anglo-Saxon Russopaths. On the other hand the perfection, negative rather than positive, of his style and narrative manner can be appreciated only by those who really know Russian, who feel the fine imponderable shades of words and know what has been left out as well as what has been put in. Lérmontovs prose is the best Russian prose ever written, if we judge by the standards of perfection and not by those of wealth. It is transparent, for it is absolutely adequate to the content and neither overlaps it nor is overlapped by it. It is different from Púshkin's in its complete freedom and in the absence of that constraint which is always present in the greater poet's prose.

The novel consists of five stories. The first (*Bèla*) relates the narrator's meeting on the road from Tiflís to Vladikavkáz with the Caucasian veteran Captain Maxím Maxímych. Maxím Maxímych tells the story of Pechórin, who was his subaltern for a time in a fort on the mountain frontier, and of Pechórin's love affair with a Caucasian girl. In the second, the narrator meets Pechórin himself and comes by his journal. The remaining three stories are extracts from the journal of Pechórin. The first, *Tamán*, relating an incident he had with some smugglers in the town of that name, is perhaps the masterpiece of Russian fiction. At least it was so considered by Chékhov, who owed much of his method to its atmospheric construction. Next comes *Princess Mary*, which itself may be regarded as a complete short novel. It is the diary of Pechórin, describing his stay at the Caucasian waters. It is analytic, and a large part of Pechórin's entries are a direct dissection of his mind in an aphoristic style closely connected with that of the French moralists and is first cousin to Stendhal's. The construction of the story is delicately suggestive of a parody of *Evgény Onégin*. The last story is *The Fatalist*, in which Pechórin is nothing but a narrator and plays no part. It is an intensified anecdote, akin to the tales of Púshkin.

Pechórin, the hero, is a strong, silent man with a poetic soul who, from noble shyness and high contempt for the herd, especially for the aristocratic herd, assumes the mask of a snob and a bully. He is capable of noble and generous passions, but life has robbed him of all opportunity to experience them, and his devastated heart is like an extinct volcano. Pechórin was not only a great literary influence—he was imitated in life as well as in fiction. To us Pechórin is redeemed from operatic cheapness by the magical atmosphere of the novel, which lifts him above the possibility of ridicule or second-rateness. It is an atmosphere difficult to define. It has a particular fine, refined quality, at once ironic, tragic, and visionary. Goethe would have called it "daimonic." The vision behind the novel is never so much as hinted at, but it is unmistakably present and gives it that air of nobility which (in spite of its complete freedom from the vice of poeticality) raises it above the level of mere prose fiction. This atmosphere, together with the perfection of the verbal and narrative form, is what has induced people by no means extravagant or paradoxical to call *A Hero of Our Times* the greatest Russian novel, thus placing it above *War and Peace*.

Another notable feature of the novel, and one that had the greatest effect on the immediate future, is the figure of Maxím Maxímych, the veteran captain of the line, the simple, humble, and casual hero of duty, kindness, and common sense, who is one of the greatest creations of Russian realism. It is a connecting link between Púshkin's Captain Mirónov and Tolstóy's humble heroes of army officers, and in this line it is, unquestionably, the fullest and most comprehensive expression of the type.

After *A Hero of Our Times* Lérmontov wrote little prose, nor had he much time to write more. The beginning of a novel of Petersburg—full of a cold and condensed romanticism that has its roots in *The Queen of Spades*—makes us lament all the more the untimely death of one who, had he lived, might have shown the Russian novel a manlier and stronger way than it actually took.

THE FIRST NATURALISTS

Under the influence of Gógol's taboo-lifting and boundary-removing work there arose towards 1840 what called itself the "Natural School." The movement ultimately culminated in the birth of the national school of realism in the memorable years 1846–7. Before that date its pioneers, apart from Gógol, were Dahl, Sollogúb, and Butkóv.

Vladímir Ivánovich Dahl (1801–72), who was of Danish origin, is remembered chiefly for his *Reasoned Dictionary of the Living Great-Russian Language* (four volumes, 1864–8), which still forms the basis of our knowledge of Russian as it was spoken by the people before the spread of standard schoolmastery. In literature Dahl desired to free Russian from its Græco-Latin-German-French fetters, but he had no real sense of style, and his stories and anecdotes, written (in the thirties and forties) in illustration of his linguistic aspirations, are not remarkable. His stories of contemporary life in the "natural style" were historically more important. He was the first to introduce the form of the "physiological sketch"; that is, of short, descriptive stories illustrating the peculiarities of this or that particular social milieu, a form that had a great vogue in the forties.

Count Vladímir Alexándrovich Sollogúb (1813–82) was an aristocratic dilettante. His best known work, *Tarantás* (1844), is a satirical journey from Moscow to Kazán in a tumble-down traveling cart. The satire, superficial and uninspired, is directed against the ideas of the Slavophils and the unpractical dreaminess of the romantic idealists. There is a greater intensity and seriousness in the work of Yákov Butkóv (*c.* 1815–56), whose *Summits* (i.e. attics) *of Petersburg* (1844–5) is the most important landmark of philanthropic' literature between Gógol's *Greatcoat* and

Dostoyévsky's *Poor Folk*. Himself a penniless proletarian and the sweated drudge of the publisher Krayévsky, Butkóv's stories are devoted to the sentimental and humorous evocation of the life of the poor government clerks of the capital.

THE PETERSBURG JOURNALISTS

Journalism flourished and its importance increased in the course of the present period. In spite of the censorship, whose rigor was never for a moment abated during the whole reign of Nicholas I, it was precisely now that the Russian magazines finally became the leaders of public opinion and acquired the peculiar form and coloring they retained till the great Revolution. Petersburg journalism was at first dominated by the notorious triumvirate—Bułháryn, Grech, and Sękowski, of whom the most talented was Joseph-Julian Sękowski (1800–59). An Arabic scholar of considerable achievement and, like Bułháryn, a Pole by birth, from 1834 he edited the *Library for Reading* and wrote in it under the pseudonym of Baron Brambeus. Fundamentally cynical, he had no respect for genius, sincerity, or generous emotion. His smart and witty reviews and critical surveys poured out contempt and obloquy on all the best authors of the time. His style, flippant, facile, tasteless, and cheaply humorous, had an immense influence on the formation of Russian journalese. Sękowski and Belínsky, so unlike in their spiritual content, were equally operative in putting an end to the elegant and distinguished "French" prose of the Karamzín-Púshkin tradition.

THE MOSCOW "CIRCLES"

The contrast, in the thirties, between bureaucratic, cynical, pleasure-seeking, meretricious Petersburg and young, idealistic, inspired, philosophical Moscow was striking. While the papers of the Petersburg triumvirate, servile and subservient, flourished, brought in big incomes, and were never so much as frowned at by the authorities, the history of the Moscow magazines is a succession of martyrdoms at the hands of the censorship, and of financial failures in the hands of dilettante publishers. The history of Muscovite idealism is much less connected with its journals than with the famous "circles."

These "circles" were invariably connected with the University. In the twenties the Wisdom-lovers had been already a typical "circle" of the kind. They were one of the germs out of which, in the thirties, grew up the Slavophil group. In the early thirties the University of Moscow contained among its undergraduates a remarkable group of young men who formed the two famous "circles" of Stankévich and of Herzen. The former devoted themselves to the enthusiastic study of German idealistic philosophy— Schelling, Fichte, and Hegel. Herzen's circle concentrated on political and social questions, and were the first to introduce the doctrines of the idealistic socialism of Saint-Simon and Fourier. The University of Moscow was a crucible wherein all classes were melted into a non-class intelligentsia. The *raznochíntsy*[1] were an increasingly important element in the mixture, and though Stankévich and others were great landowners, the principal leader of the Westernizers was Belínsky, a plebeian, with a strong plebeian pride.

In spite of this growing plebeian element, the Moscow "circles" retained a semi-aristocratic character and maintained a close connection with the intellectual part of Moscow society. The debates on philosophical, historical, and literary subjects that were such a prominent and famous feature of intellectual Moscow in the later thirties and forties took place at the *salons* of the Elágins, of the Sverbéyevs, at the Khomyakóvs', at Chaadáyev's, at Caroline Pávlova's. It was in these *salons* that a new Russian culture was forged. Though many of the great intellectuals of the thirties and forties, partly owing to the rigors of the censorship, partly owing to a deeply embedded aristocratic dilettantism, have left few traces in literature, it has become the tradition to include at least a mention of the principal leaders of intellectual Moscow in every history of literature.

The oldest of them was Peter Yákovlevich Chaadáyev

[1] Raznochíntsy (singular raznochínets) means literally "men of various classes." They included all those who, having received an education, had ceased to be members of the lower classes but had not become nobles.

(1794?–1856), who in his early years had been a Hussar of the Guards, a Liberal, and a friend of Púshkin's. In the twenties he underwent a conversion to mystical Christianity, with a strong leaning to Rome. About 1830 he wrote his *Philosophical Letters* (in French) on the meaning of history. They contained a ruthless criticism of Russian history from the point of view of Roman Catholicism. They were not originally intended for publication, but Chaadáyev was persuaded to have them printed in Nadézhdin's *Telescope*. The first letter appeared in 1836. It passed the censorship, but when it was out, it produced the effect of a bombshell. The *Telescope* was suppressed, and Chaadáyev was officially declared a lunatic and placed under medical supervision. He continued to live in Moscow, surrounded by a halo of martyrdom and courage in the eyes of the young Westernizers, who, in spite of his Romanism, looked up to him as a leader and a patriarch. His striking figure, with his high and bald forehead, was a principal ornament of the intellectual *salons*, where to the last he waged his war of words with the nationalists. His writings, though so exiguous in extent, give him an important place in the history of Russian thought, for, whatever we think of his conclusions, he stated some of the most essential problems of Russian history and Russian civilization with unique historical grasp and ruthless courage.

The most remarkable of the Moscow journalists was Michael Petróvich Pogódin (1800–75). The son of a serf and of a self-made man, he was at the University of Moscow with the future Wisdom-lovers and became their friend. He was later made Professor of Russian History, and in his untiring researches accumulated an exceptionally valuable collection of old Russian documents. Being by birth more businesslike than his aristocratic friends, he became their publisher and the editor of their magazines, the most important of which was the *Moskvityánin* (1841–56).

Pogódin is one of the most curious and comprehensive characters of modern Russian history, a strange blend of the most contrasting characteristics: morbidly close, but disinterested in his love of Old Russia; highly cultured, but essentially retaining the mentality of a provincial merchant; naturally a coward, yet capable of such real civic courage as the remarkable memoranda that he addressed, during the Crimean War, to Nicholas I with an outspoken criticism of his whole reign. All people who knew him were more or less disgusted by him; and yet there were in him a power and a message that made that great and erratic genius Apollón Grigóriev look up to him as his only master and guide. For fifty years Pogódin was the center of literary Moscow, and his biography (in twenty-four volumes!) by N. P. Barsukóv is practically a history of Russian literary life from 1825 to 1875. But his literary work need not detain us long. As an historian he had no constructive genius. As a publicist he was handicapped by lack of sincerity and courage (except in the memoranda). Nor does his early imaginative work give him a high place as a writer, though in his tales he was one of the first swallows of national realism.

Pogódin's associate, Stepán Petróvich Shevyrëv (1806–64), Professor of Literature at the University of Moscow, was one of the most cultured and European men of his generation and a critic of great merit. His essays on Púshkin (*Moskvityánin*, 1841) are one of the most illuminating criticisms of the great poet.

THE SLAVOPHILS

Slavophilism in the strict sense was a creation of Khomyakóv and the Kiréyevskys in the thirties, but Slavophil feelings had long been alive in many Russian minds. I have spoken already of the naïve nationalism of Admiral Shishkóv. S. T. Aksákov was a living link between these older forms and the developed creed of the thirties and forties. The latter included liberal and semi-anarchistic elements, and may be perhaps best defined as conservative anarchism. The primacy of the moral and religious law, of ancestral tradition, and of the spontaneous sense of the right and just over the written laws and regulations of the state, and the primacy of the whole unreflecting reason over the lower logical and dissecting reason were the principal tenets of the Slavophils. This they found in Old Russia and in the Orthodox Church, but not in western Europe and in the Roman Church, where logical reason and formal law had from time immemorial got the upper hand of whole reason. Peter the Great and the Petersburg monarchy had abjured the national ideals and gone to the school of the godless absolutism of the West. They had enslaved and humiliated the Church, which only in its secret heart had preserved its true light and was on the surface Europeanized and secularized.

The greatest of the Slavophils was Alexéy Stepánovich Khomyakóv (1804–60), who belongs to literary history as a poet, a philosopher of history, and a theologian.

His early poetry is coldly brilliant and full of conceits. Later he abandoned this manner and made his verse the mouthpiece of his political and religious feelings. He is not a great poet, but in what is perhaps poetic eloquence rather than poetry he has few rivals in Russia. His religious poems, especially that wonderful poem *The Laborer* (1858), are (with the possible exception of some of Fëdor Glínka's) the best in the language for profound sincerity of the (unmystical) feeling and the noble simplicity of the expression. His political verse is on Slavophil themes. The best of it is inspired by indignation at Russia's unworthiness of her great historical and religious mission. The poems written during the Crimean War have a particularly high place in the anthology of Russian political verse.

Khomyakóv's great work was to be a treatise on the philosophy of history. It remained unfinished and is little more than a curious monument of constructive imagination. He is far more important as a theologian. His central idea was the idea of liberty, of the spontaneous, unforced love of man for God, and of the spontaneous acceptance of the law of God, not as law, but as freedom. In theory Khomyakóv was equally opposed to Roman Catholicism and Protestantism, but the edge of his criticism is much more often directed against the former. Like all the Slavophils, he greatly preferred the Protestant to the Catholic nations of Europe. He had a particular liking for England and the Anglicans. But the England he liked was only the traditional England of the Tories and not the progressive England of the Whigs. He recognized in the former, in its neglect of written law, in its fidelity to custom and to unwritten understanding, his favorite ideals of conservative anarchism.

Khomyakóv's theology did not receive the sanction of

the official Church, and his theological works were even not allowed to be published till 1879. But all Orthodox thinking in Russia has ever since followed his lead, and today he is practically (though not explicitly) regarded as a Doctor of the Church.

As a writer of prose Khomyakóv is remarkable for the clearness, fullness, and beautiful ease of his Russian, which is free both from the Gallicisms of the Karamzín-Púshkin school and from the untidiness and vulgarity of later nineteenth-century journalism. In non-narrative prose Khomyakóv has a place similar to Aksákov's in narrative prose.

Next to Khomyakóv the two most remarkable older Slavophils were the two brothers Kiréyevsky, Iván (1806–56) and Peter (1808–56). Their mother, remarried to a Mr. Elágin, was the hostess of one of the most famous intellectual *salons* in Moscow. Peter hardly belongs to the history of literature, for his few articles are not particularly important. But he was, as it were, a keeper of the sacred fire of the Slavophil religion. He spent much of his life wandering over Russia collecting the songs of the people.

Iván's literary career was misshapen and thwarted. His criticisms published in the late twenties marked him out as the best critic hitherto born in Russia. In 1832 he started editing a big literary review, the *European,* which was almost immediately suppressed. After this venture he ceased writing for many years. Partly under the influence of his brother and of Khomyakóv, from a follower of Schelling he became a Slavophil and an Orthodox churchman. In 1845 he took over the editorship of Pogódin's *Moskvityánin,* but failed to get on with him and retired before the end of the year. In 1852 he once more published an article in a purely Slavophil miscellany, for which the miscellany was suppressed.

Kiréyevsky was the master of a beautiful style, which, unlike Khomyakóv's, is closely akin to Karamzín's and Púshkin's. He was the first Russian intellectual layman to resume the long-lost contact with the profoundest and most alive mystical currents inside the Orthodox Church, and in this respect he is, with Khomyakóv, the fountainhead of all modern Orthodox culture.

BELÍNSKY

The movement of the Westernizers took form about 1840, when the philosophical idealists of Stankévich's circle and the socialist idealists of Herzen's circle became united in one movement, equally opposed to official Russia and to Slavophilism. They were anticlerical, and in politics liberal or socialist.

Of the two circles of the thirties, the principal leaders were Timothy Granóvsky (1813–55), a brilliant lecturer and an elegant writer, but not an original scholar; Herzen, whose work belongs mainly to a later period; and, most important of all, Belínsky.

Vissarión Grigórievich Belínsky was born in 1811, the son of a poor army doctor. In 1829 he entered the University of Moscow and there soon became intimate with Stankévich and other young idealists. After three years at the University he was dismissed and never received a degree. His education was acquired, much more than by regular study, by omnivorous reading and personal contact with fellow students. Of all foreign languages, he knew only French, and that imperfectly. German and English books he could read only in translations. For his philosophical information (the great thing in the Moscow circles of the time) he depended on his better-educated friends. On leaving the University, Belínsky engaged in journalism and soon joined Nadézhdin's *Telescope*. In 1834 he published the famous *Literary Musings*, which may be regarded as the beginning of Russian intelligentsia journalism. In it and in his subsequent articles Belínsky displayed from the outset that eminently pugnacious and enthusiastic temperament which earned him the nickname of the "furious Vissarión." His articles were inspired with a youthful irreverence for all that was old and respected in Russian letters, and an equally youthful enthusiasm for the new ideas of idealism and for the creative forces of the young generation. He rapidly became the bogy of the conservative and the leader of the young.

In 1836 the *Telescope* was suppressed, and Belínsky left without a regular job. At first he engaged in tutorial work and wrote a Russian grammar. Then for some time he was editor of *Moskóvsky nablyudátel* (*Moscow Observer*), which his friend and (then) philosophical authority Bakúnin had acquired from Pogódin. Neither Bakúnin nor Belínsky was businesslike, and the venture was a failure. At last, in 1839, Belínsky was invited by Krayévsky to be principal critic of *Otéchestvennye zapíski* (*Notes of the Fatherland*). He went to Petersburg and settled there. Though grossly underpaid and sweated by Krayévsky, he was at least saved from all danger of absolute destitution.

During his work with Nadézhdin, Belínsky had been inspired by the romantic idealism of Schelling, with its high idea of poetic and artistic creation. Afterward he was led away by Bakúnin towards the moral idealism of Fichte and thence to Hegel. He came to Petersburg full of the latter philosopher. His first articles in Krayévsky's review caused considerable consternation among his readers by their unexpectedly enthusiastic conservatism and "official nationalism." The public was not aware of the hidden logic of the critic's philosophical evolution, and that he was now living up to Hegel's famous proposition: "All that is, is rational." The proposition led Belínsky (who did not like stopping halfway) to the conclusion that the existing social and political regime was rational. This "conservative Hegelism," however, was only a transient stage in Belínsky, and by 1841 his ideas assumed their final form, historically the most important. This last change was owing partly to the influence of the way Hegel's thesis was interpreted by the "Left Hegelians"; partly to that of Herzen and his socialism; but above all it was a natural reaction of the "furious" critic's temperament, which was that of a fighter and a revolutionary. Henceforward Belínsky became the moving spirit of the progressive Westernizers and the herald of the new literature, which was to be neither classical nor romantic, but modern. That literature should be true to life and, at the same time, inspired by socially significant ideas, became his principal demand, and Gógol and George Sand its fullest incarnations. In 1846–7 Belínsky had the gratification of seeing the birth of a school of realistic literature that precisely answered to the ideals he had heralded.

In 1846 Nekrásov and Panáyev, men of Belínsky's
party and partly of his making, purchased Púshkin's
Sovreménnik from Pletněv, and Belínsky left Krayévsky
to become the critic of the *Sovreménnik*. In 1847, owing
to his failing health, he went abroad, and there, once free
from the censorship and from the inquisitiveness of the
Russian post, wrote his famous letter to Gógol on the
occasion of the latter's *Correspondence with Friends*. The
letter is full of passionate and wounded indignation at the
"lost leader" (Gógol had never really been a leader), and
is perhaps the most characteristic statement of the faith
that animated the progressive intelligentsia from 1840 to
1905. Soon after his return to Russia, Belínsky died (May
26, 1848). He had remained unmolested by the police
and suffered comparatively little from the censorship, for
he had learned the art of adapting his words to its exigencies. But had he lived a little longer, there is small
doubt that, terrorized as the government was by the events
of 1848, he would have in one way or another become a
martyr and perhaps shared the fate of Dostoyévsky.

Belínsky's historical importance can scarcely be exaggerated. Socially he marks the end of the rule of the
gentry and the advent of the *raznochíntsy* to cultural leadership. He was the first in a dynasty of journalists who exercised an unlimited influence on Russian progressive
opinion. He was the true father of the intelligentsia, the
embodiment of what remained its spirit for more than
two generations—of social idealism, of the passion for im-
proving the world, of disrespect for all tradition, and of
highly strung, disinterested enthusiasm.

There is much to be said both for and against Belínsky. It remains to his lasting credit that he was the most
genuine, the most thoroughgoing, the most consistent of
literary revolutionaries. He was inspired by a love of the
immediate future, which he foresaw with wonderful intuition. Perhaps never was a critic so genuinely in
sympathy with the true trend of his times. And, what is
more, he discerned almost unerringly what was genuine
and what meretricious among his contemporaries. His
judgments on writers who began their work between 1830
and 1848 may be accepted almost without qualification.
This is high praise for a critic, and one that few deserve.

In his judgments of the literature of the preceding age and generation, he was handicapped by party feeling, or rather by certain too definite standards of taste which, to our best understanding, were wrong. He understood only a certain kind of literary excellence (it happened to be practically the only kind practiced by men of his generation) and was blind to other kinds. He judged the writers of the eighteenth century and of the Golden Age from the point of view of his own idealistic realism. The selection he made of them imposed itself on Russian literary opinion for two thirds of a century. We have emancipated ourselves from it. But from his point of view it was admirably judicious and consistent. His judgments of foreign literature were on the whole much less happy, which is hardly astonishing considering his linguistic limitations. All said and done, he cannot be denied the name of an exceptionally sensitive and prophetic critic.

His faults, however, are also serious. First of all comes his style, which is responsible for the dreadful diffuseness and untidiness (as Sękowski's is for the disgusting vulgarity) of Russian journalese (I mean high journalese) in the second half of the nineteenth century. Certainly no writer of anything like Belínsky's importance ever wrote such an execrable lingo.

Secondly, the message of Belínsky as a critic is hardly capable of kindling any enthusiasm today. Not that the civic note he introduced in the forties was avoidable or harmful. It was necessary, and it was in tune with the times. The civic attitude to literature in the later years of Nicholas I's reign was shared by all who were of any value, and was merely an expression of civic conscience. It is his *literary* doctrine that is difficult not to quarrel with. He was not entirely responsible for it, but he was, more than anyone, effective in so widely propagating it. It was Belínsky, more than anyone else, who poisoned Russian literature by the itch for expressing ideas, which has survived so woefully long. It was he also who was instrumental in spreading all the commonplaces of romantic criticism —inspiration, sincerity, genius, and talent, contempt for work and technique, and the strange aberration of identifying imaginative literature with what he called "thinking in images." Belínsky (not as the civic, but as the romantic, critic) is largely responsible for the contempt of form and workmanship which just missed killing Russian literature in the sixties and seventies. It is, however, only fair to say that, if the most influential, Belínsky was not the only man who contributed to the infection. The weight of the sin rests on the whole generation.

6

The Age of Realism:
The Novelists (I)

THE realistic novel (a term that must be made to include shorter and less definite narrative forms as well as the full-sized novel) dominated Russian literature (roughly) from 1845 to 1905, almost to the exclusion of other forms of imaginative writing. To most foreign readers it is the most interesting thing in the whole language. It is Russia's principal contribution to *European* literature, if we take that term as denoting, not the sum total of the national literatures of Europe, but the international literature belonging in an equal degree to all European mankind.

From Aksákov and Turgénev to Chékhov, and even to Górky, Búnin, and other writers of their generation, the Russian realistic novel may and must be regarded as one literary growth, with a unity even greater than, for instance, that of the Elizabethan drama. Of course there was movement and change inside the school. Chékhov's and Búnin's work is in many ways different from Aksákov's and Goncharóv's, but, taken all in all, it answers to the same standards of taste and to the same conceptions of the function of art; while the work of Púshkin and Gógol in the earlier period, of Rémizov and Bély in later days, proceeds from different conceptions and has to be judged by different standards.

Russian realism[1] was born in the second half of the forties, more exactly in the years 1846–7. Its genealogy is mixed. In substance it is a cross between the satirical naturalism of Gógol and an older sentimental realism revived and represented in the thirties and forties chiefly by the then enormously influential George Sand. Gógol and George Sand were the father and mother of Russian realism and its accepted masters during the initial stages. Other foreign examples, especially that of Balzac, were not without their importance. The classical realism of Púshkin and Lérmontov presided over the fusion of the heterogenous elements, and *Evgény Onégin* and *A Hero of Our Times* influenced Russian realistic fiction very powerfully. Finally a factor of considerable importance in giving the Russian novel its idealistic and civic character was the evolution of the intellectual Moscow circles of the thirties and forties and the definite form their idealism took in the latter decade. Belínsky especially played a part that can hardly be exaggerated. His critical writings of 1841–5 practically foretold the whole movement. Never did a literary development so exactly answer to the expectations entertained by a leading critic.

In the preceding chapter I have analyzed the "naturalism" of Gógol and spoken of his first followers. The fully developed Russian realism is different from the school of Gógol in that while Gógol's naturalism is suited only for the representation of the baser sides of humanity in their most vulgar and grotesque aspects, the realists emancipated themselves from this one-sidedness and took possession of the whole of life, not only of its ugly aspects. The task before them was to find satisfactory realistic forms for the painting of the higher and middle levels of humanity, of mixed good and evil, of the ordinary man, considered, not as a caricature of mankind, but as a human being. Gógol himself had given hints in this direction by his sentimental treatment of vegetable life in *Old-World Landowners,* and by the "philanthropic" (as the

[1] It will be noted in the course of the following that the term "realism" is used in Russia with a different shade of meaning from what it has in English.

phrase went) attitude to the small and ridiculous man in
The Greatcoat. The "philanthropic" attitude was strengthened by George Sand (and to a less extent by Dickens),
but the main influences that emancipated Russian realism
from pure satire were Púshkin and Lérmontov. Not that
there was any "philanthropic" sentimentality in their works,
but they gave the example of an equal, level, human treatment of all humanity. The "philanthropic" attitude in its
more sentimental forms did not much survive the forties,
but its substance, a sympathetic attitude to human beings,
without distinction (not only of class but) of intrinsic
moral significance, became a principal characteristic of
Russian realism. People are not good or bad; they are only
more or less unhappy and deserving of sympathy—this
may be taken as the formula of all the Russian novelists
from Turgénev to Chékhov. This was what Europe accepted as their message to mankind when they were first
revealed to the West.

Taken as a whole, Russian realism has little in common with Gógol, its professed master. What it inherited
from him may be reduced to the following: In the first
place, it retained his great attention to detail, vivifying
and enlivening—not only the detail of outer things, but,
above all, the detail of a person's appearance and movements. In this respect the continuer of Gógol was Tolstóy,
otherwise so unlike him, who in his later work (after 1880)
was the first to react against the method of "superfluous
detail." In the second place, the realists endorsed Gógol's
taboo-lifting work—the admission to the freedom of fiction
of the vulgar, base, unprepossessing, and unedifying aspects
of life. But no further taboos were lifted by them—the
physical side of sex, as well as of disease and death, continued to be concealed, and though the rules of reticence
in Russian realistic fiction were not the same as in Victorian England, it was as reticent in substance as the
Victorian novel. A new taboo-lifting period was begun only
half a century later by Tolstóy, in his later work, and by
Górky. In the third place, the realists inherited from Gógol
his satirical attitude to the existing forms of life. This is
not quite so true of all the school as the preceding gener-
alization, but on the whole a satirical attitude towards
vegetable life and social routine pervades the Russian novel of the later nineteenth century.

Another characteristic that, though not common to all the realists, is typical of them as a school is their relative neglect of narrative construction and narrative interest, and the concentration on extra-narrative interests, on character and introspection. In this respect the Russian novel, especially Tolstóy, was far ahead of the European novel of the times and was outdone by Western novelists only in the later work of Henry James, in that of Proust and of James Joyce.

Another important and general characteristic of the Russian realistic novel is quite opposed to the example of Gógol—this is its artistic simplicity, a consistent effort to make its style as unobtrusive and as unstriking as possible. The realists avoided all fine writing. What they regarded as good prose was prose adequate to the thing described, prose that answered to the reality it spoke of, transparent prose that should not be noticed by the reader. This is the antithesis of Gógol's method, and was very largely because of the example of Púshkin and of Lérmontov, especially of the latter.

Another obligation generally recognized by the realists was the duty of choosing their subjects exclusively from contemporary or almost contemporary Russian life. This was owing not only to their honest desire to speak of nothing but what they actually knew, but also the social position of fiction in mid- and late-nineteenth-century Russia. The novelists were expected to react, sensitively and significantly, to the current life of the nation. Partly owing to the severity of the censorship for other branches of literature, fiction, from the forties onward, became an important and widely listened-to mouthpiece of social thinking, and the critics demanded that every time a novelist gave his work to the world, it should contain things worth meditating on and worth analyzing from the point of view of the social issues of the day. As a rule, the novelists took the obligation very seriously and never ignored it, at least in their more ambitious work. This "social" (*obschéstvenny*) or "civic" (*grazhdánsky*) coloring is a general characteristic of the European novel of the mid-nineteenth century, but it is nowhere more apparent than in Russia. It gives it an almost journalistic character and makes it tempting as an actual source of information on Russian social history. It has been used in that way more than once by Russian and foreign authors, but of course this is bad method. Only persons ignorant alike of the nature of imaginative literature and of that of historical evidence will attempt to use Russian fiction as a historical source unless its evidence is corroborated by extra-literary sources, in which case it becomes superfluous.

DOSTOYÉVSKY'S EARLY WORK

The first great success of the new school was Dostoyévsky's maiden novel, *Poor Folk*. In it and in the other early novels and tales of Dostoyévsky the connection of the new realism with Gógol is particularly apparent. This consideration makes it profitable to begin the survey of the individual realists with Dostoyévsky. On the other hand, Dostoyévsky's later work is so in advance of its time, so closely connected with later developments, and went home to the reading public so much later, that it is advisable, in a general history of Russian literature, to divide Dostoyévsky in two, an operation facilitated by the long break in his literary career caused by his conviction and deportation in 1849. His writings after his release from prison will be reserved for a following chapter.

Fëdor Mikháylovich Dostoyévsky was born October 30, 1821, in Moscow, where his father was a doctor at a big public hospital. The Dostoyévskys were a family of southwestern (Volynian) origin, while Dostoyévsky's mother was the daughter of a Moscow merchant; so he united Ukrainian and Muscovite blood. Very early Fëdor and his elder brother Michael (afterwards his associate in journalism) developed a passion for reading, and Dostoyévsky's cult of Púshkin dates also from very early. The brothers studied at a private school in Moscow, whence in 1837 Fëdor went to Petersburg, to the Military Engineers' School. He remained there for four years, not very deeply interested in engineering but much more in literature and reading. In 1841 he obtained a commission but continued his studies at the school for another year, after which he received a post in the engineering department. In return for his five years at school he was obliged to serve two years in the army. He did not remain in the service any longer than was obligatory but resigned his commission in 1844. Dostoyévsky was not penniless, his father having left a small fortune, but he was impractical and improvident and thus often in financial difficulties. On leaving the service he decided to devote himself to literature and in the winter of 1844–5 wrote *Poor Folk*. Grigoróvich, a beginning novelist of the new school, advised him to take the novel to Nekrásov, who was then planning the publication of a literary miscellany. On reading it Nekrásov was overwhelmed with admiration and took it to Belínsky. "A new Gógol has arisen!" he exclaimed, breaking into the critic's room. "Gógols grow like mushrooms in your imagination," Belínsky replied, but took and read the novel and was impressed with it as Nekrásov had been. A meeting was arranged between Dostoyévsky and Belínsky, and the latter poured out to the young novelist all his enthusiasm, exclaiming: "Do you yourself understand *what* you have written?" Dostoyévsky, remembering the whole business thirty years later, said that this was the happiest day of his life. *Poor Folk* appeared in January 1846 in Nekrásov's *Petersburg Miscellany*. It was rapturously reviewed by Belínsky and by other critics friendly to the new school and received with great favor by the public. Dostoyévsky did not take his success lightly—he was puffed with pride; and curious anecdotes are recorded of his overbearing vanity. His second novel, *The Double* (1846), had a much cooler reception. Dostoyévsky's relations with Belínsky and his friends began to spoil. The vanity he had shown on the occasion of his first novel was intensified by their disillusionment in his subsequent work. He was teased and ridiculed by Turgénev and he ceased to frequent their company. His works continued appearing but met with little approval. Though his friendship with the advanced literary coterie did not last, Dostoyévsky continued a radical and a Westernizer. He was a member of the socialist circle of Petrashévsky, who gathered to read Fourier, to talk of socialism, and to criticize the existing conditions. The reaction that followed the Revolution of 1848 was fatal to the Petrashevskians: in April 1849 they were arrested. Dostoyévsky was confined in the Peter and Paul Fortress for eight months while a court-martial was deciding on the fate of the "conspirators." Dostoyévsky was found guilty of "having taken part in criminal plans, of having circulated the letter of the journalist Belínsky (to Gógol) full of insolent expressions against the Orthodox Church and the Supreme Power, and of having attempted, together with others, to circulate anti-Government writings with the aid of a private press." He was sentenced to eight years' penal servitude. The sentence was commuted by the Emperor to four years, after which he was to serve as a private soldier. But instead of simply communicating the sentence to the prisoners, the authorities enacted a wantonly cruel tragicomedy: a sentence of death was read out to them, and preparations were made for shooting them. Only when the first batch of prisoners had already been tied to the posts, were the real sentences read. All the prisoners naturally took the death sentence quite seriously. One of them went mad. Dostoyévsky never forgot the day: he remembers it twice in his writings—in *The Idiot* and in *An Author's Diary for 1873*. This took place December 22, 1849. Two days later Dostoyévsky was taken off to Siberia, where he was to serve his term. For nine years he drops out of literature.

For his own sake it is convenient to regard the young Dostoyévsky as a different writer from the author of his later novels; a lesser writer, no doubt, but not a minor one, a writer with a marked originality and an important place among his contemporaries. The principal feature that distinguishes him is his particularly close connection with Gógol. Like Gógol, he concentrated on style. His is as tense and saturated as Gógol's, if not always as unerringly right. Like the other realists, he seeks, in *Poor Folk*, to transcend Gógol's purely satirical naturalism by infusing it with elements of sympathy and human emotion. But while the others sought to solve the problem by adopting a middle way between the extremes of the grotesque and of the sentimental, Dostoyévsky in a much more truly Gogolian spirit, and continuing, as it were, the tradition of *The Greatcoat*, sought to combine extreme grotesque naturalism with intense sentiment; without losing their individuality in a golden mean, the two elements are fused together. But the message of *Poor Folk* is not Gógol's. It is not disgust at the vulgarity of life, but pity, intense sympathy for the downtrodden, half-dehumanized, ridiculous, and still noble human being. *Poor Folk* is the acme of the "philanthropic" literature of the forties, and has a foretaste

of the wracking visions of pity that are such a lurid feature
of the Dostoyévsky of the great novels. It is a novel of
letters between a young girl who ends by going wrong
and her elder friend the government clerk Makár Dévush-
kin. It is long, and the concentration on style tends to
lengthen it. But it is a carefully and cleverly constructed
work of art in which all the details are made to contribute
to the complex effect of the whole.

His second story, *The Double,* is also rooted in Gógol
and still more original. It is the story, told in great detail
and in a style intensely saturated with phonetic and
rhythmical expressiveness, of a government clerk who goes
mad, obsessed by the idea that a fellow clerk has usurped
his identity. It is painful, almost intolerable reading. With
the cruelty later on marked out by Mikhaylóvsky as his
characteristic feature, Dostoyévsky dwells with convincing
power on the sufferings of the humiliated human dignity
of Mr. Golyádkin. In its own, perhaps illegitimate, kind
of cruel literature (cruel although, or rather because,
intended to be humorous) *The Double* is a perfect work of
art. Closely connected with it is the still stranger and mad-
der *Mr. Prokhárchin* (1846), the story, in places deliberately obscure and unintelligible, of the death of a
miser who had accumulated a fortune while living in abject
filth in a wretched slum.

The Landlady (1847) is unexpectedly romantic. The
dialogue is in an elevated, rhetorical style, imitative of the
diction of folk poetry and strongly reminiscent of Gógol's
Terrible Vengeance. The story is far less consistent and
perfect than the first three, but there is in it a more definite
foretaste of the later Dostoyévsky. The heroine seems to
be a foreboding of the demon-ridden women of the great
novels. But in style and composition it is derivative—
too deeply dependent on Gógol, Hoffmann, and Balzac.
Nétochka Nezvánova (1849) was planned on a vaster scale
than any one of the preceding novels. Its completion was
interrupted by Dostoyévsky's arrest and conviction. It remains a powerful and somewhat mysterious fragment, full
of that heavy and overstrung tension familiar to readers
of *The Idiot* and *The Brothers Karamázov.* The heroine,
a poor musician's stepdaughter brought up in a rich house,
is the first of those proud women of Dostoyévsky's, a
predecessor of Dúnya (*Crime and Punishment*), of Agláya

(*The Idiot*), and of Katerína Ivánovna (*The Brothers Karamázov*).

AKSÁKOV

Dostoyévsky's method of evolving a new style by the *fusion* of extremes was not followed by any of his contemporaries, who preferred to arrive at a golden mean by the avoidance of extremes. This triumph of a *middle* style is the characteristic feature of Russian realism from the forties to Chékhov. It was first achieved in the work of three writers, all of them belonging to the settled and propertied class of gentlemen and not to the rootless plebeian intelligentsia: Aksákov, Goncharóv and Turgénev.

The oldest of them was Sergéy Timoféyevich Aksákov (1791–1859). He was a man of a much older generation, older even than either Púshkin or Griboyédov, and has consequently many features to distinguish him from the strictly realistic generation. But he was born to literature through the influence (exercised to a rather unexpected result) of Gógol, and all his work belongs to the period of the realistic triumph.

Aksákov had dabbled in literature ever since boyhood. But the nationalists and conservatives, with whom he principally associated, had nothing to show him in the way of literary forms but those of French classicism; and classicism, especially in its higher *genres,* was profoundly uncongenial to the rural mind of Aksákov. In 1832 Aksákov met Gógol and recognized in him what he had failed to see in Púshkin or any other man—a purely Russian genius. Aksákov's house, a stronghold of pure Russianism in Moscow society, became the temple of the cult of Gógol, and Aksákov its high priest. Gógol's genius was in essence as profoundly uncongenial to Aksákov's as Racine's or Kheráskov's, but it was Gógol who revealed to Aksákov the possibility of a new attitude towards reality, an attitude that had not been foreseen by the classicists— the possibility of taking life as it comes, of making use of the whole material of life, without necessarily forcing it into the molds of classical form. Of course this truth might have been revealed to Aksákov in some other way besides the evidently more-than-that route of Gógol, but it so happened that it was Gógol's art that removed the film of obligatory stylization from Aksákov's eyes. His first attempt in a new, realistic manner was a short descriptive story, *The Blizzard,* printed in 1834. It is distinctly experimental and immature. Towards 1840, urged by Gógol, Aksákov began writing *A Family Chronicle,* substantial fragments of which were published anonymously in 1846 in a Slavophil miscellany. In the following years Aksákov published a series of books on sport in his native Orenbúrg country. They were enthusiastically reviewed by Turgénev, and Gógol wrote to the author: "Your birds and fishes are more alive than my men and women." When in 1856 *A Family Chronicle* (together with *Recollections*) appeared, Aksákov saw himself recognized by the most influential critics as the foremost living writer. He increased his literary output. In 1858 he published *Years of Childhood of Bagróv-Grandson,* and wrote the greater part of the contents of his collected works in his last remaining years.

The principal characteristic of Aksákov's work is its objectivity. His art is purely receptive. Even when he is introspective, as he is in the greater part of *Years of Childhood,* he is objectively introspective. He remains unmoved by any active desire except to find once again the time that has been lost—*"retrouver le temps perdu."* The Proustian phrase is not out of place, for Aksákov's sensibility is curiously and strikingly akin to that of the French novelist; only he was as sane and normal as Proust was perverse and morbid, and instead of the close and stuffy atmosphere of the never aired flat of the boulevard Haussmann, there breathes in Aksákov's books the air of the open steppe. Like Proust, Aksákov is all senses. His style is transparent. One does not notice it, for it is entirely adequate to *what* it expresses. It possesses, moreover, a beautiful Russian purity and an air of distinction and unaffected grace that gives it a fair chance of being recognized as the best, the standard, Russian prose. If it has a defect, it is the defect of its merit—a certain placidity, a certain excessive "creaminess," a lack of the thin, "daimonic," mountain air of poetry. It is of the earth earthy: the air one breathes in it is a fresh and open air, but it is the air of the lowermost atmospheric layers of a country without mountains. This is why, all said and done, it must be regarded as second in quality when compared with Lérmontov's.

The most characteristic and Aksakovian of Aksákov's books is unquestionably *Years of Childhood of Bagróv-Grandson*.[2] It is the story of a peaceful and uneventful childhood, exceptional only for the exceptional sensibility of a child encouraged by an exceptionally sympathetic education. The most memorable passages in it are perhaps those which refer to nature, for instance the wonderful account of the coming of spring in the steppe. Many readers who prefer incident to the everyday, and the exceptional to the humdrum, find *Years of Childhood* tedious. But if ordinary life, unruffled by unusual incident, is a legitimate subject of literature, Aksákov, in *Years of Childhood*, wrote a masterpiece of realistic narrative. In it he came nearer than any other Russian writer, even than Tolstóy in *War and Peace*, to a modern, evolutionary, continuous presentation of human life, as distinct from the dramatic and incidental presentation customary to the older novelists.

A Family Chronicle is less exclusively personal and more entertaining. It is fuller of incident, and, being the story of the author's grandparents and parents before his own birth, it is necessarily free from introspection. It is also strikingly and unusually objective. The story of a great pioneering serf owner is told, and the picture of the golden age of the serf owners under Catherine is drawn without wrath or love. It is so dispassionate that it could be used by socialists as a weapon to strike at the Russian gentry, and by the conservatives to defend it. Russian rural life, especially on the thinly peopled borderlands (Aksákov's grandfather had been among the first to plant a colony of Russian serfs in the Bashkirian steppe), was strongly reminiscent of mediæval, or rather even of patriarchal, conditions. The landlord had nothing above him except God, with whom he felt himself in essential understanding, and the Tsar, who sanctioned his power and had practically no way of reaching him. These conditions bred men of Biblical dimensions. Stepán Mikháylovich Bagróv is a patriarch, strong, righteous, kind, generous, fearless, but strongly conscious of his rights and with no sentimental scruples as to using them. Another aspect of a great serf-

---

[2] Here and in *A Family Chronicle* Aksákov uses fictitious names for real places and people. Bagróv and Bagróvo are Aksákov and Aksákovo. In *Recollections* the real names are used.

owner is drawn in the wicked Kuralésov, who marries
Bagróv's cousin and is ultimately brought back to the
ways of lawfulness by Bagróv. The latter part of the book
narrates the story of the wooing of Sophie Zúbova by
Aksákov's father. Here also there is a monumental, Biblical, Homeric simplicity that gives the figure of Sophie
Zúbova something like heroic proportions. Aksákov's father
is treated much less heroically—he is one of the most remarkable figures of the *ordinary* man in Russian fiction.
The whole episode is perfect from beginning to end and
is quite unique in modern literature for its tone at once
so primævally magnifying and so scrupulously objective.

The other works of Aksákov are of less universal appeal. *Recollections,* the story of his life from eight to sixteen, is interesting rather as a picture of Russian provincial
culture about 1805 than as a revelation of a great literary
temperament. The same may be said of his *Literary and
Theatrical Reminiscences,* in which he tells of his relations
with the actors and playwrights of 1810–30. They are
delightful and at times amusing, but the portraits he paints
are visual impressions left on a sensitive retina, not profound intuitions into other people's souls. The same ap-
plies to his delightful sketch of Admiral Shishkóv (who
had been an early patron of Aksákov's) but not to the
remarkable *Recollections of Gógol.* These have a place
apart. Aksákov was not as a rule a student of other people's
minds. He took people as they came, as parts of his world,
and gave them a sensual, rather than a mental, reality.
But in the case of Gógol the elusive and evasive personality of the great writer caused him such bitter disappointment and disillusionment that he was forced to make an
exceptional effort to understand the workings of the strange
man's mind, where genius and baseness were so strangely
mingled. The effort was painful but extraordinarily successful, and Aksákov's memoir is to this day our principal
approach to the problem of Gógol.

Aksákov's objectivity and impartiality are enough to
mark him off from the rest of the Russian novelists of
the mid-nineteenth century. The latter, all of them, either
were, or seemed to be, or tried to be, novelists with a
purpose; and their work may almost invariably be described
as problem stories. Two of the greatest successes of the
literary spring of 1846–7 were the two problem novels,

Whose Fault? by Herzen, and *Pólinka Sachs,* by Druzhínin. But the greatest of the problem novelists are of course Turgénev and Goncharóv.

GONCHARÓV

Iván Alexándrovich Goncharóv (1812–91), born in Sim-bírsk of a wealthy merchant family, grew up in the conditions typical of the provincial gentry. He studied at the University of Moscow at the same time as Lérmontov and Belínsky but mixed with neither. On taking his degree he entered the Civil Service, where he remained all his life, at first in the Ministry of Finance, later, when in 1856 it was decided to liberalize the censorship, as a censor. The only events of his life are his literary activities and his voyage to the Far East. His first novel, *A Common Story,* appeared in 1847 and was greeted by Belínsky as, next to *Poor Folk,* the masterpiece of the incipient realistic school. It was followed in 1849 by *The Dream of Oblómov,* which was the first germ of his most famous novel. Having casu-ally expressed the wish to go to the Far East as secretary to a mission to Japan, he was taken at his word, and only when it was too late, he realized that he was obliged to go, at the risk of appearing ridiculous. He did not enjoy the long sea voyage—he found the ocean shockingly devoid of orderliness. But he avidly absorbed every kind of new visual and human impression and kept a diary. During the voyage war broke out with England, and Goncharóv had to return to Petersburg by the exceedingly long and incon-venient way of Okhótsk, Yakútsk, and Irkútsk. He was happy to be back in his comfortable flat in Petersburg and, now it was over, to remember his heroic journey. His travel notes appeared in 1855–7 under the title of *The Frigate "Palláda."* In 1859 he completed and published *Oblómov,* begun more than ten years earlier. Its success was immense and definitely made him a national classic. He had begun working at a third novel, *The Precipice,* almost simultaneously with *Oblómov* and continued work-ing at it after the publication of the latter. It took him almost twenty years to complete it. It appeared in 1869 and met with much less success, partly owing to its lesser merits, partly owing to the hostility of the radicals, who resented the caricature he made of them in one of the characters. *The Precipice* is connected with a curious development in Goncharóv's life that borders on insanity. At an early stage of the novel's progress he had read fragments of it to Turgénev, and ever since then he was obsessed by the notion that Turgénev had stolen all the ideas contained in them, and was not only making use of them in his own work, but communicating them to all his Russian and foreign friends. Not only *Fathers and Sons*, but novels by Auerbach and Flaubert's *Éducation sentimentale* were recognized by Goncharóv as plagiarized from *The Precipice*. He ascribed his novel's lack of success to its thus having been robbed before its publication. He wrote an account of his wrongs as they appeared to him in a curious document entitled *An Uncommon Story*. This psychopathic document, published only in 1924, revealed an unexpected side of a writer who had always been regarded as the incarnation of staid respectability.

After *The Precipice* Goncharóv wrote little—some recollections of his early years; an essay on Griboyédov, which has had the good, or ill, fortune of being singled out by schoolmasters and professors of literature for special admiration; and a series of sketches on *Old Servants*, which have had the equally doubtful advantage of being used in England as texts for beginners in Russian. Goncharóv's place as a Russian classic is almost entirely based on the second of his three novels—*Oblómov*. The other two are on a distinctly inferior level. *A Common Story* is a neatly constructed *roman à thèse*, showing in an almost mathematically elegant succession of episodes the disillusionment of a young idealist in his generous, but unpractical ideals. The success of *A Common Story* rested chiefly on its thesis and was a sign of the times, which were shifting their allegiance from the generous ideals of the thirties to the positive and practical progressiveness of the reign of Alexander II. Nor is *The Precipice*, the third of Goncharóv's novels, a masterpiece. It displays all his shortcomings: an absence of imagination; an extreme subjectivity in psychological painting, and the consequent lifelessness of all the characters that are not founded on introspection; an absence of poetry and of real inspiration; and an unsurmountable *smallness* of soul. It may be said that all is unsatisfactory in *The Precipice* except the picture, based on his reminiscences of childhood, of the patriarchal, despotic, and kindly grandmamma, and of her life, at once spacious and economical, in her vast, almost rural estate in the city overhanging "the precipice" above the Volga. The ineffective hero, Ráysky, is a pale and generalized reflection of the author's self. The proud and passionate heroine, Vera, is badly drawn, and the nihilist, Mark Vólokhov, is simply flat and absurd.

Oblómov is a different business. It is a great book. The current schoolmaster and professor-of-literature view of Goncharóv is that he was a great stylist and a great *objective* painter of reality. This view is ludicrously wrong: in both cases almost the contrary is true. Goncharóv's prose is, like Aksákov's and Turgénev's, a golden mean, but while Aksákov's and Turgénev's has all the beauty of measure, Goncharóv's has all the flatness of mediocrity. It lacks both the beautiful plenitude and abundance of Aksákov's and the grace and sweetness of Turgénev's. As to his objectivity, Goncharóv was as incapable of seeing into another human being as Gógol had been. He was capable of seeing and recording external things, and he was capable of evolving out of his inner self more or less sublimated reflections. The greatest of these reflections is Oblómov. Oblómov is more than a character; he is a symbol. The fact that he is drawn with the aid of none but purely and modestly realistic methods only enhances the force of the symbolism. He obviously was, and was immediately recognized to be, the embodiment of a whole side of the Russian soul, or rather of a side of the soul of the Russian gentry—its sloth and ineffectiveness. He has a high sense of values. He is open to generous aspirations but incapable of effort or discipline. The fragment of *Oblómov* that first appeared in print— *Oblómov's Dream*—is a vast, synthetically intended picture of the life of the Russian rural gentry, the soil of vegetable comfort, easy wealth, and irresponsibility, that produced the flower of Oblómov. *Oblómov's Dream* is contained in the first part of the novel, the best known and the most frequently commented on. We are shown Oblómov in his Petersburg flat—the way he spends his day between his bed and his dressing gown. The slow and leisurely narrative is calculated to enhance the impression of being hopelessly and irremediably stuck in slimy sloth. It takes Oblómov a whole chapter to get out of bed. His spacious dressing gown, to quote Miss Harrison, dominates the whole story, as "an Ibsenian symbol of the impossibility of being well groomed, physically or mentally." Oblómov's manservant, Zakhár, is in complete harmony with his master. Then the contrast to Oblómov is introduced, the practical and energetic Stolz, characteristically represented as half German, a devotee to work and efficiency. It is here that Goncharóv's intellectual and moral insufficiency comes out: Stolz is hopelessly uninteresting and flat. Of course the whole of the author's subconscious and imaginative sympathy is with Oblómov, but Goncharóv, the bureaucrat and the littérateur, in trying to endow the hero of work, Stolz, with all he could imagine of efficient virtue, only revealed his own smallness. In the second part Oblómov is shown in a love affair that falls flat because he cannot tear himself away from the torpor of his slovenly habits, and finally disgusts the long-patient lady. Like all Goncharóv's love stories (and in spite of its autobiographical foundation), it is very inadequate, and the heroine as unconvincing as Vera in *The Precipice*. The third and fourth parts are less often quoted and read in schools, but they are unquestionably the highest achievement of Goncharóv.[3] Oblómov, yielding more and more to his slovenly indolence, which always remains poisoned by a sting of dissatisfaction, drops out of society. His landlady, an uneducated young woman, Agáfia Mikháylovna, loves him and becomes his mistress. She loves him sincerely and pathetically, but she is dominated by her people, unscrupulous rascals who exploit Oblómov's love for her to cajole and blackmail him out of all his possessions. In spite of the energetic intervention of the ever energetic and efficient Stolz, Oblómov sinks lower and lower into the ooze of his new surroundings and dies in the arms of Agáfia Mikháylovna, to her despair and to the rejoicing of her people. The atmosphere of inevitable doom gradually descending on Oblómov—the irrevertible action of the slime sucking him in—is conveyed with truly wonderful power. Russian realistic fiction is rich in stories of overpowering gloom, but none of them (with the exception of Saltykóv's great novel) excels in this respect the high

[3] In one English translation they are abridged out of all recognition.

achievement of Goncharóv in the third and fourth parts of
Oblómov.

Goncharóv, like Aksákov, and more than Turgénev,
is characteristic of the tendency of the Russian novel to
do without all narrative interest. There are no events or
happenings in *Oblómov;* there are in *The Precipice,* but
dealt with in so flat and puerile a manner that the less
said the better. There is nothing but the continuous, evolutionary unfolding of an inevitable development. This is
what Miss Harrison has called the "imperfective" tendency
of the Russian novel—the "imperfective" being that form
of the Russian verb which views the action *in the process*
of happening. The tendency dominates all Russian fiction
after the times of Lérmontov, except the plebeian novelists—Leskóv and Písemsky. But nowhere is it so all-pre-
vailing and so justified as in *Oblómov,* for here the
evolutionary determinism of the manner (which is in fact
the negation of the efficacy of human will) is in complete
harmony with the indolent and impotent determinism of
the hero.

TURGÉNEV

Iván Sergéyevich Turgénev was born on October 28, 1818,
in Orël. His father, a handsome but impoverished squire
who had served in the cavalry, was married to an heiress
older than himself. She had had a very unhappy childhood
and girlhood and adored her husband, who never loved
her. This combined with the control of a large fortune to
make of Mme Turgénev an embittered and intolerable
domestic tyrant. Though she was attached to her son, she
treated him with exasperating despotism, and with her
serfs and servants she was plainly cruel. It was in his
mother's house that the future author of *A Sportsman's
Sketches* saw serfdom in its least attractive form.

In 1833 Turgénev entered the University of Moscow,
but remained there only one year, for in 1834 his mother
moved to Petersburg and he went over to the other university. He studied under Púshkin's friend, Professor
Pletnëv, and had occasion to meet the great poet himself.
His first verses were published in Pletnëv's, formerly Púsh-

kin's, *Sovreménnik* (1838). This connection with the "literary aristocracy" is of importance: alone of all his contemporaries, Turgénev had a living link with the age of poetry. After taking his degree he went to Berlin to complete his philosophical education at the university that had been the abode and was still the temple of Hegel—the divinity of the young generation of Russian idealists. Several of them, including Stankévich and Granóvsky, Turgénev met at Berlin, and henceforward he became the friend and ally of the Westernizers. His three years at Berlin (1838–41) imbued him with a lifelong love for Western civilization and for Germany. When in 1841 he returned to Russia he at first intended to devote himself to a university career. As this did not come off, he entered the Civil Service, but there also he remained only two years, and after 1845 abandoned all pursuits except literature. His work at first was chiefly in verse, and in the midforties he was regarded, chiefly on the strength of the narrative poem *Parásha* (1843), as one of the principal hopes of the young generation in poetry.

In 1845 Turgénev fell out with his mother, who ceased to give him money, and for the following years, till her death, he had to live the life of a literary Bohemian. The reason for Mme Turgénev's displeasure was partly that she resented her son's leaving the Civil Service and becoming a scribbler of a dangerous, revolutionary kind, but especially that she strongly disapproved of his infatuation for the famous singer Pauline García (Mme Viardot). This infatuation proved to be the love of his life. Mme Viardot tolerated it and liked Turgénev's company, and so he was able most of his life to live near her. In 1847 he went abroad, following her, and returned only in 1850, at the news of his mother's dangerous illness. On her death he found himself the possessor of a large fortune.

Meanwhile Turgénev had abandoned verse for prose. In 1847 Nekrásov's *Sovreménnik* started the publication of the short stories that were to form *A Sportsman's Sketches.* They appeared in book form in 1852, and this, together with the publication, about the same time, of other stories, gave Turgénev one of the first places, if not the first, among Russian writers. *A Sportsman's Sketches* was a great social as well as literary event. On the background of the complete silence of those years of reaction, the *Sketches,* seemingly harmless if taken one by one, produced a cumulative effect of considerable power. Their consistent presentation of the serf as a being, not only human, but superior in humanity to his masters, made the book a loud protest against the system of serfdom. It is said to have produced a strong impression on the future Emperor Alexander II and caused in him the decision to do away with the system. Meanwhile the authorities were alarmed. The censor who had passed the book was ordered to leave the service. Shortly after that an obituary notice of Gógol by Turgénev, written in what seemed to the police a too enthusiastic tone, led to his arrest and banishment to his estate, where he remained eighteen months (1852–3). When he was released he came to Petersburg already in the full glory of success. For several years he was the *de facto* head of Petersburg literature, and his judgment and decisions had the force of law.

The first years of Alexander II's reign were the summer of Turgénev's popularity. No one profited more than he from the unanimity of the progressive and reforming enthusiasm that had taken hold of Russian society. He was accepted as its spokesman. In his early sketches and stories he had denounced serfdom; in *Rúdin* (1856) he paid homage to the idealism of the elder generation while exposing its inefficiency; in *A Nest of Gentlefolk* (1859) he glorified all that was noble in the old Orthodox ideals of the old gentry; in *On the Eve* (1860) he attempted to paint the heroic figure of a young girl of the new generation. Dobrolyúbov and Chernyshévsky, the leaders of advanced opinion, chose his works for the texts of their journalistic sermons. His art answered to the demands of everyone. It was civic but not "tendentious." It painted life as it was, and chose for its subjects the most burning problems of the day. It was full of truth and, at the same time, of poetry and beauty. It satisfied Left and Right. It was the mean term, the middle style for which the forties had groped in vain. It avoided in an equal measure the pitfalls of grotesque caricature and of sentimental "philanthropy." It was perfect. Turgénev was very sensitive to his success, and particularly sensitive to the praise of the young generation and of advanced opinion, whose spokesman he appeared, and aspired, to be.

The only thing he had been censured for (or rather, as everyone believed in the photographic veracity of

Turgénev's representation of Russia, it was not he, but
Russian life, that was found fault with) was that while he
had given such a beautiful succession of heroines, he had
failed to give a Russian hero; it was noticed that when he
had wanted a man of action, he had chosen a Bulgarian
(Insárov in *On the Eve*). This led the critics to surmise
that he believed a Russian hero an impossibility. Now
Turgénev decided to make up for this shortcoming and give
a real Russian man of action—a hero of the young generation. This he did in Bazárov, the nihilist hero of *Fathers
and Sons* (1862). He created him with love and admiration, but the result was unexpected. The radicals were indignant. This, they said, was a caricature and no hero. This
nihilist, with his militant materialism, with his negation of
all religious and æsthetic values and his faith in nothing
but frogs (the dissection of frogs was the mystical rite of
Darwinian naturalism and anti-spiritualism), was a caricature of the young generation drawn to please the reactionaries. The radicals raised a hue and cry against Turgénev,
who was proclaimed to have "written himself out." A little
later, it is true, a still younger and more extreme section of
radicals, in the person of the brilliant young critic Písarev,
reversed the older radicals' verdict, accepted the name of
nihilist, and recognized in Bazárov the ideal to be followed.
But this belated recognition from the extreme Left did not
console Turgénev for the profound wound inflicted on
him by the first reception given to Bazárov. He decided to
abandon Russia and Russian literature. He was abroad
when *Fathers and Sons* appeared and the campaign against
him began. He remained abroad in the shade of Mme
Viardot, at first in Baden-Baden and after 1871 in Paris,
and never returned to Russia except for short periods. His
decision to abandon literature found expression in the fragment of lyrical prose *Enough*, where he gave full play to
his pessimism and disillusionment. He did not, however,
abandon literature, and continued writing to his death. But
in by far the greater part of his later work he turned away
from contemporary Russia, so distasteful and unresponsive
to him, towards the times of his childhood, the old Russia
of before the reforms. Most of his work after 1862 is
either frankly memoirs, or fiction built out of the material
of early experience. He was loath, however, to resign himself to the fate of a writer who had outlived his times.

Twice again he attempted to tackle the problems of the day in big works of fiction. In *Smoke* (1867) he gave full vent to his bitterness against all classes of Russian society; and in *Virgin Soil* (1877) he attempted to give a picture of the revolutionary movement of the seventies. But the two novels only emphasized his growing estrangement from living Russia, the former by its impotent bitterness, the latter by its lack of information and of all sense of reality in the treatment of the powerful movement of the seventies. Gradually, however, as party feeling, at least in literature, sank, Turgénev returned into his own (the popularity of his *early* work had never diminished). The revival of "æsthetics" in the later seventies contributed to a revival of his popularity, and his last visit to Russia in 1880 was a triumphant progress.

In the meantime, especially after he settled in Paris, Turgénev became intimate with French literary circles—with Mérimée, Flaubert, and the young naturalists. His works began to be translated into French and German, and before long his fame became international. He was the first Russian author to win a European reputation. In the literary world of Paris he became an important personality. He was one of the first to discern the talent of the young Maupassant, and Henry James (who included an essay on Turgénev in a volume on *French* novelists) and other beginning writers looked up to him as to a master. When he died, Renan, with pardonable lack of information, proclaimed that it was through Turgénev that Russia, so long mute,[4] had at last become vocal. Turgénev felt much more at home among his French confreres than among his Russian equals (with most of whom, including Tolstóy, Dostoyévsky, and Nekrásov, he sooner or later quarreled), and there is a striking difference between the impressions he produced on foreigners and on Russians. Foreigners were always impressed by the grace, charm, and sincerity of his manner. With Russians he was arrogant and vain, and no amount of hero-worship could make his Russian visitors blind to these disagreeable characteristics.

Soon after his last visit to Russia Turgénev fell ill. He died on August 22, 1883, in the small commune of Bougival, on the Seine below Paris.

[4] One will remember the words of Carlyle on "mute Russia" written in 1840, three years after the death of Púshkin.

Turgénev's first attempt at prose fiction[5] was in the wake of Lérmontov, from whom he derived the romantic halo round his first Pechórin-like heroes (*Andréy Kólosov, The Duelist, Three Portraits*) and the method of the intensified anecdote (*The Jew*). In *A Sportsman's Sketches*, begun in 1847, he was to free himself from the romantic conventions of these early stories by abandoning all narrative skeleton and limiting himself to "slices of life." But even for some time after that date he remained unable in his more distinctly narrative work to hit on what was to become his true manner. Thus, for instance, *Three Meetings* (1852) is a story of pure atmosphere woven round a very slender theme, saturated in its descriptions of moonlit nights, with an excess of romantic and "poetical" poetry. *The Diary of a Superfluous Man* (1850) is reminiscent of Gógol and of the young Dostoyévsky, developing as it does the Dostoyevskian theme of humiliated human dignity and of morbid delight in humiliation, but aspiring to a Gógol-like and very un-Turgenevian verbal intensity. (The phrase "a superfluous man" had an extraordinary fortune and is still applied by literary and social historians to the type of ineffective idealist portrayed so often by Turgénev and his contemporaries.) At last *Mumú* (1854), the well-known story of the deaf serf and his favorite dog, and of how his mistress ordered it to be destroyed, is a "philanthropic" story in the tradition of *The Greatcoat* and of *Poor Folk*, where an intense sensation of pity is arrived at by methods that strike the modern reader as illegitimate, working on the nerves rather than on the imagination.

A Sportsman's Sketches, on the other hand, written in 1847–51, belongs to the highest, most lasting, and least questionable achievement of Turgénev and of Russian realism. The book describes the casual and various meetings of the narrator during his wanderings with a gun and a dog in his native district of Bólkhov and in the surrounding country. The sketches are arranged in a random order and have no narrative skeleton, containing nothing but accounts of what the narrator saw and heard. Some of them are purely descriptive, of scenery or character; others consist of conversation, addressed to the narrator or overheard. At times there is a dramatic *motive*, but the development

[5] For the poetic work of Turgénev see Chapter V; for his dramatic work, Chapter VII.

is only hinted at by the successive glimpses the narrator gets of his personages. This absolute matter-of-factness and studious avoidance of everything artificial and made-up were the most prominent characteristics of the book when it appeared—it was a new genre. The peasants are described from the outside, as seen (or overseen) by the narrator, not in their intimate, unoverlooked life. As I have said, they are drawn with obviously greater sympathy than the upper classes. The squires are represented as either vulgar, or cruel, or ineffective. In the peasants, Turgénev emphasized their humanity, their imaginativeness, their poetical and artistic giftedness, their sense of dignity, their intelligence. It was in this quiet and unobtrusive way that the book struck the readers with the injustice and ineptitude of serfdom. Now, when the issue of serfdom is a thing of the past, the *Sketches* seem once more as harmless and as innocent as a book can be, and it requires a certain degree of historical imagination to reconstruct the atmosphere in which they had the effect of a mild bombshell.

Judged as literature, the *Sketches* are frequently, if not always, above praise. In the representation of rural scenery and peasant character, Turgénev never surpassed such masterpieces as *The Singers* and *Bézhin Meadow*.[6] *The Singers* especially, even after *First Love* and *Fathers and Sons*, may claim to be his crowning achievement and the quintessence of all the most characteristic qualities of his art. It is the description of a singing-match at a village pub between the peasant Yáshka Túrok and a tradesman from Zhízdra. The story is representative of Turgénev's manner of painting his peasants; he does not one-sidedly idealize them; the impression produced by the match, with its revelation of the singers' high sense of artistic values, is qualified by the drunken orgy the artists lapse into after the match is over and the publican treats Yáshka to the fruit of his victory. *The Singers* may also be taken as giving Turgénev's prose at its highest and most characteristic. It is careful and in a sense artificial, but the impression of absolute ease and simplicity is exhaled from every word and turn of phrase. It is a carefully *selected* language, rich, but curiously avoiding words and phrases, crude or journalese, that might jar on the reader. The beauty of the land-

[6] It is interesting to note that these pieces are precisely those Henry James singles out for particular praise.

scape painting is due chiefly to the choice of exact and delicately suggestive and descriptive words. There is no ornamental imagery after the manner of Gógol, no rhetorical rhythm, no splendid cadences. But the sometime poet's and poets' disciple's hand is evident in the careful, varied, and unobtrusively perfect balance of the phrases.

The first thing Turgénev wrote after the *Sketches* and *Mumú* was *The Inn*. Like *Mumú* it turns on the unjust and callous treatment of serfs by their masters, but the sentimental, "philanthropic" element is replaced for the first time in his work by the characteristic Turgenevian atmosphere of tragic necessity. *The Inn* was followed in 1853–61 by a succession of masterpieces. They were divided by the author himself into two categories: novels and *nouvelles* (in Russian, *romány* and *póvesti*). The difference between the two forms in the case of Turgénev is not so much one of size or scope as that the novels aim at social significance and at the statement of social problems, while the *nouvelles* are pure and simple stories of emotional incident, free from civic preoccupations. Each novel includes a narrative kernel similar in subject and bulk to that of a *nouvelle,* but it is expanded into an answer to some burning problem of the day. The novels of this period are *Rúdin* (1856), *A Nest of Gentlefolk* (1859), *On the Eve* (1860), and *Fathers and Sons* (1862); the *nouvelles, Two Friends* (1854), *A Quiet Spot* (1854), *Yákov Pásynkov* (1855), *A Correspondence* (1856), *Faust* (1856), *Ásya* (1858), and *First Love* (1860). It will be noticed that the civic novels belong chiefly to the age of reform (1856–61), while the purely private *nouvelles* predominate in the reactionary years that precede it. But even "on the eve" of the Emancipation, Turgénev could be sufficiently detached from civic issues to write the perfectly uncivic *First Love*.

The novels of Turgénev are, thus, those of his stories in which he, voluntarily, submitted to the obligation of writing works of social significance. This significance is arrived at in the first place by the nature of the characters, who are made to be representative of phases successively traversed by the Russian intellectual. Rúdin is the progressive idealist of the forties; Lavrétsky, the more Slavophil idealist of the same generation; Eléna, in *On the Eve,* personifies the vaguely generous and active fermentation of the generation immediately preceding the reforms; Bazárov, the militant materialism of the generation of 1860. Secondly, the social significance is served by the insertion of numerous *conversations* between the characters on topics of current interest (Slavophilism and Westernism, the ability of the educated Russian to act, the place in life of art and science, and so on). These conversations are what especially distinguished Turgénev's novels from his *nouvelles*. They have little relation to the action, and not always much more to the character of the representative hero. They were what the civic critics seized upon for comment, but they are certainly the least permanent and most dating part of the novels. There frequently occur characters who are introduced with no other motive but to do the talking, and whom one would have rather wished away. But the central, representative characters—the heroes—are in most cases not only representative, but alive. Rúdin, the first in date, is one of the masterpieces of nineteenth-century character drawing. An eminent French novelist (who is old-fashioned enough still to prefer Turgénev to Tolstóy, Dostoyévsky, and Chékhov) has pointed out to me the wonderfully delicate mastery with which the impression produced by Rúdin on the other characters and on the reader is made gradually to change from the first appearance in the glamour of superiority to the bankruptcy of his pusillanimous breach with Natália, then to the gloomy glimpse of the undone and degenerate man, and to the redeeming flash of his heroic and ineffective death on the barricades of the faubourg St. Antoine. The French writer thought this delicate change of attitude unique in fiction. Had he known more Russian, he would have realized that Turgénev had merely been a highly intelligent and creative pupil of Púshkin's. Like Púshkin in *Evgény Onégin*, Turgénev does not analyze and dissect his heroes, as Tolstóy and Dostoyévsky would have done; he does not uncover their souls; he only conveys their atmosphere, partly by showing how they are reflected in others, partly by an exceedingly delicate and thinly woven aura of suggestive accompaniment—a method that at once betrays its origin in a *poetic* novel. Where Turgénev attempts to show us the *inner* life of his heroes by other methods, he always fails—the description of Eléna's feelings for Insárov in *On the Eve* is distinctly painful reading. Turgénev had to use all the power of self-criticism and self-restraint to avoid the pitfall of false poetry and false beauty.

Still, the characters, constructed though they are by means of suggestion, not dissection, are the vivifying principle of Turgénev's stories. Like most Russian novelists he makes character predominate over plot, and it is the characters that we remember. The population of Turgénev's novels (apart from the peasant stories) may be classified under several heads. First comes the division into the Philistines and the elect. The Philistines are the direct descendants of Gógol's characters—heroes of *póshlost,* self-satisfied inferiority. Of course there is not a trace in them of Gógol's exuberant and grotesque caricature; the irony of Turgénev is fine, delicate, unobtrusive, hardly at all aided by any obvious comical devices. On the other side are the elect, the men and women with a sense of values, superior to those of vegetable enjoyment and social position. The men, again, are very different from the women. The fair sex comes out distinctly more advantageously from the hands of Turgénev. The strong, pure, passionate, and virtuous woman, opposed to the weak, potentially generous, but ineffective and ultimately shallow man, was introduced into literature by Púshkin, and recurs again and again in the work of the realists, but nowhere more insistently than in Turgénev's. His heroines are famous all the world over and have done much to spread a high reputation of Russian womanhood. Moral force and courage are the keynote to Turgénev's heroine—the power to sacrifice all worldly considerations to passion (Natália in *Rúdin*), or all happiness to duty (Líza in *A Nest of Gentlefolk*). But what goes home to the general reader in these women is not so much the height of their moral beauty as the extraordinary *poetical* beauty woven round them by the delicate and perfect art of their begetter. Turgénev reaches his highest perfection in this, his own and unique art, in two of the shorter stories, *A Quiet Spot* and *First Love*. In the first, the purely Turgenevian, tragic, poetic, and rural atmosphere reaches its maximum of concentration, and the richness of suggestion that conditions the characters surpasses all he ever wrote. It transcends mere fiction and rises into poetry, not by the beauty of the single words and parts, but by sheer force of suggestion and saturated significance. *First*

Love stands somewhat apart from the rest of Turgénev's work. Its atmosphere is cooler and clearer, more reminiscent of the rarefied air of Lérmontov. The heroes—Zinaída and the narrator's father (who is traditionally supposed to portray the author's own father)—are more *animal* and vital than Turgénev usually allows his heroes to be. Their passions are tense and clear-cut, free from vagueness and idealistic haze, selfish, but with a selfishness that is redeemed by self-justifying vitality. Unique in the whole of his work, *First Love* is the least relaxing of Turgénev's stories. But, characteristically, the story is told from the point of view of the boy admirer of Zinaída and of his pangs of adolescent jealousy for his rival and father.

At the height of his popularity, in 1860, Turgénev wrote a famous essay on *Hamlet and Don Quixote*. He considered these characters as the two prototypes of the elect intellectual portion of mankind, which was divided into self-conscious, introspective, and consequently ineffective, Hamlets, and enthusiastic, single-minded, courageous at the risk of seeming ridiculous, Quixotes. He himself and the great majority of his heroes were Hamlets. But he had always wanted to create Quixotes, whose freedom from reflection and questioning would make them efficient, while their possession of higher values would raise them above the Philistines. In the later forties the critics, who had taken note of the consistent inefficiency of Turgénev's heroes, clamored for him to produce a more active and effective hero. This he attempted in *On the Eve*. But the attempt was a failure. He made his hero a Bulgarian patriot, Insárov. But he failed to breathe into him the spirit of life. Insárov is merely a strong, silent puppet, at times almost ludicrous. In conjunction with the stilted and vapid Eléna, Insárov makes *On the Eve* distinctly the worst of all Turgénev's mature work.

The best of the novels and ultimately the most important of Turgénev's works is *Father and Sons,* one of the greatest novels of the nineteenth century. Here Turgénev triumphantly solved two tasks that he had been attempting to solve: to create a living masculine character not based on introspection, and to overcome the contradiction between the imaginative and the social theme. *Fathers and Sons* is Turgénev's only novel where the social problem is distilled without residue into art, and leaves no bits of undigested journalism sticking out. Here the delicate and poetic narrative art of Turgénev reaches its perfection, and Bazárov is the only one of Turgénev's men who is worthy to stand by the side of his women. But nowhere perhaps does the essential debility and feminineness of his genius come out more clearly than in this, the best of his novels. Bazárov is a strong man, but he is painted with admiration and wonder by one to whom a strong man is something abnormal. Turgénev is incapable of making his hero triumph, and to spare him the inadequate treatment that would have been his lot in the case of success, he lets him die, not from any natural development of the nature of the subject, but by the blind decree of fate. For fate, blind chance, crass casualty, presides over Turgénev's universe as it does over Hardy's, but Turgénev's people submit to it with passive resignation. Even the heroic Bazárov dies as resigned as a flower in the field, with silent courage but without protest.

It would be wrong to affirm that after *Fathers and Sons* Turgénev's genius began to decline, but at any rate it ceased to grow. What was more important for his contemporaries, he lost touch with Russian life and thus ceased to count as a *contemporary* writer, though he remained a permanent classic. His attempts again to tackle the problems of the day in *Smoke* (1867) and in *Virgin Soil* (1877) only emphasized his loss of touch with the new age. *Smoke* is the worst-constructed of his novels: it contains a beautiful love story, which is interrupted and interlarded with conversations that have no relation to its characters and are just dialogued journalism on the thesis that all intellectual and educated Russia was nothing but smoke. *Virgin Soil* is a complete failure, and was immediately recognized as such. Though it contains much that is in the best manner of Turgénev (the characters of the bureaucratic-aristocratic Sipyágin family are among his best satirical drawings), the whole novel is disqualified by an entirely uninformed and necessarily false conception of what he was writing about. His presentation of the revolutionaries of the seventies is like an account of a foreign country by one who had never seen it.

But while Turgénev had lost the power of writing for the times, he had not lost the genius of creating those wonderful love stories which are his most personal contribution

to the world's literature. Pruned of its conversations,
Smoke is a beautiful *nouvelle*, comparable to the best he
wrote in the fifties, and so is *The Torrents of Spring*
(1872). Both are on the same subject: a young man loves
a pure and sweet young girl but forsakes her for a mature
and lascivious woman of thirty, who is loved by many and
for whom he is the plaything of a fleeting passion. The
characters of Irína, the older woman in *Smoke*, and of
Gemma, the Italian girl in *The Torrents of Spring*, are
among the most beautiful in the whole of his gallery. *The
Torrents of Spring* is given a retrospective setting, and in
most of the other stories of this last period the scene is set
in the old times of pre-Reform Russia. Some of these
stories are purely objective little tragedies (one of the best
is *A Lear of the Steppes*, 1870); others are non-narrative
fragments from reminiscences, partly continuing the manner and theme of *A Sportsman's Sketches*. There are also
the purely biographical reminiscences, including interesting
accounts of the author's acquaintance with Púshkin and
Belínsky and the remarkable account of *The Execution of
Troppmann* (1870), which in its fascinated objectivity is
one of the most terrible descriptions ever made of an execution.

There had always been in Turgénev a poetic or romantic vein, as opposed to the prevailing realistic atmosphere of his principal work. His attitude to nature had always been lyrical, and he had always had a lurking desire
to transcend the limits imposed on the Russian novelist by
the dogma of realism. Not only did he begin his career as
a lyrical poet and end it with his *Poems in Prose*, but even
in his most realistic and civic novels the construction and
atmosphere are mainly lyrical. *A Sportsman's Sketches* includes many purely lyrical pages of natural description,
and to the period of his highest maturity belongs that remarkable piece *A Tour in the Forest* (1857), where for
the first time Turgénev's conception of indifferent and
eternal nature opposed to transient man found expression
in a sober and simple prose that attains poetry by the simplest means of unaided suggestion. His last period begins
with the purely lyrical prose poem *Enough* and culminates
in the *Poems in Prose*. At the same time the fantastic element asserts itself. In some stories (*The Dog, Knock!
Knock! Knock!* and *The Story of Father Alexis*) it appears

only in the form of a suggestion of mysterious presences in an ordinary realistic setting. The most important of these stories is his last, *Clara Mílich* (1883), written under the influence of spiritualistic readings and musings. It is as good as most of his stories of purely human love, but the mysterious element is somewhat difficult to appreciate quite whole-heartedly today. It has all the inevitable flatness of Victorian spiritualism. In a few stories Turgénev freed himself from the conventions of realistic form and wrote such things as the purely visionary *Phantoms* (1864) and *The Song of Triumphant Love* (1881), written in the style of an Italian *novella* of the sixteenth century. There can be no greater contrast than between these and such stories of Dostoyévsky as *The Double* or *Mr. Prokhárchin*. Dostoyévsky, with the material of sordid reality, succeeds in building fabrics of weird fantasy. Turgénev, in spite of all the paraphernalia introduced, never succeeded in freeing himself from the second-rate atmosphere of the medium's consulting room. *The Song of Triumphant Love* shows up his limitation of another kind—the inadequacy of his language for treating subjects of insufficient reality. This limitation Turgénev shared with all his contemporaries (except Tolstóy and Leskóv). They did not have a sufficient feeling of words, of language as language (as Púshkin and Gógol had had), to make it serve them in unfamiliar fields. Words for them were only signs of familiar things and familiar feelings. Language had entered with them on a strictly limited engagement—it would serve only in so far as it had not to leave the everyday realities of the nineteenth century.

The same stylistic limitation is apparent in Turgénev's last and most purely lyrical work, *Poems in Prose* (1879–83). (Turgénev originally entitled them *Senilia;* the present title was given them with the author's silent approval by the editor of the *Messenger of Europe,* where they first appeared.) They are a series of short prose fragments, most of them gathered round some more or less narrative kernel. They are comparable in construction to the objectivated lyrics of the French Parnassians, who used visual symbols to express their subjective experience. Sometimes they verge on the fable and the apologue. In these "poems" is to be found the final and most hopeless expression of Turgénev's agnostic pessimism, of his awe of unresponsive nature and

necessity, and of his pitying contempt for human futility
The best of the "poems" are those where these feelings are
given an ironic garb. The more purely poetical ones have
suffered from time, and date too distinctly from about
1880—a date that can hardly add beauty to anything connected with it. The one that closes the series, *The Russian
Language,* has suffered particularly—not from time only,
but from excessive handling. It displays in a condensed
form all the weakness and ineffectiveness of Turgénev's
style when it was divorced from concrete and familiar
things. The art of eloquence had been lost.

Turgénev was the first Russian writer to charm the
Western reader. There are still retarded Victorians who
consider him the only Russian writer who is not disgusting.
But for most lovers of Russian he has been replaced by
spicier food. Turgénev was very nineteenth century, perhaps the most representative man of its latter part, whether
in Russia or west of it. He was a Victorian, a man of compromise, more Victorian than any one of his Russian contemporaries. This made him so acceptable to Europe, and
this has now made him lose so much of his reputation there.
Turgénev struck the West at first as something new, something typically Russian. But it is hardly necessary to insist
today on the fact that he is not in any sense representative
of Russia as a whole. He was representative only of his
class—the idealistically educated middle gentry, tending
already to become a non-class intelligentsia—and of his
generation, which failed to gain real touch with Russian
realities,[7] which failed to find itself a place in life and
which, ineffective in the sphere of action, produced one of
the most beautiful literary growths of the nineteenth century. In his day Turgénev was regarded as a leader of
opinion on social problems; now this seems strange and
unintelligible. Long since, the issues that he fought out
have ceased to be of any actual interest. Unlike Tolstóy or
Dostoyévsky, unlike Griboyédov, Púshkin, Lérmontov,
and Gógol, unlike Chaadáyev, Grigóriev, and Herzen—
Turgénev is no longer a teacher or even a ferment. His
work has become pure art—and perhaps it has won more
from this transformation than it has lost. It has taken a

[7] What Turgénev was in touch with were not the raw realities of
Russian life, but only their reflection in the minds of his generation
of intellectuals.

permanent place in the Russian tradition, a place that stands
above the changes of taste or the revolutions of time. We
do not seek for wisdom or guidance in it, but it is impossible to imagine a time when *The Singers, A Quiet Spot,
First Love,* or *Fathers and Sons* will cease to be among the
most cherished of joys to Russian readers.

THE SENTIMENTAL PHILANTHROPISTS

Turgénev in *A Sportsman's Sketches* was not the first of
the realists to take his subjects from peasant life. He had
been preceded by Dmítry Vasílievich Grigoróvich (1822–
99), whose stories of peasant life, *The Village* and *Antón
Goremýka,* published respectively in 1846 and 1847, were
among the principal events of those eventful two years.
They produced a strong impression on the partisans of the
new literature by a deliberate effort to paint peasant life
from the point of view of the characters themselves. But
the intention was better than the execution, and the stories
can hardly be regarded as satisfactory or intrinsically
significant. Grigoróvich has a more important place in
literary biography than in literature, for it was he who, in
1845, introduced Dostoyévsky to Nekrásov and Belínsky
and, more than forty years later, played a principal part in
the discovery of Chékhov.

After *The Village* and *A Sportsman's Sketches* the
sentimental, "philanthropic" presentation of peasant life
became one of the set subjects of the novelists of the
realistic school. Only one writer, however, made a name on
it. This was Marie Alexándrovna Márkovich, née Velínsky
(1834–1907), who wrote in both Ukranian and Russian
under the name of Márko-Vovchók. Her stories are folk
tales, with clear-cut characters, which leave no doubt as
to their moral value, and a good deal of healthy and orthodox melodrama. The peasants are all painted white; their
oppressors, the landlords, black. In spite of this somewhat
naïve monochromy the narrative merit of her stories is so
great that they quite justify her place as a classic in the
Ukrainian tradition.

PÍSEMSKY

Alexéy Feofiláktovich Písemsky (1820–81) came of a noble, but very poor family and may in many ways be regarded as a plebeian. At twenty he went to the University of Moscow, but was not infected by the metaphysical and social idealism prevalent there. A sort of skeptical common sense remained forever the foundation of his mentality, coupled with an intense Russian feeling, which took no interest in foreign things, but neither idealized Russia and the Russians nor shared the nationalist idealism of the Slavophils. After taking his degree he entered the Civil Service and, with several intervals, remained most of his life a civil servant. In 1847 he presented to the censorship his novel *Boyárshina,* but it was not passed, the censor finding too gloomy the picture it presented of Russian life. So the first novel by Písemsky to appear was *The Muff* (1850). Soon after its publication Písemsky became a member of the so-called "young editorial staff of the *Moskvityánin,*" a group of highly gifted young men (the leaders were Ostróvsky and Grigóriev). They were inspired by a love of Russia that was more democratic and less dogmatic than Slavophilism. Písemsky was attracted by their enthusiasm for originality and raciness. But his independence and distrust of all theories and ideas prevented him from identifying himself with them altogether. Their spirit is easily recognized in the populár stories he wrote in the early fifties. Throughout the fifties Písemsky continued producing masterpieces that met with increasing recognition. He attained the height of his popularity after the publication of the novel *A Thousand Souls* (1858) and the realistic tragedy *A Hard Lot* (1859). But in spite of his success he was out of tune with the times: he lacked the reforming zeal, the enthusiasm for rational progress, the faith in social theories that inspired the Russia of his day. In 1858 he rashly ventured into journalism, and when, after 1861, the atmosphere changed and violent party feeling took the place of the unanimous enthusiasm of the preceding years, Písemsky was one of the first to suffer. He conducted his review in a spirit of skepticism and of disbelief in progress and in the young generation. Some rather harmless skeptical remarks on Sunday schools (one of the pet toys of the time) were enough to provoke a storm of indignation that forced Písemsky to close his review, to retire to Moscow, and to seek readmission to the Civil Service. In 1863 he published a new novel, *Troubled Seas,* which contained a satirical presentation of the young generation. This naturally increased the hostility of the radicals. Písemsky became a profoundly embittered man. He began to loathe not only the radicals but everything around him. In particular he was moved to wrath by the orgy of unbridled money-making that was such a feature of the years following the Emancipation. His gloom was aggravated by the suicide of his son. He became a victim to hypochondria, which poisoned his last years. He courageously fought against it, forcing himself to write a certain number of hours each day, but his talent steadily declined and his popularity still more. By the time of his death he had long ceased to be regarded as a living literary force.

Písemsky is different in many ways from his contemporaries. Most of the essential features I have spoken of as common to the Russian realists are absent from his work. To begin with, he is free from all idealism, and this in two senses—he has no use for ideas and theories, and he does not take an optimistic view of mankind. In the painting of human baseness, meanness, and smallness he has no rivals and he is the true successor of Gógol. But he is infinitely more objective than either Gógol or any of the realists. He painted life as he saw it, without breaking it to any preconceived idea. The people who inhabit his stories are not subjective creations, ultimately based on the exteriorization of personal experience, like Gógol's and like those of most of the realists, but really *other* people, seen with the eyes and understood by the sense of kind. Another feature of Písemsky is the predominance in his work of outline over atmosphere. His people do not move about in a mellow autumnal haze like Turgénev's, but stand out in the fierce glare of sunlight. Closely connected with this feature is a far greater element of narrative interest than is usual in Russian fiction. Like others among the Russian realists Písemsky is gloomy rather than otherwise, but again in a different way—his gloom is not, like Turgénev's, a hopeless surrender to the mysterious forces of the universe, but a hearty and virile disgust at the vileness of the majority of mankind and at the futility in particular of the Russian educated classes. All these characteristics, together with his somewhat cynical attitude to life, make Písemsky unlike the main current of Russian realism and much more like the French naturalists. He has points in common with Balzac and is anticipatory of Zola and of Maupassant. But the Russian characteristics of Russian realism that we do not find in Písemsky are not so much typical of the Russian mind as of a very particular phase of it—the mind of the idealist of the forties. Písemsky, who kept himself uncontaminated by idealism, was in his own time regarded as much more characteristically Russian than his more cultured contemporaries. And this is true, Písemsky was in much closer touch with Russian life, in particular with the life of the uneducated middle and lower classes, than were the more genteel novelists. He was, together with Ostróvsky, and before Leskóv, the first to open that wonderful gallery of Russian characters of *non-noble* birth which is one of the greatest things in Russian literature yet to be discovered by the West. Písemsky's great narrative gift and exceptionally strong grip on reality make him one of the best Russian novelists, and if this is not sufficiently realized, it is (apart from considerations of fashion) because of his regrettable lack of culture. It was lack of culture that made Písemsky too weak to hold out against the ravages of age and permitted him to degenerate so sadly in his later work. It was lack of culture also that made him so unsatisfactory a stylist, for he had a command of language (his peasant dialogue is infinitely superior to anything before of its kind), but he was undone by his lack of respect for the individual work—which is after all the beginning and end of the craft of letters. It is chiefly for this reason that he has to be placed below Leskóv.

Písemsky's first novel, *Boyárschina* (written, 1845; published, 1858), already possessed most of his best qualities. It has even more narrative tensity than his later stories, and a substantial element of melodrama, which is absent from his maturer work but reappears in the dramas he wrote in the sixties. The painting of provincial society is powerfully scornful, and Písemsky already displays an art in which he was to excel—the art of relating with wonderfully vivid convincingness the growth and spread of scandal and calumny. Here also appears the first of these strong men of the people, the peasant squire Savély, said to be a reminiscence of the writer's father.

The Muff is free from the melodramatic and idealistic residue of *Boyárschina*. It is a distinctly unpleasant story. It has no sympathetic characters and, at the same time, no villains. All are equally mean and small; but nothing is to blame except everyone's insincerity in pretending to be something better than he really is. The story of the unhappy marriage of two equally mediocre and despicable people is told with extraordinary power, which in spite of the triviality of the souls involved rises to the level of tragedy. *The Muff* was followed by a succession of stories and by the wonderful *Sketches of Peasant Life,* which introduced an entirely new attitude to the people, poles away from the superior compassion of Grigoróvich and Turgénev. The peasant (it must be remembered that the peasants of Písemsky's native province are not agriculturists but traders and craftsmen, who make their money in the towns) is represented not as a poor creature to be sympathized with for his humanity and pitied for his sufferings, but as a strong and shrewd man, the superior, in moral strength and will power, of his social superior—a man untainted by the vulgarity of provincial gentility, unpoisoned by the weakness of emasculated feelings, who knows what he wants, can yield to his passions, and can control them. The greatest of Písemsky's popular creations is the drama *A Hard Lot,* but the *Sketches* also contain masterpieces of character drawing, vigorous narrative, and racy Russian.

A Thousand Souls (1858) was Písemsky's most ambitious work. It is the story of Kalínovich, a young man of talent and promise, whose one desire is to *parvenir,* to become somebody. He fails in literature, but he succeeds in marrying an heiress (the owner of "a thousand souls") with powerful family connections but with a doubtful past. Thanks to her connections, and especially to her lover and cousin, Prince Iván, Kalínovich reaches a degree of importance in the official world, where he feels himself independent enough to get rid of his steppingstones. He casts aside his wife. He is made a provincial governor and shows himself a fierce champion of honesty and integrity. He prosecutes the dishonest and powerful Prince Iván but, in his zeal to undo his enemy, goes beyond the limits of

legality and has to leave the service. The story is as unsweetened and ruthless in its unidealized view of mankind
as any story of Písemsky's, but its gloom and squalor are
redeemed by the person of Kalínovich's first fiancée, and
later mistress, Nástya, in her courageous womanhood one
of the most charming figures in Russian fiction.

Troubled Seas, which sealed Písemsky's quarrel with
the radicals, is not so good as *A Thousand Souls.* The first
three parts are quite on his best level, but the last three are
a scurrilous and unfair satire on the young generation, too
profoundly distorted by the personal embitterment of the
author.

The novels he wrote after that date are on a still lower
level. Though he always retained his power of narrative
development, it glided down into the cheaply melodramatic.
His characters lose their vitality, his Russian becomes intolerable journalese, and his values are hopelessly distorted
by bitterness and hypochondria.[8]

NOVELISTS OF PROVINCIAL CHARACTER

Písemsky's stories of popular life were part of a movement. Other young writers belonging to the "young staff of
the *Moskvityánin*" cultivated what we may call the literature of popular *character,* as opposed to the "philanthropic"
peasant fiction of the Westernizers. They approached the
lower and uneducated classes of Russian society not as ob-
jects of pity, but as the purest and finest expression of
Russian national originality. Except for Písemsky and
Ostróvsky none of the writers of this school are of the first
rank, and all are more or less forgotten.

After the general awakening of 1856 numerous writers
devoted themselves to the study of the various forms of
the people's life. The literature produced by the eth-
nographers takes every intermediate form between pure
fiction and pure journalistic or scientific description.

Pável Ivánovich Mélnikov (pseudonym "Andréy
Pechérsky," 1819–83) described the life of the Old Believers in the backwoods beyond the middle Vólga (opposite Nízhny-Nóvgorod). His works are not really first-class
literature and are disfigured by a meretricious pseudo-

[8] For Písemsky's dramatic work see Chapter VII.

poetical style, imitative of folklore. But the interest of the milieu described and the author's knowledge of it are so great that they make absorbingly interesting reading. The life of that stubborn and conservative community of Old Believers is strikingly unlike the life of the genteel intelligentsia. Rising on a foundation of imperfectly subdued, exuberant, and lusty heathenism, and held in check by the powerful discipline of ascetic and fanatical religion, it offers a powerfully picturesque picture.

Here is probably the best place to introduce Nadézhda Stepánovna Sokhánsky (1825–84, "Kokhanóvskaya"). Although she took the subject matter of her stories from the life of the provincial gentry, she resembles the novelists of popular character in bringing out the peculiarities and the old-fashioned originality of the class she describes, the small, uneducated squires of her native province of Khárkov. She was herself the daughter of such a squire, and her work is inspired by a love for the simple and backwater provincial life of her class of people and a devotion to the Slavophil ideals of family unity and paternal authority. Her stories of contemporary life may be regarded as a continuation of the tradition of Gógol's *Old-World Landowners*. In the use of language, racy, picturesque, and varied, she is also a more worthy disciple of the great novelist than most of her contemporaries. Better even than her stories of contemporary manners are those which revive the more spacious life of the great provincial squires of the age of Catherine. Her pictures of that life need not fear comparison with Aksákov's *Family Chronicle*. They are in a different key—more romantic—and the characters, drawn, like Aksákov's, bigger than nature, are heroic in a different way—heroes of romance rather than of epic.

7

The Age of Realism: Journalists, Poets, and Playwrights

WHEN, in 1846, Belínsky left Krayévsky's review for Nekrásov's *Sovreménnik,* his part of chief critic in the former was taken by a young man of unusual promise, Valérian Nikoláyevich Máykov (1823–47), brother of the poet Apollón Máykov. He possessed an amount of common sense, a breadth of understanding, and a sense of literary values that it would be vain to look for in any other Russian critic of the "intelligentsia" age. His early death was a real calamity: like Venevítinov before him and Pomyalóvsky after him, he was one of those who, had they been granted a longer life, might have turned the course of Russian civilization into more creative and less Chekhovian ways. Máykov was a civic critic and a socialist. But he was a *critic,* one of the small number of genuine critics in Russian literature. His criticism of Dostoyévsky's early work can even now be accepted almost without qualifications, and he was the first to give public appreciation to the poetry of Tyútchev.

After the deaths of Máykov and Belínsky the critical leadership of the Westernizing press passed to the right-wing Westernizers, the non-civic, æsthetic critics for whom art was an ultimate expression of ideas that were above the problems of today and a matter of enjoyment, not of values.

The most notable were Alexander Vasílievich Druzhínin (1824–64), already mentioned as the author of the problem novel *Pólinka Sachs,* and Pável Vasílievich Ánnenkov (1812–87). Ánnenkov was at one time Gógol's secretary and afterward became the intimate friend of Turgénev. In 1853–6 the two together and Nekrásov formed a sort of triumvirate that practically controlled Russian (at least Petersburg) literature. Ánnenkov's book on *Púshkin in the Reign of Alexander I* (1875) is a master-piece of social history, indispensable to any student of Russian civilization. Equally shrewd and suggestive are his numerous memoirs and biographical sketches of his con-temporaries. Together they form a richly suggestive picture of those crucial years in the life of the Russian intellectual mentality.

Apollón Alexándrovich Grigóriev (1822–64) was born in Moscow, in the heart of the merchants' quarter—a part of the town where the superficial veneer of interna-tional and genteel civilization was scarcely apparent, and where Russian character survived and throve in more or less unfettered forms. In due course Grigóriev went to the University, and there before long he was thoroughly soaked in the romantic and idealistic spirit of his age. Schiller, Byron, Lérmontov, and, above all, the theater—with Shakspere, and Mochálov to interpret him—became the air he breathed.

In 1847 he came in contact with a group of gifted young men whose center was Ostróvsky. They were united by a bubbling and boundless enthusiasm for Russian originality and for the Russian people. Under their action Grigóriev's early, vaguely generous romanticism took the form of a cult of the Russian character and Russian spirit. Ostróvsky, especially, produced an enormous impression by his wholeness and common sense, and at the same time by the new and purely Russian spirit of his dramatic work. Henceforward Grigóriev became the herald and prophet of Ostróvsky.

In 1850 Grigóriev persuaded Pogódin to hand over to him the editorship of the *Moskvityánin.* Grigóriev, Ostróv-sky, and their friends became known as "the young staff of the *Moskvityánin.*" The shortsighted miserliness of Pogódin gradually forced the best writers of the "young staff" to desert to the Westernizing reviews of Petersburg. In 1856, at last, the *Moskvityánin* came to an end, and Grigóriev moved to Petersburg in search of employment. But as a journalist he was unacceptable to the majority of editors, who disapproved of his enthusiastic nationalism. He fell on evil times and had to look for non-literary employment. At one time he got an excellent situation as tutor to a young aristocrat abroad, but his connection with the family ended in one of the most notorious scandals of his generally scandalous life. In 1861 he came in touch with the Dostoyévsky brothers and Strákhov and took part in their publication *Vrémya.* He found in them a kindred spirit and a sympathetic understanding, but he was too far gone to be redeemed from his irregular life. A great part of his last years was spent in a debtor's prison. In 1864, when the *Vrémya* (suppressed in 1863) was revived as the *Epoch,* Grigóriev was invited by the Dostoyévskys to be chief critic. In the few months left him Grigóriev wrote what is probably his most significant prose work, *My Literary and Moral Wanderings* and *Paradoxes of Organic Criticism.* The *Wanderings* may be described as a cultural autobiography. It is not the complete history of his soul, but the history of his experience as related to the cultural milieu that produced him and to the cultural life of the nation during his early years. Grigóriev was extraordinarily sensitive to the movement of history, and no one was more capable than he of reviving the smell and taste of a particular phase of time. The book is almost unique in kind—the only other book that in any sense approaches it is Herzen's *My Past and Thoughts,* different in tone but similar in the power of historical intuition.

As a poet he is typical of the post-Lérmontov period, when all technical effort was practically discarded and poetry relied on inspiration pure and simple. Grigóriev's narrative poems are unreadably diffuse. His best verse belongs to the days of his carousals with the "young staff." Published some years later in second-rate newspapers, it remained uncollected until Blok's edition of 1915. The best of these poems were inspired by his intimacy with the gypsy choruses. His address to his guitar and the wonderful lyric fugue beginning *Two Guitars* can rank with the most purely and beautifully inspired lyrics in the language. The latter poem, though uneven, crude, and excessively long, is certainly a wonderful flight of lyrical genius, forestalling in a certain sense Blok's famous *The Twelve*.

As a critic Grigóriev is chiefly remembered for the theory of "organic criticism," which insisted on the necessity of art and literature's being an organic growth of the national *soil* (*póchva;* hence the name of *póchvenniki* for his followers.) This *organic* quality he found in Púshkin and in his contemporary Ostróvsky, whose herald he prided himself on being. Grigóriev loved all that was Russian for being Russian, and apart from all other considerations. "Meekness" was to him the characteristic of the Russian character, as opposed to the "predatory" quality of European man. The "new word" that he hoped would be uttered by Russia was the creation of "meek types"; the first indication of it he discerned in Púshkin's Bélkin and in Lérmontov's Maxím Maxímych. He did not live to see what he might have accepted as its final expression, Dostoyévsky's *Idiot*.

But the "predatory" type incarnate in Lérmontov (and his Pechórin) and, above all, in Byron had an unconquerable fascination for Grigóriev. In fact nothing that was romantic was alien to him, and for all his love of the classical and balanced geniuses of Púshkin and Ostróvsky, his innermost sympathy went to the most exuberant of the romanticists and to the sublimest of the idealists. Byron, Victor Hugo, and Schiller were his most intimate preferences. He was also a great admirer of Carlyle, of Emerson, and of Michelet. With Michelet his affinities are particularly great. What is perhaps the most valuable part of all the critical theories of Grigóriev, his intuition of life as an organic, complex, self-conditioned unity, is strongly reminiscent of the great French historian. Of course he does not come near to Michelet as an artist of words— Grigóriev's writings are all more or less unkempt and slovenly journalism where flashes of genius and intuition are stifled by the overgrown weeds of verbosity. Only in *My Literary and Moral Wanderings* and in *Paradoxes of Organic Criticism* does he really reach something like adequate expression. The latter was written in answer to an invitation from Dostoyévsky to give a definite statement of his *Weltanschauung*. It contains these words, the quintessence of his intuition "Life is something mysterious and inexhaustible, an abyss that engulfs all finite reason, an unspannable ocean, the logical conclusion of the wisest brain—something even ironical, and at the same time full of love, procreating one world after another. . . ."

HERZEN

Alexander Ivánovich Herzen (1812–70), although an illegitimate child, grew up in every respect as the son of a rich nobleman. He received the usual, French and unpractical, education and was much less of a *déclassé* than Turgénev or Nekrásov. His lifelong friendship with N. P. Ogarëv began very early. The two boys were strongly impressed by the Decembrist Revolt and vowed themselves to the completion of the work of the defeated rebels. In the University (where Herzen was in the early thirties) the two friends became the center of a circle that concentrated on political ideas and on socialism. In 1834 the members of the circle were arrested, and Herzen was exiled to the provinces, not as a prisoner, but as a clerk in the Civil Service. In 1840 Herzen was allowed to return, and he immediately became a prominent figure. He had a decisive influence on Belínsky, and it was from the contact of the two men that Russian Westernism arose in its definite form. In literature he began making a name by a series of articles on progress and natural science (over the signature of Iskander) that were the first symptoms of the general turn of the Russian mind from romantic idealism to scientific positivism. In 1846–7 he also published several stories, including the novel *Whose Fault?* In 1847, after the death of his father, he came into a large fortune. Not without difficulty he succeeded in obtaining a foreign passport and left Russia for Paris. From Paris he sent to Nekrásov's *Sovreménnik* four remarkable *Letters from the Avenue Marigny,* which were a rather open assertion of socialist ideas in the teeth of the censorship. Soon after Herzen's arrival in Paris there broke out the February Revolution. He greeted it enthusiastically and openly, thus destroying for himself all possibility of returning to Russia. Henceforward he identified himself with the revolutionary movement of Europe. Expelled from France after the victory of Cavaignac, he went to Rome; and, after the failure of the Roman Revolution, to Switzerland, where he was naturalized a Swiss citizen; to Nice; and ultimately to England. The failure of the Revolution was a profound wound to Herzen. Under its immediate influence he wrote that series of essays and dialogues *From the Other Shore* (first published in German, as *Vom andern Ufer*) which is probably his masterpiece and his greatest claim to immortality. In 1852 Herzen settled in England and there founded the first Russian free press abroad. After the Crimean War, when the general awakening of Russia gave new hopes to Herzen, he turned his interest from European revolution to Russian reform. In 1857 he founded the *Bell* (*Kólokol*), a weekly paper that at once acquired an enormous influence and, though officially prohibited, poured into Russia in numerous copies. It was read by everyone, and not least by those in power. Its revelations of abuses and misgovernment often led to immediate official action in removing the most objectionable culprits. In the years 1857–61 the *Bell* was the principal political force in Russia. This was owing very largely to Herzen's gift of political tact: without surrendering a tittle of his extreme socialistic and federalistic theories, in practice he was ready to give his support to a reforming monarchy as long as he believed in the sincerity of its good intentions. This made it possible for him actively to influence the solution of the peasant problem. But after 1861 his influence declined. His openly pro-Polish position in 1861–3 repelled from him all that section of opinion which was not openly revolutionary, while on the other hand his theories were beginning to seem backward and his mentality antiquated to the young radicals. In 1864 he left London for Geneva, where he continued sporadically publishing numbers of the *Bell*, but with nothing like the former success. He died in 1870 in Paris and was buried in Nice.

Herzen has an equally important place in political history, in the history of ideas, and in purely literary history. A more detailed account of his political activities than I have already given in the foregoing paragraph would be out of place in a history of literature. Nor can I here give his ideas the detailed treatment they would claim in any history of Russian thought. Herzen was the pioneer in Russia of the positivist and scientific mentality of nineteenth-century Europe and of socialism. But he was deeply rooted in the romantic and aristocratic past, and though the content of his ideas was materialistic and scientific, their tone and flavor always remained romantic. The first stimulant of his thought was the French socialist Saint-Simon, and his gospel of the "emancipation of the flesh" from the traditional fetters of religion always remained one of Herzen's fundamental watchwords.

Socialism to Herzen was not so much a positive program as an incentive and a ferment that was to destroy the outworn civilization of the West and to rejuvenate the senescent tissues of European humanity. He was the first to lay the foundations of Russian agrarian socialism, which hoped to build a socialistic Russia not so much on a Europeanized proletariat as on the communistic tradition of the Russian peasant and the revolutionary initiative of an enlightened and generous minority. But he was always more political than social, and the inspiration of his thought was always liberty rather than equality. Few Russians have felt individual freedom and the rights of man as keenly as Herzen.

Herzen's socialism has a distinctly national coloring. He believed in Russia's vitality as he did not believe in that of the West, and he loved Russia with a passionate love. He hated the government of Nicholas I and the forces of reaction, but he loved not only the people, but also all that was sincere and generous in the intellectual classes; he had a warm feeling for the Slavophils, with whose Christianity he was in no sort of sympathy but from whom he derived much of his faith in the Russian people. In the West, though at one time he gave himself entirely to the European revolution, he had sympathy with the workman only, especially the French workman, in whom he saw a force that was to destroy the selfish bourgeois civilization he loathed.

What makes Herzen, however, much more than a mere teacher of revolutionary doctrines, and conciliates with him even those who are least inclined to share his aspirations, is his intellectual fairness and capacity for detachment. In spite of the extremeness of his views, he could understand his enemies and judge them by *their* standards. His historical intuition, his ability to see history in broad outline, to understand the significance of details and to *relate* them to the main lines, is marvelous. His thought is mainly historical, and the way he understood history as a spontaneous, unpredestined, incalculable force continuing the equally spontaneous and unpredestined evolution of nature makes him, like Grigóriev, akin to Bergson. He saw the "creativeness" of the process of becoming, the novelty of every future in relation to every past, and the pages he devotes to the confutation of all idea of predestination, all notion of an extrinsic *idea* guiding human history, are among the most eloquent he wrote.

As a writer Herzen lives chiefly by what he wrote between his departure from Russia and the foundation of the *Bell* (1857). His writings after that date are of much greater importance for the political than for the literary historian, and his early work written before he left Russia gives only a foretaste of the essential Herzen. His stories and his novel do not give him a place among the greater novelists, in spite of their considerable psychological interest and delicacy of observation.

But the works written during his first ten years abroad (1847–57) secure for Herzen a permanent place among the national classics. They include *Letters from France and Italy* (1847–50), *From the Other Shore* (1847–50), a series of propaganda pamphlets written in the early fifties, and *My Past and Thoughts,* an autobiography written mainly in 1852–5 but continued fragmentarily after that date and to which he was still adding in the sixties.

By far the most important of Herzen's political writings are his eight articles (three of them are in dialogue form) that compose *From the Other Shore.* The book was called forth by the failure of what Herzen had hoped would be the dawn of a revolutionary and socialist Europe. Although distinctly dated in most of the details, it still reads as one of the most significant things ever written on human history and is perhaps particularly suggestive and appropriate reading in our own days, even though we find it often impossible to endorse Herzen's reading of historical facts. Alone of all Herzen's political writings, it was not written for propaganda purposes, and the edge of its irony is directed not against the old Europe, but against the idealistic optimism of revolutionaries, who expected too much and too early and were either too soon disillusioned or held too firmly to their errors and superstitions. To destroy the *religion* of revolution and socialism, with its rhetoric and its official optimism, and to replace it by a clear and sober *will* for revolution were Herzen's aim. It is here that his intuition of life receives full expression —a hopeful and active acceptance of the "stream of history" viewed as a *creative* process, not as preordained necessity, is the keynote of the book.

His other political writings are different in being primarily propaganda and written not in the disinterested pursuit of truth for itself, but with the aim of influencing other men's actions and opinions. It is in them, however, that Herzen's eloquence comes out especially well. It is a French and romantic type of eloquence—loosely built, spacious, varied, abundantly availing itself of repetition and purely emotional effects, never losing an opportunity to make a side stroke or score a point in a parenthesis or subordinate clause. The best example of this kind of writing is his letter to Michelet, on *The Russian People and Socialism,* an eloquent assertion of the difference between the people and the state and a defense of the former from all responsibility for the crimes of the latter, in particular in relation to Poland.

The same characteristics of his style, but in an even more unfettered and spontaneous form, still more like conversation and relatively free from rhetoric, recur in his autobiography, *My Past and Thoughts.* To the majority of readers it will ever remain his principal work. Its attraction lies above all in its freedom and obvious sincerity. Not that there is no pose in it—Herzen was too French and too romantic to do without a pose. He was, in fact, a rare example of a Russian not afraid of an obvious pose. The absence of self-conscious and excessive sincerity, the superficiality, the somewhat matter-of-course theatricality of *My Past and Thoughts,* are its essential charm to the open-minded reader. Apart from the tone of the voice, there is little self in Herzen's memoirs and less introspection. The relative conventionality of his psychology makes it all the simpler and truer, for he speaks of himself in universal and accepted terms. The best part of the book from this point of view is the wonderful account of his wife's love affair with the German revolutionary poet Herwegh. Here the impression of absolute human sincerity is attained precisely because Herzen openly and sincerely speaks of the relations in terms of current fiction; and this relating the true emotions of two real people to the accepted clichés of current psychological thinking produces that impression of universal humanity which no one who reads those pages can fail to have.

But the greater part of the book is not subjective, and its most frequently memorable pages are those in which he speaks of the outer world. Herzen is a great portrait painter, an impressionist—and the impressions he left of his father and other relations, of the Moscow idealists, and of the leaders of the European revolution are unforgettably vivid. His lightness of touch, which never insists and always moves on, gives them a wonderfully convincing mobility. Not the least remarkable passages of the book are those in which he gives a wider historical background to the narrative: the first parts devoted to his life before his exile contain the broadest, truest, and most penetrating view of Russian social and cultural history in the first half of the nineteenth century. They are a great historical classic.

THE RADICAL LEADERS

The influence of Herzen as a begetter of ideas and a ferment of thought and also as a purely political journalist was very great, but he was too individual and too complex a personality to be a representative man or to become the adequate mouthpiece of a movement, and no group of Russian radicals ever adhered to him as a teacher or recognized him for a leader. The leadership of the radical intelligentsia, vacant since the death of Belínsky, was from 1856 onward exercised by a succession of truly representative men—Chernyshévsky, Dobrolyúbov, Písarev, Lavróv, and Mikhaylóvsky.

The first two had much in common. Both were the sons of comparatively prosperous and highly venerated priests. While rejecting all the traditional ideas of their homes, they retained much of the moral atmosphere they had been brought up in: they were puritans—almost ascetics—and fanatics. Herzen called them the "bilious set," and Turgénev said to Chernyshévsky on one occasion:

"You are a snake, but Dobrolyúbov is a rattlesnake." They were plebeians, uncontaminated by the artistic and æsthetic culture of the educated gentry, and they simply had no use for any non-utilitarian cultural values. To them Russian literature before their time was concentrated in Belínsky and in Gógol, interpreted as a purely social satirist. The literature of their time they regarded as a collection of texts for utilitarian sermons or as a map of contemporary life, of which the only merit lay in its handiness and accuracy. All that was traditional and romantic they rejected. Their faith was in only two gods—in Western science as the principle of progress, and in the Russian peasant as the depository of socialistic ideals. A new plebeian intelligentsia, risen from the people and imbued with scientific rationalism, was to build a new Russia in place of the corrupt land of serfdom.

The older of the two, Nikoláy Gavrílovich Chernyshévsky, (1828–89) published a doctoral thesis in 1855 on *The Æsthetic Relations of Art to Reality*, in which he contended that art, being nothing but a more or less adequate imitation of reality, is always inferior to the reality it represents. In the following years he published *Studies of the Age of Gógol*, which laid the foundation of the utilitarian, civic criticism of literature and revived the cult of Belínsky, whose name had been taboo in the years of extreme reaction. After 1857 he concentrated on economic and social questions. He became the recognized leader of the radical young generation. After 1861, dissatisfied by the Emancipation, he passed to more active revolutionary action, and round him grew up the first nucleuses of Revolutionary Socialism. They did not go further than the printing of proclamations, but in 1862 Chernyshévsky was arrested. For two years he was confined in the Fortress of Petersburg and there wrote his famous novel *What to Do?* the first and most influential of a long succession of tendentious radical novels. In the person of the hero, Rakhmétov, he represented the ideal radical, pure and strong—a populist and an ascetic. In 1864 Chernyshévsky was deported to Siberia, where he remained at first in a convict prison, then in the isolated northeastern town of Vilyúysk. In 1883 he was allowed to live in Ástrakhan, and afterward in his native Sarátov. He died in 1889.

Nikoláy Alexándrovich Dobrolyúbov (1836–61) began contributing to the *Sovreménnik* in 1856, and from
1857 to his early death was its chief critic. Like
Chernyshévsky he came to be regarded as a saint by the
radical intelligentsia. He was the most famous and influential of the critics after Belínsky: all the radical intelligentsia from 1860 to 1905 were brought up on him.
Although all his criticism is about works of imaginative
literature, it would be grossly unjust to call it literary
criticism. Dobrolyúbov had, it is true, a certain sense of
literary values, and the choice of works he consented to
use as texts for his sermons was, on the whole, happy,
but he never so much as attempted to discuss their literary
aspects. All his most famous articles—*What Is Oblómov-
ism?* (Goncharóv's *Oblómov*), *A Kingdom of Darkness*
(Ostróvsky's early plays), *A Ray of Light in the Kingdom
of Darkness* (Ostróvsky's *Thunderstorm*), *When Will
There Be Really Day?* (Turgénev's *On the Eve*)—are
criticisms of Russian life as reflected in those works. His
task was to create a democratic intelligentsia that would
be inspired by faith in progress and a desire to serve the
people and that might take the place of the romantic and
æsthetic, lazy and ineffective, educated gentry—of which he
regarded Oblómov as the true incarnation. All Old Russia
—the gentry, the merchants, the traditions of Church and
State—he hated with equal violence, and to tear the intelligentsia and the people away from everything connected
with old times was his one aim.

Dobrolyúbov died the year of the Emancipation, and
about the same time a new generation of radicals came to
the forefront, concentrating on the propaganda of materialism. Natural science became the order of the day and
the principal enemy, not so much of the government, as
of the old superstitions of idealism, art, and everything
romantic. The descent of man from apes became the first
article of the new creed, and the dissection of frogs a
symbolic rite of their religion. The new radicals called
themselves "thinking realists" but did not resent the appellation of "nihilists" given them by their enemies. Their
leader was Dmítry Ivánovich Písarev (1840–68), a squire
by birth, but thoroughly imbued with the new anti-romantic
and materialistic ideas. Like Chernyshévsky and Dobrolyúbov, he was a man of high moral character and, though

an apostle of the emancipation of the flesh, a puritan in life. In 1862 he was involved in the printing of proclamations and sentenced to four years' imprisonment in the Fortress. There it was he wrote most of his articles. After his release, in 1866, he almost ceased writing. Two years later he was drowned while bathing. Písarev was unquestionably a man of brilliant gifts. Though diffuse, like all Russian journalists, and truculent, like all those of the sixties, he was a born polemist and a past master in the art of killing his enemies. In the domain of literary criticism he rejected all art, admitting "art with a purpose" only in so far as it was immediately useful for the purposes of educating a scientific intelligentsia. His famous uncrowning of Púshkin, for all its naïveté, may still be read with pleasure. It is healthily sincere and outspoken. At any rate Písarev shows very well in it the entire wrongness of Belínsky's idealistic interpretation of the great poet.

After Písarev's death the spirit of nihilism begins to degenerate; socialism and revolution once more come to the fore. The seventies are the age of the populists (*naródniki*), the successors of Herzen and Chernyshévsky. Their most influential journalistic leaders were Lavróv and Mikhaylóvsky. Peter Lávrovich Lavróv (1823–1900) was a man of the older, pre-Reform generation. At the end of the sixties he emigrated, and after the death of Herzen he became the principal figure of the Russian political emigration. His principal work was the *Historical Letters* (1870), in which he explains all progress as the effect of the action of "critically thinking individualities." The book is a powerful assertion of the role of the individual in history and became the gospel of revolutionary action. It was made particularly wide use of to justify political terror.

Nikoláy Konstantínovich Mikhaylóvsky (1842–1904) was one of that generation of the young gentry whom it is customary to call "conscience-stricken nobles"—nobles who were dominated by a peculiar complex of social guilt: to wipe out the guilt of their serf-owning ancestors by sacrificing their lives to the people was their one aim in life. Mikhaylóvsky took no part in revolutionary or illegal propagandist activities, considering it his duty to preserve as far as possible an open tribune for the propaganda of radical views. His influence in the seventies was enormous and, together with Lavróv's, practically all-powerful among the young generation of radicals. The starting point of Mikhaylóvsky's socialism was the idea of right and justice, and its moral and idealistic tone colored the whole of Russian socialism till the advent of Marxism. Mikhaylóvsky was primarily a sociologist, and his most important work is *What is Progress?* (1873) directed against the mechanical struggle-for-life conception of the English evolutionists. In literary criticism Mikhaylóvsky was a man of strong party feeling and made his criticism quite subservient to civic ends. But he was not devoid of genuine critical insight, and his articles on Tolstóy (1873) and Dostoyévsky (1882) will ever give him a place among genuine critics. In the former he foresaw with wonderful acumen the essentially anarchistic foundation of Tolstóy's thought, which was to lead him to his later social doctrines. The latter is still one of the most forceful statements of the case against Dostoyévsky.

SLAVOPHILS AND NATIONALISTS

The Slavophil movement, started by Khomyakóv and the Kiréyevskys, was continued by men of the next generation —Yúry Samárin (1819–76) and the two Aksákovs, the sons of S. T. Aksákov, Constantine (1817–60) and Iván (1823–86).

The latter is the greatest literary name among the younger Slavophils. He carried the initial idealistic impulse of Slavophilism undiminished and undiluted into the gloomy days of Alexander III, and in a time of violent party hatred he was one of the few public men respected by his opponents. He began his literary career as a poet (*v. infra*), but it was as a political publicist that he became famous. He was exceptionally outspoken and (unlike most of the radicals) refused to learn the art of evading the censorship by circumlocution. He was always particularly courageous in insisting on the rights of free speech. The height of his influence was reached in 1876–8, when he was the mouthpiece of the general enthusiasm for the liberation of the Balkan Slavs. Next to Herzen, Aksákov is the greatest of Russian political journalists. His style is vigorous and straightforward, less rhetorical than

Herzen's. His Russian, like Khomyakóv's, retains the distinction of the preceding age without its Gallicisms. Aksákov was married to a daughter of Tyútchev, and, after his father-in-law's death, wrote the latter's *Life,* which, though it dwells chiefly on the political aspects of Tyútchev's activities, contains pages that are among the best in all Russian literary criticism.

The pure Slavophilism of the older generation, idealistic and (not so much in doctrine as in tone) aristocratic, came to an end with Iván Aksákov. Only minor men of the younger generation carried on its traditions. But new types of Slavophilism arose in the fifties and sixties. These were the democratic Slavophilism of Grigóriev and Dostoyévsky, and the biological nationalism of N. Danilévsky. Of the former I have already spoken in connection with Grigóriev and shall speak again in connection with Dostoyévsky. Besides these two great men its most eminent partisan was Nikoláy Nikoláyevich Strákhov (1828–95), the friend of Tolstóy, a philosopher and a critic of considerable eminence. The doctrine of "biological nationalism" was first voiced by Nikoláy Yákovlevich Danilévsky (1822–85), whose *Russia and Europe* (1869) is still a living influence.

The reign of Alexander II was an age not only of reform and revolution, but also of wars and of rapid military expansion. The heroes of this expansion, Generals Chernyáyev and Skóbelev, were immensely popular, particularly among the Slavophils. There grew up a sort of Slavophil doctrine of strategy and tactics that insisted on the existence of a Russian school of warfare and on the great tradition of Suvórov. The principal exponent of this was General M. I. Dragomírov (1830–1908), a man of considerable literary gifts, famous in his later years for his cutting epigrams and witticisms, and General Rostisláv Fadéyev (1824–83), the brother of "Zinaída R-va" and the uncle of Count Witte, a brilliant writer on military subjects as well as a remarkable political journalist.

The growth of the revolutionary movement and the Polish rebellion of 1863 brought into existence a new reactionary movement. Its principal mouthpiece was Michael Nikíforovich Katkóv (1818–87), next to Herzen and Iván Aksákov the most influential political journalist of his time. Never in the course of Russian history was a journalist so attentively listened to by the government or so often responsible for the government's policy. But he was in no sense a creator of ideas, and besides mere security of the State he had really no superior principles to lean against. As a writer he is distinctly inferior to Herzen and to Aksákov.

THE ECLECTIC POETS

After the death of Lérmontov it became the general con-viction that the age of poetry was over. In the fifties there was a certain revival of interest in poets and poetry. But in the sixties the school of Písarev launched a systematic campaign against all verse, and some of the most prominent poets were actually hooted into silence. With few exceptions the poets of this Silver Age lack vitality, and with hardly an exception their technique is lax and insufficiently conscious. A feature common to the poets of the period, which they do not share with the novelists, is their *eclecticism*, their submission to a compromise. They did not believe in the rights of the poetical imagination and sought to reconcile it with the modern spirit of science and positive knowledge. Only two poets remained free from this eclecticism: Fet, who had a genuinely tran-scendent poetic vision, and Nekrásov, who was truly in tune with the stream of history. But Fet was appreciated only by the extreme literary right, and Nekrásov only by the left—the middle poets met with much more universal and unquestionable approbation.

The characteristic feature of a central group of poets of the generation of the forties might be defined as their "imagism," which was partly due to the German-born theory of Belínsky that poetry was by definition "thinking in images." It was a parallel development to French Parnas-sianism and the poetry of the English Keatsians. It ex-pressed itself in a predilection for visual subjects, among which nature and classical antiquity were particularly popular.

The most famous in his own day of these "imagists," and altogether the most representative poet of the age, was Apollón Nikoláyevich Máykov (1821–97). Máykov's verse answered admirably to the taste of an age which had forgotten that poetry was the art of words. It had lost all interest in romantic feeling but did not want to go without all poetical enjoyment. It could not conceive that poetry might and ought to cease being "poetical," and so its one resource was images. Máykov was mildly "poetical" and mildly realistic; mildly tendentious, and never emotional. Images are always the principal thing in his poems. Some of them (always subject to the restriction that he had no style and no diction) are happy discoveries, like the short and very well-known poems on spring and rain. But his more realistic poems are spoiled by sentimentality, and his more "poetic" poems hopelessly inadequate—their beauty is mere mid-Victorian tinsel. Few of his more ambitious attempts are successful. The best is the delightful idyl on *Fishing* (1855), where for once he recovered the relative sense of style he had displayed in his early poems. Máykov always aspired to express ideas. His *opus magnum* was to be a large tragedy on the subject of the struggle between Imperial Rome and the early Christians. Published in final form in 1882, under the title of *Two Worlds,* it contains numerous passages that prove Máykov had a strong brain, but the verse is flat and the conception of the whole is a failure, chiefly owing to his entire lack of sympathy with early Christianity. There is reason to think that Máykov the poet did not come up to the caliber of Máykov the man. At any rate Dostoyévsky had more respect for him than for any of his contemporaries and found in him the most stimulating and responsive of correspondents.

Of the other "imagists" of the mid nineteenth century I shall mention only Nikoláy Fëdorovich Scherbína (1821–69) and Leo Alexándrovich Mey (1822–62). The former had in him the stuff of a true poet; he had something to say and a personal vision of the world. His mother was a Greek, and his vision of antiquity has something homely and intimate in it that can be explained only by racial affinity.

The "imagists" imagined themselves to be continuers of the "objective" tradition of Púshkin. But the romantic "subjective" tradition of Lérmontov also survived. The most romantic of the mid-nineteenth-century eclecticists was Yákov Petróvich Polónsky (1819–98), for sheer gift of song one of the greatest poets of his generation. He is the most typical instance of that conflict between the rights of poetry and of modern thought of which I have spoken. His poetical experience was purely romantic, but he was afraid to give himself away to it and considered it his duty to write well-meaning verse on the light of progress, on freedom of speech, and other modern subjects. But the really valuable part of his poetry is quite uncivic and quite free from the expression of ideas. He is the only Russian poet capable of evoking the delicate, forest effects of the German romanticists, and next to Lérmontov the only one who had a vision of a distant land beyond the clouds of sunset. He has also Lérmontov's power of making the most delicate and poignant poetry out of the common stuff of everyday life and words. His romanticism is very Russian, genuinely akin to the spirit of Russian folk song and folk tales. Of all Russian poets, Polónsky, in his best lyrics, is the one who is surest to captivate the English reader of Russian poetry, for he has both the qualities that the English romanticist regards as synonymic with all poetry, and a simplicity and modest, realistic grace that are peculiarly, and obviously, Russian. It is no wonder that he was a special favorite of Maurice Baring.

A. K. TOLSTÓY

The most popular, the most versatile, and ultimately the most personally significant of the eclectic poets was Count Alexéy Konstantínovich Tolstóy (1817-75), a distant cousin of the great novelist. He began his literary career in 1841 with a fantastic story (*The Vampire*) in the style of the German romanticists, but it was only by 1854 that his poetic individuality assumed a mature form and he began regularly publishing his verse. A little earlier, together with his two cousins Zhemchúzhnikov, he had begun publishing satirical, humorous, and nonsense verse and prose under the joint pseudonym of Kuzmá Prutkóv. "Kuzmá Prutkóv" flourished from 1853 to 1863. Besides two volumes of lyrical narrative verse, A. Tolstóy is the author of a historical novel, *Prince Serébryany* (1862), and a dramatic trilogy (1866–70) (*v. infra*).

Like Máykov and Polónsky, A. Tolstóy was an eclectic, but his eclecticism was the natural expression of an internal harmony and a balance of adjusted forces. A many-sided and versatile serenity firmly grounded in an ideal-istic (Platonic) philosophy is the main characteristic of his poetry. He is the least tragic, the least disharmonious of Russian poets, but his harmony is free from complacency and placidity. It is very clean and noble. From top to toe, in poetry as in life, Alexéy Tolstóy was a gentleman.

Not being a sufficiently great and original poet to transcend the limitations of his degenerate age, Tolstóy shared with his contemporaries a certain technical inef-ficiency, an occasional flabbiness and indistinction of rhythm, and an uncertainty of diction. But he had a sense of the value of words, which ultimately muddled him through into style. His command of expression ranged over a great variety of manner and subject matter. He is by far the greatest of Russian humorous and nonsense poets, and at the same time he was, in his generation, without rivals in the grand manner. There is nothing after Derzhá-vin to compare with the solemn beauty of his paraphrase of St. John Damascene's prayer for the dead, used in the requiem of the Orthodox Church. His lyrics are some-times the worse for wear and show too much banality and sentimentality, but many of them have preserved all their freshness and still produce the impression of ex-quisitely clear dewdrops. One of the chief charms is that poetical realism which seems to be an almost exclusive monopoly of the Russian nineteenth century. A charm-ing example is the one translated by Maurice Baring in the preface to *The Oxford Book of Russian Verse*.

Alexéy Tolstóy's ballads are often operatic and date too distinctly from about 1860. But in some of them his sense of language and his unique power of making use of proper names are displayed at their best. Of his longer narrative poems, *The Dragon* (1875) contains long pas-sages of grandly sonorous verse, really evocative of Dantesque majesty—as, for instance, the splendid invective of the Guelph narrator against the traitorous Ghibelline cities of Upper Italy, where the mere enumeration of the names of the Lombard cities produces an effect of thunder-ing beauty. The most original and exquisite of the longer poems is *The Portrait* (1874), a romantic, humorous poem in octaves in a style descended, through Lérmontov, from Byron's *Don Juan,* relating the love of the adolescent poet for an eighteenth-century portrait of a lady. The blend

of humor and semi-mystical romance is perfectly successful, and the feeling of ironical and wistful homesickness
for a distant land is expressed with exquisite delicacy.

The Portrait is first cousin to the purely humorous
poems of Alexéy Tolstóy, of which *The Dream of Councilor Popóv* is likewise in octaves. It is the purest glory of
Russian humorous poetry—a mixture of keen and pointed
satire (aimed at the popularity-seeking minister Valúyev
and at the Secret Police) with sheer delight in preposterous
fun. It is today probably the least questionable of Tolstóy's
claims to immortality. Another delightful humorous poem
is the *Mutiny in the Vatican,* where a risqué subject (the
revolt of the papal *castrati*) is treated with delightful
ambiguity and playfulness.

But the most famous of Alexéy Tolstóy's humorous
creations is Kuzmá Prutkóv, which he shares with the
two Zhemchúzhnikovs. Kuzmá Prutkóv is a sort of Russian
Prudhomme. He is a clerk in the Ministry of Finance (a
side hit at the poet Benedíktov) and the incarnation of
self-centered and arrogantly naïve complacency. The
character of Prutkóv is chiefly given in his biography and
in his proudly platitudinous fables. But he is also made
the pretext for witty parodies of contemporary poets, while
his father and grandfather are made to contribute plays
and anecdotes that are a mixture of excellent parody of
old styles with sheer absurdity and nonsense. Kuzmá
Prutkóv became the founder of a whole school of nonsense
poetry. Its most eminent members in the later nineteenth
century were Vladímir Soloviëv and his friend, the gifted
dilettante designer, Count Fëdor L. Sollogúb.

FET

Afanásy Afanásievich Fet (1820–92) was the son of a
squire named Shenshín and a German lady, whose marriage, contracted abroad, was invalid in Russia. It was
not until 1876 that he was authorized by an imperial decree
to assume the name of Shenshín. He retained his former
name in literature until his death.

In 1840 Fet published, at his own expense, a first
volume of very immature verse, which contains hardly any

promise of a future poet. But already in 1842 he published in the *Moskvityánin* some of his most lasting and perfect lyrics. On leaving the University he entered the military service and for fifteen years served in various cavalry regiments, firmly intent on obtaining the grade that gave nobility. His ill luck was such that during his service this grade was twice raised, and only in 1856, on being promoted to Captain of the Guards, could he leave the service with the satisfaction of being at last a Russian noble. After a short journey abroad he married (very practically and unsentimentally) and settled down on a small estate to make a fortune. Meanwhile his poems had made him a reputation, and in the later fifties he was one of the most prominent figures in the literary world. He contracted lasting friendships with Turgénev and Tolstóy, who appreciated his common sense and did not dislike his extreme reserve. It is from Fet that we know the details of the famous quarrel of the two great novelists. It was he also who afterward brought them together once more. Meanwhile the young generation of anti-æsthetic radicals, provoked by the overtly uncivic character of his poetry and by his notoriously reactionary sympathies, started a systematic campaign against him. They eventually succeeded in hooting him into silence; after the publication in 1863 of a third edition of his poems Fet disappeared from the printed page for twenty years. His poetic genius continued maturing during these years of apparent silence. In 1883 at last he once more appeared before the public and from that date onward published a succession of small volumes under the title of *Evening Lights*. He was never prolific as a poet, and he gave his spare time to vast enterprises of a more mechanical nature: he wrote three volumes of memoirs and translated his favorite Roman poets and his favorite philosopher, Schopenhauer.

Fet is a typical example of a poet with a double life. In his student years he was, like all his contemporaries, expansive and naïvely open to generous and ideal feelings, but later on he disciplined himself into a guarded reserve that had all the appearance (and a good deal of the substance) of callousness. Hence that strange inadequacy which struck his contemporaries between the staid and ordered life of his old age and the saturated passionateness of his late lyrics, built of the complete and disinterested *poetic* exploitation of repressed and sublimated emotions. The self of real life is present in some of his odes, in some second-rate epigrams, and above all in his remarkable, unusually reticent, and yet fascinating memoirs.

In poetry Fet was first and foremost the uncompromising champion of the rights of pure poetry. He was no eclecticist, but entirely devoted himself to the true expression of his poetic experience, which was in sympathy with many of his best contemporaries but was much against the grain of the leaders of critical opinion.

His early verse includes purely "imagist" poems of classical subjects, which are better than Máykov's or Scherbína's but would not be sufficient to single out Fet as the greatest "art-for-art" poet of his age. The real early Fet is contained in the wonderful nature lyrics and "melodies," the art of which he seems to have learned from no one. They have much in common with Verlaine, except that Fet's robust pantheism is very unlike the morbid sensibility of the French poet. Such poems, deliberately excluding all but the music of emotion and associations, do not strike us today as very exceptional. But to the mid-nineteenth-century Russian critics (*not* to a creative artist, like Turgénev, Tolstóy, or Nekrásov, all of whom were fervent admirers of Fet) they seemed little better than downright moonshine.

After 1863, and especially in the eighties, Fet became more metaphysical. He more frequently tackled philosophical subjects and brooded on the eternal problems of artistic perception and expression. His syntax becomes more difficult and condensed, at times obscure, sometimes not unlike that of the sonnets of Shakspere. The highest summits of Fet's later poetry are reached in his love poems, certainly the most extraordinary and concentratedly passionate love poems ever written by a man of seventy (not excepting Goethe). In them Fet's method of utilizing nothing but his repressed emotions for his poetry wins its most brilliant victories. They have a saturation that makes them look as if they were the quintessence of a life of passion, and they are among the most precious diamonds of our poetry.

REALISTIC POETS

All the preceding poets were bracketed by their contemporaries as the party of "pure art" or "art for art's sake." This was not quite correct, as almost all of them used their verse to grind some ax or other. But they were united by a common traditional conception of poetical beauty, a beauty of subject matter, that was above and apart from current life. They were contrasted to the civic poets, who were the conscious mouthpieces of contemporary political and social feeling, and who, like the novelists, used the material of contemporary life for their poetry. The strength of the traditional conception of poetry as a thing unrelated to life may be gauged by the fact that while in the novel no subject matter was made use of that was not directly taken from contemporary Russian life, only a minority of the poets had the courage to introduce into their verse details of Russian reality. Poetry for the majority continued to be romantically conceived as a land of escape.

Civic poetry, in the hands of its more significant representatives, did become realistic, but the rank and file of civic bards were often as eclectic as, and more conventional than, the "pure art" poets. Such, for instance, is the flat and tiresome poetry of the very amiable and respectable A. N. Pleschéyev (1825–93), a member of the Petrashévsky circle. Most of the civic poets were radicals of some kind or other, but one of the first and best was the Slavophil Iván Aksákov, whose publicistic poems written in the forties and fifties, in which he calls the Russian intellectual to work and discipline, and inveighs against his Oblómov-and-Rúdin ineffectiveness and sloth, are admirable for their unadorned and straightforward strength. His narrative, realistic poem *The Tramp* (1852) was the first Russian *poem* of peasant life and in many ways forestalls Nekrásov. There is much in common with Iván Aksákov's in the poetry of Alexéy Mikháylovich Zhemchúzhnikov (1821–1908), a first cousin of Alexéy Tolstóy's, and a co-creator with him of "Kuzmá Prutkóv." His serious poetry belongs chiefly to his old age and is inspired by indignation at the abandonment by the generation of the eighties of the high ideals of the age of reform.

Somewhat less civic and more eclectic is the poetry of Iván Sávvich Nikítin (1824–61), whose principal claim to attention lies in his realistic poems of the life of the poor. He was inclined sometimes to idealize and sentimentalize them, but his best things are free from this sin. There is an almost epic calm in the long, uneventful, and powerful *Night Rest of the Drivers,* and an unsweetened realism in such poems of tragic misery as *The Tailor.* In *Kulák,* his *opus magnum,* Nikítin introduced into poetry the methods of realistic prose. He succeeds in evoking pity and terror by the simple account of sordid and trivial misery. But he was not strong enough to create a really new art or a really new attitude to poetry. And Russian poetical and civic realism would have to be regarded as a rather second-rate growth were it not for the great name of Nekrásov.

NEKRÁSOV

Nikoláy Alexéyevich Nekrásov (1821–78) published his first volume of verse in 1840. It contained very little promise and was severely criticized by Belínsky. Unsupported by his father, a rude hunting squire and a brutal bully, Nekrásov had to give up his studies at the University of Petersburg and engage in literary and theatrical hack work and in publishing enterprises, where he gave proof of considerable business ability. By 1845 he stood on his own legs and had become virtually the principal publisher of the young literary school. A series of literary miscellanies published by him had a considerable financial success. One of them was the famous *Peterbúrgsky sbórnik,* which contained Dostoyévsky's *Poor Folk* and the first mature poems of Nekrásov himself. He became an intimate friend of Belínsky, who was as enthusiastic about his new verse as he had been severe to the 1840 volume. In 1847 Nekrásov acquired from Pletnëv what had been Púshkin's *Sovreménnik,* and, from the valetudinarian antique that it had become in the hands of the remnants of the "aristocracy," it became a splendidly paying concern and the best and most living literary review in Russia. It weathered the bad times of reaction and in 1856 became the rallying ground of the extreme left. It was suppressed in 1866 dur-

ing the official panic that followed on the first attempt
on Alexander II's life. But two years later Nekrásov, together with Saltykóv, took over the *Otéchestvennye zapíski*
and remained the publisher and editor of that principal
radical review until his death. Nekrásov was an editor of
genius: his ability to get the best literature and to find
the right man to write on current subjects was marvelous.
As a publisher, however, he was a businessman, unscrupulous, some said, and, all agreed, harsh and grasping. Nor
was his personal life up to the standards of radical puri-
tanism. He gambled heavily and regularly. He spent much
money on his table and on his mistresses. He was not
free from snobbery and liked the company of his social
superiors. All this, in the opinion of many contemporaries,
was not in harmony with the "philanthropic" and democratic character of his poetry. But what especially served
against him was his cowardly behavior on the eve of the
suppression of the *Sovreménnik*, when, to save himself and
his review, he composed and recited in public a poem in
praise of the dictator Count Muraviëv, the most ruthless
and determined of reactionaries. But, though Turgénev,
Herzen, and most of his contemporaries hated Nekrásov,
the radicals who had to work with him admired and loved
him unreservedly and pardoned as venial his private and
even his public sins. His funeral was one of the most striking demonstrations of popularity ever accorded to a Russian
writer.

In spite of his enormous popularity among the radicals, in spite of the tribute given to him as a poet by
enemies like Grigóriev and Dostoyévsky, Nekrásov can
hardly be said to have had his due during his lifetime.
Even his admirers admired the matter of his poetry rather
than its manner, and many of them believed that Nekrásov
was a great poet only because matter mattered more than
form, and in spite of his having written inartistically. To
the æsthetes he was frankly unpalatable. According to
Turgénev, "Poetry never so much as spent a night in his
verse." Perhaps Grigóriev, with his profound intuition of
values, was alone capable of really gauging the greatness of
Nekrásov. After Nekrásov's death his poetry continued to
be judged along party lines, rejected en bloc by the right
wing and praised in spite of its inadequate form by the
left. Only in relatively recent times has he come into his

own, and his great originality and newness been fully appreciated. This has been owing, first of all, to our increased ability to understand "non-poetic" poetry. It is
also owing to the displacement of Nekrásov the legendary
radical saint (which he most certainly was not, in the
sense in which Belínsky, Chernyshévsky, Dobrolyúbov,
Gleb Uspénsky were) by a better-known and more real
Nekrásov, a complex, not always edifying, but profoundly
human and original, personality.

So different in most respects from his contemporaries,
Nekrásov shared with them a lack of conscious craftsmanship and of artistic culture. He only dimly and subcon-
sciously knew what he was after, and, though an excellent
critic of other people's verse, he had no judgment of his
own. He wasted much of his creative energy on ungrateful
subjects that were not really congenial to him. He had a
dangerous verse-writing facility that he had developed during his years of hack work in writing vaudevilles and
rhymed *feuilletons*. He was essentially a rebel against all
the stock in trade of "poetic" poetry, and the essence of his
best work is precisely the bold creation of a new poetry unfettered by traditional standards of taste. But his own
creative taste was not always unerring, and though he
came very near creating a new and self-justified style
(especially in his great satiric poem *Who Is Happy?*), he
never obtained a secure command of it. But the inspiration,
the sheer poetic energy of many of even his most questionable poems, is so great that one has to accept the occasional
bathos as an ingredient of the whole. For originality and
for energy Nekrásov holds one of the very first places
among Russian poets and need not fear a comparison with
Derzhávin.

The main subject of Nekrásov's poetry was, in his own
phrase, "the sufferings of the people." But his inspiration is
subjective and individual rather than social. Except in
those of his poems in which he approaches nearest to the
spirit of folk song and thus frees himself from the all too
personal, his poetry is always personal, never group poetry.
The social wrongs of contemporary Russia are for Nekrásov not so much an objective fact as a torturing subjective
experience. One can speak of a "social compassion" complex in Nekrásov. It is precisely compassion (suffering with
the other), not pity (condescending to the other's suffering),

that animates the poetry of Nekrásov. For all the political seriousness and sincerity of Nekrásov's democratic feelings, psychologically speaking, "the sufferings of the people" were to him an emanation, a symbol of his own sufferings— from poverty, from illness, from gloom, from the pangs of conscience. He had an unusual power of idealization, and the need to create gods was the most profound of his needs. The Russian people was the principal of these gods; next to it stood the equally idealized and subjectively conditioned myths of his mother and of Belínsky. His idealized conception of the people of course tended towards sentimentality, and he did not always avoid this pitfall, but at his (frequent) best all suspicion of sentimentality is purged by the red heat of his poetic energy and poetic sincerity. Questions of taste and good form are supremely idle and irrelevant in the presence of such elemental creative processes as produced, for instance, the realistic myth poem of *Frost the Red-Nosed*. But Nekrásov's people were not only an object of compassion and worship. He could sympathize with their humor and their laughter as well as their sufferings, and of all Russian poets of the nineteenth century, he was the only one who was genuinely and creatively akin to the spirit of popular songs; he did not imitate it—he simply had in him the soul of a popular singer.

All Nekrásov's work may be divided into two sections: that in which he uses forms conditioned (though often only negatively conditioned) by the preceding development of literary poetry, and that in which he worked in a spirit of folk song. It may be generally said that in the former he is subjective; in the latter, objective and impersonal. The two aspects of Nekrásov are very different, but it is the combination of the two that makes his unique personality. On the whole the traditionally literary part of his work is much the more uneven of the two. Its lower strata merge in the absolutely inartistic and mechanical verse-mongery in which he engaged in the early forties and which he never abandoned. Much of that which was particularly highly praised by his contemporaries for its civic and humanistic contents today seems rather a negative item in the legacy of Nekrásov. On the other hand, his ironic and satirical poems probably find more response in us than they did in our fathers and grandfathers. The biting and bilious, tersely concentrated sarcasm of such a condensed masterpiece as

The Thief is enough to place Nekrásov in the front rank of the world's greatest satirists. And in most cases his poems of rhetorical invective have won from the action of time more than the lesser Nekrásov has lost. Personally I think that such a poem as the elegy *Home* is one of the highest pinnacles of Russian poetry, and leaves most of the poetical invective of Lérmontov simply nowhere. Another group of Nekrásov's poems that have won by the lapse of time are his love lyrics—remarkably original in their unsweetened, unsentimental, poignantly passionate, and tragic accounts of a love that brings more pain than joy to both parties. Lastly, among his very earliest poems (1846) there is that veritably immortal poem which so many people (Grigóriev, among others, and Rózanov) have felt and experienced as something more than poetry, that poem of tragic love on the brink of starvation and moral degradation which begins: "Whether I am driving in the night down a dark street" (*"Édu li nóchiu po úlitse tëmnoy"*). The same intensity is often present in the poems written during his last illness (*Last Songs*).

Of his objective and narrative poems, *Sásha* (1856), which he was accused of plagiarizing from Turgénev's *Rúdin*, is an attempt at a problem story in verse and, though it contains some beautiful passages, compares very poorly with the novels of Turgénev. Much more interesting are the numerous chiefly short and dramatic narrative poems of peasant life. Among the most famous is *Vlas* (1854), one of those poems in which Nekrásov gave proof of his sympathy, not only with the people's sufferings, but also with their religious ideals. The most ambitious of his poems not in folk-song style is the majestic and statuesque *Frost the Red-Nosed* (1863), with its almost mythological idealization of the Russian peasant woman and the grand pictures of the silent and frozen forest.

In his folk-song poetry Nekrásov transcends his *moi haïssable*, frees himself from his torturing obsessions of suffering, and becomes the poet of more than individual expression. This is already noticeable in the poems for children, especially in the delightful *General Toptýgin* (where a performing bear is taken by a terrorized postmaster for an angry general). But it is especially apparent in the most singing of all Nekrásov's poems, *The Pedlars* (1861) a story ultimately of tragic content but told in a lusty and vigorous major key. The opening of the poem in particular has been appropriated by the people as a folk song. It is perhaps the most genuinely popular snatch of song in the whole range of Russian literary poetry. A very different note is struck in the same poem by the weirdly effective *Song of the Wanderer,* one of the most powerful and purely original ever written by Nekrásov. It is one of those poems which are human because (in Synge's phrase, so often applicable to Nekrásov) they are brutal.

Nekrásov's greatest achievement in the folk-song style, and perhaps his greatest achievement altogether, is the vast, realistic satire *Who Is Happy in Russia?* at which he worked in the seventies. The poem relates how seven peasants, to settle the question as to who lives happily in Russia, set out on foot to walk the round of the country. They meet representatives of various classes of society, the Squire, the Parson, the Peasant Woman, and so on. They are told tales of extraordinary moral achievements, heroism, and crime, and the poem ends on a note of joyful confidence in the future of the people with the help of the new democratic intelligentsia. The style is full of originality, wonderfully racy and vigorous. The poet never lets himself fall into his usual subjective lamentations, but conducts the story in a tone of keen and often good-humored, shrewd satire, in a popular style, with frequent scenes of strong and simple realism, and occasionally a heroic note when speaking of the virtues of the strong Russian peasant. Full of remarkable verbal expressiveness, vigor, and inventiveness, the poem is one of the most original productions of nineteenth-century Russian poetry.

THE UTTER DECLINE OF POETRY

From 1860 to the end of the seventies there appeared no new poet of even tolerable mediocrity. Both parties—the civic poets and the partisans of "pure art"—were equally poor. The latter, it is true, produced in Constantine Sluchévsky (1837–1904) a poet of real significance. But after a short first appearance in 1857–60, he, like Fet, disappeared from the scene for almost twenty years, not to reappear before the end of the seventies. He had a genuinely original vision of the world, the foundation of real genius, and he seemed the man to create a really new, really modern poetry, but his ill luck in falling on times of exceptionally low technical culture never allowed him to develop into anything better than a stammerer.

The only other poet of the period worth mentioning is Dmítry Nikoláyevich Sadóvnikov (1843–83), a native of Simbírsk, who attempted to create a sort of local Volga poetry, of which the most famous example is the well-known, but now anonymous (for no one remembers the authorship) ballad of *Sténka Rázin and the Persian Princess*.

In the absence of original poetry there developed in the sixties and seventies an enormous translating activity. Very severe to native poets, the extreme anti-æstheticians retained a degree of reverence for certain foreign reputations, especially for those which were in some way or other connected with revolution—Byron, Béranger, and Heine. Byron retained much of his old reputation—and was given lip service even by Písarev. And it is hardly an exaggeration to say that Béranger and Heine, in translation, were more popular with the wide mass of the intelligentsia than any Russian poet.

THE DRAMA

Realism had a simpler and more unilinear development on the Russian stage than it had in the Russian novel. Its history may be summed up in a few representative names in a way the parallel periods of fiction cannot. Its three phases are dominated, the first (roughly 1830–50) by a great actor, the second (1850–95) by a great playwright, the third by a great producer. They are respectively Schépkin, Ostróvsky, and Stanislávsky. Schépkin was the pioneer of realistic acting. But his roots were deep in the classical tradition of universal human truths, and the realism he sought was not that of the particular, but of general human nature. His art was an art of psychological, not of social, types. The second phase of Russian scenic realism concentrated on social realism, on the least universal, and most individual, aspects of a given social milieu. It became "ethnographical" realism—or, to use the technical

Russian term, the realism of *byt,* which means life considered in its local and temporal aspects.

This phase found its complete expression in the plays of Ostróvsky and in the acting of Prov Sadóvsky (1818–72), the personal friend of the dramatist. The first representation of a play by Ostróvsky (1853) inaugurated the new theatrical era, which lasted for half a century.

Ostróvsky gives his name and impress to the period. Like the contemporary novel, the drama in his hands tended to become a selected arrangement of slices of life, with the minimum of adaptation to scenic demands. The same tendency is apparent in the dramatic work of Turgénev, who at the beginning of his career hesitated for some time between devoting himself to drama and devoting himself to fiction. With the exception of Písemsky, Turgénev, of all the novelists, is the most important as a playwright.[1] His plays belong to the years 1843–52. They are largely experimental gropings after an adequate personal form of expression. The most stageable is the *Provincial Lady,* a delicately characterized light comedy (1851). The most interesting historically is *A Month in the Country* (1850), a psychological play on the time-honored theme of the rivalry in love between a mature woman and a young girl, which in style and construction (absence of apparent action and complexity of inner psychological and atmospheric pattern) has an obvious foretaste of Chékhov.

OSTRÓVSKY

Alexander Nikoláyevich Ostróvsky (1823–86) was born in Moscow, on the south side of the river, in the center of the merchant residential quarter. His father was a government clerk and afterward a sort of lawyer whose practice was among the merchants of the South Side. The dramatist went to the University, but in 1843, after a row with the University authorities, left and entered the government service as a clerk of the Commercial Court. The eight years he spent at the court were an important addition to

[1] Of the other great novelists, Saltykóv wrote the comedy *The Death of Pazúkhin,* which was staged by Stanislávsky in 1914. Most of Tolstóy's plays belong to the period after 1880.

his early experiences at home in the Moscow merchant community and served him well in his later knowledge of its *byt*. His first work was published in 1847. This was a fragment of a comedy, *The Bankrupt*, which was completed in 1849. The first of his plays to be produced on the stage were *Stick to Your Station* and *The Poor Bride*, in 1853. After that, and till his death, no year passed without a new, original play of his appearing on the stage of the imperial theaters. The height of his popularity was reached simultaneously with that of Turgénev, Goncharóv, and Písemsky in the years 1856–60. After the latter date Ostróvsky's popularity, though it did not decline, came to a standstill, and critics and public began to insist on the superiority of his earlier to his new plays.

Between 1847 and 1886 Ostróvsky wrote about forty plays in prose[2] besides eight in blank verse. They are of unequal merit, but taken as a whole, doubtless the most remarkable body of dramatic work in Russian. Griboyédov and Gógol had written great and original plays, and each of them is a man of greater genius than Ostróvsky, but it was left to Ostróvsky to create a school of Russian drama, a Russian theater that may be put by the side of the national theaters of the West, if not on equal, at least on comparable terms. The limitations of Ostróvsky's art are obvious. His plays (with few exceptions) are neither tragedies nor comedies, but belong to the middle and bastard kind of drama. The dramatic skeleton in most of them, sacrificed to the exigencies of the slice-of-life method, lacks the firm consistency of classical art. With few exceptions his plays are devoid of poetry, and even where poetry is present, as it is in *The Thunderstorm*, it is a poetry of atmosphere, not of words and texture. Though an admirable master of individualized and typical dialogue, Ostróvsky is not a master of language in the sense Gógol, Leskóv, or (to use an English instance) Synge was. His language is purely representational; he uses it truthfully, but uncreatively. His very raciness of the Russian soil is in a certain sense a limitation, for his plays are always narrowly native and do not have universal significance. Were it not for this limitation, and had he been universal in his nationality, Ostróvsky's place would have been among the greatest. The breadth, the

[2] Among other things, he translated *The Taming of the Shrew* and the interludes of Cervantes.

grasp, the variety of Ostróvsky's vision of Russian life are almost infinite. He is the least subjective of Russian writers. His would be a hopeless case for the psychoanalyst. His characters are not in any sense emanations of himself. They are genuine reflections of "the other." He is no psychologist; his characters are not, as Tolstóy's are, inner worlds to which we are introduced by a supreme power of intuition; they are just people as seen by other people. But this superficial realism is not the external, pictorial realism of Gógol and Goncharóv, but a truly dramatic realism, for it gives the characters in their relations to the other characters, which is the simplest and oldest way of narrative and dramatic characterization by speech and action, enriched only by an enormous wealth of social, ethnographic detail. And in spite of this superficiality, they have the individuality and the uniqueness we recognize in our fellow creatures, even without getting inside their skull.

These general remarks on the art of Ostróvsky refer chiefly to his early and most characteristic work, up to about 1861. The subject matter of these plays is taken for the most part from the life of Moscow and provincial merchants and of the lower strata of the official world. The vast and varied picture of the conservative and un-Europeanized life of the Russian merchants was what struck his contemporaries most strongly in the work of Ostróvsky, for the reality underlying literary creation interested them more than the art that transformed it. The critics of the fifties spilled endless ink over the elucidation of Ostróvsky's attitude towards the conservative mainstays of the merchant class. He himself gave disconcertingly abundant food for such discussions and for every kind of interpretation, for his artistic sympathy is distributed in different ways in different plays. Every interpretation, from the most enthusiastic idealization of stolid conservatism and patriarchal despotism to the fierce denunciation of the merchants as an unredeemed kingdom of darkness, could find a peg to hang on in the text of the plays. As for Ostróvsky's own attitude, it was simply unstable, or, to be more exact, the moral and social attitude was a secondary thing to him. His task was to build plays out of the elements of reality as he saw it. An attitude of sympathy or antipathy was to him entirely a matter of dramatic expediency, of pure technique, for, though an "anti-artificial" realist, he felt very keenly the inner laws along which, and not along those of life, he had to construct each play. So his moral judgment over the tyrannical merchant paterfamilias depended on his dramatic function in the particular play. Apart from this it is extraordinarily difficult to extract a social and political *Weltanschauung* out of Ostróvsky.

Technically speaking, the most interesting of all Ostróvsky's plays are the first two, *The Bankrupt* (written 1847–9, published in 1850 under the title *Among Friends One Always Comes to Terms*) and *The Poor Bride* (published 1852, acted 1853). The former was as striking and sensational a beginning for a young author as there is on record in Russian literary history. Gógol in *Marriage* had given an example of a characteristic painting of the merchant milieu. In particular the character of the professional matchmaker practicing among the merchants was already abundantly exploited. In the inclusion of none but unsympathetic characters Ostróvsky also followed the example of Gógol in *Revizór*. But here he went one better and discarded the most time-honored of all traditions of comedy—the poetic justice that punishes vice. The triumph of vice, and precisely of the most unredeemed of all the characters, gives Ostróvsky's play its particular note of bold originality. It was this which incensed even such an old realist as Schépkin, who thought the play cynical and dirty. The realism of Ostróvsky, in spite of the obvious influence of Gógol, is in substance of an opposite nature to Gógol's. It is free from all expressiveness for the sake of expressiveness; it keeps clear of caricature and farce; it is based on a solid, intimate, first-hand knowledge of the life described. The dialogue aims at truthfulness to life, not at verbal richness. The art of using realistic speech without producing the effect of grotesqueness and without obtruding it is a characteristic art of the Russian realists, but it reaches its perfection in Ostróvsky. Finally the untheatrical construction is entirely un-Gogolian, and in the deliberate discarding of all tricks and contrivances at scenic effect Ostróvsky from the outset attains his best. The mainstay of the play is the characters, and the plot is entirely a result of the characters. But the characters are taken in their social aspect. They are not men and women in general, but Moscow merchants and assistants, and cannot be torn away from the social setting.

The Poor Bride is entirely different in tone and atmosphere from The Bankrupt. The milieu is not merchants but minor officials. The unpleasantness of it is redeemed by the character of the heroine, a strong girl, in no way inferior to and more actively alive than the heroines of Turgénev. She ends characteristically, after being let down by her romantic, ideal admirer, in submitting to her fate and marrying the successful brute Benevolénsky, who can alone save her mother from imminent ruin. All the characters are masterpieces, and Ostróvsky's skill at building the action entirely on the characters is at its best. But what is especially remarkable is the last act—a bold technical novelty. The play ends on a mass scene, where the crowd discusses the marriage of Benevolénsky and where a wonderfully new note is introduced by the appearance in the crowd of his former mistress. The delicacy and pregnancy of these last scenes, in which the heroes hardly appear, were really a new word in dramatic art. Ostróvsky's power of creating atmospheric poetry is revealed for the first time in this fifth act of The Poor Bride. In Poverty Is No Crime (1854) Ostróvsky went still further in detheatricalizing the theater, but with less intrinsic success. The immediate success of the play was great, owing to the original and Slavophil character of the noble drunkard, the ruined merchant Lyubím Tortsóv, who has remained one of the most popular roles in the Russian repertory. But as a play it is much less satisfactory, and the "sliciness" of the technique inclines to mere looseness.

Of the plays written in 1856–61, The Ward (1859) attains to almost intolerable power in the painting of a character that often reappears in his later work—the selfish, rich, and self-righteous old woman. The three short comedies united by the character of the silly and conceited young clerk Balzamínov (1858–61) are his masterpieces in the comic vein for the characters of Balzamínov and of his mother, fondly doting and yet fully conscious of her son's extreme silliness, and for the saturated painting of their social environment. In another comedy of the same period Your Drink—My Hangover (V chuzhóm pirú pokhmélie, 1856), Ostróvsky concentrated into the character of the merchant Kit Kítych all the essence of the samodúr—the willful domestic tyrant who is decided to make everyone do "what my left toe wishes," but who is easily bulliable.

By far the most significant work of this period, and
ultimately the masterpiece of Ostróvsky, is *The Thunderstorm* (1860). It is the most famous of his plays and has
been most abundantly written about. Dobrolyúbov took it
as the text for one of his most effective and influential
sermons against the dark forces of conservatism and tradition, and Grigóriev saw in it the highest expression of
Ostróvsky's love for the traditional life and character of the
undefiled Russian middle classes. In reality it is a purely
poetical work, a purely atmospheric creation, a great poem
of love and death, of freedom and thralldom. It is intensely
local and Russian, and the saturation of the atmosphere
with the very essence of Russian *byt* and Russian poetical
feeling makes it hardly understandable to a foreigner. For
every detail of it is intensified by the background of a
whole emotional tradition (expressed perhaps best of all in
the lyrical songs of the Russian people), and without this
background it loses most of its appeal. *The Thunderstorm*
is a rare example of a supreme masterpiece built of exclusively national material.

After 1861 Ostróvsky sought new ways. He devoted
himself at one time to historical plays (*v. infra*), and in his
prose plays he departed from much of his original novelty.
He almost abandoned the merchant milieu, which under
the influence of the Reforms and of the spread of education
was rapidly transforming into a drabber middle class, and
he more and more submitted to the traditional method of
playmaking, never, however, condescending to use the
mere artificial and improbable tricks of the French school.
Owing to his example, Russia, unlike most other countries,
succeeded in keeping clear from the all-pervading school of
Scribe and Sardou. Still there is more intrigue and plot
in most of his later than in his early plays, and though the
critics as a rule disapproved of them, some later plays of
Ostróvsky (*Enough Simplicity in Every Wise Man*, 1868;
The Forest, 1871; *Wolves and Sheep*, 1875) proved even
greater favorites with the public than his more characteristic early masterpieces. The first two are distinctly among
his best work, and *The Forest* shares with *The Thunderstorm* the honor of being regarded as his masterpiece. Less
exclusively original, the comedy is extraordinarily rich in
its character drawing. Of all Ostróvsky's plays, it is the one
in which the essential nobility of man is most triumphantly

asserted. But it also contains the most unsweetened types of cynical and complacent meanness and selfishness in the whole of Russian literature.

Ostróvsky never stood still, but always sought for new ways and methods. In his later plays (*The Dowerless Girl*, 1879) he attempted a more psychological method of character-drawing. But on the whole his later plays mark a certain drying-up of his creative sources. At the time of his death he dominated the Russian stage by the mass of his work. But the successors he left were minor and uncreative men, who were capable only of writing plays with "grateful parts" for the excellent actors and actresses brought up in the school of Schépkin and of Ostróvsky, but not of carrying on a vital tradition of literary drama.

SUKHOVÓ-KOBÝLIN, PÍSEMSKY, AND MINOR DRAMATISTS

The only two contemporary dramatists who come at all near to Ostróvsky, if not for the quantity, at least for the quality of their work, were Sukhovó-Kobýlin and Písemsky, both of whom are more traditional, more "artificial," and more theatrical than he.

Alexander Vasílievich Sukhovó-Kobýlin (1817–1903) was a typical educated nobleman of his generation, soaked in Hegel and in German idealism. He considered metaphysics his true vocation, and playwriting was only a short episode in his life. The wonderful thing is that neither his metaphysical bent nor the unprofessionality of his playwriting has left any impress on his plays. They are curiously free from ideas, and as for sheer stagecraft they have no rivals in Russian literary drama. The one important event in Sukhovó-Kobýlin's life was the murder of his mistress in 1850. He was suspected of being guilty of the crime, and for seven years he was under trial (at one time in prison); only in 1857 was he finally acquitted. The episode, which brought him face to face with the horror and ineptitude of the pre-Reform law courts, left a profound trace in him and filled him with that bitter hatred for all the official class which informs his two later plays. All his work consists of only three comedies: *The Wedding of Krechínsky* (acted 1855), *The Affair*, and *The Death of Tarélkin*. The latter two appeared in print in 1869, but were prohibited for the stage till much later. *The Wedding of Krechínsky* is a pure comedy of picaresque intrigue in which the rogue triumphs over the stupidity of the virtuous characters. The critics found it lacking in ideas and too dependent in plot, too French in style. But the public made it a tremendous success, and it became one of the favorite and securest plays of the Russian repertory. For general familiarity with the text it rivals *Góre ot umá* and *Revizór*.

The Affair and *The Death of Tarélkin* are very different in tone. They are satires that, in the author's own phrase, are calculated, not to make the audience laugh, but shudder. The savage bitterness of the satire is such that by their side Saltykóv seems harmless. They were too much even for the radicals of the sixties. Sukhovó-Kobýlin used in them methods of grotesque exaggeration and improbable caricature in the way Gógol had used them, but much more fearlessly and savagely—methods that were profoundly alien to the spirit of Russian realism. *The Death of Tarélkin* is a thing unique in its way, combining, as it were, the wisely calculated cruelty of Ben Jonson with the passionately serious rage of Swift.

Písemsky began his dramatic career with comedies (*The Hypochondriac*, 1852), in which he abundantly availed himself of the Gogolian tradition of farce and obvious incongruity. But his greatest achievement was in realistic tragedy. This genre is represented in Russian literature by practically only two plays—Písemsky's *A Hard Lot* (1859) and Tolstóy's *Power of Darkness*. For all the intensity and power of the latter, an unprejudiced critical judgment can hardly fail to conclude that, if the two are equal in human and tragic significance, Písemsky's is the greater play, the completer artistic success. It has the tensity and inevitability of the classical drama, and while *Power of Darkness* is best of all defined as a morality play, *A Hard Lot* is a genuine tragedy with that supreme logical unity which is the great characteristic of the plays of Racine. The subject, like those of Racine, is simple, almost geometrical. A squire, a weakling of the Hamlet, idealist type, has seduced, in the absence of her husband, the wife of one of his serfs. The husband is a strong character of the type that occurs in Písemsky's and Leskóv's popular stories. Though a serf, he is a prosperous tradesman and has made money in Petersburg. He returns home (this is the initial situation) and by degrees discovers the guilt of his wife and reacts accordingly. The squire is the master of the husband, while the husband is the master of his wife— so it is a conflict between, on the one hand, the squire's rights as a serf-owner and the dignity of his serf; on the other, between the rights of free love (an essential point is that the squire and the serf's wife do love each other) and the rights of the master of the house over his wife. The double conflict is unfolded with supreme mastery, and the spectator's sympathy is held in balance between the rights of human dignity and the rights of free love. The tragedy ends in the husband's killing the lovers' child and then (a trait particularly praised by Russian critics but suggested to Písemsky by the actor Martýnov) delivering himself into the hand of the law.

Písemsky's later plays do not come up to the high standard of *A Hard Lot*. They consist of two cycles—a series of historical melodramas of the eighteenth century and a series of dramas satirizing the money-making frenzy of the sixties and seventies. The former are tantalizing and strange creations. Their dramatic manner is terse, almost sketchy. They are full of rapid and melodramatic incident. The dramatist seems willfully to avoid the finer touch, and gives an almost puppet-theater psychology. Yet these plays have a strange fascination and, if revived on the stage, should prove extraordinarily effective. The satirical plays of contemporary life are akin to Sukhovó-Kobýlin's in the savageness of their satire. But they are long and technically imperfect and show a distinct decline of the writer's creative forces.

The numerous minor dramatists of the period partly endeavored to assimilate Ostróvsky's methods in the portrayal of Russian *byt*, partly wrote what were called "plays of exposure," that is to say, denunciations of various official and social vices, especially of pre-Reform conditions. Here also the lead had been given by Ostróvsky in *A Profitable Post*. The real rival, in the public favor, of the literary realistic drama of Ostróvsky was the operetta of Offenbach, which in the latter half of the sixties flooded the Russian stage and relegated into a comparative unpopularity all other forms of dramatic art. But it remained a purely imported commodity, and no attempt was made by Russian authors to imitate it.

THE COSTUME PLAY

By the end of the forties the pseudo-romantic drama of Kúkolnik and his like had lost all credit. It was not till some ten years later that there began a new movement to revive the verse drama. Its starting point was the example of Púshkin's *Borís Godunóv*. The first to begin the movement was the poet Mey, whose *Maid of Pskov* (1860), a conventionally pretty drama of the times of Iván the Terrible, started a continuous series of plays on subjects from Old Russian history before the time of Peter the Great, chiefly from the Moscow period. In spite of the solid historical knowledge at the basis of most of these plays, they are, as a whole, remarkably lacking in Old Russian flavor. Old Russia was to the authors, and still more to the public, above all a land of picturesque and luxurious "boyar costumes." Its life was seen through the prism of the European romantic drama, and the motive of romantic love, so alien to the spirit of real Muscovy, was almost inevitably introduced into every play. The great drawback of all these plays is their language (which is the conventional language of contemporary poetry larded with idioms from old documents and from folklore), and especially their meter—blank verse. Besides the technical laxity common to the verse write˙ s of the period, Russian blank verse, even in Púshkin's hand, has always been the least Russian of meters, and is always suggestive of translation; the only really effective romantic blank verse in the language is Púshkin's in the Little Tragedies, which all deal with subjects from foreign life.[3] The use of it in dramas of Muscovite life is particularly inappropriate. Lastly, the example of *Borís Godunóv* and of the common model, the histories of Shakspere, is responsible for the excess detail and the overcrowding of the stage with secondary personages. Altogether the school as a whole must be regarded as unsatisfactory and one of the least original and least significant of Russian literary developments.

[3] And, it is true, in *Rusálka*, but *Rusálka* is, in the exact sense of the word, unique, a miracle and no example; besides, the Russian element in *Rusálka* is not Muscovite, and is, as it were, universalized.

This is not to say that the plays of its best representatives are devoid of merit. Ostróvsky's chronicles (1862–8) are distinctly the poorest part of all his work, though *historically* they are often interesting and suggestive. Infinitely better is *The Snow Maiden* (*Snegúrochka*), which is the only really poetical romantic comedy in the language. Based on somewhat naïvely interpreted mythological material, it is full of that atmospheric poetry of which Ostróvsky gave such a masterpiece in *The Thunderstorm*. But in *The Snow Maiden* the nature poetry is all transfused with a delicate humor, owing to which even the ineffective blank verse of Ostróvsky loses much of its inadequacy. And in the songs he finally transcended all his limitations and unexpectedly created genuinely folklore-like poetry that can almost be compared with Nekrásov's.

Alexéy Tolstóy is superior to Ostróvsky as an historical dramatist. Though all the strictures on the school in general apply to him as well, his famous historical trilogy (*The Death of Iván the Terrible*, 1866; *Tsar Theodore*, 1868; and *Tsar Borís*, 1870) deserves to a certain extent its high reputation. The plays are intellectually *interesting* and suggestive. They are full of excellent character drawing. In most cases it is, perhaps, intelligent and shrewd rather than genuinely imaginative. But in the character of Tsar Theodore, Alexéy Tolstóy succeeded in creating one of the most interesting figures in Russian literature—the good and weak sovereign, with an unerring sense of values and a complete inability to impose his good will on his crafty councilor.

The principal interest of all this drama is its connection with the far more vigorous growth of the Russian opera; Rímsky-Kórsakov's librettist, Bélsky, was one of its best writers, and above all it can claim kinship with the greatest Russian tragic poet of the period, Modést Musórgsky. Musórgsky himself wrote the libretto of *Khovánschina* and adapted with great skill Púshkin's *Borís Godunóv* to make his popular opera. That he had dramatic as well as musical genius cannot be denied, but the literary historian unfortunately has no right to appropriate him or to sever the dramatic from the musical texture of his dramas. The *spirit* of Musórgsky was very different from that of his contemporary dramatists, and his real spiritual kin in literature were Nekrásov and Dostoyévsky.

8

The Age of Realism: The Novelists (II)

TOLSTÓY (BEFORE 1880)

TWENTY years ago[1] there was no difference of opinion outside Russia as to who was the greatest of Russian writers—Tolstóy dominated Russian literature in a way that no writer had dominated a national literature in the eyes of the world since the death of Goethe, or even, if we think of the enormous extraliterary prestige of Tolstóy, since the days of Voltaire. Since then the wheel of fashion, or the laws of growth of the occidental mind, has displaced Tolstóy from his place of ascendancy and substituted for his the idols of Dostoyévsky and, in these last years (strangest of occidental whims), of Chékhov. It is left to the future to show whether the wheel will turn again, or whether the advanced elite of the Western world has definitely reached a stage of mental senility that can be satisfied only by the autumnal genius of Chékhov.

For his own compatriots Tolstóy, though often pre-

[1] This passage (with a few others in similar tone) has been preserved for its special interest for the English-speaking reader, who should remember that it was first published in 1927. (Ed.)

ferred to all other writers, never was the center or the symbol of Russian literature as a whole—a part irrevertibly belonging to Púshkin. The enormous moral and personal prestige he enjoyed in the last twenty-five years of his life was not inevitably linked with a recognition of his absolute literary supremacy. But the permanence of Tolstóy has never been put to question, and, as far as we can see ahead, never will be. To compare him to Chékhov is as impossible to a level-headed Russian as it is to say that Brussels is a bigger city than London. The actuality, the influence of Tolstóy may have its ebb and flow; we may (as we happen to do today) find nothing we should like ourselves to imitate in *War and Peace*; but the star of Tolstóy will never be eclipsed by any other body. Humanly speaking, it is impossible to deny that he was the biggest man (not the best, nor perhaps even the greatest, but just morally the bulkiest) that trod the Russian soil within the last few lifetimes; the biggest man, if not the greatest artist, in all Russian literary history.

The bigness of Tolstóy has seemed to me sufficient to justify a procedure that would have been disastrously unfair to anyone of lesser bulk: I have cut him in two, and the reader will find an account of his work after 1880 in the following chapter. If I were mainly concerned with Tolstóy the man, this halving him between two chapters would be unjustifiable—the essential unity of the young and the old Tolstóy is an all-important point to every student of his personality and, especially, of his ideas. But literary history is concerned with literature, which is a supra-personal growth, and in which biography and psychology are matters of secondary importance as compared to the supra-personal evolution of a nation's literature as a whole and of its component parts, the evolutions of the individual genres. It so happens that Tolstóy's conversion, about 1880, to the religion of his later years coincided with a profound change in his artistic views and aims that was partly conditioned by that conversion but was also an independent literary development with a definite place of its own in the general evolution of Russian literature, and was almost a negation of the whole achievement of the realistic school. In this chapter I am concerned only with that of Tolstóy's work in which he is a typical, even an extreme (if in certain points eccentric), representative of the main tendencies of the Russian realistic school, its finest flower and highest æsthetic justification.

Count Leo Nikoláyevich Tolstóy was born on August 28, 1828, on his father's estate of Yásnaya Polyána, in the Province of Túla. The Tolstóys are a family of old Russian nobility, and the writer's mother was born a Princess Volkónsky. His father and mother are respectively the starting points for the characters of Nicholas Rostóv and Princess Márya in *War and Peace*. They belonged to the best Russian nobility, and this fact of belonging by birth to the upper layer of the ruling class marks off Tolstóy very distinctly from the other writers of his time. He always remained a class-conscious nobleman (even when this class consciousness became purely negative) and kept aloof from the intelligentsia.

Tolstóy's childhood and boyhood were passed between Moscow and Yásnaya Polyána, in a large family of several brothers. He has left us an extraordinarily vivid record of his early human environment in the wonderful notes he wrote for his biographer P. I. Biryukóv. He lost his mother when he was two, and his father when he was nine. His subsequent education was in the hands of his aunt, Mlle Érgolsky, who is supposed to be the starting point for Sónya in *War and Peace*. In 1844 Tolstóy matriculated at the University of Kazán, where he studied first oriental languages and afterward law, but which he left in 1847 without receiving a degree. In 1849 he settled down at Yásnaya Polyána, where he attempted to be useful to his peasants but soon discovered the ineffectiveness of his uninformed zeal. Much of the life he led at the University and after leaving it was of a kind usual with young men of his class, irregular and full of pleasure-seeking—wine, cards, and women—not entirely unlike the life led by Púshkin before his exile to the south. But Tolstóy was incapable of that lighthearted acceptance of life as it came. From the very beginning, his diary (which is extant from 1847) reveals an insatiate thirst for a rational and moral justification of life, a thirst that forever remained the ruling force of his mind. The same diary was his first experiment in forging that technique of psychological analysis which was to become his principal literary weapon. To the year 1851 belongs his first attempt at a more ambitious and more definitely creative kind of writing.

In the same year, sick of his empty and useless life in Moscow, he went off to the Caucasus, where he joined an artillery unit garrisoned in the Cossack country on the Térek, as a *junker*—that is to say, a volunteer of private rank, but of noble birth. In 1852 he completed his first story (*Childhood*) and sent it to Nekrásov for publication in the *Sovreménnik*. The story had a considerable and immediate success and gave Tolstóy a definite place in literature.

In his battery Tolstóy lived, in agreeable billets, the rather easy and unoccupied life of a *junker* of means. He had much spare time, and most of it was spent in hunting. In the little fighting he saw, he did very well. In 1854 he received his commission and was, at his request, transferred to the army operating against the Turks in Wallachia, where he took part in the siege of Silistria. In November of the same year he joined the garrison of Sevastópol. There he saw very serious fighting. He took part in the defense of the famous Fourth Bastion and in the battle of Chërnaya Réchka, the bad management of which he satirized in a humorous song, the only piece of verse he is known to have written.[2] In Sevastópol he wrote his famous *Sevastópol Stories,* which, appearing as they did in the *Sovreménnik* while the siege was still on, greatly increased the general interest in their author. Soon after the abandonment of the fortress, Tolstóy went on leave of absence to Petersburg and Moscow, and the following year he left the army.

These years after the Crimean War were the only time in Tolstóy's life when he mixed with the literary world. He was welcomed by the littérateurs of Petersburg and Moscow as one of their most eminent fellow craftsmen. As he confessed afterwards, his vanity and pride were greatly flattered by his success. But he did not get on with them. He was too much of an aristocrat to like this semi-Bohemian intelligentsia. They were too self-consciously plebeian for him, while they resented the way he obviously preferred "society" to their company. Cutting epigrams on this subject passed between him and Turgénev. On the other hand, all

[2] Professor George R. Noyes has pointed out to me that this statement is not quite correct. There is also a letter in verse, written to Fet on November 12, 1872. (Ed.)

the structure of his mind was against the grain of the progressive Westernizers. The way they stated their problems
was uninteresting to him. He did not believe in progress or
culture. His lack of sympathy with the literary world was
increased by their disappointment in his new work. All he
had written since *Childhood* had shown no advance from
the point of view of artistic perfection, and his critics
failed to realize the experimental value of this imperfect
work. All this made his connection with the literary world
short-lived. It culminated in a resounding quarrel with
Turgénev (1861), whom he challenged and afterward
apologized to for so doing. The whole story is very characteristic and revelatory of his character, with its profound
and sensitive self-consciousness and impatience of other
people's assumed superiority. The only writers with whom
he remained friends were the reactionary and "landlordist"
Fet and the democratic Slavophil Strákhov, both of them
men entirely out of tune with the main current of contemporary progressive thought.

The years 1856–61 were passed between Petersburg,
Moscow, and Yásnaya, and foreign countries. In 1857 (and
again in 1860–1) he traveled abroad, and returned disgusted by the selfishness and materialism of European
bourgeois civilization. In 1859 he started a school for peasant children at Yásnaya, and in 1862 published a pedagogical magazine, *Yásnaya Polyána,* in which he astonished
the progressive world by contending that it was not the intellectuals who should teach the peasants, but rather the
peasants the intellectuals. In 1861 he accepted the post of
Arbiter of the Peace, a magistrature that had been introduced to supervise the carrying into life of the Emancipation Act. Meanwhile his insatiate quest for moral stability
continued to torment him. He had now abandoned the wild
living of his youth, and thought of marrying. In 1856 he
made his first unsuccessful attempt to marry (Mlle
Arséniev). In 1860 he was profoundly affected by the death
of his brother Nicholas, which was for him the first en-
counter with the inevitable reality of death. In 1862, at
last, after long hesitations (he was convinced that since he
was old—thirty-four!—and ugly, no woman could love
him) he proposed to Sophie Andréyevna Behrs and was
accepted. They were married in the September of the same
year.

His marriage is one of the two most important land-marks in the life of Tolstóy, the other being his conversion. He was always dominated by one preoccupation—how to justify his life before his conscience and thus attain a stable moral welfare. In his bachelor years he oscillated between two opposite desires. One was a passionate and hopeless aspiration after that whole and unreflecting "natural" state which he found among the peasants, and especially among the Cossacks in whose villages he had lived in the Caucasus —a state that has no need to justify life because it is free from the consciousness that demands such a justification. He tried to find such an unquestioning state in a deliberate surrender to the animal impulses—in living the life of his friends and (here he was nearest to attaining it) in his favorite occupation of hunting. But he seemed incapable of finding it for good, and the other equally passionate de-sire—to find a rational justification of life—tore him away every time he hoped he had attained the goal of self-satis-faction. His marriage was for him the gate towards a more stable and lasting "natural state." Family life, and an un-reasoning acceptance of and submission to the life to which he was born, now became his religion.

For the first fifteen years of his married life he lived in this blissful state of confidently satisfied vegetable life, whose philosophy is expressed with supreme creative power in *War and Peace*. In his family life he was excep-tionally and shamelessly happy. Sophie Andréyevna, almost a girl when he married her, was easily molded into the form he desired, and informed with his new philosophy, of which, to the later undoing of the household, she became the impregnable rock and unalterable depository. She proved an ideal wife and mother and mistress of the house. She was, moreover, a devoted help to her husband in his literary work, and the story is well known how she copied out *War and Peace* seven times from beginning to end. The family fortune, owing to Tolstóy's efficient management of his estates and to the sales of his works, was prosperous, making it possible to provide adequately for the increasing family. But Tolstóy, though absorbed and largely satisfied by his self-justified life, though glorifying it with unsur-passed imaginative power in his greatest novel, was not capable of being merged in family life as his wife had be-come merged. Nor could his "life in art" absorb him as it did his fellow craftsmen. The worm of moral thirst, reduced at one time to negligible proportions, could never die. Tolstóy was constantly agitated by moral problems and moral urges. In 1866 he was counsel (unsuccessfully) before a court-martial for a soldier accused of striking an officer. In 1873 he published articles on popular education which enabled that shrewd critic Mikhaylóvsky practically to predict the later developments of his ideas. *Anna Karénina,* written in 1873–7, is appreciably less "vegetable" and more moralistic than *War and Peace.* While he was writing that second novel, the crisis overcame him that led to his conversion, described with Biblical power in *A Confession.* It was caused by a growing obsession of the reality of death, which again brought forward the unquenchable thirst and need for ultimate justification. At first it led Tolstóy to the Orthodox Church. But his all-pervading rationalism led him on to a purely rational religion that accepted only the moral without the theological and mystical doctrines of Christianity, and that became at last the final justification for which his spirit had yearned. In 1879 the process was at an end, and in 1880 he began *A Confession.* Only in 1884, largely under the influence of Chertkóv, Tolstóy began an active propaganda for his new religion. In his personal life his conversion led to an estrangement from his wife, whom he was this time unable to mold nearer to his heart's changed desire. The story of his later years, up to his death in 1910, is outlined in the following chapter.

Tolstóy's conversion coincided with an important change in the style and manner of his imaginative writings. He discarded the methods he had used in his earlier work, the dissecting analysis of the subconscious and semiconscious workings of the human mind, and all that he later on (in *What Is Art?*) condemned as "superfluous detail." In his early work he was a representative man of the Russian realistic school, which relied entirely on the method of "superfluous detail" that had been introduced by Gógol. It was "superfluous" detail that gave the particular and individual convincingness that is the very essence of the realistic novel. The general effect of such detail is to bring out the particular, the individual, the local, and the temporary at the expense of the general and the universal. At its logical

term it produced the purely ethnographical *byt* realism of
Ostróvsky. This particularity which excludes a universal
appeal and emphasizes social and national differences was
what the old Tolstóy condemned in the methods of realistic
fiction. In his early work he had entirely adopted them and
carried them farther than his predecessors. In physical
description of character he outdid Gógol and has never
been surpassed. But he is different from his compeers in
that he never inclined towards *byt*. The interest of his work
is always psychological, never ethnographical. The essence
of Tolstóy's early art was to push analysis to its furthest
limit; hence it is that the details he offers are not complex
cultural facts, but, as it were, *atoms* of experience—the
indivisible units of immediate perception. An important
form of this dissecting and atomizing method (and one that
survived all the changes of his style) is what Victor
Shklóvsky has called "making it strange." It consists in
never calling complex things by their accepted name, but
always disintegrating a complex action or object into its
indivisible components. The method strips the world of the
labels attached to it by habit and by social convention, and
gives it a "dis-civilized" appearance, as it might have appeared to Adam on the day of creation. It is easy to see
that the method, while it gives unusual freshness to imaginative representation, is in essence hostile to all culture
and all social form, and is psychologically akin to anarchism. This method is the principal feature that distinguishes
the work of Tolstóy from that of other realists. The universality of Tolstóy's realism is increased by his concentration on the inner life, and especially on its more
elusive experiences. When arrested and expressed in words,
they give a particularly keen feeling of unexpected familiarity, for it seems that the author is aware of the reader's
most intimate, secret, and inexpressible feelings. This
mastering of the elusive is irresistible and overwhelming, at
least to people who have grown up in a roughly similar
emotional ambient. How far this particular side of Tolstóy
strengthens his appeals to a Chinese or to an Arab I cannot say. Tolstóy himself in his old age believed it did not,
and in his later work intended for the world, irrespective
of race and civilization, he avoided this method of what
Constantine Leóntiev called "psychological eavesdropping."

But within certain limits the "eavesdropping" only enhances the human and universal as against the local and
social appeal of the early Tolstóy.

Again the subject matter of Tolstóy and his way of
approaching it increase the universal as much as they
diminish the ethnographical appeal of his work. The issues
of his stories are not the public issues of contemporary
Russia. Except for certain parts of *Anna Karénina* (and
for the posthumous comedy, *A Contaminated Family*),
contemporary issues are absent from Tolstóy's work. This
disqualified it for being used as texts for the civic sermons
of Chernyshévsky and Dobrolyúbov, but has also prevented it from dating. The issues and the conflicts are
moral and psychological, not social, a considerable asset
in winning the unqualified understanding of the foreign
reader. In his later work this feature is only further developed. His universality gives Tolstóy a somewhat eccentric
standing among the Russian novelists of his time. But in
another respect he is again eminently representative of the
movement. He carried further than anyone (except Aksákov) the deliberate neglect of narrative interest and the
deliberate avoidance of artificial construction. He also
carried to the furthest the purity of his prose from all
extra-representational elements. His style is deliberately
prosaic—purged to chemical purity of all "poetry" and
rhetoric—sternly puritanical prose. His syntax, especially
in the earliest work, is sometimes clumsy and exaggeratedly
involved. But at its best it is beautifully adequate and
transparent—a prose admirably adapted to its task and
perfectly obedient to what it is made to express. The *language* of Tolstóy also deserves special notice for the pains
he took to avoid the bookish vocabulary of literature and
to use with consistent purity the spoken vocabulary of
his class. It is the best example (after Griboyédov and
after Púshkin's epistolary prose) of the spoken Russian of
the nobility. But his syntax is based on the example of
the French analysts and uses all the means at its disposal
for complicated logical subordination. This combination of
a very pure colloquial vocabulary with a very complicated
and logical syntax makes the peculiar individuality of
Tolstóy's Russian. In his dialogue, on the other hand,
especially from *War and Peace* (and *A Contaminated
Family*) onward, he achieved a purity and convincingness

of colloquial idiom and intonation that have not been surpassed. The highest achievement of his art of dialogue,
however, belongs to his last period and is to be found in
his last plays, *The Light Shines in the Darkness* and *The
Living Corpse*.

The roots of Tolstóy's art are to be found in his
diary, which we know from 1847 onward. Like Stendhal,
with whom as a psychologist he has much in common,
and whom he recognized as one of his masters, Tolstóy is
particularly interested in discovering the semiconscious suppressed motives of his actions, in exposing the insincerity
of the superficial, as it were, official, ego. A detail that
cannot fail to strike the reader of Tolstóy's diaries (as
well as of certain of his stories written in the fifties) is
his inordinate love for classifications, which he marshals
under numbered headings. It is a minor, but significant,
detail. It has often been affirmed that Tolstóy was an
eminently natural, subconscious, elemental man, and that
in this he was akin to primitive man, as yet imperfectly
differentiated from nature. Nothing can be more misleading. He was on the contrary a rationalist to the marrow,
one of the greatest that ever lived. Nothing was safe from
the lancet of his analysis. His art is not the spontaneous
revelation of the subconscious but the conquest of the
subconscious by lucid understanding. Tolstóy was a predecessor of Freud, but the striking difference between the
artist and the scientist is that the artist is incomparably
less imaginative, more matter-of-fact and levelheaded than
the scientist.

From the beginnings of his diary to the time he wrote
War and Peace, writing was to Tolstóy above all a struggle
to master reality, to found a method and a technique of
reducing it to words. To this, from 1851, he added the
problem of transforming notation of fact into literature.
Tolstóy did not achieve it at a single stroke. His first attempt at imaginative writing, a fragment entitled *An Account of Yesterday*, is apparently the beginning of an
account of an actual twenty-four hours spent by him, with
no invention, nothing but notation. It was only to be
fuller and less selective than the diaries and subordinated
to a general design. In point of detail the *Account* is
almost on a Proustian if not a Joycean scale. The author
revels, as it were, in his analysis. He is a young man in

possession of a new instrument, who has unbounded confidence in his command of it. The same impression is never again given in any of his later work. This exuberance wanted repression and disciplining before it was ready to be shown to the public. It wanted a more literary, a less immediately "recording" appearance. It wanted the discipline of convention. For all his pioneering courage, Tolstóy did not have the audacity to continue in this line of extensive notation. It is almost a pity he did not. The sheer originality of *An Account of Yesterday* remains unsurpassed. If he had continued in that line, he would probably have met with less immediate recognition, but he might have ultimately produced an even more astounding body of work.

In the light of *An Account of Yesterday, Childhood* seems almost a surrender to all the conventions of literature. Of all Tolstóy's writings it is the one where extraneous literary influences (Sterne, Rousseau, Töpfer) are most clearly apparent. But even now, in the light of *War and Peace, Childhood* retains its unique and unfading charm. It has already that wonderful poetry of reality which is attained without the slightest aid of poetical device, without the aid of language (the few sentimental, rhetorical passages rather tend to destroy it), by the sole help of the choice of significant psychological and real detail. What struck the world as a new thing, hitherto done by no one, was this gift of evoking memories and associations, recognized by everyone as his own intimate and unique memories, by the choice of details memorable to everyone, but rejected by everyone as insignificant and not worth while. It needed the avid rationalism of Tolstóy to fix for ever these moments which *were* but had remained unrecorded since the beginning of time.

In *Childhood* Tolstóy succeeded for the first time in transposing the raw material of recorded experience into art. For a moment Tolstóy abandoned his pioneering energy and was content to draw up a balance of what he had already acquired, in a form not too unlike the accepted conventions of literature. In all he wrote after *Childhood* and up to *War and Peace* he continued his forward movement, experimenting, forging his instrument, never condescending to sacrifice his interest in the process of production to the artistic effect of the finished product. This is apparent in the sequels of *Childhood*—*Boyhood* (1854) and *Youth* (1857)—when the poetic, evocative atmosphere of *Childhood* becomes thinner and thinner and the element of sheer untransformed analysis protrudes more and more. It is still more apparent in his stories of war and of the Caucasus: *A Raid* (1853), *Sevastópol in December, Sevastópol in May* (1855), *Sevastópol in August* (1856), *A Wood Felling* (1855). In them he set out to destroy the existing romantic conceptions of those two arch-romantic themes. To be understood in their genesis, these stories have to be felt against their background of romantic literature, against the romances of Bestúzhev and the Byronic poems of Púshkin and Lérmontov. The unromanticizing of Caucasus and war is achieved by Tolstóy's usual method of ever advancing analysis and of "making it strange." Battles and skirmishes are not described in terms of military history, with its grand nomenclature, nor in terms of battle-painting, but in the ordinary and unprepossessing details that strike the actual observer and are only afterward transformed by a name-ridden memory into heroic battle scenes. Here more than anywhere Tolstóy followed in the steps of Stendhal, whose account of Waterloo he recognized as a perfect example of military realism. The same process of destroying the heroic convention was further promoted by the ruthless analysis of the psychological workings that result in the display of courage, which are composed of vanity, lack of imagination, and stereotyped thinking. But in spite of this exposure of war and military virtues, the general effect of Tolstóy's military stories is not unheroic or anti-militarist. It results much rather in the glorification of the unconscious and unambitious at the expense of conscious and ambitious heroism, of the private soldier and professional army officer at the expense of the smart young officer from Petersburg who has come to the front to taste of the poetry of war and to win his St. George's Cross. The casual, matter-of-fact courage of the plain soldier and officer is what strikes the reader most of all in these stories. These humble heroes of Tolstóy's early war stories are descendants of Púshkin's Captain Mirónov and of Lérmontov's Maxím Maxímych, and landmarks on the way to the soldiers and army officers of *War and Peace*.

In the stories written in the second half of the fifties and early sixties Tolstóy's center of interest is shifted from

analysis to morality. These stories—*The Memoirs of a*
Billiard Marker, Two Hussars, Albert, Lucerne, Three
Deaths, Family Happiness, Polikúshka, and *Kholstomér,*
the Story of a Horse—are frankly didactic and moralistic,
much more so than any of the stories of his last, dogmatic
period. The main moral of these stories is the fallacy of
civilization and the inferiority of the civilized, conscious,
sophisticated man, with his artificially multiplied needs, to
natural man. On the whole they mark an advance neither,
as the war stories did, in Tolstóy's method of annexing
and digesting reality, nor in his skill in transferring the raw
experience of life into art (as in *Childhood* and *War and*
Peace). Most of them are crude, and some (as, for
instance, *Three Deaths*) did not need a Tolstóy to write
them. Contemporary criticism was right in regarding them,
if not as a decline, at least as a standstill in the development of his genius. But they are important as an expression
of that moral urge which was finally to bring Tolstóy to
A Confession and to all his later work and teaching.
Lucerne, for its earnest and bitter indignation against the
selfishness of the rich (which, it is true, he was inclined
at that time to regard, semi-Slavophilwise, as a peculiarity
of the materialistic civilization of the West) is particularly
suggestive of the spirit of his later work. As a sermon in
fiction it is certainly one of the most powerful things of
its kind. The nearest approach to complete artistic success
is *Two Hussars,* a charming story that betrays its purpose
only in the excessively neat parallelism between the characters of the two Hussars, father and son. The father is an
"unconscious," "natural" man who lives a rather unedifying life, but who, precisely on account of his unconscious-
ness and proximity to nature, is noble even in his vices
and reveals the essential nobility of man. The son in
circumstances similar to those of his father shows himself
a coward and a cad precisely because he is contaminated
by the evil influences of civilization, and what he does, he
does self-consciously. Lastly, *Kholstomér, the Story of a*
Horse is certainly one of the most characteristic and curious
of all Tolstóy's writings. It is a satire upon civilized mankind from the point of view of a horse. The method of
"making it strange" is pushed to its furthest limits. It is
essentially a descendant of the Persian, Chinese, and such-
like letters of the eighteenth century, where oriental ob-

servers were introduced just to expose the absurdities of contemporary life by making it strange. Here more than elsewhere Tolstóy is the faithful disciple of French rationalism. It is interesting, however, that the keenest point of the satire is turned against the institution of property, and it is characteristic that the story, written just before his marriage, was published only after his conversion.

Apart from the rest of his earliest work stands *The Cossacks*. It was written during his life in the Caucasus, but Tolstóy remained unsatisfied with it, returned to it again, and, still unsatisfied, would not have published it were it not for the necessity he found himself in of paying a debt at cards. It appeared in 1863 in a form Tolstóy regarded as unsatisfactory. What he would have done with it ultimately we do not know, but as it is, it is probably his masterpiece before *War and Peace*. It is the story of the life of Olénin, a young volunteer of noble birth and university education, in a Cossack village on the Térek. The main idea is the contrast of his sophisticated and self-conscious personality to the "natural men" that are the Cossacks. Unlike the "natural man" of Rousseau (and of Tolstóy's own later teaching), "natural man" in *The Cossacks* is not an incarnation of good. But the very fact of his being natural places him above the distinction of good and evil. The Cossacks kill, fornicate, steal, and still are beautiful in their naturalness, and hopelessly superior to the much more moral, but civilized and consequently contaminated, Olénin. The young Cossack Lukáshka, the Cossack girl Mariánka, and especially the old huntsman Eróshka are among the most memorable and lasting creations of Tolstóy. They are his first great successes in the objective painting of the human figure. But the objective painting of the human soul he was to achieve only in *War and Peace*, for in his early work his analyzed and dissected heroes are either emanations of his own self or else only more or less abstract and generalized human material for dissection, like the "other" officers in the Sevastópol stories, who are not more psychologically alive than the horse Kholstomér. The processes that go on in them are convincing, but the details of this psychological mechanism are not welded into a whole to form an individuality.

Tolstóy's first literary work after his marriage was

the (posthumously published) comedy *A Contaminated Family*. It shows already the conservative trend of his married mind. It is a satire of the nihilist, ending in the triumph of the meek, but fundamentally sensible, father over his rebellious children. It is a masterpiece of delicate character-drawing and dialogue. It contains more genuine and good-humored humor than any other of his works. At one time Tolstóy was very keen on having it acted. But it was rejected by the Imperial Theater, probably for fear of offending the younger generation.

Soon after his marriage Tolstóy began to be attracted by the recent past of the Russian society, and planned a novel on the subject of the Decembrists. Some fragments of this novel were written and published, but before long he found himself unable to understand the Decembrists without a study of the preceding generation, and this led to the writing of *War and Peace*. It took him over four years. A first fragment under the title *1805* appeared in 1865. The whole novel was completed and published in 1869.

War and Peace is, not only in size, but in perfection, the masterpiece of the early Tolstóy. It is also the most important work in the whole of Russian realistic fiction. If in the whole range of the European novel of the nineteenth century it has equals, it has no superiors, and the peculiarities of the modern, as opposed to the pre-nineteenth-century, novel are more clearly seen in it than in such rivals as *Madame Bovary* or *Le Rouge et le Noir*. It was an advanced pioneering work, a work that widened, as few novels have done, the province and the horizon of fiction. In a textbook, where space is limited, it is impossible to speak at all adequately of the great novel. Besides, more than anything else in Russian literature, it belongs to Europe as much as it does to Russia. A history of the European novel would have to place it, not so much in its Russian, as in its international, setting, on the line of development that leads from the novels of Stendhal to those of Henry James and Proust. In many respects *War and Peace* is a direct continuation of the preceding works of Tolstóy. The methods of analysis and of "making it strange" are the same, only carried to a greater perfection. The use of apparently elusive, but emotionally significant detail for the creation of poetic atmosphere is a direct

development of the methods of *Childhood*. The presentation of war as an unromantic and sordid reality, but one
that is nevertheless pregnant with heroical beauty in the
courage of its unconscious heroes, is a direct continuation
of the Sevastópol stories. The glorification of "natural
man," of Natásha and Nicholas Rostóv at the expense of
the sophisticated Prince Andrew, and of the peasant Platón
Karatáycv at the expense of all the civilized heroes, continues the line of thought of *Two Hussars* and of *The
Cossacks*. The satirical representation of society and of
diplomacy is completely in line with Tolstóy's disgust at
European civilization. However, in other respects it is different from the earlier work. First of all it is more objective. Here for the first time Tolstóy becomes capable
of stepping out of himself and of seeing into the other.
Unlike *The Cossacks* and *Childhood* the novel is not
egocentrical. There are several heroes with equal rights,
none of whom is Tolstóy, though the two principal ones,
Prince Andrew and Pierre Bezúkhov, are no doubt trans-
positions of Tolstóy. But the most wonderful difference of
War and Peace from the earlier stories are the women,
Princess Maria and especially Natásha. There can be no
doubt that it was his increased knowledge of feminine
nature, due to marriage, that enabled Tolstóy to annex
this new province of psychological experience. The art of
individualization also attains to unsurpassable perfection.
The little details that made the unique and unprecedented
charm of *Childhood* are used here with a supreme and
elusive perfection that transcends art and gives the book
(and *Anna Karénina*)—alone, perhaps, among all books
—the appearance of actual life. To many of Tolstóy's
readers his personages are not classified with other
characters of fiction, but with men and women of actual
experience. The roundness, the completeness, the liveness
of the characters, even of the most episodic, are perfect
and absolute. This is attained, of course, by the extraordinary subtlety, delicacy, and variety of the analysis (we
are far removed from the crudish and schematic methods
of *Sevastópol*), but it is also attained by the means of more
elusive detail, of "accompaniment," and especially of language. The speech Tolstóy lends his characters is something that surpasses perfection. In *War and Peace* he
attains for the first time to a complete mastery of this

medium. It gives the reader the impression of actually hearing the different individual voices of the characters. You recognize the voice of Natásha, or Vera, or Borís Drubetskóy as you recognize the voice of a friend. In this art of individualized intonation Tolstóy has only one rival—Dostoyévsky. There is no need to dwell on the individual characters. But it is impossible not to insist once more on the supreme creation of Natásha, certainly the most wonderfully made character in any novel. Natásha is also the center of the novel, for she is the symbol of "natural man," the ideal.

The transformation of reality into art is also more perfect in *War and Peace* than in anything that preceded it. It is almost complete.[3] The novel is built along its own laws (Tolstóy has let escape him some interesting hints as to these laws) and contains few undigested bits of raw material. The narrative is a miracle. The vast proportions, the numerous personages, the frequent changes of scene, and the close and necessary interconnection of all give the impression of being really a record of a society, not only of so many individuals.

The philosophy of the novel is the glorification of nature and life at the expense of the sophistications of reason and civilization. It is the surrender of the rationalist Tolstóy to the irrational forces of existence. It is emphasized in the theoretical chapters and it is symbolized in the last volume in the figure of Karatáyev. The philosophy is profoundly optimistic, for it is confidence in the blind forces of life, a profound belief that the best one can do is not to choose, but to trust in the goodness of things. The passive and determinist Kutúzov embodies the philosophy of wise passivity as against the ambitious smallness of Napoleon. The optimistic nature of the philosophy is reflected in the idyllic tone of the narrative. In spite of the horror—by no means veiled—of war, and the ineptitude —assiduously unmasked—of sophisticated and futile civilization, the general message of *War and Peace* is one

---

[3] Not so complete as in certain works of other great realists; not for instance so complete as in *Madame Bovary*. But then neither Flaubert nor anyone else absorbed so much of reality in the transforming process. The quantity of transforming energy utilized in *War and Peace* is greater than in any work of realistic fiction.

of beauty and satisfaction that the world should be so beautiful. It is only the sophistication of conscious reason that contrives to spoil it. The general tone may be properly described as idyllic. The inclination towards the idyllic was from first to last an ever present possibility in Tolstóy. It is the opposite pole to his unceasing moral uneasiness. Before the time of *War and Peace* it pervades *Childhood*, and it strangely and unexpectedly crops up in his auto-biographical notes written in his last years for Biryukóv. Its roots are in a sense of unity with his class, with the happy and prosperous *byt* of the Russian nobility. And it is, after all, no exaggeration to say that, all said and done, *War and Peace* is a tremendous "heroic idyl" of the Russian nobility.

There are two conceivable strictures on *War and Peace*, the figure of Karatáyev, and the theoretical chapters on history and warfare. Personally I do not admit the validity of the latter drawback. It is an essential of Tolstóy's art to be not only art, but knowledge. And to the vast canvas of the great novel the theoretical chapters add a perspective and an intellectual atmosphere one cannot wish away.[4] I feel it more difficult to put up with Karatáyev. In spite of his quintessential importance for the idea of the novel, he jars. He is not a human being among human beings, as the other two ideally natural characters, Natásha and Kutúzov, are. He is an abstraction, a myth, a being with different dimensions and laws from those of the rest of the novel. He does not fit in.

After *War and Peace* Tolstóy, pursuing his historical studies, ascended the stream of Russian history to the age of Peter the Great. The period appeared to him as critical in bringing about the cleft between the people and the educated classes and in poisoning the latter with European civilization. He tried several plans and wrote several beginnings of a novel of those times, but in the course of his studies Tolstóy became so disgusted with the person of the great Emperor—the embodiment of all he hated— that he gave it up. Instead he began in 1873 to write a

---

[4] It may be remarked that as an historian of war Tolstóy gave proof of remarkable insight. His reading of the battle of Borodinó, which he arrived at by sheer intuition, has been since corroborated by documental evidence and accepted by military historians.

novel of contemporary life—*Anna Karénina*. The first in-
stalments appeared in 1875, and the publication of the
novel was completed in 1877.

Anna Karénina is in all essentials a continuation of
War and Peace. The methods of Tolstóy are the same in
both, and the two novels are justly named together. What
has been said of the personages of *War and Peace* may
be repeated of those of *Anna Karénina*. The figures of
Anna, of Dolly, of Kitty, of Stíva Oblónsky, of Vrónsky,
of all the episodic and secondary personages, are as memorable as those of Natásha and of Nicholas Rostóv. Perhaps
there is even a greater variety and a more varied sympathy
in the characters of *Anna Karénina*. Vrónsky particularly
is a genuine and fundamental addition to the world of
Tolstóy; more than any other of Tolstóy's characters, he
is fundamentally different from the author and in no way
based on subjective vision. He and Anna are perhaps Tolstóy's greatest achievements in the understanding of "the
other." But Lëvin is a much less happily transformed Tolstóy than are his emanations in *War and Peace*, Prince
Andrew and Pierre. Lëvin is a return to the subjective,
diaristic Nekhlyúdovs and Olénins of the early stories, and
he jars in the story as much as does Platón Karatáyev in
War and Peace, though in an exactly opposite way. Another
difference between the two novels is that *Anna Karénina*
contains no separate philosophical chapters, but a more
obtrusive and insidious moral philosophy is diffused
throughout the story. The philosophy is less irrational and
optimistic, more puritan, and is everywhere felt as distinct
from and alien to the main groundwork of the novel.
The groundwork has the idyllic flavor of *War and Peace*.
But in the philosophy of the novel there is an ominous
suggestion of the approach of a more tragic God than the
blind and good life-God of *War and Peace*. The tragic
atmosphere thickens as the story advances towards the
end. The romance of Anna and Vrónsky, who had trans-
gressed the moral and social law, culminates in blood and
horror to which there is no counterpart in the earlier novel.
Even the idyllic romance of the good and obedient-to-
nature Lëvin and Kitty ends on a note of confused perplexity. The novel dies like a cry of anguish in the desert
air. Both the great novels have an indefinite ending, but
while in *War and Peace* it suggests only the infinite con-

tinuity of life, of which the given narrative has been only a detached fragment, in *Anna Karénina* it definitely suggests a no-thoroughfare, a path gradually losing itself before the steps of the wayfarer. And in fact before Tolstóy had finished *Anna Karénina*, he had already entered on the crisis that was to bring him to his conversion. The perplexed ending of the novel is only a reflection of the tragic perplexity he was himself experiencing. He was never again to write a novel like these two. After finishing *Anna Karénina* he attempted to resume his work on Peter and the Decembrists, but it was soon forsaken, and instead, two years after the completion of his last idyl, he wrote *A Confession.*

Anna Karénina leads up to the moral and religious crisis that was so profoundly to revolutionize Tolstóy. Before he began it he had already begun to cast his eyes on new artistic methods—abandoning the psychological and analytical manner of superfluous detail and discovering a simpler narrative style that could be applied not only to the sophisticated and corrupt educated classes, but to the undeveloped mind of the people. The stories he wrote for the people in 1872 (*God Sees the Truth* and *The Captive in the Caucasus,* which, by the way, is merely a translation into unromantic terms, a sort of parody, of the poem of Púshkin) already announce the popular tales of 1885–6. They are not yet so pointedly moral, but they are all concentrated on narrative and action and are entirely free from all "eavesdropping."

DOSTOYÉVSKY (AFTER 1849)

From January 1850 to January 1854 Dostoyévsky[5] served his term of penal servitude at Omsk convict prison. During the whole term he had no books to read but a Bible and he was never for a moment alone. During these years he underwent a profound religious crisis: he rejected the social and progressive ideas of his youth and became converted to the religion of the Russian people, in the sense that he began not only to believe in what the people believed, but to believe in it *because* the people believed. On the other hand his four years of hard labor greatly injured

[5] For the early life and work of Dostoyévsky see Chapter VI.

his health, and his epilepsy became more marked and more frequent.

On completing his term he was transferred as a private soldier to an infantry battalion garrisoned at Semi-palátinsk. In October 1856 his commission was restored to him. He was now free to write and receive letters and to resume his literary work. In 1857, while staying at Kuznétsk, he married the widow Isáyeva. This first marriage was not a happy one. He remained in Siberia till 1859. During these five years he wrote, besides some shorter stories, the novel *The Manor of Stepánchikovo,* which appeared in 1859, and began *Memoirs from the House of Death.* In 1859 he was allowed to return to European Russia. Later in the same year he was finally amnestied and came to Petersburg.

He arrived in the midst of the great reform movement and was immediately sucked into the journalistic whirl-pool. Together with his brother Michael he started the review *Vrémya (The Time),* which began appearing in January 1861. In the first two years he contributed to the review a novel, *The Humiliated and Insulted,* and *Memoirs from the House of Death,* besides a great number of articles. Though the position that the Dostoyévskys took up fitted in with no party, their review was a success. What they stood for was a sort of mystical populism that did not want to make the people happy along Western and progressive lines, but to assimilate the ideals of the people. They found a valuable ally in Strákhov. Their other ally, Grigóriev, was of little use at the time, as he was traversing the most chaotic and anarchic period of his life. Dostoyévsky himself worked furiously, and often suc-cumbed to the overstrain. But he was exhilarated by success and by the atmosphere of struggle. In 1862–3 he traveled for the first time abroad, visiting England, France, and Germany, and recorded his impressions of the West in *Winter Notes on Summer Impressions,* which appeared in 1863. In them he attacked and condemned the impious bourgeois civilization of the West from a point of view that is connected at once with Herzen's and with that of the Slavophils. In 1863, like a bolt from the blue, came the suppression of *Vrémya* for an article on the Polish question by Strákhov, which had been, quite literally, misread by the censorship. The misunderstanding was cleared up before long, and the Dostoyévskys were allowed to resume their review in January 1864 under a new name (*The Epoch*), but the financial damages caused them by the suppression were incalculable. For eight years Dostoyévsky was unable to free himself from them. Meanwhile he was undergoing a crisis of greater significance than his conversion in Siberia. To the years 1862–3 belongs his liaison with Apollinária Súslova, the most important love affair of his life. After the suppression of *Vrémya* he traveled with her abroad. It was on this journey that for the first time he lost heavily at roulette. Mlle Súslova (who afterwards married the great writer Rózanov) was a proud and (to use a Dostoyevskian epithet) "infernal" woman, with unknown depths of cruelty and of evil. She seems to have been to Dostoyévsky an important revelation of the dark side of things.

The Epoch began under the worst auspices. The action of the authorities prevented it from being advertised in due time, and it never succeeded in recovering the good will of the subscribers of *Vrémya*. Soon after it was started, Dostoyévsky's wife and, almost simultaneously, Michael Dostoyévsky both died. The death of Grigóriev in the autumn of the same year was a further blow to the review. Dostoyévsky found himself alone, and with the whole family of his brother to provide for. After fifteen months of heroical and hectic labor he gave in, recognizing that *The Epoch* could not be saved. The review was closed. Dostoyévsky was bankrupt. It was in the terrible year 1864 that Dostoyévsky wrote the most unique of all his works, *Memoirs from Underground*.

To meet his enormous liabilities he set down to work at his great novels. In 1865–6 he wrote *Crime and Punishment*. He sold the copyright of all his works for the ludicrous sum of three thousand roubles ($1,500) to the publisher Stellóvsky. The contract stipulated that besides all previously published work Dostoyévsky was to deliver to Stellóvsky by November 1866 a full-length unpublished novel. To meet this obligation he began writing *The Gambler*, and, to be able to finish in time, he engaged a shorthand secretary, Anna Grigórievna Snítkin. Owing to her efficient help, *The Gambler* was delivered in time. A few months later he married his secretary (February 1867).

Anna Grigórievna proved the best of wives, and in the long run it was owing to her devotion and practical sense (as much as to his own enormous working capacity) that Dostoyévsky freed himself from his debts and was able to spend the last ten years of his life in comparatively easy circumstances. But the first years after their marriage were beset with the most cruel ordeals. Very soon after the wedding Dostoyévsky had to leave Russia, and for four years remained abroad for fear of falling into the hands of his creditors if he returned to Russia. His difficulties were aggravated by a new access of gambling frenzy in the summer of 1867. Only gradually, by dint of hard and hurried labor at his great novels, and with the aid of Anna Grigórievna, he once more stood on his feet and in 1871 could return to Russia. The years between the suppression of *Vrémya* and his return to Russia after four years' life abroad were, both in quantity and in significance, the most productive of his whole life. *Memoirs from Underground, Crime and Punishment, The Gambler, The Idiot* (1868–9), *The Eternal Husband* (1870), and *The Possessed* (1871–2), all belong to this period, while the plan of *The Life of a Great Sinner,* planned in the same year, contains the germ of *The Brothers Karamázov.*

When they returned to Petersburg, the Dostoyévskys, though not at first free from all difficulties, began to have better luck. The publication in book form, at their own expense, of *The Possessed* (Russian title *Bésy* "Devils" 1873) was a success. In the same year Dostoyévsky became editor of Prince V. Meschérsky's weekly *The Citizen.* This gave him a settled income. In 1876 he himself began publishing *An Author's Diary,* which had a considerable sale. The political ideas of Dostoyévsky were now more in tune with the times, and his influence grew. He felt a more sympathetic atmosphere round him. The high-water mark of his popularity was reached in the year preceding his death, when *The Brothers Karamázov* appeared. The culmination was his famous address on the occasion of the unveiling of the Púshkin memorial in Moscow, delivered on June 8, 1880. The address evoked an enthusiasm that had no precedents in Russian literary history. The following winter he fell seriously ill, and, on January 28, 1881, he died.

Both psychologically and historically Dostoyévsky is

a very complex figure, and it is necessary to distinguish not only between the various periods of his life and the various currents of his mind, but between the different *levels* of his personality. The higher—or rather, deeper—level is present only in the imaginative work of his last seventeen years, beginning with *Memoirs from Underground*. The lower—or rather, more superficial—level is apparent in all his work, but more particularly in his journalistic writings and in the imaginative work of before 1864. The deeper, the essential, Dostoyévsky is one of the most significant and ominous figures in the whole history of the human mind, one of its boldest and most disastrous adventures in the sphere of ultimate spiritual quest. The superficial Dostoyévsky is a man of his time, comparable—and not always favorably comparable—to many other Russian novelists and publicists of the age of Alexander II, a mind that had many rivals and that cannot be placed in any way apart from, or above, Herzen, Grigóriev, or Leóntiev. The other one, the essential Dostoyévsky, for the profundity, complexity, and significance of his spiritual experience, has only two possible rivals in the whole range of Russian literature—Rózanov and of course Tolstóy, who, however, seems to have been given to the world for the special purpose of being contrasted with Dostoyévsky.

The comparison between Tolstóy and Dostoyévsky has for many years been, with Russian and foreign critics, a favorite subject of discussion. Much has been said of the aristocratic nature of the former and the plebeian nature of the latter; of the one's Luciferian pride and the other's Christian humility; of the naturalism of the one and the spiritualism of the other. Apart from the difference of social position and education, a main difference between the two is that Tolstóy was a puritan, and Dostoyévsky a symbolist. That is to say that for Dostoyévsky all relative values were related to absolute values and received their significance, positive or negative, from the way they reflected the higher values. For Tolstóy the absolute and the relative are two disconnected worlds, and the relative is in itself evil. Hence Tolstóy's contempt for the meaningless diversity of human history, and Dostoyévsky's eminently historical mode of thinking, which relates to all the main line of higher Russian thought—to Chaadáyev, the Slavophils, Herzen, Grigóriev, Leóntiev, and Soloviëv.

Dostoyévsky is one of them: his thought is always historically related. Even in their most purely spiritual form, his
problems are not concerned with an eternal, static, and immutable law, but with the drama that is being played out
in human history by the supreme forces of the universe.
Hence the great complexity, fluidity, and many-sidedness
of his thought as compared to the rigidly geometrical and
rectilinear thinking of Tolstóy. Tolstóy (in spite of his
sensitiveness to the infinitesimals of life) was in his moral
philosophy, both on the high level of *A Confession* and
on the much lower level of his anti-alcoholic and vegetarian
tracts, a Euclid of moral quantities. Dostoyévsky deals in
the elusive calculus of fluid values. Hence also what
Strákhov so happily called the "purity" of Tolstóy and
what may be called the obvious "impurity" of Dostoyévsky. He was never dealing with stable entities, but with
fluid processes; and not seldom the process was one of
dissolution and putrefaction.

On a more social and historical plane it is also important to note that while Tolstóy was an aristocrat and
(alone of his literary contemporaries) culturally had his
roots in the old French and eighteenth-century civilization
of the Russian gentry, Dostoyévsky was, to the core, a
plebeian and a democrat. He belonged to the same historical and social formation that produced Belínsky, Nekrásov,
and Grigóriev, and to this is due, among other things,
that absence of all grace and elegance, whether internal
or external, which characterizes all his work, together with
an absence of reserve, discipline, and dignity, and an excess
of abnormal self-consciousness.

The great, later novels of Dostoyévsky are ideological
novels. The idea of the novel is inseparable from the imaginative conception, and neither can it be abstracted from
the story nor the story stripped of the idea. But this does
not apply to the novels of his middle period, 1857–63,
which are in many ways a continuation of his early work
(1845–9) rather than an anticipation of what was to follow. The work of 1857–63 belongs to the same superficial
level as Dostoyévsky's earlier work. The deeper abysses
of his consciousness are not yet revealed in it. It is different, however, from the work of the forties in that it
is free from the immediate influence of Gógol and from
the intense stylistic preoccupation that marks *Poor Folk*

and *The Double*. The principal works of this period are *The Manor of Stepánchikovo and its Inhabitants* (1859; in Mrs. Garnett's translation, *The Friend of the Family*), *The Humiliated and Insulted* (1861), and *Memoirs from the House of Death* (1860–2). Of these, *The Humiliated and Insulted* is a novel closely connected in style and tone with the French romantic novel of social compassion and with the later and less humorous novels of Dickens. The religion of compassion, verging often on melodramatic sentimentality, finds there its purest expression, as yet uncomplicated by the deeper problems of the next period.

Stepánchikovo also lacks the intellectual passionateness and richness of the essential Dostoyévsky, but in other respects it is one of the most characteristic of his works. All his great novels have a construction that is dramatic rather than narrative. *Stepánchikovo* is the most dramatic of all (it was originally planned as a play)— only, of course, it is far too long for the theater. It is also interesting for the way it displays what Mikhaylóvsky called the "cruelty" of Dostoyévsky. Its subject is the intolerable psychological bullying inflicted by the hypocrite and parasite, Fomá Opískin, on his host, Colonel Rostánev. The imbecile meekness with which the colonel consents to be bullied and allows all around him—his friends, and servants—to be bullied by Opískin, and the perverse inventiveness of Fomá in devising various psychological humiliations for his victims, produce an impression of intolerable, almost physical pain. Fomá Opískin is a weird figure of grotesque, gratuitous, irresponsible, petty, and ultimately joyless evil that together with Saltykóv's Porfíry Golovlëv and Sologúb's Peredónov form a trinity to which probably no foreign literature has anything to compare. *Stepánchikovo* was intended for a comical and humorous story with a touch of satire (aimed, it would seem, at Gógol, as revealed by *A Correspondence with Friends*), but it must be confessed that though the element of humor is unmistakably present, it is a kind of humor that requires a rather peculiar constitution to enjoy.

The same "cruelty" in an even more elaborate form is to be found in the most characteristic of the shorter stories of this period—*A Bad Predicament* (1862), in which, with a detail on the scale of *The Double*, Dostoyévsky describes the sufferings of humiliated self-conscious-

ness experienced by a superior civil servant at a wedding
of a minor clerk of his, where he comes uninvited, behaves
himself ridiculously, gets drunk, and involves the poor
clerk in heavy expenses.

Apart from these stories stand *Memoirs from the
House of Death* (1860–2), during the lifetime of Dostoyévsky his most famous and most universally recognized book.
It is the account of a term of penal servitude spent by a
convict of the educated classes in a Siberian prison, based
mainly on autobiographical material. Like the other works
of Dostoyévsky before 1864, it is free from his later complex and deeper experience. Its ultimate message is one of
human and optimistic sympathy. Even the moral degradation of the most hardened criminals is not represented
so as to make one lose faith in human nature. It is rather
a protest against the inefficiency of punishment. In spite
of the dreadful, sordid, and degrading details of crime
and cruelty, *The House of Death* is, after all, a bright and
glad book, full of "uplift," and well made to fit in with
an age of optimistic social idealism. The main motif of
the book was the tragic estrangement between the educated
convict and the people: even at the end of his term the
narrator feels himself an outcast in a world of outcasts.
Stripped of all external social privilege and placed in equal
conditions with several hundreds of simple Russian people,
he discovers that he is rejected by them and will ever
remain an outcast from their midst for the mere fact of
belonging to the educated class that had torn itself away
from the people's ideals. This idea closely relates *The
House of Death* to the journalistic writings of Dostoyévsky.

Dostoyévsky's non-imaginative writings belong to two
principal periods: the articles he contributed in 1861–5 to
Vrémya and *The Epoch,* and *An Author's Diary* of 1873–
81. On the whole his political philosophy may be defined
as a democratic Slavophilism or a mystical populism. It
has points of contact with Grigóriev and the Slavophils,
but also with Herzen and the populists. Its main idea is
that Russian educated society must be redeemed by a
renewal of contact with the people, and by an acceptance
of the people's religious ideals—that is to say, of Orthodoxy. On the whole it may be said that the democratic
and populist element predominates in the writings of the
sixties, while in the seventies, under the influence of the

growth of revolutionary socialism, the nationalist and conservative element tends to get the upper hand. But on the
whole Dostoyévsky's journalism is more or less of a piece
from beginning to end. His religion is Orthodoxy *because*
it is the religion of the Russian people, whose mission it
is to redeem the world by a reassertion of the Christian
faith. Christianity is to him the religion not so much of
purity and salvation, as of charity and compassion. All
this is obviously connected with the ideas of Grigóriev and
his teaching of meekness as the essential message of Russia to the world. Dostoyévsky's enemies were the atheistic
radicals and socialists, and all the impious forces of
Western, atheistic civilization. The victory of Christian Russia over the godless West was his political and historical
faith. The taking of Constantinople is a necessary symbolic
item of his program as the sanction of the universal mission of the Russian nation.

Somewhat apart, and once more strongly inclining to
the left, stands the Púshkin address, the most famous and
concentratedly significant of his unimaginative writings.
Here he praises Púshkin for the virtue of "pan-humanity,"
which is the gift of understanding all peoples and civilizations. It is the main feature of the Russian people.
The union of all humanity is the message and mission of
Russia to the world—a strange prophecy of the Third
International. In the same address, largely retracting from
his previous writings, he extolled the "Russian wanderer,"
by which term he covertly designated the Revolutionaries
and their predecessors. He discerned in them a yearning
after religious truth that was only temporarily obscured by
the lure of atheistic socialism. In commenting on the
Gypsies, moreover, he expounded something like a theory
of mystical anarchism and proclaimed the wickedness of
all violence and punishment, thus unexpectedly forestalling
Tolstóy's doctrine of non-opposition. The Púshkin address
did much to reconcile the radicals with Dostoyévsky.

It also displays one of the most attractive features of
Dostoyévsky the publicist—his boundless faculty of enthusiasm and admiration. The greatest portion of it went to
Púshkin. But he speaks with equal enthusiasm of Racine,
and there have been few nobler tributes to the memory
of a literary and political enemy than Dostoyévsky's obituary of Nekrásov.

Dostoyévsky's style in his journalistic writings is of course unmistakably personal. But like all the journalistic press of the time, it is diffuse and formless. The individual vices of Dostoyévsky as a prose writer are a certain nervous shrillness and uneasiness of tone, which reappear in his novels wherever he has to speak in his own person.

The dialogue of the novels and the monologue of those of his writings that are written in the person of some fictitious character are also marked by a nervous tension and an exasperated (and perhaps exasperating) "on-end-ness" that was their creator's own. They are all agitated, as it were, by a wind of desperate spiritual passion and anxiety, rising from the innermost recesses of his subconsciousness. In spite of the *air de famille* of all his characters, Dostoyévsky's dialogue and personative monologue are incomparable for his wonderful art of individualization. There is an enormous variety of individuality in the comparatively limited and narrow compass of Dostoyévsky's mankind.

In all the later imaginative work of Dostoyévsky (from *Memoirs from Underground* to *The Brothers Karamázov*) it is impossible to separate the ideological from the artistic conception. These are novels of ideas, in which the characters, for all their enormous vitality and individuality, are after all only atoms charged with the electricity of ideas. It has been said of Dostoyévsky that he "felt ideas," as others feel cold and heat and pain. This distinguishes him from all other imaginative writers —the same faculty of "feeling ideas" is to be discovered only in certain great religious thinkers, in St. Paul, St. Augustine, Pascal, and Nietzsche.

Dostoyévsky is a psychological novelist, and his principal means of expression is analysis. In this he is the twin and counterpart of Tolstóy. But both the object and the method of his analysis are quite different from Tolstóy's. Tolstóy dissects the soul in its vital aspects; he studies the physiological basis of the mind, the subconscious workings of the will, the anatomy of the individual act. The higher spiritual states, when he comes to them, are discovered to be *outside* and on a different plane from life. They have no dimensions; they are entirely irrational to the ordinary stream of experience. Dostoyévsky, on the contrary, deals in those psychic strata where the mind and will are in constant contact with higher spiritual entities, where the ordinary stream of experience is constantly deflected by ultimate and absolute values and agitated by a never subsiding wind of the spirit. It is interesting to compare the treatment of the same feeling—the feeling of self-consciousness—by Tolstóy and by Dostoyévsky. Both were painfully self-conscious. But in Tolstóy it is purely social sensitiveness, the consciousness of the unfavorable impression produced by one's own personal appearance and conduct on persons one would like to impress favorably. Hence, with the growth of his social independence and the extinction of his social ambitions, the theme ceases to occupy Tolstóy. In Dostoyévsky the torture of self-consciousness is the torture of the ultimate and absolute value of a human personality, wounded, unrecognized, and humiliated by other human personalities. Dostoyévsky's "cruelty" finds a particularly rich field to feed on in the analysis of wounded and suffering human dignity. Either Tolstóy's self-consciousness is social or it ceases to operate; Dostoyévsky's is metaphysical and religious and can never disappear. This again brings forward the "purity" of Tolstóy and the "impurity" of Dostoyévsky: Tolstóy could overcome all his human failures and become a "naked man" before eternity. In Dostoyévsky his very spirit was inextricably entangled in the symbolical meshes of "relative reality." Hence also Tolstóy's later condemnation of the superfluous details of realism, with their absence of bearing on essential things, and Dostoyévsky's inability ever to transcend the limit of the temporal.

Dostoyévsky's method of analysis is also different from Tolstóy's. He does not dissect, but reconstructs. Tolstóy's question is always *why?* Dostoyévsky's *what?* This enables Dostoyévsky in many of his novels to do without all direct analysis of feelings and to reveal the inner life of his characters by their acts and speeches. For what they are is inevitably reflected in what they do and say. This is the symbolist attitude, with its faith in the necessary and real interconnection of the relative (behavior) and the absolute (personality); while for the "puritan" mentality of Tolstóy, behavior is only a veil cast over the non-dimensional core of the soul.

Memoirs from Underground, the work that introduces us, chronologically, to the "mature" Dostoyévsky, contains

at once the essence of his essential self. It cannot be regarded as imaginative literature pure and simple. There is
in it quite as much philosophy as literature. It would have
to be connected with his journalistic writings were it not
that it proceeded from a deeper and more significant
spiritual level of his personality. The work occupies a
central place in the creation of Dostoyévsky. Here his
essential tragical intuition is expressed in the most unadulterated and ruthless form. It transcends art and literature, and its place is among the great mystical revelations
of mankind. The faith in the supreme value of the human
personality and its freedom, and in the irrational religious
and tragic foundation of the spiritual universe, which is
above reason, above the distinction of good and evil (the
faith, ultimately, of all mystical religion), is expressed in a
paradoxical, unexpected, and entirely spontaneous form.
The central position of *Memoirs from Underground* in the
work of Dostoyévsky was first discerned by Nietzsche and
Rózanov. It stands in the center of the writings of Shestóv,
the greatest of Dostoyévsky's commentators. Viewed as
literature, it is also the most original of Dostoyévsky's
works, although also the most unpleasant and the most
"cruel." It cannot be recommended to those who are not
either sufficiently strong to overcome it or sufficiently
innocent to remain unpoisoned. It is a strong poison, which
is most safely left untouched.

Of the novels, *The Gambler, The Eternal Husband,
The Adolescent* are not philosophical in the same sense as
the four great novels are. *The Gambler* is interesting as
being demonstrably self-revelatory in its description of the
gambling fever, and as giving in the figure of Pauline one
of the most remarkable expressions of Dostoyévsky's favorite type of the proud and demoniac woman, which seems to
be connected with the real person of Apollinária Súslova.
The Eternal Husband belongs to the most "cruel" of his
writings. It turns round the irreparable spiritual injury
inflicted on the wronged human dignity of a husband by
the lover of his wife, and his subtle and slow revenge (a
torture to himself as to the other) on his wronger. *The
Adolescent* (1875) of all Dostoyévsky's writings is most
closely connected with the journalistic *Author's Diary,* and
is ideologically on a lower plane than the four great novels.
Crime and Punishment (1866), *The Idiot* (1868), *The*

Possessed (1871–2), and *The Brothers Karamázov* (1880), the four great novels, form, as it were, a connected cycle. They are all dramatic in construction, tragical in conception, and philosophical in significance. They are very complex wholes: not only is the plot inextricably woven into the philosophy—in the philosophy itself the essential Dostoyévsky, whom we have in a pure form in *Memoirs from Underground*, is inseparably mixed with the more journalistic Dostoyévsky of *An Author's Diary*. Hence the possibility of reading these novels in at least three different ways. The first, the way their contemporaries read them, relates them to the current issues of Russian public and social life of 1865–80. The second views them as the progressive disclosure of a "new Christianity," which found its final expression in the figures of Zosíma and Alësha Karamázov in the last of the four novels. The third connects them with *Memoirs from Underground* and the central tragic core of Dostoyévsky's spiritual experience. At last our contemporaries have discovered a fourth way of reading them, which pays no attention to their philosophy and takes them as pure stories of melodramatic incident.

His contemporaries, who kept to the first set of readings, regarded Dostoyévsky as a writer of great natural gifts but questionable taste and insufficient artistic discipline, who had original views on matters of general interest and a considerable power to make his characters live. They deplored his lack of taste, his grotesque misrepresentation of real life, his weakness for crudely sensational effects, but admired his great knowledge of morbid human types and the power of his psychopathic analysis. If they were conservatives, they recognized truth in the picture he drew of the nihilists; if they were radicals, they lamented that a man who had been ennobled by political martyrdom should stoop to be the ally of dirty reactionaries.

The Dostoyevskians of the following generation accepted the novels as a revelation of a new Christianity in which ultimate problems of good and evil were discussed and played out with ultimate decisiveness, and which, taken as a whole, gave a new doctrine, complete in all points, of spiritual Christianity. The tragic failure of Raskólnikov to assert his individuality "without God"; the saintly idiocy of Prince Mýshkin; the dreadful picture of godless socialism in *The Possessed;* above all, the figure of the "pure" Alësha Karamázov and the preachings of the holy Zosíma; these were accepted as dogmatic revelations of a new ultimate form of religion. This attitude towards Dostoyévsky, dominant in the early years of this century, has still numerous partisans among the older generation. To them Dostoyévsky is the prophet of a new and supreme "universal harmony," which will transcend and pacify all the discords and tragedies of mankind.

But the truth is (and here lies the exceptional significance of Dostoyévsky as a spiritual case) that the tragedies of Dostoyévsky are irreducible tragedies that cannot be solved or pacified. His harmonies and his solutions are all on a lower or shallower level than his conflicts and his tragedies. To understand Dostoyévsky is to accept his tragedies as irreducible and not to try to shirk them by the contrivances of his smaller self. His Christianity in particular is of a very doubtful kind. It is impossible to overlook the fact that it was no ultimate solution to him, that it did not reach into the ultimate depths of his soul, that it was a more or less superficial spiritual formation which it is dangerous to identify with real Christianity. But these issues are too complicated, too important, and too debatable to be more than pointed at in a book of the present kind.

The ideological character of Dostoyévsky's novels is in itself sufficient to mark him off from the rest of the Russian realistic school. It is obviously different in kind from the social messages of the novels of Turgénev or Goncharóv. The interests at stake are of a different order. The fusion of the philosophical and imaginative fabric is complete; the conversations are never irrelevant, because they *are* the novel (as the analysis can never be irrelevant in Tolstóy's, or the atmosphere in Turgénev's, novels). Novels of the same kind have been written only under the direct influence of Dostoyévsky by novelists of the symbolist school, but of them only Andréy Bély has succeeded in being original and creative.

Another feature that distinguishes Dostoyévsky from the other realists is his partiality for sensationalism and elaborate intrigue. In this he is a true disciple of Balzac, of the French sensational school, and of Dickens. His novels, however charged they may be with ideas and philosophy, are in substance novels of mystery and suspense. He was in complete control of the technique of this kind of novel. The devices he uses to lengthen the suspense and mystery of his novels are numerous. Everyone remembers the ultimately unsolved mystery of the murder of old Karamázov and the cat-and-mouse game of Porfíry, the examining magistrate, with Raskólnikov. A characteristic device is also the omission in *The Idiot* of all account of the life of Prince Mýshkin, Rogózhin, and Nastásia Filípovna in Moscow in the period between the first and second parts, to which allusion is often mysteriously made in an offhand manner as if to explain their subsequent relations. The atmosphere of tension to bursting point is arrived at by a series of minor devices, familiar to every reader of every novel of Dostoyévsky, that are easily reducible to a common principle. This combination of the ideological and sensational elements is, from the literary point of view, the most striking feature of Dostoyévsky's "developed manner."

In his interestedness in current social issues, in his "philanthropic" sympathy for the suffering, insignificant man, above all in his choice of milieu, and in the elaboration of concrete, realistic detail, especially in the speech of his characters, Dostoyévsky belongs to the realistic school. It would, however, be a mistake to regard his novels as *representations* of Russian life under Alexander II—not only because it is in general dangerous to regard even realistic fiction as a representation of life, but because Dostoyévsky is in substance less true to life than any other writer. Aksákov, Turgénev, Goncharóv, Tolstóy, did at least honestly try to represent Russian life as they saw it. Dostoyévsky did not. He dealt in spiritual essences, in emanations of his own infinitely fertile spiritual experience. He only gave them the externally realistic garbs of current life and attached them to current facts of Russian life. But *The Possessed* is no more a true picture of the terrorists of the sixties than Gógol's Plyúshkin is the true picture of a typical miser. They are exteriorizations of the author's self. Hence their latent "prophetic" and universal significance. They are distinctly on a different scale from the Russian life of the time. *The Possessed*, though a novel of terroristic conspiracy, is about something quite different from what the actual terroristic movement was about. Dostoyévsky's Russia is no more the real Russia of Alexander II than the characters of *Wuthering Heights* are the real West Riding of the early nineteenth century. They are related to it and symbolical of it, but they belong to another order of existence.

The essential units of Dostoyévsky's novels are the characters, and in this respect he is in the true tradition of Russian novel-writing, which regards the novelist as primarily a maker of characters. His characters are at once saturated with metaphysical significance and symbolism, and intensely individual. Dostoyévsky is as great a master as Tolstóy in giving individuality to the people of his creation. But the nature of this individuality is different: Tolstóy's characters are faces, flesh and blood, men and women of our acquaintance, ordinary and unique, like people in real life. Dostoyévsky's are souls, spirits. Even in his lewd and sensual sinners, their carnal self is not so much their body and their nerves as the spiritual essence of their body, of their carnality. Flesh—real, material flesh— is absent from the world of Dostoyévsky, but the idea, the spirit of flesh, is very present, and this is why in that world the spirit can be assailed by the flesh on its own spiritual ground. These spiritual extracts of the flesh are among the most terrible and tremendous creations of Dostoyévsky— and no one has ever created anything approaching the impure grandeur of old Karamázov.

The portrait gallery of Dostoyévsky is enormous and varied. It is impossible to enumerate the portraits or to give briefly characteristics of them: their vitality, reality, and complexity, and their quantity are too great. They live in every one of the great novels (and in the minor novels too) a strange, morbid, dematerialized life, of terribly human demons or terribly live ghosts—with their "cracks" (nadrýv, a word used in a sense not unlike Freud's "complex") and wounds, their spiritual intensity and intense personality, their self-consciousness, their pride (the "proud women" especially), and their knowledge of good and evil—a suffering, tormented, and never-to-be-pacified race. Of the individual novels, the most rich in persons is perhaps The Possessed, which contains at least three creations that come at the top of the list—the terrible and weirdly empty figure of the hero, Stavrógin; the "pure" atheist, Kirílov, perhaps next to Memoirs from Underground, the most ultimately profound creation of Dostoyévsky; and the no less terrible "little demon," the mean and strong plotter, flatterer, idolater, and murderer, Peter Verkhovénsky. These three figures are enough to indicate in their maker a creative force in which he has had no human rivals.

Though influential as a publicist, and always recognized (chiefly, however, on the strength of *Poor Folk* and *The House of Death*) as a very eminent novelist, Dostoyévsky during his lifetime did not get anything like adequate recognition. This is only natural: his mentality was "prophetic" and belonged historically, not to his own time, but to that preceding the great Revolution. He was the first and the greatest symptom of the spiritual decomposition of the Russian soul in its highest levels which preceded the final break-up of Imperial Russia.

His literary influence during his lifetime and in the eighties was insignificant and limited to a certain revival of the theme of pity and compassion, and to a certain vogue of morbid psychology among a few second-rate novelists. Nor was his influence in the strictly literary sense important even afterwards. Very few writers can in any strict sense be called his literary progeny. But the influence of Dostoyévsky as a whole and complete phenomenon cannot be exaggerated. The pre-Revolutionary generation, especially that born between 1865 and 1880 (that is to say, by a curious coincidence, between the dates of the first and last of his great novels), was literally soaked with his ideas and his mentality. Since then the younger generation has become more indifferent to him. Not that his greatness is put to question, not even that he is less read or less written about. But our organism has grown immune to his poisons, which we have assimilated and ejected. The most typical attitude of our contemporaries towards Dostoyévsky is to accept him as an absorbingly interesting novelist of adventure. The young men of today are not very far from putting him on a level with Dumas, an attitude that testifies of course to a very limited sensitiveness to his essential individuality. But it would be wrong to lament this attitude; for the real Dostoyévsky is food that is easily assimilated only by a profoundly diseased spiritual organism.

SALTYKÓV-SCHEDRÍN

The civic and social element already so prominent in the work of Turgénev and of the other novelists of the forties was further emphasized by the writers of the reign of Alexander II. The anti-æsthetic movement on the one hand, and the increased possibility of exposing and satirizing existing social and administrative conditions on the other, led to the formation of a literary genre that stood halfway between fiction and journalism. The first and the most remarkable of these semi-novelists and semi-journalists, as well as the only one who was to win more or less general recognition and to be included in the number of classics, was Michael Evgráfovich Saltykóv (1826–89), better known in his own time under the pseudonym of N. Schedrín.

Born of a family of country squires, Saltykóv was educated at the same Lyceum where Púshkin had studied. In 1844, on the completion of his studies, he entered the Civil Service. At the same time he came in touch with the progressive circles of the young generation and began writing for the Westernizing press. Two stories by him, in the style of the "natural school," appeared in 1847–3, over pseudonyms. Their appearance coincided with the turn towards extreme reaction, and Saltykóv, for having written them, was suddenly transferred to the northeastern city of Vyátka (where Herzen had been transferred fourteen years earlier). In Vyátka, Saltykóv remained in the Civil Service and, in spite of his disgrace, even rose to a rather important and responsible post in the administrative board controlling the provincial police. After the accession of Alexander II he was transferred back to Petersburg and in 1858 appointed vice-governor of a province. In 1856 he resumed his literary work. *Provincial Sketches,* a series of satirical sketches of provincial officialdom, appeared in Nekrásov's *Sovreménnik* over the pseudonym of N. Schedrín. In the reforming atmosphere of 1856–61 his writings were received with general approval, and he soon became one of the most universally recognized authors. In 1868 he left the Civil Service to consecrate himself entirely to literature, and, together with Nekrásov, became the editor of *Otéchestvennye zapíski,* which was to replace the *Sovreménnik,* suppressed by the authorities in 1866. Henceforward Saltykóv became one of the leaders of the radical intelligentsia and retained this position till his death. His review was the most advanced of all the left organs of the home press. The reaction that followed the assassination of Alexander II was fatal to it; it was suppressed in 1884. In the eighties Saltykóv remained a last remnant of the heroic age of reform and progress, universally venerated by all the advanced intelligentsia.

The greater part of Saltykóv's work is a rather nondescript kind of satirical journalism, for the most part with no narrative skeleton, and intermediate in form between the classical "character" and the modern *feuilleton*. Enormously and universally popular though it was in its own time, it has since lost much of its attraction simply because it satirizes conditions that have long ceased to exist and much of it has become unintelligible without comment.

His early works (*Provincial Sketches*, 1856–7; *Pompadours and Pompadouresses*, 1863–73, and others) are a "smiling" satire, more humorous than scornful, of the vices of the pre-Reform provincial officials. There is little earnestness and positive value in these early satires, and the extreme nihilist Písarev was not quite in the wrong when he condemned them as irresponsible and uninspired joking in a famous article entitled *Flowers of Innocent Humor* that scandalized the other radicals.

In 1869–70 appeared *The History of a Town*, which sums up the achievement of Saltykóv's first period. It is a sort of parody of Russian history, concentrated in the microcosm of a provincial town, whose successive governors are transparent caricatures of Russian sovereigns and ministers, and whose very name is representative of its qualities—Glúpov (Sillytown).

Saltykóv's later work is inspired by a keener sense of indignation and higher feeling for moral values. The satire is directed against the new post-Reform men: the "enlightened," but essentially unchanged, official; the unrooted, but unregenerate, squire; the grasping and shameless capitalist risen from the people. The intrinsic value of these books (*Gentlemen of Tashként*, 1869–72; *In the Realm of the Moderate and of the Exact*, 1874–7; *The Sanctuary Mon-Repos*, 1878–79; *Letters to Auntie*, 1881–2, and others) is greater than that of the earlier ones, but the excessive topicality of the satire makes them date very distinctly. Besides, they are written in a language that Saltykóv himself called Æsopic. It is one continuous circumlocution in view of the censorship and demands a constant running commentary. The style, moreover, is deeply rooted in the bad journalese of the period, which goes back to Sękowski's and which today invariably produces an impression of painfully elaborate vulgarity.

On a higher level of literary achievement stand the *Fables,* written in 1880–5, in which Saltykóv achieved a greater degree of artistic tightness, and occasionally (as in the admirable *Konyága,* in which the destinies of the Russian peasant are symbolized in the figure of an old downridden jade) a concentration that almost attains to poetry.

But, after all, Saltykóv's place in Russian literature would be only that of an eminent journalist were it not for his masterpiece—his only genuine novel—*The Golovlëv Family* (1872–6). This one book places him in the very front line of Russian realistic novelists and secures him a permanent place among the national classics. It is a social novel—the natural history of a family of provincial squires, intended to show up the poverty and bestiality of the civilization of the serf-owning class. The reign of brute matter over human lives has never been portrayed with greater force. Spiteful, greedy, selfish, without even any family feeling for each other, without even any satisfaction or any possibility of happiness in their dull and dark souls, the Golovlëvs are an unrelieved wilderness of animal humanity. The book is certainly the gloomiest in all Russian literature—all the more gloomy because the effect is attained by the simplest means without any theatrical, melodramatic, or atmospheric effects. Together with Goncharóv's *Oblómov* before, and Búnin's *Sukhodól* after it, it is the greatest *monumentum odiosum* erected to the memory of the Russian provincial gentry. The most remarkable single figure in the novel is Porfíry Golovlëv, nicknamed Iúdushka (little Judas), the empty and mechanical hypocrite who cannot stop talking unctuous and meaningless humbug, not for any inner need or outer profit, but because his tongue is in need of constant exercise. It is one of the most terrible visions of ultimately dehumanized humanity ever conceived by an imaginative writer.

In his last years Saltykóv undertook a large work of retrospective painting—*Old Years in Poshekhónie* (1887–9)—a chronicle of the life and surroundings of a family of the middle provincial gentry shortly before the abolition of serfdom. It contains numerous reminiscences of his own childhood. "Tendentious" and unrelievedly gloomy, it abounds in powerful painting but lacks that concentration and inevitability which *The Golovlëv Family* has, and which alone would have raised it above the level of mere "literature with a purpose."

THE DECLINE OF THE NOVEL IN THE SIXTIES AND SEVENTIES

By about 1860 the rank of universally approved authors was filled in, and no new novelist who appeared after that date was able to command general recognition. This was owing to two co-operative causes: the growing intensity of party feeling, which was breaking Russian opinion into more exclusive compartments and categories; and the very evident and distinct decline of creative force among the writers of the younger generation. The only novelist after 1860 who had nothing to fear from a comparison with the men of the forties was Nicholas Leskóv (1831–95). But the exasperated state of party feeling and his inability to fit in with any party precluded his general recognition—he was hooted down by the radical press and even placed under boycott. The late recognition of Leskóv, as well as the fact that his work has features that mark it off distinctly from that of all his contemporaries, has made me decide to discuss him in a later chapter.

In his early work, however—the reactionary novels *No Way Out* (1864) and *At Daggers Drawn* (1870–1)— Leskóv is little more than a typical "tendentious" anti-radical whose novels are scarcely superior to the common run of reactionary novels that were written in great quantities in the sixties and seventies to satirize the new movement and the young generation. This kind of fiction includes, it is true, such superior—and different—works as Písemsky's *Troubled Seas* (1863, the first of the lot), Turgénev's *Smoke,* Goncharóv's *The Precipice,* and even Dostoyévsky's *The Possessed.* But the typical reactionary novel is on a much lower level of literary significance. It is usually the story of an aristocratic and patriotic hero who fights single-handed, in spite of the insufficient support of the authorities, against Polish intrigue and nihilism. The most typical and popular purveyor of such novels was

Bolesław Markiéwicz. Other practitioners in the kind were
Victor Klyúshnikov, V. G. Avséyenko, and Vsévolod Kres-
tóvsky.

The reactionary novel had its counterpart in the
"tendentious" radical novel, which early became equally
conventionalized. The most notable of these novels was the
first of them, Chernyshévsky's *What to Do?* (1864), which
had a considerable influence on the formation of the radical
youth. Other famous and influential novels were *Signs of
the Times,* by Daniel Mordóvtsev, and *Step by Step,* by
Innocent Omulévsky. The most prolific of the radical
novelists was A. K. Scheller-Mikháylov. All these novels
are about ideal radical young men and girls victoriously
struggling against hostile social conditions. From a literary
point of view they are all quite worthless. But they contributed to the formation of the idealistic intelligentsia of
the seventies.

In the seventies a third kind of "tendentious" novel
was added to these two: the populist (*naródnik*) novel. It
did not represent the individual virtues of the heroes of the
educated classes, but the collective virtues of the peasant
commune in its struggle against the dark faces of big and
small capitalists. The most notable of these populist novelists were N. N. Zlatovrátsky (1845–1911) and P. V.
Zasodímsky (1843–1912).

Other novelists continued the traditions of Turgénev
and the men of the forties without exaggerating the "tendentious" element, but emphasized the social at the expense
of the artistic element of their realism. Peter Dmítrievich
Boborýkin (1836–1922) tried to rival Turgénev in his
sensitiveness to the changes of mood of the Russian intelligentsia, and his innumerable novels form a sort of chronicle
of Russian society from the sixties to the twentieth century.
A more genuine spirit of the school of Turgénev will be
found in the rural novels of Eugene Márkov. Another rural
novelist of some importance was Sergéy Terpigórev, whose
Impoverishment (1880) was intended as a vast picture of
the social decay of the middle gentry of central Russia after
the abolition of serfdom.

Somewhat apart from the other fiction of his time
stand the unpretentious and quite enjoyable stories of naval
life by Constantine Stanyukóvich, the only Russian novelist
of the sea in the nineteenth century. Still more apart stand

the fairy tales by N. P. Wagner ("Kot-Murlýka"), Professor of Zoology at the University of Petersburg, the only writer of the time who attempted to write in a style that was not dominated by the canons of the "natural school."

These canons invaded the historical novel as well as the novel of contemporary life. The romantic and moderately realistic historical novel in the style of Scott breathed its last breath in the operatic *Prince Serébryany* (1863) of Alexéy Tolstóy, a work that is considerably below the level of his poetical, and even of his dramatic, achievement. The new historical novel was a sort of vulgarization of the method used by the other Tolstóy in *War and Peace*. Its principal practitioner was Count Eugène Salias de Tournemir. Other historical novelists, greatly in vogue in the last quarter of the century among the less sophisticated, but as a rule looked down upon by the advanced and the literate, were G. P. Danilévsky and Vsévolod Soloviëv, son of the historian and brother of the famous philosopher.

All this novel-writing was frankly and obviously derivative and second-rate. In so far as the younger generation (apart from Leskóv) produced anything, if not quite first-class, at least genuine, it all came from a group of young men of plebeian origin and radical convictions, who are somewhat loosely grouped by literary historians as the "plebeian novelists of the sixties" (*belletrísty raznochíntsy*).

THE "PLEBEIAN" NOVELISTS

The most notable of the plebeian novelists was Nikoláy Gerásimovich Pomyalóvsky (1835–63). He was the son of a deacon of a Petersburg suburb and was educated at a clerical seminary, which left in him, as was usual, none but the gloomiest impressions. His subsequent life was one continuous struggle for existence, which led him, as it did so many others of his time and class, to an early surrender to drink. He died at the age of twenty-eight after a particularly acute access of delirium tremens. All his work was done in the last three years of his life. His most famous book, and the one that made his reputation, was *Seminary Sketches* (1862–3), in which by the mere sober and matter-of-fact accumulation of realistic detail he succeeded in producing an impression of almost infernal horror. In

Bourgeois Happiness and in its sequel, *Mólotov* (1861),
Pomyalóvsky drew the character of a man of the young
generation. He did not idealize his hero, nor did he even
represent him as an idealist, but as a strong man intent on
finding for himself a place in life. When Pomyalóvsky died
he was working at a vast social novel, *Brother and Sister,*
picturing the life of a family of small Petersburg towns-
people. The fragments that remain make us bitterly regret
the loss of a novelist of vast outlook, original imagination,
and powerful grasp of reality. His unsweetened and unidealized, but by no means flat, realism; his careful avoidance of everything poetical and rhetorical; and his strong
sense of the grim poetry of ugliness—all were an individual
and new note in the orchestra of Russian realism. There
were also in Pomyalóvsky a cement of practical sense that
is unusual in a Russian intellectual and only transiently a
feature of the first generation of plebeian intellectuals that
came after the generation of the forties.

The same anti-romanticism and anti-æstheticism, a
natural reaction against the idealism of the forties, produced in the sixties an attitude towards the Russian peasant
that was opposed to the sentimental philanthropism of the
preceding age. It did not emphasize the human values that
can be discovered in the peasant, but the brutishness to
which he had been reduced by centuries of oppression and
ignorance. This attitude, with a touch of cynical flippancy,
is apparent in the witty sketches and dialogues of Nicholas
Uspénsky (1837–89; a first cousin of the more important
Gleb Uspénsky, of whom presently), which appeared in
1861 and were greeted by Chernyshévsky as the dawn of
a new and more sensible attitude to the people than that of
the sentimental "philanthropists." The same attitude is apparent in a less trivial form in the work of Vasíly Alexéyevich Sleptsóv (1836–78), one of the most characteristic
figures of the sixties. A nobleman and an exceedingly handsome man, Sleptsóv had a powerful attraction for the other
sex. He put into practice the ideals of free love to which his
generation was devoted. To the indignation of the radicals,
he was transparently lampooned by Leskóv in the reactionary novel *No Way Out.* As a writer Sleptsóv is particularly
remarkable for his brilliant command of realistic dialogue.
The dialogue of his peasants, often intensely comical, pre-
serves all the spoken intonations and all dialectal peculiari-

ties, and has the merit of a phonographic record without forfeiting the workmanlike tensity of genuine art. Sleptsóv's most ambitious work, *Hard Times* (1865), is a satirical picture of the liberal society of the sixties.

The same unsentimental attitude to the peasants, but raised to a more earnestly tragic power, inspires the work of Fëdor Mikháylovich Reshétnikov (1841–71), whose life story is almost identical with Pomyalóvsky's except that he was born in the far-off Province of Perm and had to surmount still greater difficulties in his struggle for a place in life. His story, portraying the life of the Finnish Permyaks of his native province, *The People of Podlípnoye* (1864), produced a tremendous impression by its ruthless representation of the peasants (the critics overlooked the fact that they were not Russian) as unmitigated, hopeless, downtrodden, and miserable brutes. The story was one of those which most powerfully promoted the movement of the "conscience-stricken nobles" by rousing in them a sense of social guilt for the state to which the people had been reduced.

The biography of Alexander Ivánovich Lévitov (1835–77) is almost the same story over again as those of Pomyalóvsky and Reshétnikov. He spent most of his life in wandering over the vast expanses of Russia, and his work is concerned chiefly with the homeless life of tramps and pilgrims. Lévitov stands out among his contemporaries for the romantic character of his work, which combines a poignantly lyrical note with a bitter irony in a way that is reminiscent of Heine's.

A very notable figure in the history of the Russian intelligentsia is Gleb Ivánovich Uspénsky (1843–1902). He began his literary career in 1866, with a series of sketches of life in the suburbs of his native city of Túla, *Manners of Rasteryáyeva Street,* in which he displayed an unmistakable gift of humor and human sympathy as well as a sober and unbiased vision of life. But his most characteristic and influential writings belong to the end of the seventies and to the early eighties, when after several years in the country he gave a series of semi-journalistic, semi-imaginative sketches of peasant life, the most important of which is *The Power of the Soil* (1882). They are marked by the same gifts of humor and intense humanity, of sober, unobscured vision. They reflected his disillusionment in the populist conception of the Russian peasant as an ideal communist. Appearing as they did in Saltykóv's radical review side by side with Zlatovrátsky's idealizations of the peasant commune, they contributed powerfully to the breakdown of dogmatic populism. But Gleb Uspénsky is interesting not only as a student of peasant life. He is in general one of the most representative and characteristic figures of the best type of Russian intellectual. Possessed of a morbidly developed moral sensitiveness, he lived the conflicts and the tragedies of the Russian radical mind with extraordinary intensity. The tragic romance of the Russian intellectual with the Russian people was played out in his soul as in a microcosm. Unfortunately his writings, diffuse and intensely topical, are obsolete even more than Saltykóv's, and few except students of the history of the Russian intelligentsia read them nowadays. In the early nineties Gleb Uspénsky became a victim to mental illness, which lasted till his death. It took the form of a morbid disintegration of personality. He felt himself divided into two beings, one of which he designated by his Christian name, Gleb; the other by his patronymic, Ivánovich. Gleb was the embodiment of all that was good; Ivánovich of all that was evil in Uspénsky—an identification characteristic of the eminently anti-traditional and rootless nature of the Russian radical intelligentsia.

At the end of the seventies another remarkable semijournalist was Andrew Novodvórsky (1853–82), who wrote under the pseudonym of A. Ósipovich. He took part in the revolutionary movement, and his stories are, as it were, fragments from the diary of an intellectual who was unable to identify himself wholeheartedly with what he thought the one important thing—revolutionary propaganda. The style of Novodvórsky is personal and full of a fine irony and incisive humor. He, alone in his generation, played with the plot and with the narrative illusion in the manner of Sterne. The obscurities and innuendoes impressed on him by the presence of the censorship contributed to enhance the whimsical and capricious character of his delightfully personal prose.

It is particularly agreeable for me to end this account with the name of Nicholas Afanásievich Kuschévsky, one of the most delightful and least recognized of Russian writers. His biography is similar to those of numerous

plebeian writers. Born in 1847 in Siberia, he came to Petersburg at the end of the sixties in search of literary employment but met with unsurmountable difficulties and suc-
cumbed to disease, destitution, and drink. While he lay
convalescent in a municipal hospital, he succeeded in
writing his one important work, the novel *Nicholas
Negórev, or The Happy Russian*. It appeared in Saltykóv's
and Nekrásov's magazine in 1871 and in book form in
1872, and had a considerable success among the radical
public. But his later work did not bear out the promise of
that book and is hardly above the level of average journalism. After five more years of hopeless struggle against
starvation, undermined by drink and consumption, Kuschévsky died in 1876.

Nicholas Negórev assumes the more or less orthodox
form of a chronicled life, the greater part of which is occupied by the childhood and boyhood of the hero. This hero,
in whose person the narrative is conducted, is a remarkable
type of moderately ambitious, moderately clever, moderately cowardly, moderately priggish boy who grows up to
be a successful, satisfied, and selfish bureaucrat. But it is
not the central figure, however finely drawn, that makes the
unique charm of the book. The other characters—
Nicholas's reckless, foolish, and generous brother Andrew;
their sister Liza; the extraordinary crank and fanatic
Ovérin; the hero's *fiancée* Sophie Vasílievna—are all figures
endowed with a convincing liveness that challenges comparison with *War and Peace*. Kuschévsky's delicacy of
touch is unique in Russian literature. For liveliness and
lightness of humor the book has no equals. On a higher
level of seriousness, the character of the fanatic Ovérin,
with his succession of dead-serious and dangerously earnest
fads while a schoolboy and his propagandist activities when
grown up, and the scene of the death of Sophie Vasílievna
belong to the greatest achievement of Russian fiction. From
the historical point of view the novel offers an unsurpassed
picture of the change that transformed the Russia of
Nicholas I into the almost anarchic Russia of the sixties.

9

The End of a Great Age

THE reign of Alexander II (1855–81) was an age of great
literary achievement, the Golden Age of the Russian novel.
It saw the making of almost every one of the great works of
Russian fiction, from Turgénev's *Rúdin* and Aksákov's
Family Chronicle to *Anna Karénina* and *The Brothers
Karamázov*. The best forces were attracted to the novel,
but by its side other forms of imaginative literature continued to flourish and helped to produce the impression
of a Golden Age. But there was a worm in the flower: all
this great achievement was by men of an older generation,
and they had no successors. Not one of the younger men
who had entered the literary career since 1856 was felt
worthy to stand beside them, and as one by one the old
men disappeared, there was no one to take their place.
The turning point came soon after 1880: Dostoyévsky died
in 1881, Turgénev in 1883. Tolstóy announced his withdrawal from literature. The great age was over.

The generation born between 1830 and 1850 was by
no means poor in talents, but these talents were directed
into other channels than literature. It was a generation of
great composers—Musórgsky, Tchaikóvsky, Rímsky-Kórsakov; of great scientists, like Mendeléyev; of eminent paint-
ers, journalists, lawyers, and historians. But its poets and
novelists were recruited from among the second-rate. It

was as if the nation had expended too much of its forces on literature and was now making up by giving all the genius it had to the other arts and sciences.

But apart from this mysterious process of restoring the balance between various spheres of intellectual activity, there were good reasons why literature should decline. The first is connected with certain essential features of Russian literature itself, and of Russian literary criticism in particular. The great Russian novelists were superb masters of their craft, even those of them who, like Tolstóy, most tried to hide it and affected to despise "form." But they *did* try to hide it and *did* affect to despise "form." At any rate, before the public they seemed to countenance the view that it was their message that signified, and not their art. The critics went further and crudely identified the value of literary work with the moral or social utility of its message. They "declared war on æsthetics," and proscribed all interest in "pure art." New beginners in literature became easily imbued with the doctrine that form was naught, and matter everything. This made impossible the transmission of those traditions of the craft which alone permit the normal development of literary art. The young were prevented from profiting by the example of their elders and betters by a taboo laid on all questions of form. They could only ape them, unconsciously and unintelligently, but not learn from them in any creative sense. The generation of 1860 made an attempt to break away from the established forms of the novel. This attempt promised to develop into a creative quest for new ways of expression, something like a premature futurist movement. But the atmosphere was unpropitious for such a development, and it ended in nothing. The most significant of the young innovators, Pomyalóvsky, died very young, and under the general pressure of utilitarianism the movement, instead of leading to a rejuvenation of old forms, resulted in a complete emancipation from all form. This stage is reached in the work of the most gifted democratic novelist of the period—Gleb Uspénsky. As for the more traditional and conservative writers, they were able only to repeat the processes and methods of the great realists, vulgarizing and cheapening them. Whether they applied the realistic manner to give a fresh appearance to the historical novel, or used it to make propaganda for or against radical ideas, or to describe the

virtues of the peasant commune and the vices of capitalistic
civilization, they are all equally unoriginal, uninteresting
and, unreadable. They can only be classified, like M. P.'s,
according to their political allegiance.

A second reason that accentuated the break of literary
tradition was the great social upheaval produced by the
Emancipation of the serfs and the other liberal reforms of
the first half of Alexander II's reign. The Emancipation
dealt a mortal blow to the economic welfare of the class
that had up to then monopolized all literary culture—the
landed gentry. Its middle strata, which were intellectually
the most active, suffered most from the blow. A new class
arose to replace them—the intelligentsia. The origin of this
class was composite. It absorbed many members of the
ruined gentry, but the groundwork consisted of men risen
from the lower, or rather *outer,* classes that had not previously taken part in modern civilization. Sons of the clergy
were especially numerous and prominent among the new
men of the sixties. One feature is common to all these new
intellectuals—complete apostasy from all parental tradition. If he was the son of a priest, he would of necessity be
an atheist; if the son of a squire, an agrarian socialist. Revolt
against all tradition was the only watchword of the class.
To preserve a literary tradition under these circumstances
was doubly difficult—and it was not preserved. Only that
was retained from the older writers which was considered
to be directly useful for the purposes of revolution and
progress.

The Reforms produced an enormous change in Russian life and opened many new channels to ambitious and
vigorous men, who under the preceding regime would most
probably have turned to writing verse or fiction. The new
law courts demanded large numbers of educated and
civilized workers. The rapid growth of capitalistic enterprises
attracted numerous workers, and the number of engineers
was many times multiplied. The rise of evolutionary
theories made science fashionable and attractive. The whole
atmosphere became freer and more propitious for every
kind of intellectual activity. Political journalism became
possible and lucrative, and direct revolutionary action
absorbed much of the best forces of the younger generation. It would be an error to believe that under freer conditions literature and the arts must necessarily prosper

more than under despotism. The contrary is more often the case. When all other activity becomes difficult, they attract all that is ambitious and wants to express itself in intellectual work. Literature, like everything else, requires time and work, and when other work is attractive and easily found, fewer persons can give their time to the muses. When new fields of intellectual activity are suddenly thrown open, as was the case in Russia about 1860, the conditions are particularly unfavorable for the progress of literary art. When they are again closed, literature again attracts the intellectual unemployed. Milton was a political pamphleteer and an administrator when his party was in power—and wrote *Paradise Lost* after the triumph of his enemies. The immediate effect on literature of the great liberal Reforms of Alexander II was a shortage of new hands. The sixties and seventies in the history of Russian literature were a period when work of the first order was done by men of a preceding generation, and the young generation, absorbed by other activities, could give to literature only its second best.

When, with the approach of the eighties, the atmosphere began to change, the younger generation had still nothing to show to compare with the work of their fathers. The few survivors of the great generation were looked up to as the solitary remnants of a bitter age, and the greatest of them, Tolstóy, was for many years after his "conversion" without comparison the greatest and most significant figure in Russian literature, a solitary giant incommensurable with the pygmies at his feet.

TOLSTÓY AFTER 1880

Tolstóy's writings after 1880 are divided by a deep cleft from all his earlier work. But they belong to the same man, and much of what appeared at first new and startling in the later Tolstóy existed in a less developed form in the early Tolstóy. From the very beginning we cannot fail to discern in him an obstinate search for a rational meaning to life; a confidence in the powers of common sense and his own reason; contempt for modern civilization with its "artificial" multiplication of needs; a deeply rooted irreverence for all the functions and conventions of State and Society; a sovereign disregard for accepted opinions and scientific and literary "good form"; and a pronounced tendency to teach. But what was disseminated and disconnected in his early writings was welded after his conversion into a solid consistent doctrine, dogmatically settled in every detail. And the doctrine was such as to surprise and repel most of his old admirers. Before 1880 he had belonged, if anywhere, to the conservative camp, and only an exceptionally acute critic like Mikhaylóvsky could as early as 1873 discern the essentially revolutionary foundation of Tolstóy's mentality.

Tolstóy had always been fundamentally a rationalist. But at the time he wrote his great novels his rationalism was suffering an eclipse. The philosophy of *War and Peace* and *Anna Karénina* (which he formulates in *A Confession* as "that one should live so as to have the best for oneself and one's family") was a surrender of his rationalism to the inherent irrationalism of life. The search for the meaning of life was abandoned. The meaning of life was Life itself. The greatest wisdom consisted in accepting without sophistication one's place in Life and making the best of it. But already in the last part of *Anna Karénina* a growing disquietude becomes very apparent. When he was writing it the crisis had already begun that is so memorably recorded in *A Confession* and from which he was to emerge the prophet of a new religious and ethical teaching.

The teaching of Tolstóy is a rationalized "Christianity," stripped of all tradition and all positive mysticism. He rejected personal immortality and concentrated exclusively on the moral teaching of the Gospels. Of the moral teaching of Christ the words, "Resist not evil," were taken to be the principle out of which all the rest follows. He rejected the authority of the Church, which sanctioned the State, and he condemned the State, which sanctioned violence and compulsion. Both were immoral, like every form of organized compulsion. His condemnation of every form of compulsion authorizes us to classify Tolstóy's teaching, in its political aspect, as anarchism. This condemnation extended to every state as such, and he had no more respect for the democratic states of the West than for Russian autocracy. But in practice the edge of his anarchism was directed against the existing regime in Russia. He allowed that a constitution might be a lesser evil than autocracy (he recommended it in *The Young Tsar,* written after Nicholas II's accession in 1894), and his attacks were often directed against the same institutions as those of the radicals and revolutionaries. His attitude towards the active revolutionaries was ambiguous. He disapproved on principle of violent methods and consequently of political murder. But there was a difference in his attitude towards revolutionary terrorism and governmental suppression. As early as 1881 he remained unmoved by the assassination of Alexander II but wrote a letter of protest against the execution of the assassins. To all intents and purposes, Tolstóy became one of the greatest forces on the side of revolution, and the revolutionaries recognized this and paid homage to the "grand old man," though they did not accept his doctrine of "non-resistance" and though they treated his followers with contempt. Tolstóy's agreement with the Socialists was further accentuated by his own communism and condemnation of private property, especially in land. The methods he proposed for the abolition of the evil were different (they included the voluntary abdication of all money and land), but the negative part of his doctrine was in this point identical with Socialism.

Tolstóy's conversion was, largely, the reaction of his fundamental rationalism against the irrationalism into which he had allowed himself to drift in the sixties and seventies. His metaphysics may be summed up as the identification of the principle of life with reason. Like Socrates, he boldly identifies absolute good with absolute knowledge. "Reason, that is, good" is a favorite phrase of his, and occupies as central a place in his doctrine as *Deus sive Natura* does in Spinoza's. Knowledge is the necessary foundation of good, and this knowledge is inherent in every man. But it is obscured and stifled by the evil fogs of civilization and sophistry. It is necessary only to listen to the inner voice of one's conscience (which he was inclined to identify with the practical reason of Kant) and not to be misled by the false lights of human sophistry, which includes the whole of civilization—art, science, social tradition, law, as well as the historical dogmas of theological religion. But for all its rationalism, Tolstóy's religion is in a sense mystical. It is true that he rejected all the accepted mysticism of the churches, declined to recognize God as a Person, and spoke with satirical scorn (which to every believer will appear as the wildest blasphemy) of the sacraments. And yet his final authority (as in fact all the final authority of every metaphysical rationalism) is the irrational human "conscience." He did his utmost to identify it in theory with reason. But the mystical *daimonion* constantly reappeared, and in all his more remarkable later works "conversion" is described as an essentially mystical experience. It is mystical in that it is personal and unique. It is the result of an intimate revelation, which may or may not be prepared by previous intellectual development, but is essentially, like every mystical experience, incommunicable. In Tolstóy's own case, as described in *A Confession*, it is led up to by his whole previous intellectual life. But all purely intellectual solutions to the essential question were unsatisfactory, and the final solution is represented as a series of mystical experiences, repeated flashes of inner light. The civilized man lives in a state of unquestioning sin. The questions of meaning and justification arise against his will—as effect of fear of death—and the answer comes as a ray of inner light—the process described thus more than once by Tolstóy—in *A Confession*, in *The Death of Iván Ilyích,* in the *Memoirs of a Madman,* in *Master and Man.* The necessary consequence of this fact is that the truth cannot be preached, but may only be discovered for oneself. This is the doctrine of *A Confession,* which does not attempt to demonstrate, but only to narrate and to "infect." Later on, however, when the original impulse had widened, he attempted to preach it in logical form. He really always disbelieved in the efficacy of preaching. It was his disciples, men of a very different cast, who made Tolstoyism a preaching doctrine and encouraged Tolstóy to preach. In its final form the mystical element of Tolstóy's teaching is practically eliminated, and his religion becomes an essentially eudæmonistic doctrine—a doctrine founded on the search after happiness. Man must be good because it is the only way for him to be happy. In a typical work of the period when his teaching became crystallized and dogmatic—*Resurrection*—the mystical motive is absent and Nekhlyúdov's regeneration is no more than an adaptation of his life to the moral law, in order to free himself from the disagreeable reactions of conscience. In Tolstóy's final conception the moral law, which acts through the medium of conscience, is a law in the strict scientific sense, in the same sense as gravitation or any other natural law.

This is powerfully expressed in the idea—borrowed from Buddhism—of Karma, a conception profoundly different from the Christian in that Karma operates mechanically, without any intervention of Divine Grace, and is a necessary consequence of sin. Morality in the finally crystallized form of Tolstoyism is the art of avoiding Karma or of adapting onself to it. Tolstóy's morality, being a morality of happiness, is also a morality of purity, not of sympathy. Love of God, that is, of the moral law inside oneself, is the primary and only virtue, and charity—love for one's fellow creatures—is only a consequence. Charity—the actual feeling of love—is not a necessity for the Tolstoyan saint. He must act as if he loves his fellow men, and that will mean that he loves God and he will be happy. Tolstoyism is thus at the opposite pole to the teaching of Dostoyévsky. For Dostoyévsky, charity—love of men, pity—is the one supreme virtue, and God is revealed only through pity and charity. Tolstóy's religion is entirely egotistic. There is no God except the moral law inside man. The end of good actions is inner peace. This makes us understand the charge of Epicureanism that has been brought against Tolstóy, and also that of Luciferism and measureless pride, for there is nothing *outside* Tolstóy to which he bows.

Tolstóy was ever a great rationalist, and his rationalism found satisfaction in the admirably constructed system of his religion. But the irrational Tolstóy remained alive beneath the hardened crust of crystallized dogma. Tolstóy's diaries reveal how difficult it was for him to inwardly live up to his ideal of moral happiness. Except during the first years when he was carried on by the initial mystical impulse of his conversion, he was never happy in the sense he wanted to be. This was partly owing to the impossibility he found himself in of practicing what he preached, and to the constant and obstinate opposition of his family to his new ideas. But, apart from this, the old Adam was always alive. The desires of the flesh were active in him till an unusually advanced age; and the desire for expansion, the desire that gave life to *War and Peace*, the desire for the fullness of life with all its pleasure and beauty, never died in him. We catch few glimpses of all this in his writings, for he subjected them to a strict and narrow discipline. But we have a picture of Tolstóy in his old age in which the irrational, the complete man stands before us in all the relief of life—this is Maxím Górky's *Recollections of Tolstóy,* a work of genius worthy of its subject.

When the news of Tolstóy's conversion spread, it became known that Tolstóy had condemned as sinful all the writings that had made him famous, and decided to abandon all further literary work in the sense of pure and disinterested art. When this news reached Turgénev, who was on his deathbed, he wrote Tolstóy a letter that has been quoted to satiety and that contains a phrase which has become hackneyed to such a nauseous extent that it is impossible to reproduce it. The dying novelist adjured Tolstóy not to abandon literature, but to think of the duty that lay on him as the greatest of Russian writers. Turgénev greatly exaggerated his influence if he hoped that a letter from him might change the decision of a man who had always been noted for obstinacy and who had just emerged from a crisis of immeasurable gravity. But Turgénev saw a danger where there was none; though Tolstóy condemned as sinful (and artistically wrong) *War and Peace* and *Anna Karénina* and subjected all his work henceforth to the exigencies of his moral philosophy, it is ridiculous to think that Tolstóy ever abandoned "art." He soon returned to the narrative form, but apart from this, even in his polemical writings, he never ceased being supremely artistic. In the most trivial of his tracts against tobacco he never ceased being, *as a craftsman,* head and shoulders above even the best writers of the "æsthetic" revival of the eighties. *A Confession* itself may without exaggeration be called in some ways his greatest artistic work. It is not a disinterested, self-contained "representation of life" like *War and Peace* or *Anna Karénina;* it is "utilitarian," it is "propaganda work," and in this sense it is less "pure art." But it possesses "æsthetic" qualities that are not present in the great novels. It is *constructed,* and constructed with supreme skill and precision. It has an oratorical movement difficult to expect from the author of *War and Peace.* It is more synthetic and universal, and does not rely for its action on little homely and familiar effects of realism, so abundant in the novels. Its analysis is simple, deep, courageous—and there is nothing in it of that "psychological eavesdropping" (the phrase is Leóntiev's) which repels many readers in his earlier works. *War and Peace* and *Anna Karénina* have been compared, somewhat far-fetchedly, with the poems of Homer. *A Confession* might with more appropriateness be placed by the side of no less supreme "world's books"—Ecclesiastes and the book of Job. So it is quite wrong to affirm that in any literary sense the change that overcame Tolstóy about 1880 was a fall. He remained forever, not only the supreme writer, but the supreme craftsman of Russian letters. Even the most dryly dogmatic of his treatises is a masterpiece of literary ability and of the best Russian. For all that, the fact remains that henceforward Tolstóy ceased to be a "writer," in the sense of a man who writes for the sake of producing good literary work, and became a preacher. And when he turned, as he did very soon, towards imaginative narrative, he wrote stories that, like everything else, were strictly subordinate to his dogmatic teaching and intended to illustrate and to popularize it.

The first of Tolstóy's works in which he preached his new teaching was *A Confession* (begun in 1880 and completed in 1882).[1] *A Confession* is altogether on a higher level than the rest—it is one of the world's masterpieces. It is a work of art, and Tolstóy's biographer would give proof of too much simple-mindedness if he used it as biographical material in the strict sense of the word. But the work is more important to us than the facts that led up to it. The facts have been, and are no more. Their history in *A Confession* remains as a κτῆμα ἐς ἀεί, a perfect work, a living entity. It is one of the greatest and most lasting expressions of the human soul in the presence of the eternal mysteries of life and death. To give the argument in one's own words would be presumption, to quote passages would be to destroy. For it is a wonderful whole, built with marvelous precision and effectiveness. Every detail, every turn of thought, every oratorical cadence, is in its right place to contribute to the one supreme effect. It is the greatest piece of oratory in Russian literature. But it is not conventional eloquence. Its rhythm is a logical, mathematical rhythm—a rhythm of ideas—and Tolstóy scorns all the devices of traditional rhetoric. It is sustained in the simplest of languages, in that wonderful language

[1] It was not at the time passed by the Russian censorship. It was printed in Geneva and circulated in manuscript in Russia.

of Tolstóy, whose secret has not yet been caught, and which is naturally lost in a translation. A good translation (like Aylmer Maude's) will preserve the oratorical movement of the original, for this is based on the succession of ideas and large syntactical units, not on the sound and quantity of words. But the effect of Tolstóy's Russian cannot be reproduced in any of the literary languages of the West, for all of them are too far divorced from their spoken forms, and the spoken languages too full of slang. Russian alone has this felicity—that it can use everyday speech to produce effects of Biblical majesty. And Tolstóy's favorite device in *A Confession*, of illustrating his idea by a parable, is in complete keeping with the general tone of the work. Tolstóy's language was largely his own creation. He achieved in *A Confession*, for the language of abstract thought, what he had attempted in his pedagogical articles and achieved for narrative prose in his novels— the creation of a new literary language free from the bookish traditions of contemporary literature and based entirely on the language actually spoken. The language thus evolved is beyond doubt the best vehicle yet used in Russian for the expression of abstract thought. The extent of Tolstóy's innovation in the literary language is singularly great—it is almost a different language from that of his contemporaries. Many of the principal terms of his teaching are words that had not been used before Tolstóy in literary Russian, and were borrowed by him from the colloquial speech of his class. Such, for instance, is one of his most frequent words—*dúrno*—bad.

Tolstóy's other moral and religious writings are not on a level with *A Confession*, though they are written in the same admirable Russian, sometimes with even greater elegance and precision. In *A Confession* he speaks with the utmost tragical earnestness of a unique and overwhelming experience. In the later tracts he lays down the "articles" of a hard and narrow creed. They have all the best qualities of Tolstóy the rationalist, the arguer, and the logician, but it would be quite out of place to compare them, as one can compare *A Confession*, with the books of the Bible. *What Are We to Do?* is a kind of continuation of *A Confession*, but on a less mystical and more social plane. It is the story of Tolstóy's experience in the slums and night refuges of Moscow soon after his conversion.

His religious views were systematized in a series of works, of which the first, *What I Believe,* was written in 1883–4. This was followed by a *Critique of Dogmatic Theology, The Kingdom of Heaven Is Within Us, An Exposition of the Gospels,* and *The Christian Doctrine. What I Believe* is the most comprehensive of his dogmatic writings. What he gave in *A Confession* in the form of a personal experience, in its process of becoming, is here crystallized and stabilized into a settled doctrine. *The Christian Doctrine* (1897) is an exposition of the same doctrine in a still more logical and fixed form, after the manner of a catechism. It is a source of infinite pleasure to those who admire most in Tolstóy his lucidity and his skill at definition and precise statement. *The Exposition of the Gospels* has less of this quality and more of a very far-fetched and not always bona fide interpretation. In *The Critique of Dogmatic Theology* he is a polemist well versed in all the little tricks of argumentative tactics, a cunning fencer, and consummate ironist. Ridicule and an appeal to common sense are his favorite polemical methods. "This is unintelligible nonsense," is his knock-out argument. His minor tracts are numerous and touch on a great variety of points of detail, or on topics of current interest. Such is *Why Do People Intoxicate Themselves?* denouncing drink and tobacco. Such is *I Cannot Be Silent,* a violent invective against the Russian government and the numerous executions during the suppression of the First Revolution.

But of all Tolstóy's non-narrative writings, that which is of greatest interest for the literary historian is *What Is Art?* (1897–8). Tolstóy's taste in literature and art always drew him towards the classical, the rational, and the primitive. He disliked everything romantic, everything ornate or exuberant. He had no understanding for "pure poetry." He liked the classic theater of Racine, the analytical novel of Stendhal, the stories of Genesis, and the songs of the Russian people. He disliked the Elizabethan exuberance of Shakspere. In his famous attack on Shakspere, Tolstóy charged him with being not only an immoral writer, but a bad poet. He preferred the pre-Shaksperian *King Leir* to Shakspere's tragedy because it was more primitive, less exuberant, less baroque. Voltaire would have agreed with much in Tolstóy's criticism of *King Lear.* He had many faults to find in other great writers. Homer was an immoral poet because he idealized wrath and cruelty; Racine and Púshkin were inferior writers because they appealed to a restricted aristocratic audience and were unintelligible to the people. But Shakspere was a bad writer because he wrote badly, and Tolstóy remained unmoved by his poetry. Now· art, according to Tolstóy, is that which "infects" with sympathetic feelings. "If a man is infected by the author's condition of soul, if he feels this emotion and this union with others, then the object which has effected this is art; but if there be no such infection, if there be not this union with the author and with others who are moved by the same work, then it is not art." Shakspere and Wagner were not art. Tolstóy opposes to them the creations of primitive popular art—the story of Joseph, the Hungarian *csárdás,* the theater of a primitive Siberian tribe, the Voguls. He quotes, as an example of genuine art, a description of a Vogul drama representing in a very simple and naïve way a reindeer hunt and the anxiety of the doe for her calf; "from the mere description, I felt that this was a true work of art," because he was infected by the feelings of the doe. Everything that does not *infect* is not art and only obscures art. Too much technique, too much magnificence in producing a play, too much realism, obscure and diminish the artistic value of a picture, a play, a book. The simpler, the barer, the better. "The author of the story of Joseph did not need to describe in detail, as would be done nowadays, the bloodstained coat of Joseph, the dwelling and dress of Jacob, the pose and attire of Potiphar's wife, and how, adjusting the bracelet on her arm, she said: 'Come to me,' and so on, because the subject matter of feelings in this novel is so strong that all details, except the most essential—such as that Joseph went out into the other room to weep—are superfluous and would only hinder the transmission of feelings. And therefore this story is accessible to all men, touches people of all nations and classes, young and old, and has lasted to our times, and will yet last for thousands of years to come. But strip the best novels of our times of their details, and what will remain?" (*What Is Art?*) Genuine art may be moral or immoral, according to the moral value of the feelings with which it infects. *The Iliad,* for instance, is *art,* but it is morally bad art because the feelings with which it infects are bad feelings. Much of modern literature, though genuine art, is morally bad because it is class art, intelligible only to the rich and cultivated, and tends to disunite, instead of uniting. Tolstóy excepts very little of modern literature from this general condemnation. He quotes only a few works—Schiller (*The Robbers*), Hugo (*Les Misérables*), Dickens (*A Tale of Two Cities, A Christmas Carol,* and *The Chimes*), George Eliot (*Adam Bede*), Dostoyévsky (*Memoirs from the House of Death*), and Harriet Beecher Stowe (*Uncle Tom's Cabin*)—as "examples of the highest art flowing from the love of God and man"—of (as he calls it) "religious art." As examples of an inferior but still good kind of art, of "art transmitting the simplest feelings of common life, but such always as are accessible to all men of the world," he quotes with great reservations *Don Quixote,* Molière, *David Copperfield,* the *Pickwick Papers,* and the tales of Gógol, Púshkin, and Maupassant. But "the exceptional nature of the feelings they transmit, and the superfluity of special detail of time and locality, and, above all, the poverty of their subject matter, make them comprehensible only to people of their own circle." Tolstóy condemned his own earlier works on grounds both moral (class exclusiveness and bad feelings) and æsthetic (superfluity of detail, all the paraphernalia of realism). But long before he had completed *What Is Art?* he had already made an effort to produce new works of fiction that would be in harmony with his new ideals. The novelty of Tolstóy's later stories is not only that they are all written with and strongly subordinate to the purpose (many of his early stories, especially those written in 1856–61 are quite as much "with a purpose"), but that he abandoned in them his early realistic and detailed manner and endeavored to approach the chastity and simplicity of outline of his favorite masterpiece—the story of Joseph.

The first stories he wrote after *A Confession* were a series of edifying short stories for the people. They were published in 1885 and the following years by the firm Posrédnik, founded for the special purpose of popularizing Tolstóy's teaching. They were written with regard to the existing conditions in Russia, that is, they were meant to satisfy the censor. Consequently they contain no violent and overt satire of the Church and State. The moral is always plainly present, often in the title—*Evil Allures, but*

Good Endures, God Sees the Truth but Waits—but is not always peculiarly Tolstoyan. About the time he was writing *Anna Karénina,* Tolstóy had made an attempt at a popular story—this is the only story he excluded from the general condemnation of his earlier work—*The Captive in the Caucasus* (1873), which he recognized as belonging to the inferior but still commendable category of "good universal art" (not religious art). The new stories aspired to be religious art. According to Tolstóy's new taste, the narrative in these stories is reduced to the essential subject matter and stripped of all the superfluous embellishments of "realism." But they remain realistic in that they all have for a setting the life familiar to the prospective reader—it is Russian peasant life, with sufficient local color to individualize it as Russian. All these stories are admirably told, and every one of them is a little masterpiece of construction, economy, and adaptation of means to ends. Manner and matter are one organic whole, and the moral tendency does not stand out as something external. One of the best is *Two Old Men,* the story of two peasants who set out on a pilgrimage to Jerusalem in fulfillment of a vow. One reached his goal and saw the Holy Land, but the other was detained on his way by meeting a starving family, and, in his efforts to save them, he spent all his money, lost all his time, was late for the boat, and returned home without seeing Jerusalem. The other, on his return journey, comes on the family saved from death by his companion, and is brought to understand that "the best way to keep one's vows to God and to do His will is for each man, while he lives, to show love and do good to others."

Later on, as his fame grew and he began to have a public all over the world, he wrote popular stories of a new kind, more universal and generalized. They approach still nearer to his ideal of being comprehensible to all men. Such are his adaptations from the French—*Françoise* (Maupassant's *La Vierge-des-Vents* pruned of realistic excrescences), *The Coffee-House of Surat,* and *Too Dear,* and his still later stories, *King Essarhadon, Work, Death, and Sickness,* and *Three Questions.* In these he approaches the style of the parable, which he had used with such powerful effect in *A Confession,* and the oriental apologue.

The stories written with a view to the educated reader are different in manner: they are much longer, much fuller of detail, more "psychological," altogether nearer in style to his earlier work. There are problem stories, written not so much to teach as to communicate his own experience. They may be grouped into two categories, stories of conversion and stories on the sexual problem. The first group consists of *The Memoirs of a Madman* (unfinished, posthumous, written in 1884), *The Death of Iván Ilyích* (1886), and *Master and Man* (1895). In all these stories the subject is the conversion of the dark and unregenerated educated or rich man before the face of death or madness. *The Memoirs of a Madman* is very much akin to *A Confession*. It conveys with dreadful force the feeling of elemental metaphysical joylessness and despair before the abysmal meaninglessness of life, the feeling Tolstóy himself must have experienced at the height of his great crisis, and which seems to have returned to him at intervals after his conversion. It is the most genuinely mystical of his writings. He left it unfinished; yet it cannot be refused a central place in his work, next to, and as a "piece of evidence" even above, *A Confession*. For it is more directly sincere, more of a document, less of a work of art. In *The Death of Iván Ilyích* the hero is not a thinking and seeking man like Tolstóy of the *Confession* or like the madman. He is an ordinary, vulgar, average man of the educated classes, a judge (the class Tolstóy detested most of all). The revelation comes to him as the direct consequence of his mortal illness. When he realizes that he is dying, he loses all taste for existence and is plunged into that elemental joylessness which comes from realizing the meaninglessness and emptiness of life. But joy comes back to him in the simple and cheerful charity of his servant Gerásim, the only person who gives him help in his mortal despair. And before he dies he sees the inner light of faith, renunciation, and love. *Master and Man* is again the story of a birth to new life in the face of death. It is one of Tolstóy's masterpieces, comparable to *A Confession* in the sustained beauty of its construction and to *The Memoirs of a Madman* in the genuineness of its mystical light. It stands halfway in style between his old realistic and new popular manner, and answers more to his ideal of religious art than any of his other works not especially intended for the people.

The "sexual" stories are *The Kreutzer Sonata* (1889) and *The Devil* (written the same year, published posthumously). The first, a study of jealousy and a diatribe against the sexual education of young men and women in modern society, is a powerful production but hardly a perfect work of art. It is not sufficiently concentrated; its preaching is not always artistically "necessary"; its manner strangely enough reminds one of the untidy and excited manner of Dostoyévsky. *The Devil* is more satisfactory. It is an extraordinary analysis of that obsession by the desires of the flesh which was so peculiar to Tolstóy and of which such shrewd things have been said by Maxím Górky. It is the story of a man who loves his young and charming wife but is impelled against his will by à purely carnal desire for a peasant woman with whom he has had relations before his marriage. He is powerless to combat it, and, to save himself from succumbing, in a state of exasperation he kills the woman. Tolstóy was not completely satisfied by this ending and wrote an alternative ending, in which the hero, instead of killing the object of his desire, kills himself. In spite of this ambiguous ending, *The Devil* is one of Tolstóy's greatest masterpieces, for both the fierce sincerity and the masterly construction; the terrible inevitableness of the hero's fall, his helplessness before his carnal instinct, grow like a terrible doom and are developed with supreme mastery.

Of all Tolstóy's late narrative works, the one that attracted the greatest attention and became most widely known, and is consequently, more often than not, taken as typical of his last period, was *Resurrection* (completed and published in 1899). It is a novel in three parts—by far the longest of all his stories since 1880, almost comparable in length with *Anna Karénina* and *War and Peace*. This is the sole reason why it has usurped a principal position among his later work and is so often quoted by the side of the two earlier novels. It has often been used to prove that Tolstóy's genius declined after he became a preacher. If the imaginative work of his last thirty years is to stand or fall according to the merit of *Resurrection*, it will be in somewhat bad case, for it is quite obvious that

Resurrection is very much inferior to *War and Peace* and *Anna Karénina*. But it is also much inferior to *Master and Man*, to *Hajjí Murád*, and to *The Living Corpse*. In spite of its size it is by no means the work into which Tolstóy put the most work and care. It was written, strange to say, for money, and would probably not have seen the press before his death were it not for the desire to find funds for the Dukhobórs. The Dukhobórs, a peasant sect of "Christian communists," were persecuted by the government for their "conscientious objection" to military service. Canada had offered hospitality to them, and the only drawback to their emigration was lack of funds. Tolstóy decided to meet the emergency by finishing in a hurry, and publishing in one of the best-selling Russian papers, a novel he had been working on. He was working then on *Hajjí Murád* and *Resurrection*, and he chose the latter because he liked it less and had fewer objections to seeing it published in an unsatisfactory form. *Resurrection* is not a perfect work of art: the moral idea, profusely supported by texts from the Gospels, is not organically fused into the fabric. The story of Nekhlyúdov's conversion is on an inferior plane to that of Tolstóy's own in *A Confession*, or of Iván Ilyích's, or of the merchant in *Master and Man*. It is not a revelation of inner light, but a cold decision to adapt himself to the moral law so as to escape the stings of conscience and acquire inner peace. *Resurrection* presents Tolstóy and his teaching from the most unattractive side. For all that, it is a book by Tolstóy. But its best qualities are not characteristic of the later Tolstóy: they are rather, in a minor degree, those of *Anna Karénina* and *War and Peace*. The best thing in the novel is the minor realistic details he condemned so severely in *What Is Art?* The early story of Máslova is the best part of the book. It is full of that elusive poetry which reminds one of the subtle poetic atmosphere that accompanies Natásha in *War and Peace*. The account of the trial is excellent—sustained, concentrated, unexaggerated satire. It has not been surpassed by Tolstóy, except perhaps in the second part of the same novel, where he satirizes the bureaucratic society of Petersburg. But his satirically blasphemous account of an Orthodox Church service, prohibited by the censorship and absent in pre-Revolutionary editions printed in Russia, can scarcely be qualified otherwise than as a grave lapse from good taste. It is quite gratuitous and unnecessary for the mechanism of the novel.

If in *Resurrection* Tolstóy is at his worst, in its twin novel he is at his best. *Hajjí Murád* was begun in 1896 and completed in 1904. It was published after his death. In it he tried to give a story that would answer to his ideal of "good universal," not religious, art. *Hajjí Murád* is a masterpiece of the highest order. It is a story of the extended war that the Caucasian mountaineers, under their military and religious leader Shamíl, waged against Russia. Hajjí Murád, a prominent mountaineer chief, from motives of personal ambition and vengeance, deserts Shamíl and goes over to the Russians, who receive him with apparent friendliness but with concealed distrust. Hajjí Murád's family has remained with Shamíl, who keeps them as hostages. The desire of once more seeing his son grows on Hajjí Murád, and he decides to escape into the mountains but is killed in the attempt. Hajjí Murád is a savage. His feelings are those of a shrewd, brave, and treacherous warrior with all the virtues and all the vices of a warlike barbarian. The story is told in what Tolstóy called the "peep-show manner"—the scene is constantly shifted, and the chapters are like a succession of slides. This method brings forward with great vividness the tragic irony of mutual misunderstanding between men of various classes and nationalities. The story is stirring tragedy conveyed by the simplest means. The final scene—the death of Hajjí Murád and his four followers surrounded by hundreds of pursuers—is one of the grandest and most tragical in all literature.

Hajjí Murád, as well as *The Memoirs of a Madman* and *The Devil*, was published only in 1911, in the collected edition of Tolstóy's posthumous works.[2] This collection also includes several plays and many other stories and fragments. One of these is *Father Sergius* (1890–8), the story of an aristocrat who became a monk and a hermit—a powerful study of spiritual pride and, once again, carnal desires. It is also an excellent example of Tolstóy's later rapid and "essential" narrative manner. Still better in this

[2] They were not published during his life, to avoid making the question of their copyright fresh fuel for the war waged by Chertkóv and the Countess Tolstóy over the person of their author.

respect is *The False Coupon* (1903–5), the admirably constructed story of a succession of evils diverging from one
initial evil action to converge by a contrasting succession
of good actions towards the common salvation of all concerned. It is impossible to list all the numerous minor
stories and fragments of these wonderful three volumes.
But one at least must be mentioned: one of the shortest—
Alësha Gorshók (1905). It is a masterpiece of rare perfection. It is the apotheosis of the "holy fool," who does
not himself realize his goodness. It is the story, told in
five or six pages, of a peasant boy who was all his life
everyone's drudge but, in his simplicity of soul and meek,
unquestioning submission (non-resistance), knew that inner light and purity of conscience, that perfect peace which
was never attained by the conscious, rational, restless soul
of Tolstóy. Concentrated into its six pages, *Alësha Gorshók*
is one of his most perfect creations, and one of the very
few that make one forget the bedrock Luciferism and pride
of the author.

Tolstóy's plays all belong to the period after 1880.
He had not the essential qualities that go to the making of
a dramatist, and the merits of his plays are not of the
strictly dramatic order. In spite of his French education
and classical tastes, his plays are constructed in a very
un-French and unclassical manner. With the exception of
The Fruits of Enlightenment, a comedy—or rather, a farce
—of intrigue, all his plays are built according to the same
scheme—which is the "peep-show" scheme of *Hajjí Murád.*
The action is not a continuous development, but scenes
are cut out so as to present the principal moments of a
story, which usually extends over a period of many years.
This concentration may in some cases approach the form
of a mediæval morality. It may also be easily adapted to
make a movie drama. The first in date of Tolstóy's plays
is the *First Distiller,* a humorous anti-liquor morality play
"for the people," published originally in 1886 in the same
series as the popular tales. The *First Distiller* is of course
the devil. He has plenty of victims from all the rich and
idle classes, but he cannot succeed in catching a single
peasant into his net, for work is the peasant's safeguard
from sin. He succeeds in corrupting him only by showing
him the way to make spirits. It is a very amusing little
play, and, as an English reviewer has remarked, would

raise grave anxiety among the liquor trade if it were acted in England. This was followed by *The Power of Darkness,* the best-known and most highly esteemed of Tolstóy's plays (1887). It is also in essence a morality—but treated in a very different manner. It is a tragedy—and a realistic tragedy. It represents the life of peasants but is intended for the educated public. There is a profound inner contradiction in the play. Planned as a morality, it is executed as a realistic drama, with all the condemned paraphernalia of "superfluous details," including phonographically exact reproduction of peasant dialect, a thing the peasant spectator resents above all things. This disharmony of plan and execution, and this abundant presence of the abominations of gratuitous realism, made Tolstóy dislike this play and condemn it as belonging to the "bad manner." Like *Resurrection,* it is one of Tolstóy's least perfect works, and its great success proves only how little the Russian and the foreign public were really in tune with the genius of Tolstóy. The Russian public liked it because it was in the familiar realistic "superfluous detail" style, and because the Russian actors, trained to the style, acted it well. Abroad it was received enthusiastically because its ruthless realism was a new and piquant thing to the Western palate. All this is not to say that it has no trace of genius in it; on the contrary, the scheme of the play is one of Tolstóy's most powerful inventions. It is the best expression he ever gave to his favorite conception of Karma— the mechanical atonement of sin—and of another favorite idea of his—the great evil-begetting power of every evil action, which is expressed in the subtitle, *If a Claw Is Caught, the Bird Is Lost.* The tragical atmosphere is thick and dark, and there are few more impressive things in Tolstóy than the third act, where we see Nikíta enjoying the first joyless fruit of his initial crime. But for all its merits, *The Power of Darkness* cannot take away from a much older play, Písemsky's *Hard Lot,* the honor of being the best Russian realistic tragedy. The same realistic tendency that mars the dialogue of *The Power of Darkness* is one of the chief attractions of Tolstóy's society plays. For in the peasant play he tried to ape a dialect that was not his; in *The Fruits of Enlightenment* and in the posthumous plays he made his characters talk his own everyday language. *The Fruits of Enlightenment* (1889) is, after all, only a trifle, but the dialogue of the society people is admirable and the satire very pointed. *The Light Shines in the Darkness* (begun in the early eighties and continued in 1900–2) remained unfinished. It has the appearance of autobiography—for it is the story of a Tolstoyan moralist who is surrounded by an unsympathizing family and whose followers are sent to prison for practicing what he preaches. But it must be said in all fairness that Tolstóy does much less than justice to himself in the character of Saryntsov. Saryntsov is not the giant of Yásnaya Polyána, but a narrow, cold, hard, pedantic fanatic—perhaps more like some inferior Tolstoyan—Chertkóv, for instance. A very different thing is *The Living Corpse*, one of Tolstóy's most attractive and lovable works. There is in it something we meet in very few of his works: a distinct note of human sympathy, free from all moralizing dogmatism. There is also something one could hardly suspect in Tolstóy: a vast mellow pity for the misformed and erring human race, a respect for the sufferings of man—even of the abandoned drunkard, even of the proud society mother. It is at the opposite pole to *Resurrection*. It is, even more than *Hajjí Murád,* the most *disinterested* of all Tolstóy's later works. It is rather loosely constructed, after the familiar "peep-show" plan, and it can hardly be called a drama in any strict sense of the word. But it has been produced; and in the hands of a cast like Stanislávsky's Moscow Art Theater it acts very well. *The Living Corpse* may be taken as the last expression of Tolstóy's genius. It is distinctly a very old man's work, with that broadness and mellowness of outlook which, if it comes, is the best ornament of old age.

The life of Tolstóy after his conversion can be given here only in the briefest outline. Soon after *A Confession* became known, he began, at first against his will, to recruit disciples. The first of these was the notorious and sinister V. G. Chertkóv, an ex-officer of the Horse Guards, a narrow fanatic and a hard, despotic man, who exercised an enormous practical influence on Tolstóy and became a sort of grand vizier of the new community. Other disciples came, among whom P. I. Biryukóv may be mentioned, the author of a *Life of Tolstoy,* the official life, written throughout in a tone of panegyrical admiration like the life of a saint, but valuable for its wealth of information. Tolstóy also established contact with certain sects of

Christian communists and anarchists, like the Dukhobórs. The external action of Tolstóy's new doctrine found its principal expression in cases of conscientious objection to military service, which sent many men to prison and Siberia. But Tolstóy himself was unmolested by the government. Only in 1901 the Synod excommunicated him. This act, widely but very unjudiciously resented both at home and abroad, merely registered a matter of common knowledge—that Tolstóy had ceased to be an Orthodox Churchman.

The dogmatic followers of Tolstóy were never numerous, but his reputation among people of all classes grew immensely. It spread all over the world, and by the last two decades of his life Tolstóy enjoyed a place in the world's esteem that had not been held by any man of letters since the death of Voltaire. Yásnaya Polyána became a new Ferney—or even more than that, almost a new Jerusalem. Pilgrims from all parts flocked there to see the great old man. But Tolstóy's own family remained hostile to his teaching, with the exception of his youngest daughter, Alexandra. Countess Sophie Andréyevna especially took up a position of decided opposition to his new ideas. She refused to give up her possessions and asserted her duty to provide for her large family. Tolstóy renounced the copyright of his new works but had to surrender his landed property and the copyright of his earlier works to his wife. This produced an external contradiction between Tolstóy's preaching of communism and contempt of material riches, and the easy and even luxurious life he led under the regime of his wife—for Sophie Andréyevna was the embodiment of Tolstóy's earlier philosophy of *War and Peace*—"that one should live so as to have the best for oneself and one's family." This contradiction weighed heavily on him, and the consciousness of it was carefully fostered by Chertkóv. This man and Countess Tolstóy became the heads of two hostile parties who disputed the possession of Tolstóy. Tolstóy was remarkably healthy for his age, but he fell seriously ill in 1901 and had to live for a long time in the Crimea. Still he continued working to the last and never showed the slightest sign of any weakening of brain power. The story of his "escape" and death is familiar to all. Ever more oppressed by the contradiction of his private life, urged

on by Chertkóv, full of a growing irritation against his
wife, he left Yásnaya, in the company of his daughter
Alexandra and his doctor, for an unknown destination.
After some restless and aimless wandering he had to stop
at Astápovo Junction (Province of Ryazán). There he was
laid up in the stationmaster's house and died on November 7, 1910.

LESKÓV

Nikoláy Semënovich Leskóv (1831–95) was only three
years younger than Tolstóy, but he was past thirty when he
first appeared before the public, and the times were no
longer the same as had given such a wholehearted and
generous reception to the great generation of novelists. It
was a time of intense party strife, when no writer could
hope to be well received by all the critics, and only those
who identified themselves with a definite party could hope
for even a partial recognition. Leskóv never identified himself with any party and had to take the consequences. His
success with the reading public was considerable, but the
critics continued to neglect him. Leskóv's case is a striking
instance of the failure of Russian criticism to do its duty.

Leskóv's father was a civil servant and the son of a
priest. His mother was of a family of gentry, and his early
life was that of an average squire's son. One of the lasting
influences of his early life was his Aunt Polly, who had
married an Englishman and followed the Quaker way of
life. When he was sixteen his parents died and he had to
leave school and enter the civil service. He served as a
copying clerk in various provincial government offices. In
this service he acquired an extensive first-hand acquaintance with various aspects of Russian reality. This knowledge of life was still more widened when he left the civil
service and was employed by an Englishman, a Mr. Scott,
a Nonconformist like Aunt Polly and chief steward of the
estates of a rich nobleman. In this employment Leskóv
acquired a far wider outlook on Russian life, and one
very different from that of the typical educated gentleman
of the day. Owing to this training, Leskóv is one of those
Russian writers whose knowledge of life was not founded
on the possession of serfs, to be later modified by university

theories of French or German origin, like Turgénev's and Tolstóy's, but on practical and independent experience. This is why his view of Russian life is so unconventional and so free from that attitude of condescending and sentimental pity for the peasant which is typical of the liberal and educated serf-owner. His first literary work consisted of business reports to Scott, who was quick to appreciate the wealth of common sense, the power of observation, and the knowledge of people displayed in them. Leskóv was twenty-nine when, in 1860, he first engaged in part-time journalism. Two years later he abandoned his other work, came to Petersburg, and became a professional journalist. It was a time of intense public excitement. Leskóv was absorbed by public interests as much as anyone, but his eminently practical mind and training made it impossible for him to join unreservedly any of the very unpractical and hot-headed parties of the day. Hence his isolation when the incident occurred that left such a lasting trace in his career. He wrote an article on the great fires that had in 1862 destroyed a large part of Petersburg and that popular rumor was inclined to impute to the "nihilists" and radical-minded university students. Leskóv did not support this rumor, but he mentioned it in an article and demanded that a thorough investigation should be carried out by the police in order that it might be either confirmed or confuted. This demand produced in the radical press the effect of a bombshell. Leskóv was accused of inciting the populace against the students and of "informing" to the police. Leskóv was put under boycott and expelled from the progressive papers. Meanwhile he passed from journalism to fiction. His first short story (*The Ovibos*, 1863) was followed by a long novel (*No Way Out*, 1864) that led to further misunderstandings. The radicals affected to recognize in some of its characters slanderous caricatures of their friends, and this sufficed to stamp Leskóv as a vile and libelous reactionary, though the principal Socialist characters in the book were represented as little short of saints. In his next "political" novel, *At Daggers Drawn* (1870–1), Leskóv went much further in the representation of the "nihilists" as a set of blackguards and scoundrels. These "political" novels are not among Leskóv's master-pieces, and they had no part in the great reputation he enjoys today. But they were sufficient to make Leskóv the nightmare of all the radical literature and to make it impossible for the most influential critics to treat him with any amount of fairness. The great Slavophil critic Apollón Grigóriev, a man of extraordinary but erratic genius, was the only critic to welcome Leskóv, to appreciate and to encourage him. But Grigóriev died in 1864, and all Leskóv's subsequent popularity was entirely owing to the unguided good taste of the public.

This popularity began especially after the publication of his "chronicle" *Soboryáne* in 1872 and the series of stories, largely of ecclesiastical life, that followed it in remarkable succession till the end of the seventies. In these stories Leskóv appeared as a champion of Orthodoxy and conservative ideals, and they attracted towards him the good will of many high-placed persons, in particular the Empress Marie Alexándrovna, the wife of Alexander II. It was through her interest that Leskóv got an official appointment in an advising board of education, practically a sinecure. In the later seventies he joined in a campaign in favor of Orthodoxy against the pietist propaganda of Lord Radstock. But Leskóv never became a thorough conservative, and even in his support of Orthodoxy against Protestantism, his principal arguments were the democratic humility of the first and the aristocratic individualism of the "Society schism," as he called Radstock's sect. His attitude towards the official government of the Church was never quite docile, and gradually his Christianity became less traditional and more critical. His stories of clerical life written in the early eighties were largely satirical, and for one of these he was asked to leave his government post. He came under the growing influence of Tolstóy and towards the end of his life became a devoted Tolstoyan. This change of attitude towards the conservative principles pushed him back towards the left wing of journalism, and in his later years he contributed mainly to moderate radical magazines. But the dictators of literary opinion still reserved their judgment and were more than cold to him. When he died, he had many readers all over Russia but few friends in the literary press. Not long before his death he is reported to have said: "Now I am read for the beauty of my imaginative work, but in fifty years hence this beauty will have faded, and my books will be read only for the ideas contained in them." This was a singularly bad prophecy.

More than ever Leskóv is read today for his qualities of form, style, and narrative, and less than ever for his ideas. In fact very few of his admirers realize what his ideas were. Not that his ideas are at all obscure or concealed, but simply that the attention is concentrated on something different.

Leskóv's most striking originality lies in his Russian. His contemporaries wrote in a level and even style, avoiding anything too striking or questionable. Leskóv avidly absorbed every unexpected and picturesque idiom. All the various forms of professional and class language, every variety of slang, were welcome to his pages. But his special favorites were the comic effects of colloquial Church Slavonic and the puns of "popular etymology." These effects are of course untranslatable. Like O. Henry, he allowed himself great liberties in this direction and was the inventor of many successful and unexpected deformations of familiar sense or familiar sound. Another striking peculiarity that Leskóv alone of all his contemporaries possesses is a superlative narrative gift. His stories are mere anecdotes, told with enormous zest and ability, and even in his longer works his favorite way of characterizing his characters is by a series of anecdotes. This was quite contrary to the traditions of "serious" Russian fiction and induced the critics to regard Leskóv as a mere jester. His most original stories are packed with incident and adventure to an extent that appeared ludicrous to the critics, who regarded ideas and messages as the principal thing. Tolstóy liked Leskóv's stories and enjoyed his verbal gambols, but he censured him for his exuberance. His chief fault, Tolstóy thought, was that he could not keep his talent in bounds and that there were too many good things in his stories. This taste for verbal picturesqueness and rapid and complicated narrative is in striking contrast to the habits of almost every other Russian novelist. There is no haze, no atmosphere, no mellowness in Leskóv's vision of the world: he chooses the most crying colors, the boldest relief, and the sharpest outline. If Turgénev's or Chékhov's world may be compared to a landscape by Corot, Leskóv's is a picture by Breughel the Elder, full of gay and bright colors and grotesque forms. Great virtue, extraordinary originality, strong vices, powerful passions, and grotesque humors are his favorite matter. He is at once a hero-worshipper and a humorist. It can almost be said that the more heroic his heroes, the more humorously he treats them. This humorous hero worship is Leskóv's most original feature.

Leskóv's political novels are now deservedly forgotten, but the short stories he wrote at the same time are very good. They are not so rich in verbal felicity as the stories of his mature period, but they present in an eminent degree his qualities as a storyteller. Unlike his later work, they are pictures of almost unrelieved wickedness and passion. A typical instance is *A Lady Macbeth of the Mtsensk District*[3] (1865), a powerful study of the criminal passion of a woman and of the gay and cynical callousness of her lover. It is bathed in a cold and crude light and written with sustained, "naturalistic" objectivity. Another remarkable story of this period is *The Amazon,* the racy study of a Petersburg procuress who regards her profession with a deliciously naïve cynicism and is sincerely and deeply hurt by the black "thanklessness" of one of the victims whom she had first pushed into the ways of shame.

These early stories were followed by a series of "Chronicles" of the imaginary town of Stárgorod, which may be called a Russian Barchester. They form a trilogy—*Old Years in Plodomásovo* (1869), *Soboryáne (Cathedral,* or rather *Minster, Folk,* 1872), and *A Decayed Family* (1874). The second of these chronicles is the most widely popular of all Leskóv's works. It deals with the Stárgorod clergy. Its head, the Archpriest Tuberózov, is one of Leskóv's most successful and noble portraits of a "just man." The Deacon Akhíla is his greatest character creation. It is one of the most wonderful in the whole portrait gallery of Russian literature. The comic escapades and unconscious mischief-making of this enormous, exuberant, very unspiritual, and quite childlike deacon, and the constant reprimands his behavior draws from Father Tuberózov, are familiar to every Russian reader; and Akhíla himself is a universal favorite. But *Soboryáne* is not at all points representative of its author—it is too leisurely, too uneventful, too placid, to be really quite Leskovian. The very idea of a comparison with Trollope would be ridiculous in reference to one of his more typical tales.

Such a typical tale is *The Enchanted Wanderer* (1874). Here his narrative power reaches the high-water

[3] Used as the basis for Dmítry Shostakóvich's opera. (Ed.)

mark. In a little over a hundred pages are told the eventful life and extraordinary adventures of an unwilling adventurer, who comes under a spell and all his life, willy-nilly, is tossed from adventure to adventure. The adventures follow in breathless succession, and each of them is told in extraordinarily rapid tempo and saturated with expressive and picturesque detail. The story is told in the first person —and this is Leskóv's favorite way of giving free play to all his power of verbal invention. *The Enchanted Wanderer* was followed in the same year by *The Sealed Angel,* another breathless story of adventure told in the racy language of an Old Believer—the thrilling story of the recovery of a holy image confiscated by the authorities. In these stories, as in so many others, Leskóv has for his subject the religious life of the Russian people. His ideal, at first very close to that of Orthodox Churchmen, in his later stories becomes more purely ethical and less Orthodox. Such already is *On the Edge of the World* (1876), the story of how a Russian missionary bishop was saved from death in the Siberian wilderness by a heathen native, and how he came to the conclusion that mission work, as it was conducted, worked only ill to the natives. Next came *The Just Men,* a series depicting extraordinary puritan and Christian virtue among most various classes of Russian society. In them, as well as in the humorous and satirical *Details of Episcopal Life,* Leskóv tends to approach pure journalism. There is no invention in these stories. The limits of the narrative form become less distinct, and the narrative is often interrupted by discussions. Soon after this, Leskóv came under the influence of Tolstóy, but he never abandoned his own idiosyncrasies, and it was in the eighties that his most exuberantly original stories were written. In such stories as *The Left-handed Smith and the Steel Flea* (1882), *A Robbery* (1887), or in most stories from the collection of *Christmas Stories* (1886) and *Appropriate Stories* (1887), there is nothing except a sheer delight in story-telling. *The Left-handed Smith* is the most extraordinary of these productions. It tells of how a steel flea of life size was made by an English smith and presented to the Emperor Alexander I. The Emperor challenges the smiths of Túla to go one better. This they do by shoeing every one of the English flea's feet in gold. The left-handed smith is taken to England but, on returning to Russia, gets into the lock-up for drunkenness. The story is told in the most wonderful language, where almost every other word is an extraordinary funny invention of Leskóv's. It stands next to *Soboryáne* in the favor of the general reader.

Still most of his later works are profoundly impregnated with his "new Christianity," which he himself identified with Tolstóy's teaching. Leskóv's Christianity, like Tolstóy's, is anti-clerical, undenominational, and purely ethical. But here the identity ends: the dominant ethical note is different. It is the cult, not of moral purity and of reason, but of humility and charity. "Spiritual pride," self-conscious righteousness, is for Leskóv the greatest of crimes, and it is doubtful whether he would have liked the hero of *The Light Shines in the Darkness*. Active charity is to him the principal virtue, and he attaches very little value to moral purity, still less to physical purity. The charity of his harlots is often pointedly contrasted with the proud and cold virtue of matrons. This feeling of sin as the necessary soil for sanctity, and the condemnation of self-righteous pride as the sin against the Holy Ghost, is intimately akin to the moral sense of the Russian people and of the Eastern Church, and very different from Tolstóy's proud Protestant and Luciferian ideal of perfection. Many of Leskóv's stories of his last years written in his early manner are among his best, and one of these is his last, bearing the title so characteristic of his cult of humility—*The Lady and the Slut*.

But the most characteristic work of his last few years, his stories of early Christian life[4] (*The Mountain, The Brigand of Ascalon, The Beautiful Áza*), are written in a new manner. The subject matter and setting prevented Leskóv from giving rein in these stories to his usual verbal liberties and eccentricities. But his exuberance did not forsake him, and for all his admiration of Tolstóy, Leskóv did not seek to imitate the "classical" manner of his popular tales. He conjures up a vivid and splendidly colored pageant of life under the late pagan or early Byzantine emperors. He has very little exact knowledge of the period, commits glaring anachronisms, and is rather at sea in ancient geography. The world he evokes owes much to the Lives of the Saints, something to Flaubert, and much to

---

[4] These are for the most part borrowed from the *Prologue* (see Chapter I).

his own imagination. There is a charming, ever present undercurrent of humor and finesse. The result is altogether queer and baroque. What was particularly new in them to the Russian reader was a boldly outspoken treatment of sensual episodes. The prudish Russian critics of the time cried out against this license, which seemed strange in a Tolstoyan. They charged Leskóv with insincerity, with treating his moral subjects as nothing but pretexts for the display of voluptuous and sensuous scenes. Leskóv, however, was quite sincere, and the morals of his stories were the most important thing in them to his conscious self. But there was more complexity in the marvelous storyteller than in his simple-minded critics, and his subconscious artistic self took quite as much pleasure in the descriptions of the doings of the Alexandrian flower girls as in the sublime humility of his chief characters. He had seen Russian life as a violent, crude, parti-colored pageant of crime, horse-play, and heroism. And now he had created for himself an equally magnificent and indecent Roman orient. For if there was one thing he hated in the world, it was self-centered and self-satisfied respectability.

To his last years belongs also *The Hare Park*, which was published only posthumously in 1917. It is one of his most remarkable works and his greatest achievement in concentrated satire. It is the story, told for the greater part in his own words, of Onópry Opanásovich Peregúd, an inmate of a lunatic asylum. In his former life he was the son of a petty Little Russian squire and was made police inspector through the influence of the bishop, who happened to be a schoolfellow of his father's. Onópry Opanásovich, who is a quite unusually weak-minded and imbecile creature, got on all right with his responsible post until the beginning of the revolutionary movement of the sixties, when he succumbed to the ambitious desire of catching a nihilist. He gets hold of several nihilists, who turn out to be law-abiding citizens (and one of them even a detective who is himself hunting for nihilists), and is ultimately hoodwinked by his own coachman, who turns out to be a genuine nihilist. The unexpected result unhinges him and so he comes to the lunatic asylum. The story contains all the best features of Leskóv's manner: wonderful racy diction, boisterous farce, extraordinary anecdotes; but it is subordinated to a unifying idea, and the figure of the hapless police inspector grows into a symbol of vast historical and moral significance.

Leskóv, in spite of the admiration for him of some English critics, like Maurice Baring, has not yet come into his own with the English-speaking reader. The Anglo-Saxon public have made up their mind as to what they want from a Russian writer, and Leskóv does not fit in to this idea. But those who really want to know more about Russian must sooner or later recognize that Russia is not all contained in Dostoyévsky and Chékhov, and that if you want to know a thing, you must first be free of prejudice and on your guard against hasty generalizations. Then they will perhaps come nearer to Leskóv, who is generally recognized by Russians as the most Russian of Russian writers and the one who had the deepest and widest knowledge of the Russian people as it actually is.

POETRY: SLUCHÉVSKY

Poetry, in the reign of Alexander II, suffered from the same causes as prose but to a much greater degree. Russian "Victorian" poetry was not in itself a very vigorous growth. It was eclectic; it had degenerated from the high standard of the age of Púshkin; it did not believe in its own right to be and tried to discover a compromise between pure art and public utility. The typical Russian "Victorians"—Polónsky, Máykov, Alexéy Tolstóy—wrote some very good verse, but they were distinctly minor men in comparison with their great prose-writing contemporaries—and not only minor in genius, but minor in craftsmanship. Poetry, as it existed in their hands, was incapable of further development. There were, beside them, other poets, who, breaking away in exactly opposite directions from the "Victorian compromise," produced poetry of a more vigorous, less decadent, and more fruitful kind. These were Nekrásov and Fet.[5] But "civic" poetry in the hands of Nekrásov's successors sank to absolute insignificance, and "art for art" poetry fell just as low.

Even if compared with the novelists of the time, the poets born between 1830 and 1850 are utterly contemptible. The chief reason was again the consistent neglect of

[5] See Chapter VIII.

craftsmanship. This is best seen in the work of Constantine Sluchévsky (1837–1904), who had in him the germs of genius but was incapable of expressing himself otherwise than in a stammer. He began publishing verse very early, but, like Fet, he was hissed into silence by the nihilist critics and, like Fet, ceased publishing. When the atmosphere became more propitious for poetry, he reappeared before the public and in 1880 published a collected edition of his poems. The radicals did not give him a better reception than that of twenty years earlier, but there was now a larger public who could appreciate him apart from utilitarian considerations. He even became a sort of head of a school, but, being what he was—a stammerer innocent of the principles of his craft—he was incapable of becoming a fruitful influence.

In spite of the low level of his poetical workmanship, Sluchévsky is a true poet and a poet of outstanding interest. Like Nekrásov, though in another way, he tried to spring the fetters of romantic convention and annex to poetry provinces that had hitherto been considered foreign. He had a philosophical mind and was deeply read in modern science. He had a wonderful vision of the world and delighted in the boundless multiplicity of beings and things. His "geographical" poems, especially those inspired by the north of Russia and the Murmán coast, are among his best. But he was still more powerfully attracted by the eternal problems of good and evil, and of life and death. He brooded over the problem of personal immortality, and some of his poems on the subject are most striking. Flashes of genius are frequent in his work, but on the whole it is ineffective and irritating, for one feels all the time that all this might have been expressed much better if Sluchévsky had not lived in such a degenerate age.

THE LEADERS OF THE INTELLIGENTSIA: MIKHAYLÓVSKY

The word "intelligentsia" has two meanings. In the broader sense, it includes all the educated and professional classes, irrespective of their political feelings and degree of political activity. In a narrower sense, it is used to denote a special section of these classes—that which is intensely and actively interested in political and social issues. By a still narrower application, it came to be applied in pre-Revolutionary Russia to only those groups which were more or less radically inclined. Slavophils and conservatives were not "intelligentsia." The intelligentsia in this sense is an inner circle, a sect, almost an order of knighthood. The Russian intelligentsia assumed this form in the sixties, and it subsisted till the Bolshevík Revolution. It never included the whole, and probably even never the majority of the intelligentsia in the wider sense. But it was a center, a sort of magnetic pole towards which the majority were attracted. Its influence was large. University students formed the main army of radicalism, but it was led by the literary press. There was inside this "Church" a great variety of opinion in detail, but all were united in several essential tenets. These were: hostility to the existing regime; faith in progress and democracy; a feeling of duty towards what was called in the sixties "the younger brother"—the uneducated working classes. Most of the radicals were socialists, but they regarded the more advanced liberals as "theirs" if they were sufficiently anti-government. The history of the ideas that dominated the intelligentsia has been many times written, and intelligentsia historians have often tried to identify the history of these ideas with the history of Russian literature. This is a gross falsification. But no literary history can overlook the main lines of the development.

In the sixties and seventies there were two main shades of radical opinion—the nihilists (or "thinking realists," as they called themselves) and the populists (*naródniki*). The nihilists laid stress on materialism and agnosticism. Science, especially natural science (Darwin), was their chief weapon. They carried furthest the anti-æsthetic movement. They were socialists, but their socialism stood in the background. Their first duty was to enlighten the people with practical knowledge and evolutionary science. Their influence was paramount in the sixties, when they had a gifted leader in the brilliant pamphleteer Písarev (1840–68), but it declined after his death and had almost disappeared towards the beginning of our period. The populists were more pronounced socialists. Their name came from their cult of the people—identified with the working classes, and more especially with the peasants. Many of them were "conscience-stricken noblemen," that is, members of the gentry

who were obsessed by the idea of sacrificing all their lives
to the people in expiation of the wrongs of serfdom. At
first they were largely non-political and hoped to achieve
social revolution by some internal process in the existing
peasant land commune. But towards the end of the seventies
they gave birth to the "People's Will" Party, which adopted
more active revolutionary methods and organized the
assassination of Alexander II. The reaction of the eighties
put an end for a time to all active revolutionism, but the
naródniki remained the most influential and numerous
group of the intelligentsia till the advent of Marxism in the
nineties. Some of them, after the defeat of the terrorists,
shifted towards a more non-political attitude, and many
populists of the eighties approached Tolstóy in his passive
anarchism, or even the more conservative and Slavophil
anarchism of Dostoyévsky. But all of them retained the
cult of the virtues of the Russian people and the motto
"Everything for the People." Populism was, after all, the
form taken in Russia by the teaching of Jean-Jacques
Rousseau.

The leaders of populism in the sixties and seventies
were the poet Nekrásov and the novelist Saltykóv. They
gave the tone to the great majority of the young generation,
but as they were imaginative writers and not theoreticians,
they could play but a small part in settling the detail of the
populist dogma. The great "doctor" of the populist
"Church" was a younger man—Nicholas Konstantínovich
Mikhaylóvsky (1842–1904), the all-authoritative expounder
of its doctrine, and in his last years, the grand old man of
Russian radicalism. He was a sociologist, and his book on
What Is Progress? was considered by the successors of the
populists as the *Summa Theologiæ* of their doctrine.
Mikhaylóvsky called his method in sociology the "subjective" method, which meant that social science was to be
studied, not disinterestedly like natural science, but in
terms of human progress. Progress for him meant the
greatest happiness, not of the greatest number, but of all
men, for human individuality was the supreme and only
value and could not be sacrificed to society. Socialism was
precisely the only order that allowed for the happiness of all
and for the full expansion of every individuality. The means
of achieving progress was the conscious action of individual
persons inspired with faith and with a sense of duty towards

the people. Populism, as expounded by Mikhaylóvsky, differs from Marxian socialism principally in two things—in its ethical foundation and in its faith in human individuality. It knows nothing either of the class morality or of the superstitious faith in the laws of evolution of Marxism.

Besides his sociological writings, Mikhaylóvsky was a great journalist; his polemical writings (though, as is the case with most polemical writings, they are often not fair play) are always brilliant and full of point. He was also a critic, and though, like all the critics of his time, he considered in the writers he criticized only their "message" and their degree of public utility, he had a wonderfully acute critical insight. He was able, as early as 1873, from certain pedagogical articles by Tolstóy, to discern the essentially destructive and anarchical nature of Tolstóy's doctrine, and largely to predict the development taken by him after 1880 (*The Left and Right Hand of Count Leo Tolstóy*). Mikhaylóvsky's critical masterpiece is his essay on Dostoyévsky (*A Cruel Talent,* 1882). It is full of suppressed but unmistakable hostility to the ideas and person of Dostoyévsky, but with wonderful precision he lays his finger on the writer's love of suffering and connects it with his morbid "sadism." He was the first to bring out the importance of *The Memoirs from Underground* and recognize the central position they occupied in Dostoyévsky's work.

THE CONSERVATIVES

In political life the radicals were the opposition. But in literature they were the majority, and the supporters of the existing order were, in their turn, the opposition. Conservative writers had a considerable influence on the government, but they had fewer readers than the radicals. The Polish Revolt of 1863, and still more the assassination of Alexander II in 1881, had turned the bulk of the upper and middle classes away from radicalism in practical politics, and the reactionary policy of Alexander III's government found substantial support in the country. But this conservatism (as conservatism so often is) was merely the outcome of fear and inertness. It was not interested in conservative *ideas.* The intellectually active part of the nation remained largely radical and atheistic. Only a small minority of thinking people—but among them perhaps the most independent, original, and sincere minds of the day—showed a critical attitude towards the dogma of agnosticism and democracy, and strove towards a creative revival of Christian and national ideas. But the public had little use for independent thought—they preferred either radicalism or radicalism-and-water, and independent conservative writers—like Grigóriev, Dostoyévsky, Leóntiev, Rózanov—had to struggle against general indifference and its consequences, unemployment and poverty. Dostoyévsky was alone successful in this struggle. Only the big men of the political press—the spokesmen of one of the two large sections of conservative opinion—could command a hearing.

These two sections were Slavophils, represented by Aksákov, and practical government nationalists, headed by Katkóv. Iván Aksákov (1823–86), the son of the great memoirist, was the last remnant of the old idealistic Slavophilism of the forties. He was a brilliant and outspoken publicist and orator, and his political influence, especially during the Turkish crisis of 1876–8, was enormous. But he was not a creator of ideas. Katkóv (1818–87) was still less creative. He was an eloquent and determined journalist, and his force of will and fixity of purpose often compelled the government to be firmer in its policy than it would have been without his support. But he was only the watchdog, not the philosopher of reaction. This title might rather be assigned to the famous Pobedonóstsev (1827–1907), *"Óber-prokurór"* of the Synod for thirty years and an enormous political influence under Alexander III and especially in the first years of Nicholas II. But his conservatism was merely negative; it arose out of a profound disbelief in every reform; it was the outcome of a skepticism that did not believe in the possibility of any rational betterment. He was at bottom a nihilist who thought that the existing order was as good as any other, and that it was better to support it by all possible means than to launch out on any uncertain experiment.

But among those less closely connected with the government and with politics, there were men who had better and more positive reasons for defending the traditional groundwork of Russian State and Church. Of the old

Slavophils, romantic idealists who believed in the inherent, God-ordained superiority of the Russian nation and in the great responsibility of Russia for this dangerous gift of Providence, Aksákov was the last. A later phase of Slavophilism—more democratic and less exclusive—had lost its greatest leaders in Grigóriev and Dostoyévsky. It was still represented by Strákhov (1828–95), a philosopher and critic, who had been the journalistic ally of Dostoyévsky but had retained little enthusiasm for his great associate— of all those who knew Dostoyévsky, Strákhov had had the most illuminating and terrible glimpses of the dark, "infernal, underground" soul of the creator of Stavrógin. Strákhov's philosophical work does not belong here, and as a critic he was not strikingly great. But he was the center of anti-radical idealism in the eighties, the principal link between the Slavophils and the mystical revival of the nineties. His place is greater in literary biography than in literary history. Besides his association with Dostoyévsky, he was an intimate friend of Tolstóy, and he became the literary godfather of the greatest writer of the mystical revival— Rózanov.

Another interesting figure was Nicholas Danilévsky (1822–85), the creator of scientific Slavophilism. He was a naturalist by training and gave his nationalism a biological foundation. His book on *Russia and Europe* (1869) develops the theory of individual, mutually watertight civilizations. In Russia and Slavdom he saw the germs of a new civilization that was to displace that of the West. He did not consider Russia in any way superior to, but merely different from, the West; and Russia's duty was to be herself, not because by being herself she would be better and holier than the West, but because as she was not of the West she could never by imitating the West become anything but an imperfect ape, not a real member of Western civilization.[6]

LEÓNTIEV

Constantine Nikoláyevich Leóntiev (1831–91) studied medicine at the University of Moscow, where he came

[6] There can be no doubt that Danilévsky's book is the principal source of the ideas of Oswald Spengler.

under the influence of the "philanthropic" literature of the time and became an ardent admirer of Turgénev. In 1851, under this influence, he wrote a play full of morbid self-analysis. He took it to Turgénev, who received him, liked it, and used his influence to place it in a magazine. But it was not passed by the censor. Turgénev continued patronizing Leóntiev and at one time considered him, next to Tolstóy, the most promising young writer of the time. In 1854, when Leóntiev was in his last year at school, the Crimean War broke out, and Leóntiev volunteered for the Crimean army as a military surgeon. He worked for the most part in hospitals—and worked hard, for he was passionately interested in his work. About this time he developed a paradoxical theory of æsthetic immoralism that took strange forms at times—thus on two occasions, as he tells us in his wonderful memoirs, he encouraged marauding in the Cossacks of a regiment he was attached to. But he remained himself scrupulously honest. He was one of the few non-combatants connected with the Crimean army who had the opportunity of enriching themselves and did not.

So when the war was over he returned to Moscow penniless. He continued practicing as a doctor, and published, in 1861–2, a series of novels that had no success. They are not great novels, but they are remarkable for the fierce intensity with which he expressed in them, always in the most striking and provoking manner, his æsthetic immoralism. This strange immoralistic pathos is best of all seen in *A Husband's Confession*, in which a middle-aged husband encourages the misconduct of his young wife, not from any idea of the "rights of woman," but because he wants her to live a full and beautiful life of passion, ecstasy, and suffering. At this period of his life he began to be attracted by the Slavophils' respect for and love of the originality of Russian life, but their moral idealism remained quite alien to him.

In 1863 he was admitted to the consular service and was appointed secretary and dragoman to the Russian consulate at Candia. He did not stay long at Candia, for he soon had to be transferred for horsewhipping the French vice-consul. This, however, did not impede his career. He moved up the ladder of consular service with great rapidity, and in 1869 he was appointed to the important and inde-

pendent post of consul at Yanina, in Epirus. All this time
his behavior was far from exemplary. His hero was
Alcibiades, and he tried to live up to his standard of a "full"
and beautiful life. He lived passionately and expensively.
He was always in some love affair—and confided them to
his wife. She did not like it, and it would seem that these
confidences were the cause of her mental illness, for after
1869 she became, with intervals, a permanent mental
invalid. This was the first shadow on the wall. In 1871 came
the next—the death of his mother, for whom he had a
deep affection.

In the same year he was transferred to Salonika and
almost immediately had a very severe attack of local
malaria. He was in imminent danger, and on his bed of
sickness he made a vow to go to Mount Athos to expiate
his sins. As soon as he was well enough, he fulfilled his
vow and spent about a year at Athos submitting to the
severe rule of the monastery and to the strict spiritual
guidance of an "elder." From this time he recognized as
sinful his life of the previous years and all his immoralistic
writings and became converted to the most ascetic form
of Byzantine and monastic orthodoxy. But his æsthetic immoralism remained in substance unchanged—it only bowed
down before the rule of dogmatic Christianity. In 1873,
finding himself in disagreement with Ambassador Ignátiev
about the Græco-Bulgarian Church schism, he left the
consular service. Ignátiev, like the Slavophil he was, and
like all official Russia, took the side of the Bulgarians because they were Slavs. To Leóntiev, the Bulgarians—Slavs
or no Slavs—were democrats and rebels to their lawful
spiritual lord, the Œcumenical Patriarch. This was characteristic of Leóntiev—he had no interest in mere Slavdom.
What he wanted was a firm conservatism in the matter of
national originality and tradition, and of this he found
more in the Greeks than in the Bulgarians, whom, with
complete justice, he suspected of being easily Europeanized
and reduced to the common level of Western democratic
civilization. But the Greeks—the conservative Greek peasants, rural tradesmen, and monks—he loved passionately.
They were to him the bulwark of what was to him the
greatest of values—Byzantine civilization.

About the same time he became acquainted with
Danilévsky's *Russia and Europe,* which produced on him a

strong impression by its scientific-biological treatment of the history of civilizations. The idea of the individual civilization as a complete and self-contained organism became his own, and he gave it a brilliant development in his remarkable essay on *Byzantinism and Slavdom*. In it he confuted Danilévsky's idea of the Slavs' being an independent cultural entity and saw the originality of Russia in her being the pupil and heir of Byzantium. Unlike the Slavophils, Leóntiev did not condemn Western civilization as a whole, but only in its last stage. Civilizations were like living beings and passed, with the necessity of a natural law, three inevitable phases of development. The first phase was initial or primitive simplicity; the second, exuberant growth and complexity of creative and beautiful inequality. This was the only valuable stage. It had lasted in Europe from the eleventh to the eighteenth century. The third phase was the "secondary simplification" of dissolution and putrefaction. These phases in the life of a nation were equivalent in the life of an individual to those of embryonic life, of life, and of dissolution after death, when the complexity of a living organism is again reduced to its constituent elements.[7] Europe, since the eighteenth century, had been in the third stage, and there was reason to believe that Russia was already infected by this putrefaction.

The essay passed unnoticed, and altogether, after leaving the consular service, Leóntiev fell on evil times. His income was insignificant, and in 1881 he had to sell his estate. He passed much of his time in monasteries. At one time he was sub-editor of a provincial official paper. Then he was appointed censor. But up to his death he was in constant difficulties. During his life in Greece he had worked at a series of stories of modern Greek life. In 1876 he published them in book form (*From the Life of Christians in Turkey*, three volumes). He placed great hopes on the success of this work, but it fell flat, and the few people who noticed it admired it only as good descriptive journalism. In the eighties, with the growth of reaction, Leóntiev felt himself a little less out of tune and less alone. But though the reactionaries respected him and opened their columns to him, they did not gauge the originality of his

[7] Leóntiev's three phases are Spengler's *Vorkultur, Kultur,* and *Zivilisation*.

genius, but regarded him as rather a doubtful and dangerous ally. Still, in the last years of his life he found more
sympathy than before. And before he died he was surrounded by a small number of devoted followers and admirers. This brought some consolation to his last years. He
spent more and more time in Óptina, the most famous of
Russian ascetic monasteries, and in 1891, with the permission of his spiritual father, the "elder" Father Ambrose, he
took monastic vows with the name of Clement. He settled
in the ancient Trinity Monastery near Moscow, where he
died in the same year.

Leóntiev's political writings (including *Byzantinism
and Slavdom*) were published in two volumes under the
title of *Russia, the East, and the Slavs* (1885–6). They are
written in a vehement, nervous, hurried, disrupted, but
vigorous and pointed style. The nervous uneasiness reflected in it reminds one of Dostoyévsky. But, unlike
Dostoyévsky, Leóntiev is a logician, and the outline of his
argument through the agitated nervousness of his style is
almost as clear as Tolstóy's. Three elements form the
philosophy (if it may be called a philosophy) of Leóntiev.
First came a biological foundation, owing to his medical
training and strengthened by Danilévsky's influence, which
made him look for and believe in natural laws in the social
and moral world. Next came his temperamental æsthetic
immoralism, which made him passionately enjoy the
multiplicity and varied beauty of life. And at last came his
unconditional submission to the guidance of monastic
orthodoxy that dominated his later years; it was more a
passionate desire than the actual presence of faith, but this
only made it more vehement and uncompromising. These
three influences resulted in his final political doctrine of
extreme reaction and nationalism. He hated the modern
West, both for its atheism and for its democratic, leveling
tendencies that destroyed the complex and varied beauty of
social life. The chief thing for Russia was to stop the
process of dissolution and putrefaction coming from the
West. This is expressed in the words (attributed to Leóntiev, though they do not occur in his works): "We must
freeze Russia, to prevent her from rotting." But in his
biological heart of hearts he did not believe in the possibility of stopping the natural process. He was a profound

anti-optimist. He did not want the world to be better. He thought pessimism *here* an essential part of religion. His political "platform" is stated in his characteristically agitated and broken style in the following formulas:

(1) The State must be many-colored, complex, strong, based on class privileges, and change with circumspection; on the whole, harsh, even to fierceness. (2) The Church must be more *independent* than at present. The Episcopate must be bolder, more authoritative, more concentrated. The Church must act as a moderating influence in the State, not the contrary. (3) Life must be poetical, multiform in its national—as opposed to the West—unity (for instance, either not dance at all, but pray to God, or else dance, but in our own way; invent or develop our national dances to a beautiful refinement). (4) The Law, the principles of government, must be severer; individuals must try to be personally kinder; one will counterbalance the other. (5) Science must develop in a spirit of profound contempt for its own utility.

In all Leóntiev did and wrote there was such a profound contempt for mere morality, such a passionate hatred of the democratic herd, such a violent assertion of the aristocratic ideal, that he has been more than once called the Russian Nietzsche. But Nietzsche's impulse was religious, and Leóntiev's was not. He was a rare instance in modern times (the thing was a rule in the Middle Ages) of an essentially unreligious man submitting consciously and obediently to the hard rule of dogmatic and exclusive religion. But he was not a seeker after God or after the absolute. Leóntiev's world is a finite world, a world whose very essence and beauty lie in its finiteness and in its imperfection, *Die Liebe zum Fernen* was quite unknown to him. He accepted and loved Orthodox Christianity, not for the perfection it promised in heaven and announced in the Person of God, but for the stress it laid on the imperfection of earthly life. Those who believed in progress and wanted to introduce their paltry and inferior perfection into this splendidly imperfect world were his worst enemies. He treats them with splendid scorn, quite worthy of Nietzsche, in his brilliant satire *The Average European as the Ideal and Instrument of Universal Destruction.*

Though Leóntiev preferred life to art and liked literature in the measure it reflected beautiful, that is, organic and varied, life, he was perhaps the only genuine literary critic of his time. For, alone of all his contemporaries, he was capable of going to the essential facts of literary art apart from the *message* of the author. His book on the novels of Tolstóy (*Analysis, Style, and Atmosphere in the Novels of Count L. N. Tolstóy,* 1890) is, for its penetrating analysis of the novelist's means of expression, the masterpiece of Russian criticism. In it he condemns (as Tolstóy did himself a few years later in *What Is Art?*) the superfluous-detail manner of the realists and praises Tolstóy for abandoning it in his then recently published stories for the people. This is characteristic of Leóntiev's critical fairness: he censures the style of *War and Peace* though he likes its philosophy, and praises the style of the popular stories though he hates their "new Christianity."

During the last years of his life Leóntiev published some fragments of his personal recollections, which for the general reader are his most interesting work. Their nervous style, their unlimited sincerity, and the great vividness of the story give them a unique place among Russian memoirs. The best fragments are those which were to contain a complete history of his religious life and conversion (but stop short with the first two chapters describing his childhood and his mother, and his literary relations with Turgénev) and the wonderfully vivid account of his part in the Crimean War and of the descent of the Allies on Kerch in 1855. It is truly "infectious." The reader himself becomes part of the agitated, passionate, impulsive soul of Leóntiev.

In his lifetime Leóntiev was judged exclusively on party lines, and as he was nothing if not paradoxical, he earned little else than ridicule from his opponents and qualified praise from his friends. The first man who recognized his genius without sympathizing with his ideas was Vladímir Soloviëv, who was struck by the powerful originality of his personality and, after his death, did much to keep his memory green by writing a sympathetic and detailed notice of him for the standard Russian *Encyclopædia.* Since then he has been revived. In 1912 and following years there appeared a collected edition of his works (in nine volumes); in 1911, a collection of memoirs dedicated to him, preceded by an excellent *Life of Leóntiev*, by his disciple Konoplyántsev. He has become generally (though sometimes tacitly) recognized as a classic.

10

The Eighties and Early Nineties

THE reign of Alexander III (1881–94) was a period of reaction in political life. The assassination of Alexander II marked the crest of the great revolutionary wave and was followed by a collapse of the whole movement. The government opened an energetic campaign of suppression and found substantial support in the opinion of the upper and middle classes. In two or three years it succeeded in making a clean sweep of all revolutionary organizations. By 1884 all active revolutionaries were either in Schlüsselburg[1] and Siberia or abroad. For almost ten years there was no revolutionary activity to speak of. The more law-abiding radicals also suffered from the reaction. Their leading magazines were suppressed, and they lost most of their hold on the masses of the intelligentsia. Peaceful and passive non-political aspirations were the order of the day. Tolstoyism became popular, not so much for its sweeping condemnation of State and Church, as for its doctrine of non-resistance—precisely the point in which it differed from revolutionary socialism. The great majority of the middle class subsided into a life of humdrum boredom and impotent aspirations—a life familiarized to the English reader by the stories of Chékhov. But the end of the reign

[1] A prison, primarily for political offenders, near St. Petersburg. (Ed.)

also saw the beginning of a new upheaval of capitalistic enterprise.

In literature, the eighties were a period of "æsthetic" reaction against the utilitarian practice of the sixties and seventies. This reaction began before 1881, so it cannot have been the result of political disillusionment. It was merely the natural and essentially healthy protest of the literary spirit against the all-pervading utilitarianism of the preceding age. The movement, as a whole, did not proclaim the doctrine of "art for art's sake," but writers began to show a greater interest in things other than immediate public utility—a greater interest in form, and for the "eternal" problems of life and death, of good and evil apart from their social implications. Even those writers of the eighties who were most "with a purpose" were at pains not to let it be seen too crudely. Poetry was revived. In prose, the new writers tried to avoid the formlessness and untidiness of the "tendentious" novelists and the journalistic tendencies of Saltykóv and Uspénsky. They reverted to the examples of Turgénev and Tolstóy, and tried to be what is called in Russian *khudózhestvenny*. This word really means "artistic," but owing to the use to which it was put by the idealist critics of the forties (Belínsky), it has a very different emotional "overtone" from its English equivalent. Among other things, it conveyed to the late-nineteenth-century Russian *"intelligént"* a certain mellowness and lack of crudeness, an absence of too-apparent "purpose," and also an absence of intellectual elements— of logic and "reflection." It was also colored by Belínsky's doctrine that the essence of "art" was "thinking in images," not in concepts. This idea is partly responsible for the great honor in which descriptions of visible things were held— especially emotionally colored descriptions of nature in the style of Turgénev.

For all this reversal to "form" and to "eternal ideas" this movement was very little of a renascence. It lacked force and originality. It was conservative and placid, eclectic and timid. It strove rather after the absence of great ugliness than after the presence of great beauty. The revival of both a really active feeling for form and really daring metaphysical speculation came only later, in the nineties and in the early years of this century.

GÁRSHIN

Vsévolod Mikháylovich Gárshin (1855–88) was the first in date and, in many ways, the most representative of the novelists of the eighties. Of gentry origin, he was a man of extraordinarily acute moral sensitiveness, and, brought up as he was in the period immediately following the Emancipation of the serfs, he naturally enough acquired the mentality of a "conscience-stricken nobleman." It did not take the direction of political work for the people, but when war broke out with Turkey (1877) he enlisted as a private soldier. He did not do this from motives of patriotism or for the love of adventure, but under the intense conviction that if the people were suffering at the front, it was his duty to suffer with them. Gárshin did well as a soldier. He was mentioned in dispatches and promoted to the grade of sergeant. In August 1877 he was wounded in the leg and invalided to Khárkov. There he wrote *Four Days*, a short story about a wounded soldier who remained four days on the battlefield unable to move and next to the putrefying corpse of a dead Turk. The story appeared in October 1877 and created a sensation. It established Gárshin's reputation once for all. He became a professional writer. Gradually his delicate moral constitution took a morbid turn and developed into a permanent and agonizing dissatisfaction with the whole of the world order. He was constantly on the brink of a mental breakdown. His conduct became eccentric. One of his first eccentricities was his visit to the Prime Minister Lóris-Mélikov, whom he endeavored to convince of the necessity of "making peace" with the revolutionaries. His personal acquaintance with the morbid states of mind helped him to write *The Red Flower* (1883), the most remarkable of all his stories. As time went on, his nervous state grew worse. He began to feel the imminent approach of madness. This aggravated his melancholy and brought him to suicide. After a particularly bad access of despair he threw himself down a staircase and broke his leg. He did not recover, but, after an agony of five days, died on March 24, 1888. All those who knew him testify to the extraordinary purity and charm of his person. His eyes especially are said to have been unique and unforgettable.

The essence of Gárshin's personality is a "genius" for pity and compassion, as intense as Dostoyévsky's but free from all the "Nietzschean," "underground," and "Karamázov" ingredients of the greater writer. This spirit of compassion and pity pervades all his writing. His work is not voluminous: it consists of some twenty stories, all of them contained in a single volume. In most of them he is an intelligent pupil of Turgénev and the early Tolstóy. In a few (*The Signal, The Legend oj Proud Aggéy*) he follows the lead given by Tolstóy's "popular" stories. *That Which Was Not* and *Attalea Princeps* are fables with animals and plants in human situations. The second of these two stories is one of his best—it is saturated with a spirit of tragic irony. In *Officer and Servant* he is a forerunner of Chékhov —it is an excellently constructed story of "atmosphere," an atmosphere of drab gloom and meaningless boredom. In *A Very Short Novel* he treats, with greater felicity, the subject of Artsybáshev's *War*, the infidelity of the woman to the crippled hero. It is a little masterpiece of concentration and lyrical irony. His best-known and most characteristic story is *The Red Flower*, the first in a long row of lunatic-asylum stories (the next in time was Chékhov's *Ward No. 6*). In it Gárshin's morbid and high-strung moral sensitiveness reaches its highest pitch. It is the history of a madman who is obsessed by the desire to challenge and defeat the evil of the world. He discovers that all evil is contained in three poppies growing in the middle of the hospital garden, and with infinite astuteness and cunning he succeeds in defeating the vigilance of his warders and picking the flowers. He dies from nervous exhaustion, but dies happy and certain of having attained his end. The story is gloomy and powerful. The oppressive atmosphere of the asylum is conveyed with effective skill. The end comcs as a relief, like death to a martyr, but there is in it also a pang of bitter irony.

Gárshin is hardly a great writer. His manner is too much that of a degenerate age. His technique is insufficient, and even in *The Red Flower* there are irritating lapses into the inadequate. But his style is sober and sincere, and even his occasional clumsiness seems preferable to the fluent rhetoric and cardboard dramatism of the school of Andréyev.

MINOR NOVELISTS

In the eighties and nineties there was a considerable output of Russian fiction. It was not of a very high quality, and even at the time no one thought that a great literary revival was going on. But some of it is not altogether insignificant. There is no need to give much attention to the novelists of the eighties—a brief survey will suffice. The oldest of them (for many years the dean of Russian letters), P. D. Boborýkin (1836–1922), was a journalist rather than a novelist; his novels are snapshots of the various states of mind through which the typical *"intelligént"* passed, and of various new social phenomena, such as the "cultured merchant." They are written in an "objective" style derived from the French naturalists. A journalist of another sort was Vasíly Nemiróvich-Dánchenko (1848–1936, to be distinguished from his brother Vladímir, founder of the Moscow Art Theater), who led the Russian reader on tours around the world, with just a touch of primitively mild sensationalism. He was read by the unsophisticated, who also enjoyed the historical novels of Vsévolod Soloviëv (1849–1903), the brother of the famous philosopher. But to indulge in this sort of literature was "bad form" for the self-respecting intellectual.

The influence of Dostoyévsky is discernible in the work of M. N. Álbov (1851–1911), who described at great length the morbid states of mind experienced by priests and clerics; and in that of Prince D. P. Golítsyn-Murávlin, who, starting with the character of Prince Mýshkin, attempted to portray pathological types of the aristocracy. Another side of Dostoyévsky is reflected in the work of K. S. Barantsévich, who wrote stories in the respectable tradition of *Poor Folk*, describing the sufferings of the poor and the oppressed. A sterner note sounded in the stories of D. N. Mámin-Sibiryák, who drew unsweetened pictures of the hard and joyless life of the miners in the Ural. Ieroním Yasínsky was a naturalist of the French type who early proclaimed the rights of art for art's sake. He was the

first Russian writer to approach sexual subjects, and in
1917 the first non-party intellectual to join the Bolshevíks.
The humorous South Russian nature found expression in
the unpretending stories of I. N. Potápenko. Another
popular humorist of the time was Chékhov's friend
Scheglóv (pseudonym of I. L. Leóntiev). His *Suburban
Husband,* an amusing picture of Russian suburbia, became
a favorite catchword, almost a new word. Another famous
humorous type was created by Mme Mikúlich (pseudonym
of Lydia I. Veselítsky). Her *Mímochka* is a witty picture
of the average *jeune fille* of Petersburg bureaucratic society
—the incarnation of placid futility.

More important than any of these writers was Alexander Ivánovich Èrtel (1855–1908). He was a populist,
but in his later years he abandoned the usual agnosticism
of the Russian *"intelligént"* and tried to evolve a more
spiritualist philosophy. This caused a considerable revival
of interest in him about 1910 when the revival of religion
was the watchword—his collected works and his letters
were published then and had a considerable success. His
first stories appeared in 1880, but his best and best-known
novel is *The Gardénins, Their Retainers, Their Friends,
and Their Enemies,* in two volumes (1898). It had the
honor, when reprinted in 1908, of a preface by Tolstóy,
who gave especial praise to Èrtel's art of dialogue. "Such
good Russian," said Tolstóy, "is not to be found in any
writer, old or new. He uses the people's speech, not only
with accuracy, force, and beauty, but with infinite variety.
. . . Who wants to know the language of the Russian
people . . . must not only read but study Èrtel's Russian."
Apart from this, *The Gardénins* is one of the best Russian novels written since the great age. It is a vast panorama
of life on a big estate in south central Russia. The hero
is the son of an estate agent (like Èrtel himself). The
characters of the peasants are infinitely varied and splendidly individualized. So are those of the rural middle class
and of the rural police, which of course is presented in
a satirical light. But the Gardénins themselves, one of
whom is a "conscience-stricken" aristocrat, are much less
happily portrayed. The novel is transfused with a very
keen poetical sense of nature. One of the most memorable
episodes is the account of a trotting match at Khrenóvaya,

which holds its own even by the side of the race scene in *Anna Karénina.*

Another writer whose work has not lost its charm was Nicholas Geórgievich Mikhaylóvsky, who wrote under the pseudonym of N. Gárin (1852–1906). He was a railway engineer by profession and took to literature rather late in life. His principal work is a trilogy describing the early life of Tëma Kartashóv—*Tëma's Childhood* (1892), *Schoolboys* (*Gimnazísty*, 1893), and *Students* (1895). The series has great charm, is written in a simple and sincere style, and was immensely popular in its day. The characters that go through the three books are drawn with great warmth, and the reader soon feels towards them as if they were boys he knew in real life. Apart from the literary qualities of the trilogy, it is an important historical document, for it is the "natural history" of a typical intelligentsia education, a school of morally inefficient and nervously unstable men.

This enumeration of minor writers may be completed by the name of Peter Filípovich Yakubóvich (1860–1911), the only active revolutionary among them. He joined the People's Will Party (after March 1st), was arrested in 1884, and spent three years in the SS. Peter and Paul Fortress and eight years (1887–95) as a convict in Siberia. This record did not allow him to appear in literature under his own name, which has remained comparatively unknown, though his two pseudonyms, P. Ya. and L. Mélshin, became very popular. He used the first to sign his poetry, which is "civic" and very poor. Under the second he published in 1896 a remarkable book of stories of convict life, *A World of Outcasts,* the first book of its kind since Dostoyévsky's *House of Death.* Though, of course, on a much inferior level to Dostoyévsky's, Mélshin's book has considerable merit. Its attitude is characteristic of the Russian revolutionary idealist. He paints, with uncompromising objectivity, the most repulsive criminals as they are, with all their crimes and cynical heartlessness, but he descries in them flashes of humanity, and the message of the book is a firm belief in human nature and a firm respect for human individuality even in the deepest degradation.

ÉMIGRÉS

Those revolutionaries who did not go to Siberia or to
Schlüsselburg found refuge abroad. Their place in literary
history is not great. Their political press between 1881 and
1900 was not very active, and even afterward it produced
nothing to compare with Herzen's *Bell*. But this period of
calm produced an interesting series of memoirs. Now at
rest, the active fighters of yesterday sat down to record their
experiences of the great struggle. Their memoirs were intended largely for a foreign audience (before 1905 they
could not be imported into Russia), and much of it was
even written in some foreign language. The idea Western
people gained of the revolutionary movement (in so far
as it was not quite fantastic) was derived from the works
of Sergéy M. Kravchínsky, who wrote under the pseudonym of S. Stepnyák (1852–95). He was a terrorist: he
had taken part in 1878 in the assassination of General
Mezentsóv, chief of the political police. In 1882 he
published in Italian *La Russia sotteranea* (*Underground
Russia*), which he himself translated into Russian. Later
on he settled down in England and wrote *The Career of
a Nihilist* (1889) in English. His stories were well suited
to the taste of the Western reader—they were vivid and
thrilling. But they have very little value as documentary
evidence. From this last point of view the memoirs of
Vladímir Debogóry-Mokriévich are much more valuable.
Nor are they without purely literary merits; their narrative is easy, straightforward, and full of humor, the
almost inevitable virtue of all Southern Russians.

The most eminent of the Russian *émigrés* of this
period was Prince Peter Kropótkin (1842–1921). He was
the descendant of a very ancient family and received his
education at the Corps des Pages. He served in a Cossack
regiment in Siberia and made himself a name as a ge-
ographer. In the seventies he joined the revolutionary
movement, was arrested, and finally escaped over the frontier. At first he lived in Switzerland and in France, but
was expelled from the former and sentenced to imprisonment in the latter, in both cases for anarchist propaganda.
For he had become the leader and theoretician of anarch-

ism. In 1886 he came to London, where he lived till 1917. He was a man of aristocratic manners and great personal charm and found many friends in various classes of English society. During the first World War his attitude was patriotic. In 1917 he returned to Russia. He remained hostile to the Bolshevíks and rejected all Lénin's approaches. He died in 1921 near Moscow. His work is voluminous; it includes, besides geographical works: propaganda tracts and more elaborate expositions of his anarchism, an optimistic philosophy based on evolutionary theories, a history of the French Revolution, and a history of Russian literature. Practically all of it is in French or English. The most interesting of his books (also originally in English) is *The Memoirs of a Revolutionary* (1899), a first-class autobiography, the most remarkable work of its kind since Herzen's *My Past and Thoughts*.

Here perhaps would also be the place to mention Marie Bashkírtseva (Baschkirtseff, 1860–84). Though she was not a political *émigrée,* she lived and wrote in France and in French. Her *Journal,* published posthumously in 1887, produced a sensation in Europe and was translated into many languages (into Russian later than into English and German). It is certainly a remarkable human document and gives proof of more than ordinary power of self-observation. But its importance has probably been overrated, and in any case it stands entirely outside the line of development of Russian literature.

KOROLÉNKO

Vladímir Galaktiónovich Korolénko (1853–1921) is undoubtedly the most attractive representative of idealist radicalism in Russian literature. If Chékhov had never lived, Korolénko would also have been *facile princeps* among the novelists and poets of his time. He was born in Zhitomír, the capital of Volynia, then a semi-Polish city, and his mother was a Polish gentlewoman. In his childhood Korolénko did not very well know to which nationality he belonged, and learned to read Polish before he did Russian. Only after the Revolt of 1863 did the family have definitely to "choose" its nationality, and they became Russians. In 1870 Korolénko went to Petersburg and became a student of the Institute of Technology, and afterward of the Moscow School of Agriculture, but he did not complete his studies at either: he was expelled for belonging to a secret political organization. In 1879 he was arrested and deported to northeastern Siberia, and spent several years in a far-off part of the Yakút region. In 1885 he was allowed to come to Russia and settled in Nízhny-Nóvgorod. The same year he reappeared in literature,[2] with *Makár's Dream*, the story of a Yakút. The next ten years he spent in Nízhny, where he wrote almost all his best stories. During the famine of 1891–2 he took part in the relief work and published a volume of impressions. In 1895 he was allowed to come to Petersburg. In 1900 he was elected a member of the Academy, but resigned the title, after the incident with Górky's election (*v. infra*). In 1900 he settled in Poltáva, where he lived until his death. After the death of Mikhaylóvsky he became the most prominent figure in the populist camp. From 1895 on, he almost abandoned literature and devoted himself to the disclosure and exposition of injustices committed by the law courts and the police. After 1906 he headed the campaign against military law and capital punishment. The only work of his last period (and perhaps his best) was a sort of autobiography, *The History of My Contemporary*, the first part of which appeared in 1910, and the other parts posthumously in 1922. In 1917 and after, he remained hostile to the Bolshevíks, and his last published work was a series of letters to Lunachársky denouncing the Bolshevíks as the enemies of civilization. He died in December 1921 in Poltáva, which during the last few years of his life had more than once been taken and retaken by the various parties in the civil war.

Korolénko's work is very typical of what the eighties and nineties called "artistic" in the peculiar sense explained above. It is full of emotional poetry and of nature introduced in Turgénev's manner. This lyrical element seems today a little stale and uninteresting, and most of us will prefer to all his earlier work his last book, in which he has almost freed himself of this facile poetry. But it was this poetry which appealed so strongly to the tastes of the Russian reading public thirty and forty years ago.

---

[2] He had begun publishing before his exile, but he never allowed this early work of his to be reprinted.

The age that made the reputation of Korolénko also revived the cult of Turgénev. Though everyone knew that
Korolénko was a radical and a revolutionary, he was received with equal enthusiasm by all parties. This non-party
reception given to writers in the eighties was a sign of
the times. Gárshin and Korolénko became recognized as
(minor) classics before Leskóv, a much greater man, but
born in worse times, was given anything like justice.
Korolénko's poetry may on the whole have faded, but his
best early work still retains much of its charm. For even
his poetry rises above the level of mere prettiness when he
has to do with the more majestic aspects of nature. The
northeast of Siberia, with its vast and empty spaces, its
short sub-polar days, and its dazzling wilderness of snow,
lives in his early stories with impressive grandeur. But
what gives Korolénko his unique flavor is the wonderful
blend of poetry with a delicate humor and with his undy-
ing faith in the human soul. Sympathy and faith in human
goodness are characteristic of the Russian populist. Korolénko's world is a fundamentally optimistic world, for
man is good by nature, and only the evil conditions created
by despotism and the brutal selfishness of capitalism make
him what he is—a poor, helpless, absurd, pitiful, and irritating creature. There is a mighty poetry in Korolénko's
first story, *Makár's Dream,* not only because of the suggestive painting of the Yakút landscape, but still more because of the author's profound, indestructible sympathy
with the dark and unenlightened savage, whose mind is so
naïvely selfish and who yet has in him a ray of the divine
light. Korolénko's humor is especially delightful. It is free
from all satirical intent and sophistication. It is wonderfully easy and natural—it has a lightness of touch that is
rare in Russian authors, and in which he is surpassed only
by that wonderful and still unappreciated author Kuschévsky. In Korolénko this humor is often subtly interwoven
with poetry—as in the delightful story *At Night,* in which
a family of children discuss in their bedroom the absorb-
ing question of how babies are made. *The Day of Atonement,* with its funny old Jewish devil, has that blend of
humor and phantasy which is so delightful in Gógol's
early stories, but Korolénko's colors are mellower and
quieter, and though he has not an ounce of the creative
exuberance of his great countryman, he has much more

human sympathy and warmth. The most purely humorous of his stories is *Tongueless* (1895), the story of three Ukrainian peasants who emigrated to America without knowing a word of any language but their own. Russian critics have called it Dickensian, and this is true in the sense that in Korolénko, as in Dickens, the absurdity of his characters does not make them less lovable.

Korolénko's last work is an autobiography, which seems to be even a singularly exact and truthful account of his life but which for some supersensitive scruple he called the history, not of himself, but of his contemporary. It is less poetical and barer than his early work, but his two principal qualities—humor and sympathy—are very much present. He gives a delightful picture of life in yet semi-Polish Volynia—of his scrupulously honest but willful father. He records his early impressions of country life, of school, of the great events he had to witness—the Emancipation and the Polish Revolt. It is full of wonderfully vivid, grotesque figures of cranks and originals, perhaps the best in his whole portrait gallery. It is certainly not thrilling, but it is a deliciously quiet story told by an old man (he was only fifty-five when he began it, but there always was something of the grandfather in Korolénko) who has ample leisure and good will and who finds pleasure in reviving the vivid memories of fifty years ago.

THE LITERARY LAWYERS

One of the most important changes introduced into Russian life in the reign of Alexander II was the reform of the law courts. It substituted for the old secret process a public procedure after European models. It made the judges independent of the executive and introduced a corporation of the bar. The independence of the judges was practically done away with under Alexander III, but the bar flourished from the very beginning and turned out an important nursery of general culture. The most brilliant men of the generation adopted this profession, and many advocates soon won an all-Russian reputation by their eloquence. Contrary to what was going on elsewhere, they did not neglect to work at the form of their utterances, and more workmanship was displayed in this field than in any department of imaginative literature. The names of the advocates W. Spasowicz, Prince A. I. Urúsov, and the crown prosecutor (later on, Minister of Justice) N. V. Muraviëv may be mentioned as those of the most brilliant speakers of the time. Nor did the lawyers neglect more strictly literary work. Spasowicz wrote notable essays on Púshkin and Byron; Anatóly F. Kóni made a name by his life of Dr. Haas, the philanthropist, and still more by several volumes of recollections. They are written in an easy and limpid style, agreeably reminiscent of the fragmentary memoirs of Turgénev. The æsthetic revival of the eighties and nineties owes much to Prince Urúsov (1843–1900). He introduced into Russia the cult of Flaubert and of Baudelaire, and was one of the best critics of literature of his time, though all his criticism was contained in conversation and private letters.

But the most remarkable of all these literary lawyers was Sergéy Arkádievich Andreyévsky (1847–1920?). He was one of the most successful advocates of his day, but his name will be remembered rather for his literary work. His verse, like practically all the verse of his time, is insignificant. But his critical essays were an important event in their day—he was the first critic to give Dostoyévsky his due place (essay on *The Brothers Karamázov*, 1888) and to begin the revival of the older poetical tradition— he "discovered" Baratýnsky. But his most important work is *The Book of Death*, which was published only posthumously, abroad. It reveals him as a delicate and refined prose writer, a diligent and intelligent pupil of Lérmontov, Turgénev, and Flaubert. The first part, written about 1891, is the most remarkable. It is the history of his first experiences of death. It contains passages of singular force and sustained beauty. Such is the wonderful chapter about his elder sister Másha, his morbid affection for her, her strange mental malady and early death. This chapter deserves a high place in Russian literature. It is wonderful for the sincere analysis of his own feelings, for the vividness of the narrative, and for the sustained rhythm, for which there is no precedent in Lérmontov or Turgénev. The whole chapter (some fifty pages) is one rhythmical whole. The rhythm is all the more perfect for being quite unobtrusive —the turn of phrase is so colloquial that an untrained ear might not suspect, or a deliberately unrhythmical delivery

might not convey to the listener, that there was anything
peculiar about it. It is one of the finest achievements of
Russian prose.

POETS

Andreyévsky was typical of his time when in one of his
essays he said that the only legitimate subject matter for
poetry was "beauty and melancholy." These two words
effectively sum up the poetical work of the eighties and
early nineties. The revival of poetry began a few years before 1881 and affected both the civic and the "art-for-art's
sake" school. But there is very little difference between
these two "schools." Their style is indistinguishable. The
"civic" poets concentrated on melancholy caused by the
evils of despotism and social injustice, but they had nothing
of the vigorous, daring realism of Nekrásov, whom they
affected to recognize as master. The "art-for-art's sake"
poets preferred to dwell on beauty and on melancholy
arising from sentimental causes, but they had neither the
high craftsmanship of Fet nor the range of interest of
Sluchévsky.

Among the "civic" poets, the most famous was Semën
Yákovlevich Nádson (1862–87), a young man of partly
Jewish descent who died of consumption at a very early
age. His poetry is inspired by the impotent desire to make
the world better and by the burning consciousness of his
own impotence. This makes him akin to Gárshin, but he
had neither Gárshin's imaginative power nor his great
spiritual intensity. Nádson's verse is smooth and skeleton-
less, it avoids ugliness, but it is quite devoid of all life and
strength. It marks the low-water mark of Russian poetical
technique; and his great popularity, the low-water mark
of Russian poetical taste. His only rival was Mínsky
(pseudonym of N. M. Vilénkin, 1855–1937), the first full-
blooded Jew to win a reputation in Russian letters. He
began before Nádson but could not compete with him—
his poetry seemed cold and intellectual. In the late eighties
he abandoned "civic" poetry and became the first swallow
of the modernist movement, together with Merezhkóvsky,
who also began under the auspices of Nádson as a civic
poet. But Merezhkóvsky from the very first gave proof of

a poetical culture superior to that of his contemporaries. The most popular of the non-civic poets was A. N. Apúkhtin (1841–93), the friend and schoolfellow of Tchaikóvsky and a popular figure in Petersburg society, where he was noted for his abnormal stoutness. He was a sort of aristocratic counterpart of Nádson—what Nádson's poetry was to the radical intelligentsia, Apúkhtin's was to the gentry and official classes. It is also a poetry of impotent regret, but his regret is for the days of his youth when he could better enjoy the love of women and the taste of wine. It is the poetry of a man who has ruined his health by too much indulgence. It is less colorless and jelly-like than Nádson's, for he does not so studiously shun all realism and all concrete detail. Some of his lyrics have become very popular as songs, as the well-known *Sleepless Nights,* one of the most popular in the "gypsy" repertoire. A more dignified poet was Count A. A. Goleníschev-Kutúzov (1848–1912). He has been called the poet of Nirvana. He tried to revive a severe and "classical" style, but it is merely still and lifeless in his hands. He is at his best when he speaks of death and destruction. The description of a snowstorm in one of his poems is not without merit. But his principal title to glory is that some of his poems were put to music by Musórgsky, who had a peculiar weakness for his poetry. Another aristocrat who wrote poetry was Count P. D. Buturlín (1859–95). He was more than half a foreigner, with Italian and Portuguese blood in him, as well as an English education. His first work was a book of English verse printed in Florence. He contributed to the *Academy* and other English papers. He never really learned to speak the language of his country. This makes his poetry inadequate, but it is interesting as an isolated instance of English influence—Buturlín was a devoted follower of Keats and of the pre-Raphaelites.

In the later eighties the anti-radical critics tried to create a boom around the poetry of Constantine Mikháylovich Fófanov (1862–1911). Quite uncultured and uneducated (he was the son of a small shopkeeper in a Petersburg suburb), he possessed what none of his contemporaries possessed—a genuine gift of song. His poetry is all about stars, and flowers, and birds—it is sometimes quite genuine, but on the whole rather uninteresting; and as he was a very poor craftsman, it is singularly unequal. The next

poetical boom was around Myrrha Lókhvitsky (1869–
1905), who appeared in 1895 with a volume of passionate
and exotic feminine poetry. Her poetry and Fófanov's
seemed the last word of beauty in the nineties, when the
real revival of poetry began with the rise of the symbolist
movement.

VLADÍMIR SOLOVIËV

The eighties were a period of (mild) reaction against the
utilitarian positivism of the preceding age. This reaction
found expression in the anæmic revival of poetry and in a
somewhat more vigorous revival of religious idealism. The
radicals were by temperament idealists, but their idealism
was based (to quote a joke of Soloviëv's) on the rather
unjustifiable syllogism, "Man is descended from monkeys:
consequently we must love each other." The eighties attempted to give this piece of reasoning a more plausible
foundation. Their religious idealism found its most popular
expression in the teaching of Tolstóy, which influenced
contemporaries precisely in so far as it was religious and
a reaction against radical materialism. Another and more
orthodox expression of the same tendency is the work of
Vladímir Soloviëv. The influence of Soloviëv's religious
philosophy, at first insignificant, in the long run proved
more important than that of Tolstoyism. Soloviëv's place
in the history of Russian thought is defined by the fact
that he was the first Russian thinker to divorce mystical
and Orthodox Christianity from the doctrines of Slavophilism. He was to a certain extent the continuer of
the less exclusive and more "occidentalist" wing of Slavophilism, which found its most complete expression in the
ideas of the publicist Dostoyévsky. But there is between
the two a substantial difference: to Dostoyévsky the supreme sanction of Orthodox Christianity was that it expressed the religious intuition of the *Russian people*. He
was a nationalist in religion, a mystical populist: Orthodoxy was true *because* it was the faith of the Russian
people. Soloviëv was quite free from this mystical nationalism, and whether he based his religion on the deductions
of idealist philosophy or on the authority of the Œcumenical Church, the religious opinion of the Russian people

is to him a matter completely irrelevant. His Orthodoxy
had a strong leaning towards Rome, as the symbol of
Christian unity, and in politics he was a Westernizing
liberal. This was the chief element in his early success,
for the liberals found him a valuable ally in their campaign
against the government and the Slavophils, all the more
valuable because in his indictment of the existing political
order he appealed, not to Darwin or Marx, but to the
Bible and to the fathers. His help came from an unexpected quarter, and for that reason was especially welcome.

Vladímir Sergéyevich Soloviëv (1853–1900) was born
in Moscow, one of a numerous family. His father was the
eminent historian S. M. Soloviëv, and he grew up in the
atmosphere of the Moscow University. He belonged to
that class of Moscow society which included the elite of
the cultured nobility and the pick of the higher intelligentsia. He early joined a highly gifted set of humorists,
who called themselves the Shakspere Society and indulged
in writing nonsense verse and staging parody plays. The
most brilliant of this set was Count Fëdor L. Sollogúb,
the best Russian nonsense poet since "Kuzmá Prutkóv."
Soloviëv himself was all his life an adept in this art. At
the same time his scholarship was brilliant and precocious.
As early as 1875 he published his *magister*'s thesis on
The Crisis of Western Philosophy, directed against positivism. In the same year he went to London, where he
spent most of his time in the British Museum studying the
mystical doctrine of Sophia the Divine Wisdom. There, in
the reading room, he had a vision and received the mystical command to go immediately to Egypt. In the desert
near Cairo he had his most important and completest
vision, which revealed to him the Person of Sophia. This
voyage into the desert was accompanied by amusing in-
cidents with the Arabs. It is highly characteristic of Soloviëv that twenty years later he described these visions (including an earlier one of 1862) in a humorous poem,
Three Meetings, in which the highly lyrical and esoteric
description of the visions is surrounded by verse in the
style of *Beppo* and *Don Juan.* On his return to Russia,
Soloviëv was appointed Reader of Philosophy at Moscow,
and soon afterward at Petersburg. His university career
was a short one: in March 1881 he made a speech against
capital punishment in which he tried to persuade the new

emperor not to execute the assassins of his father. His motive was that by going "counter to the natural inclination of his heart and to every consideration of earthly wisdom, the Tsar would rise to a superhuman level and in the very fact demonstrate the divine source of his royal power." In spite of this motive, he found himself compelled to leave the university. During the eighties he worked at the idea of a universal theocracy, which brought him nearer and nearer to Rome. He went to Zagreb and became intimate with Bishop Strossmayer, the opponent in 1870 of papal infallibility but by now a docile servant of the Vatican. The work of this period is summed up in his French book *La Russie et l'Eglise Universelle* (1889), in which he took up an extremely pro-Roman position, defending both the infallibility and the Immaculate Conception, describing the Popes as the only rock of orthodoxy throughout the ages, and denouncing the Russian Church as State-governed. The book could not appear in Russia, but produced a certain sensation abroad. However, Soloviëv never actually became a Roman Catholic, and the appellation of a "Russian Newman" given him by the French Jesuit d'Herbigny (in his book *Un Newman russe*) is grossly misleading. *La Russie et l'Eglise Universelle* marks the high-water mark of his Romish tendencies. They soon began to decline, and in his last work he represented the final Union of Christian Churches as a union between three *equal* Churches—Orthodox, Catholic, and Protestant, with the Pope as only *primus inter pares*. In the late eighties and nineties he conducted an energetic campaign against the nationalist policy of Alexander III's government. These articles brought him a high reputation in liberal spheres. His mystical life, however, continued, though his visions of Sophia ceased with the Egyptian one. In the nineties his mysticism became less orthodox and took the form of a strange "mystical love affair" with the Finnish Lake Saima, which found abundant expression in his poetry. He also had diabolical visitations. In the last year of his life he entered on a correspondence with Anna Schmidt, a provincial newspaper hack who believed herself to be the incarnation of Sophia, and Soloviëv of the person of Christ. (There is a striking chapter on Anna Schmidt in Górky's *Fragments from a Diary*.) Soloviëv's answers to her were humorous in form but sympathetic in substance, and he lent himself to her singular adoration. But his mystical life remained little known to his contemporaries. They knew him as an idealist philosopher and an outspoken liberal polemist. This last capacity placed him high in the eyes of the intelligentsia, and he was invited by the radical editors of the standard *Encyclopædia* to be editor of the philosophical department, which was consequently conducted in a spirit strongly opposed to agnosticism and materialism. He also found more devoted followers who took up and developed his philosophical doctrines. First among them were the brothers Prince Sergéy and Prince Eugene Troubetzkóy. In 1900 he published his last and, from the literary point of view, most important work, *Three Conversations on War, Progress, and the End of Human History, to Which Is Added a Short History of Antichrist.* The conversations were at once recognized as masterpieces, but the *History of Antichrist* produced a certain consternation by its strangely concrete faith in that personage. Soloviëv was by this time worn out by a too-intense intellectual, spiritual, and mystical life. He went to seek repose in Úzkoye, the Troubetzkóys' estate near Moscow. There he died on July 31, 1900, of general exhaustion.

Soloviëv's personality was extraordinarily complex, and its variations and contrasts are greater than we usually find in a single man. It is difficult to include in one formula this strange and inseparable blend of high-strung religious and moral earnestness with an invincible turn for the most nonsensical humor; his extraordinarily acute sense of orthodoxy with curious proclivities towards Gnosticism and undisciplined mysticism; his equally acute sense of social justice with the lack of fair play in his polemical writings; his profound faith in personal immortality with utterances of gaily cynical nihilism; his earthly asceticism with a morbidly developed erotic mysticism. This complexity and multiplicity of his person seem to have found their expression in his weird, uncanny laugh—which was what all who knew him considered most striking and unforgettable.

Soloviëv was a most brilliant writer, brilliant in everything he undertook. In prose he commanded a trenchant and coldly splendid style, especially suited for polemics. His more serious prose works are perhaps his least characteristic, for in them he had to suppress both his merriment and his mysticism. But they are important for their ideas, and of course it was on them that his reputation grew and is still largely based. His early works are devoted to the enunciation of the first principles of his philosophy; those written in the eighties deal chiefly with questions of Church policy *sub specie æternitatis*. *The Justification of Good* (1898) is a treatise on moral theology, mainly directed against the "non-resistance" teaching of Tolstóy. Soloviëv is considered Russia's most important philosopher in the "professional" sense of the word. He was a great scholar in philosophy, and his knowledge of ancient and modern philosophy was enormous, but he cannot in any sense be put on a level with the world's greatest philosophers, and in a universal history of philosophy he may be overlooked. His philosophy was Neoplatonic, and the Gnostics had always a great attraction for him. But I am in no way competent, and it is in the present connection irrelevant, to give any epitome of his metaphysics. As for his theology, his relations with Roman Catholicism have already been mentioned. He is studied in Roman Catholic schools, though of course he is not recognized as a Doctor. In the Orthodox Church his position is ambiguous—it is recognized that he gave the best existing definitions of Orthodoxy as opposed to every individual heresy, but his leanings towards Rome and visible Unity, as well as the undisciplined and dubious character of his mystical life, make him suspect.

The cold brilliancy of his manner is nowhere more apparent than in his polemical writings. They are splendid examples of the higher journalism, but, as has already been pointed out, when disputing with opponents who had no support in public opinion (for example, Strákhov, Rózanov, the Decadents), he preferred to use arguments that were most likely to give him easy victory in the eyes of the reader rather than to go out of his way to be intellectually fair. Far more remarkable from the literary point of view than his other prose writings are the *Three Conversations*, a true masterpiece in a difficult field. In them he gave free rein to his exuberant humor and to his sparkling wit, and succeeded in creating a work that is at once as amusing as Mark Twain and as earnest as William James. And this he achieves without the aid of paradox, that favorite weapon of all "laughing philosophers." He revels in puns and anecdotes and quotations from nonsense verse, and each of the personages in the dialogue is delightfully individualized. But each (except the purely ridiculous Lady "to whom nothing human is alien") supports his thesis with admirable logic and consistency, and uses his best arguments. The *dialogi personæ* are (besides the Lady): the General, who maintains the rights of force as the just chastiser of brute evil; the Politician, who supports modern civilization as an advance against savagery; the Prince, who is a Tolstoyan and preaches non-resistance, and who is the villain of the play; and Mr. Z., who is Soloviëv's mouthpiece and recognizes the General and the Politician as the exponents respectively of a *partial* truth that must be merged in the higher synthesis of active Christianity. The *Conversations* are followed by the *History of Antichrist*. This is a curiously vivid and detailed story of the end of the world and of the events immediately preceding the day of judgment. Soloviëv saw in the rise of China and Japan (he wrote in 1900) a great danger for Christendom, and considered it one of the precursors of Antichrist. But Antichrist himself is a European, a philologist and a Roman bishop *in partibus* who is also a magician and a Superman according to Nietzsche.

Those admirers of Soloviëv who think his mysticism the principal aspect of his work place a particular value on his poetry. In this art he was a follower of Fet, with whom he was on intimate terms and whose militant atheism he deplored as precluding any chance of their meeting in the next world. But, like all his contemporaries, he was incapable of acquiring (perhaps even of distinguishing) Fet's superior technique, and, like all of them, he suffered from a slackness and thinness of form. Still he was a true poet—certainly the best poet of his generation. He used the usual romantic vocabulary, but in his hands it received a new significance, for its hackneyed stock words were used to denote concrete mystical facts. His poetry is mystical throughout, and for a complete understanding of it, the fundamental conceptions of his mystic experience must be constantly kept in mind. His most productive period was in the early nineties, when he wrote the beautiful series of lyrics addressed to Lake Saima, of which he speaks as of a living being. Those who want to understand any-

thing in Soloviëv must realize that it is no poetical metaphor, but the actual feeling of a mystical person, when he
addresses the lake as "gentle lady" and speaks of its eyes,
its moods, and its dreams. His longest poem, *Three Meetings,* though not the best, is in many ways the most characteristic, for in it his mysticism is closely elbowed by his
humorous irreverence. Soloviëv was prolific in the purest
nonsense verse. It includes witty parodies, biting satire,
"cautionary tales," and the Russian equivalent of limericks,
but the element of pure nonsense and reckless absurdity is
always very apparent. By a procedure opposite to that of
Three Meetings, he introduced into one of his most nonsensical plays (*The White Lily*) passages of intense
mystical significance and gave the whole play a mystical
"second meaning." His love of nonsense is also apparent
in his letters, which seethe with puns and delightfully irrelevant quotations. When they are published, most people's
letters written with the view of amusing the addressee fail
to amuse the reader, who has the disagreeable feeling that
he is required to laugh and does not feel inclined to. Soloviëv's fun is always as amusing to the general reader—
unless he feels an aversion to all forms of nonsense—as
it was to the person who first read it. Only in writing to
such particularly important and respectable people as
Bishop Strossmayer does Soloviëv refrain from his jokes.
But even apart from their nonsense his letters are full of
wit and humor and are delightful reading. Next to Púshkin
(who has no rivals), Soloviëv is no doubt the best of
Russian letter writers, with Chékhov as a good third.

CHÉKHOV

Antón Pávlovich Chékhov (1860–1904) was born at
Taganróg, on the sea of Azóv. His grandfather had been
a serf on the estate of V. G. Chertkóv's grandfather but
had acquired considerable wealth by trade and was able to
purchase his freedom and that of all his family. Chékhov's
parents were simple, half-educated, very religious people,
with a strong family feeling. The family consisted of several
sons and a daughter. They were all given a liberal education. Antón, who was the youngest but one, was sent
to the gymnasium (secondary school) of Taganróg. But

while he was there the prosperity of the Chékhovs came to an end. The building of a railway through the neighboring Rostóv was a severe blow to the commerce of Taganróg, and Paul Chékhov soon saw himself forced to close his business. In 1876 he left Taganróg and went to seek employment in Moscow. Antón remained alone in Taganróg. In 1879 he finished his time at the gymnasium and went to Moscow to join his family. He was matriculated as a student of the Faculty of Medicine. After the normal course of five years, he took his degree in 1884. From his arrival in Moscow to his death he never parted from his parents and sister, and as his literary income soon became important, he early became the mainstay of his family. The Chékhovs were an exceptionally united family —a case exceedingly rare among the intelligentsia, and owing, of course, to their peasant and merchant origins.

Chékhov began working in the comic papers the year he came to Moscow, and before he left the university he had become one of their most welcome contributors. So on taking his degree, he did not settle down to practice as a doctor, but fell back on his literary work for subsistence. In 1886 some of his comic stories were collected in book form. The book had an immediate success with the public and was soon followed by another volume of comic stories. The critics, especially the radical critics, took little notice of the book, but it attracted the attention of two influential men of letters—the veteran novelist Grigoróvich and Suvórin, editor of the pro-government *Nóvoye vrémya*, the largest daily paper of the day. The shrewd and clever Suvórin at once saw the great possibilities of Chékhov and invited him to contribute to his paper, where he even started a special weekly literary supplement for Chékhov. They became close friends, and in Chékhov's correspondence his letters to Suvórin form undoubtedly the most interesting part. Chékhov had now gained a firm footing in "big literature" and was free from the tyranny of the comic papers. This change in his social position was followed by a change in his work—he abandoned comic writing and developed the style that is most characteristically his. This change is apparent in the stories written by him in 1886–7. At the same time Chékhov wrote his first play, *Ivánov*, which was produced in Moscow in December 1887 and in Petersburg a year later. It is characteristic of this period of transition that Chékhov continued working at these pieces after their first publication; The *Steppe* and *Ivánov* that are now reproduced in his *Works* are very different from what first appeared in 1887. Henceforward Chékhov's life was rather uneventful, and what events there were, are closely connected with his writings. An isolated episode was his journey to Sakhalín, the Russian Botany Bay. He went there in 1890, traveling through Siberia (before the days of the Trans-Siberian) and returning by sea via Ceylon. He made a very thorough investigation of convict life and published the result of it in a separate book (*Sakhalín Island*, 1891). It is remarkable for its thoroughness, objectivity, and impartiality, and is an important historical document. It is supposed to have influenced certain reforms in prison life introduced in 1892. This journey was Chékhov's greatest practical contribution to, the humanitarianism that was so near to his heart. In private life he was also very kindhearted and generous. He gave away much of his money. His native town of Taganróg was the recipient of a library and a museum from him.

In 1891 Chékhov was rich enough to buy a piece of land at Melíkhovo, some fifty miles south of Moscow. There he settled down with his parents, sister, and younger brother, and lived for six years. He took part in local life and spent much money on local improvements. In 1892–3, during the cholera epidemic, he worked as the head of a sanitary district. Here it was he wrote many of his best and most mature stories. He remained at Melíkhovo till 1897, when the state of his health forced him to move. Consumption had set in, and he had to spend the rest of his life mainly between the south coast of the Crimea and foreign—French and German—health resorts. This was not the only change in his life. All his surroundings changed, owing to his new connection with the Moscow Art Theater and his more decided political orientation towards the left. This latter led to his breach with Suvórin, to whom he wrote a very angry letter in connection with the Dreyfus affair (even in Russia the *Affaire* was a hotbed of quarrel!) and to his friendship with the younger generation of writers, headed by Górky and distinctly revolutionary. During these last years (especially after 1900, when he settled down in Yálta) he saw much of Tolstóy.

In the popular opinion of that time, Chékhov, Górky, and Tolstóy formed a sort of sacred trinity symbolizing all that was best in independent Russia as opposed to the dark forces of Tsarism. Chékhov lived up to his liberal reputation, and when the Academy, following a hint of the government, excluded Górky from its membership almost immediately after electing him, Chékhov, like the veteran socialist Korolénko, resigned his membership. But from the literary point of view this phase is hardly of much importance—it introduced no new elements into his work. Far more important is his connection with the Art Theater. After *Ivánov*, Chékhov had written several light one-act comedies that had a considerable success with the public but added little to his intrinsic achievement. In 1895 he turned once more to serious drama and wrote *The Seagull* (as it is called in the English translation, rather absurdly —the Russian *Cháyka* means just *Gull*). It was produced at the State Theater of Petersburg in 1896. It was badly understood by the actors and badly acted. The first night was a smashing failure. The play was hissed down, and the author, confounded by his defeat, left the theater after the second act and escaped to Melíkhovo, vowing never again to write a play. Meanwhile K. S. Stanislávsky (Alekséyev), a wealthy merchant of Moscow, and the dramatist Vladímir Nemiróvich-Dánchenko founded the Art Theater, which was to be such an important landmark in the history of the Russian stage. They succeeded in getting *The Seagull* for one of their first productions. The cast worked at it with energy and understanding, and when the play was acted by them in 1898, it proved a triumphant success. Chékhov turned with new energy towards dramatic writing, and wrote his most famous plays with a direct view to Stanislávsky's casts. *Uncle Ványa* (which had been planned as early as 1888) was produced in 1900, *The Three Sisters* in 1901, and *The Cherry Orchard* in January 1904. Each play was a greater triumph than the preceding one. There was complete harmony among playwright, actors, and public. Chékhov's fame was at its height. However, he did not become so rich as to compare with Kipling, or D'Annunzio, or even with Górky. For like his favorite heroes, he was eminently unpractical: in 1899 he sold all the works he had hitherto written to the publisher Marx for 75,000 rubles ($37,500). It turned out after the transaction that Marx was not aware of the extent of his writings—he had reckoned on four volumes of short stories, and he had unconsciously bought nine! In 1901 Chékhov married an actress of the Art Theater, Olga L. Knípper; so his life became further changed. These last years he lived mostly at Yálta, where he had built a villa. He was constantly besieged by importunate admirers, with whom he was very patient and kind. In June 1904 his illness had so advanced that he was sent by the doctors to Baden-weiler, a small health resort in the Black Forest, where he died. His body was brought to Moscow and buried by the side of his father, who had preceded him in 1899.

Chékhov's literary career falls into two distinct periods: before and after 1886.[3] The English reader and the more "literary" Russian public know him by his later work, but it may be safely asserted that a much greater number of Russians know him rather as the author of his early comic stories than as the author of *My Life* and *Three Sisters*. It is a characteristic fact that many of his most popular and typical comic stories, precisely those which are sure to be known to every middle-class or semi-educated Russian (for example, *A Horse Name, Vint, The Complaint Ledger, Surgery*), were not translated into English. It is true that some of these stories are very difficult to translate, so topical and national are the jokes. But it is also evident that the English-speaking admirer of Chékhov has no taste for this buffoonery but looks to Chékhov for commodities of a very different description. The level of the comic papers in which Chékhov wrote was by no means a high one. They were a sanctuary of every kind of vulgarity and bad taste. Their buffoonery was vulgar and meaningless. They lacked the noble gift of nonsense, which of all things elevates man nearest the gods; they lacked wit, restraint, and grace. It was mere trivial buffoonery, and Chékhov's stories stand in no striking contrast to their general background. Except for a higher degree of craftsmanship, they are of a piece with the rest. Their dominant note is an uninspired sneer at the weaknesses and follies of mankind, and it would need a more than lynx-eyed critic to discern in them the note of human sympathy and of the higher humor that is so familiar to the reader of Chékhov's mature

[3] A great inconvenience of the English edition of Chékhov is that it entirely disregards dates and arranges the tales in an arbitrary order.

work. The great majority of these stories were never re-printed by Chékhov, but still the first and second volumes of his collected edition contain several dozen of the kind. Only a few—and all of them of a less crude variety—have had the honor of an English translation. But even in the crudest, Chékhov stands out as a superior craftsman, and in the economy of his means there is a promise of *Sleepy* and *At Christmas-time*. Before long, Chékhov began to deviate from the straight line imposed on him by the comic papers, and as early as 1884 he could write such a story as *The Chorus Girl,* which may yet be a little primitive and clumsy in its lyrical construction but on the whole stands almost on a level with the best of his mature work. *Parti-colored Stories,* which appeared in 1886 and laid the foundation of Chékhov's reputation in the literary circles, contained, besides many exercises in crude buffoon-ery, stories of a different kind that presented a gay appear-ance but were sad in substance—and that answered admir-ably to the hackneyed phrase of Russian critics, "tears through laughter." Such, for instance, is *Misery:* on a wet winter night a cabman who has just lost his son tries to tell his story to one after another of his fares and does not suc-ceed in kindling their sympathy.

In 1886, as has been said, Chékhov was able to free himself from the comic papers and could now develop a new style that had begun to assert itself somewhat earlier. This style was (and remained) essentially poetical, but it was some time before he finally settled the main lines of what was to be the characteristic Chekhovian story. In his stories of 1886–8 there are many elements that have been yet imperfectly blended—a strain of descriptive journalism (in its most unadulterated form in *Uprooted*); pure anecdote, sometimes just ironical (*The First-Class Passen-ger*), sometimes poignantly tragi-comical (*Vánka*); the lyrical expression of atmosphere (*The Steppe, Happiness*); psychological studies of morbid experience (*Typhus*); parables and moralities laid out in a conventional, un-Russian surrounding (*The Bet, A Story without a Title*). But already one of the favorite and most characteristic themes asserts its domination—the mutual lack of under-standing between human beings, the impossibility for one person to feel in tune with another. *The Privy Councilor, The Post, The Party, The Princess,* are all based on this idea—which becomes something like the leitmotiv of all Chékhov's later work. The most typical stories of this period are all located in the country of his early life, the steppe between the Sea of Azóv and the Donéts. These are *The Steppe, Happiness, The Horse-Stealers*. They are planned as lyrical symphonies (though the last one is also an anecdote). Their dominant note is superstition, the vague terror (Chékhov makes it poetical) before the presences that haunt the dark and empty steppe, the profound uninterestingness and poverty of the steppe peasant's life, a vague hope of a happiness that may be discovered, with the help of dark powers, in some ancient treasure mound. *The Steppe*, at which Chékhov worked much and to which he returned again after its publication, is the central thing in this period. It lacks the wonderful architecture of his short stories—it is a lyrical poem, but a poem made out of the substance of trivial, dull, and dusky life. The long, monotonous, uneventful journey of a little boy over the endless steppe from his native village to a distant town is drawn out in a hundred pages to form a languid, melodious, and tedious lullaby. A brighter aspect of Chékhov's lyrical art is in *Easter Eve*. The monk on night duty on the ferryboat tells a passenger about his dead fellow monk, who had the rare gift of writing lauds to the saints. He describes with loving detail the technique of this art, and one discerns Chékhov's sincere sympathy for this unnoticed, unwanted, quiet, and unambitious fellow craftsman. To the same period belongs *Kashtánka*, the delightful history of a dog that was kidnaped by a circus clown to form part of a troupe of performing animals and escaped to her old master in the middle of a performance. The story is a wonderful blend of humor and poetry, and though it certainly sentimentalizes and humanizes its animals, one cannot help recognizing it as a masterpiece. Another little gem is *Sleepy*, a real masterpiece of concentration, economy, and powerful effectiveness.[4]

In some stories of this period we find already the manner that is pre-eminently Chekhovian. The earliest story where it is quite distinctly discernible is *The Party*

[4] Tolstóy is said to have held this story in high esteem, and one cannot help noticing a certain similarity it bears to his own masterpiece *Alësha Gorshók*, written eighteen years later.

(1887), on which Chékhov himself laid a great value, but which is not yet perfect; he confesses in a letter to Suvórin that he "would gladly have spent six months over *The Party*. . . . But what am I to do? I begin a story on September 10th with the thought that I must finish it by October 5th at the latest; if I don't, I shall fail the editor and be left without money. I let myself go at the beginning and write with an easy mind; but by the time I get to the middle, I begin to grow timid and fear that my story will be too long. . . . This is why the beginning of my stories is always very promising . . . the middle is huddled and timid, and the end is, as in a short sketch, like fireworks." [5] But the essential of Chékhov's mature style is unmistakably present. It is the "biography" of a mood developing under the trivial pinpricks of life, but owing in substance to a deep-lying, physiological or psychological cause (in this case the woman's pregnancy). *A Dreary Story*, published in 1889, may be considered the starting point of the mature period. The leitmotiv of mutual isolation is brought out with great power. We may date the meaning that has come to be associated in Russia with the words "Chekhovian state of mind" (*Chékhovskoye nastroyénie*) from *A Dreary Story*. The atmosphere of the story is produced by the professor's deep and growing disillusionment as to himself and the life around him, the gradual loss of faith in his vocation, the gradual drifting apart of people linked together by life. The professor realizes the meaninglessness of his life—and the "giftlessness" (*bezdárnost*, a characteristically Chekhovian word) and dullness of all that surrounds him. His only remaining friend, his former ward Kátya, an unsuccessful disillusioned actress, breaks down under an intenser experience of the same feelings. And though his affection for her is sincere and genuine, and though he is suffering from the same causes as she is, he fails to find the necessary language to approach her. An unconquerable inhibition keeps him closed to her, and all he can say to her is:

"Let us have lunch, Kátya."
"No, thank you," she answers coldly.
Another minute passes in silence.

[5] *Letters of Anton Tchehov*, translated by Constance Garnett, p 101, Chatto & Windus, London.

"I don't like Khárkov," I say; "it is so grey here —such a grey town."

"Yes, perhaps. . . . It's ugly. . . . I am here not for long, passing through. I am going on to-day."

"Where?"

"To the Crimea . . . that is, to the Caucasus."

"Oh! For long?"

"I don't know."

"Kátya gets up and, with a cold smile, holds out her hand, looking at me. I want to ask her: 'Then you won't be at my funeral?' but she does not look at me; her hand is cold and, as it were, strange. I escort her to the door in silence. She goes out, walks down the long corridor, without looking back. She knows that I am looking after her, and she will look back at the turn. No, she did not look round. I've seen her black dress for the last time; her steps have died away! . . . Farewell, my treasure!" [6]

This ending on a minor note is repeated in all Chékhov's subsequent stories and gives the keynote to his work.

A Dreary Story opens the succession of Chékhov's mature masterpieces. Besides the natural growth of his genius, he was now free to work longer over them than he could when he was writing *The Party*. So his stories written in the nineties are almost without exception perfect works of art. It is mainly on the work of this period that Chékhov's reputation now rests. The principal stories written after 1889 are, in chronological order, *The Duel, Ward No. 6* (1892), *An Anonymous Story* (1893), *The Black Monk, The Teacher of Literature* (1894), *Three Years, Ariadne, Anna on the Neck, An Artist's Story* (in Russian: *The House with the Maisonette*), *My Life* (1895), *Peasants* (1897), *The Darling, Iónych, The Lady with the Dog* (1898), *The New Villa* (1899), *At Christmas-time, In the Ravine* (1900). After this date (it was the period of *Three Sisters* and *The Cherry Orchard*) he wrote only two stories, *The Bishop* (1902) and *Betrothed* (1903).

Chékhov's art has been called psychological, but it is psychological in a very different sense from Tolstóy's,

[6] *The Wife and Other Stories,* translated by Constance Garnett, pp. 218–19. (N. Y. 1916–22)

Dostoyévsky's, or Marcel Proust's. No writer excels him in conveying the mutual unsurpassable isolation of human beings and the impossibility of understanding each other. This idea forms the core of almost every one of his stories, but, in spite of this, Chékhov's characters are singularly lacking in individual personality. Personality is absent from his stories. His characters all speak (within class limits and apart from the little tricks of catchwords he lends them from time to time) the same language, which is Chékhov's own. They cannot be recognized, as Tolstóy's and Dostoyévsky's can, by the mere *sound of their voices*. They are all alike, all made of the same material—"the common stuff of humanity"—and in this sense Chékhov is the most "democratic," the most "unanimist," of all writers. For of course the similarity of all his men and women is not a sign of weakness—it is the expression of his fundamental intuition of life as a homogeneous matter but cut out into watertight compartments by the phenomenon of individuality. Like Stendhal and the French classicists, and unlike Tolstóy, Dostoyévsky, and Proust, Chékhov is a student of "man in general." But unlike the classicists, and like Proust, he fixes his attention on the infinitesimals, the "pinpricks" and "straws" of the soul. Stendhal deals in psychological "whole numbers." He traces the major, conscious, creative lines of psychical life. Chékhov concentrates on the "differentials" of mind, its minor, unconscious, involuntary, destructive, and dissolvent forces. As art, Chékhov's method is active—more active than, for instance, Proust's, for it is based on a stricter and more conscious *choice* of material and a more complicated and elaborate disposition of it. But as "outlook," as "philosophy," it is profoundly passive and "non-resistant," for it is a surrender to the "micro-organisms," of the soul, to its destructive microbes. Hence the general impressions produced by the whole of Chékhov's work that he had a cult for inefficiency and weakness. For Chékhov has no other way of displaying his sympathy with his characters than to show in detail the process of their submission to their microbes. The strong man who does not succumb in this struggle, or who does not experience it, is always treated by Chékhov with less sympathy and comes out as the "villain of the play"—in so far as the word "villain" is at all applicable to the world Chékhov moves in. The strong man in this world of his is merely the insensate brute, with a skin thick enough not to feel the "pinpricks," which are the only important thing in life. Chékhov's art is constructive. But the construction he uses is not a narrative construction—it might rather be called musical; not, however, in the sense that his prose is melodious, for it is not. But his method of constructing a story is akin to the method used in music. His stories are at once fluid and precise. The lines along which he builds them are very complicated curves, but they have been calculated with the utmost precision. A story by him is a series of points marking out with precision the lines discerned by him in the tangled web of consciousness. Chékhov excels in the art of tracing the first stages of an emotional process; in indicating those first symptoms of a deviation when to the general eye, and to the conscious eye of the subject in question, the nascent curve still seems to coincide with a straight line. An infinitesimal touch, which at first hardly arrests the reader's attention, gives a hint at the direction the story is going to take. It is then repeated as a leitmotiv, and at each repetition the true equation of the curve becomes more apparent, and it ends by shooting away in a direction very different from that of the original straight line. Such stories as *The Teacher of Literature, Iónych,* and *The Lady with the Dog* are perfect examples of such emotional curves. The straight line, for instance, in *Iónych* is the doctor's love for Mlle Túrkin; the curve, his subsidence into the egoistical complacency of a successful provincial career. In *The Teacher of Literature* the straight line is again the hero's love; the curve, his dormant dissatisfaction with selfish happiness and his intellectual ambition. In *The Lady with the Dog* the straight line is the hero's attitude towards his affair with the lady as a trivial and passing intrigue; the curve, his overwhelming and all-pervading love for her. In most of Chékhov's stories these constructive lines are complicated by a rich and mellow atmosphere, which he produces by the abundance of emotionally significant detail. The effect is poetical, even lyrical: as in a lyric, it is not interest in the development that the reader feels, but "infection" by the poet's mood. Chékhov's stories are lyrical monoliths; they cannot be dissected into episodes, for every episode is strictly conditioned by the whole and is without significance apart from it. In architectural unity Chékhov surpasses all Rus-

sian writers of the realistic age. Only in Púshkin and
Lérmontov do we find an equal or superior gift of design.
Chékhov thought Lérmontov's *Tamán* was the best short
story ever written, and this partiality was well founded.
Tamán forestalled Chékhov's method of lyrical construction. Only its air is colder and clearer than the mild and
mellow "autumnal" atmosphere of Chékhov's world.

Two of his best stories, *My Life* and *In the Ravine*,
stand somewhat apart from the rest of his mature work.
My Life is the story of a Tolstoyan, and one cannot help
thinking that in it Chékhov tried to approach the clearer
and more intellectual style of Tolstóy. There are a directness of narrative and a thinness of atmosphere that are
otherwise rare in Chékhov. In spite of this relative absence
of atmosphere, it is perhaps his most poetically pregnant
story. It is convincingly symbolical. The hero, his father,
his sister, the Azhógins, and Anyúta Blagóvo stand out with
the distinctness of morality characters. The very vagueness
and generality of its title helps to make it something like
an *Everyman*. For poetical grasp and significance *My Life*
may be recognized as the masterpiece of Chékhov—unless
it is surpassed by *In the Ravine*. This, one of his last
stories, is an amazing piece of work. The scene is the
Moscow industrial area—it is the history of a shopkeeper's family. It is remarkably free from all excess of
detail, and the atmosphere is produced, with the help of
only a few descriptive touches, by the movement of the
story. It is infinitely rich in emotional and symbolical
significance. What is rare in Chékhov—in both these stories
there is an earnestness, a keenness of moral judgment that
raises them above the average of his work. All Chékhov's
work is symbolical, but in most of his stories the symbolism
is less concrete and more vaguely suggestive. It is akin to
Maeterlinck's, in spite of the vast difference of style between the Russian realist and the Belgian mystic. *Ward
No. 6*, the darkest and most terrible of all Chékhov's
stories, is an especially notable example of this suggestive
symbolism. It is all the more suggestive for being strictly
realistic. (The only time Chékhov attempted to step out of
the limits of strict realism was when he wrote the only
story that is quite certainly a failure—*The Black Monk*.)
But this symbolism reached its full development in his
plays, beginning with *The Seagull*.

Chékhov's first attempt to use the dramatic form was *On the High Road* (1885). This is an adaptation of an earlier story of his. It did not see the stage; it was suppressed by the dramatic censorship as too "gloomy and filthy." It was published only after his death. In 1886 Chékhov wrote his first full-size play, *Ivánov*. Like *The Party* and other stories of the period, *Ivánov* is a transitional work and betrays a somewhat wavering hand that has not yet acquired a complete command of its material. *Ivánov* was successful on the stage, and, stimulated by success, Chékhov almost immediately began writing a new play, *The Forest Spirit*. But the cold reception given it by the few friends he showed it to made him put it aside and abandon serious dramatic work. Instead he wrote a series of one-act comedies (*The Bear, The Wedding,* and others) in a style closely connected with his early comic stories. These comedies were well received by the admirers of Chékhov's comic writings and became widely popular. They are still a favorite item in every provincial repertoire, and are especially often staged in private theatricals. In 1896 Chékhov returned to serious drama—and produced *The Seagull*. I have already told the story of its original failure and subsequent success. After that, Chékhov returned to *The Forest Spirit,* which became *Uncle Ványa,* to be followed by *Three Sisters* and *The Cherry Orchard*. These four famous plays form Chékhov's theater. They have received, especially the two last ones, even extravagant praise from English critics, who seem to lose the famous English virtue of "understatement" the moment they have to do with Chékhov. *The Cherry Orchard* has been described as the best play since Shakspere, and *Three Sisters* as the best play in the world. Tolstóy thought differently, and though he had an intense dislike for Shakspere, he preferred his plays to Chékhov's. Tolstóy, who considered subject matter the chief thing in plays and novels, could not have thought otherwise: there is no subject matter in Chékhov's plays, no plot, no action. They consist of nothing but "superficial detail." They are, in fact, the most undramatic plays in the world (if, however, they are not surpassed in this respect by the plays of Chékhov's bad—they were all bad—imitators). This undramatic character is a natural outcome of the Russian realistic drama. The plays of Ostróvsky, and especially of Turgénev, contain the germs of much that

reached its full development in Chékhov. The Russian
realistic drama is essentially static. But Chékhov carried to
the extreme limit this static tendency and gave his name
to a new type in drama—the undramatic drama. On the
whole, his plays are constructed in the same way as his
stories. The differences are owing to the differences of
material and are imposed by the use of dialogue. As a
general rule, it may be said that the principal difference is
that the plays have less backbone, less skeleton, than the
stories, and are more purely atmospheric creations. In his
stories there is always one central figure that is the main
element of unity—the story is conducted from the standpoint of this central figure. But the use of dialogue excludes
this monocentric construction and makes all the characters
equal. Chékhov amply avails himself of this fact and dis-
tributes the spectator's attention among all his people with
wonderful fairness. His *dramatis personæ* live in a state of
ideal democracy—where equality is no sham. This method
was admirably adapted to the principles of the Moscow Art
Theater, which aimed at creating a cast in which there
would be no stars but all actors of equal excellence. The
dialogue form is also admirably suited to the expression of
one of Chékhov's favorite ideas: the mutual unintelligibil-
ity and strangeness of human beings, who cannot and do
not want to understand each other. Each character speaks
only of what interests him or her, and pays no attention to
what the other people in the room are saying. Thus the
dialogue becomes a patchwork of disconnected remarks,
dominated by a poetic "atmosphere" but by no logical
unity. Of course this system is entirely an artistic convention. No one in real life ever spoke as Chékhov's people do.
Again it reminds one of Maeterlinck, whose plays (as
Chesterton has remarked) have a meaning only if one is
quite in tune with the poet's very exclusive mood; otherwise
they are mere nonsense. Chékhov's plays are "infectious,"
as Tolstóy wanted all art to be—in fact nothing if not infectious. But, though the moods are perhaps less exclusive
and more universal than Maeterlinck's, unless one has a
sympathy with his moods, the dialogue is meaningless. Like
his stories, Chékhov's plays are always saturated with
emotional symbolism, and in his research for suggestive
poetry he sometimes oversteps the limits of good taste—
such lapses are, for instance, the bursting of a string in

The Cherry Orchard, and the last scene in the same play, when Firs, the old servant, is left alone in the deserted house, where he has been locked in and forgotten. Even more consistently than in his stories, the dominant note of Chékhov's plays is one of gloom, depression, and hopelessness. The end of every one of them is managed in the same way as the end of *A Dreary Story*. They are all in the minor key and leave the spectator in a state of impotent—perhaps deliciously impotent—depression. Judged by their own standards (which can hardly be accepted as the normal standards of dramatic art), Chékhov's plays are perfect works of art, but are they really as perfect as his best stories? At any rate, his method is dangerous and has been imitated only at the imitator's imminent peril. No play written by an imitator of Chékhov is above contempt.

Chékhov's English admirers think that everything is perfect in Chékhov. To find spots in him will seem blasphemy to them. Still it is only fair to point out these spots. I have already referred to the complete lack of individuality in his characters and in their way of speaking. This is not in itself a fault, for it belongs to his fundamental intuition of life, which recognizes no personality. But it is not a virtue. It is especially noticeable when he makes his characters speak at length on abstract subjects. How different from Dostoyévsky, who "felt ideas" and who made them so splendidly individual! Chékhov did not "feel ideas," and when his characters give expression to theirs, they speak a colorless and monotonous journalese. *The Duel* is especially disfigured by such harangues. This is perhaps Chékhov's tribute to a deep-rooted tradition of Russian intelligentsia literature. Their speeches may have had some emotional significance in their time but certainly have none today. Another serious shortcoming is Chékhov's Russian. It is colorless and lacks individuality. He had no feeling for words. No Russian writer of anything like his significance used a language so devoid of all raciness and nerve. This makes Chékhov (except for topical allusions, technical terms, and occasional catchwords) so easy to translate. Of all Russian writers, he has the least to fear from the treachery of translators.

Chékhov's direct influence on Russian literature was not important. The success of his short stories contributed to the great popularity of that form, which became the predominant form in Russian fiction. But Górky, Kúprin, and Búnin, to name but the foremost of those who regarded him as their master, can hardly be recognized as his pupils. Certainly no one learned from him the art of constructing his stories. His dramas, which looked so easy to imitate, were imitated, but the style proved a pitfall. Today Russian fiction is quite free from any trace of Chékhov's influence. Some of the younger writers began, before the Revolution, as his more or less unintelligent imitators, but none of them remained true to him. In Russia, Chékhov has become a thing of the past—of a past remoter than even Turgénev, not to speak of Gógol or Leskóv. Abroad, things stand differently. If Chékhov has had a genuine heir to the secrets of his art, it is in England, where Katherine Mansfield did what no Russian has done—learned from Chékhov without imitating him. In England, and to a lesser degree in France, the cult of Chékhov has become the hallmark of the high-brow intellectual. Curiously enough, in Russia, Chékhov was always regarded as a distinctly "lowbrow" writer; the self-conscious intellectual elite was always conspicuously cool to him. The highbrows of the beginning of the century even affected to (or sincerely did) despise him. His real stronghold was in the heart of the honest Philistine in the street. Nowadays Chékhov has of course become the common property of the nation. His place as a classic—a major classic, one of the "ten best"—is not challenged. But he is a classic who has been temporarily shelved.

Index

PRINCE DMITRY SVYATOPOLK MIRSKY was born in Russia in 1890 and was educated at the University of St. Petersburg. After five years of military service he went to England, where he lectured at King's College, London University, from 1922 to 1932. He then returned to Russia, where he was a member of the Union of Soviet Writers, a contributor to various Russian papers, and the author of a number of published books of history and of literary criticism. Mirsky occupied a unique position as an interpreter of English literature to his own countrymen and of Russian literature to English readers. His best-known books are *A History of Russian Literature, Contemporary Russian Literature* (from which two books the Vintage Book is drawn), and *The Intelligentsia of Great Britain*. No official news has been published about Mirsky's fate, but there is evidence that he was exiled and died in Siberia in the late 1930's.

FRANCIS J. WHITFIELD was born in Springfield, Massachusetts, in 1916. He has taught at Harvard and the University of Chicago, and, as a visitor, at Columbia and the University of Michigan. At present he is Professor of Slavic Languages and Literatures at the University of California at Berkeley.

A free catalogue of VINTAGE BOOKS *will be sent at your request. Write to* Vintage Books, 457 Madison Avenue, New York, New York 10022.

VINTAGE BELLES-LETTRES

A free catalogue of VINTAGE BOOKS *will be sent at your request. Write
to* Vintage Books, 457 Madison Avenue, New York, New York 10022.